A LIFE IN A YEAR

THE AMERICAN INFANTRYMAN IN VIETNAM, 1965–1972

James R. Ebert

BALLANTINE BOOKS • NEW YORK

A Presidio Press Book
Published by The Random House Publishing Group
Copyright © 1993 by James R. Ebert

Presidio Press and colophon are trademarks of Random House, Inc.

www.presidiopress.com

ISBN 0-89141-829-6

Manufactured in the United States of America

First Hardcover Edition: December 1993
First Trade Paperback Edition: August 2003
First Mass Market Edition: March 2004

OPM   10   9   8   7   6   5   4   3   2   1

This book is dedicated to:

> Eddie Austin, Jeffrey Beatty, Leonard Dutcher, and Ed Iwasko, who sacrificed everything in Vietnam and did not come home.

And to:

> Jack Freitag, Ed Hoban, and Vernon Janick, who returned home with wounds both visible and invisible. I miss you but hope that in your passing you find the peace you battled so long to achieve.

Finally, to Ed Woods, 103d Infantry Division, World War II:

> Thank you for your example. You showed me that a man can soldier with dignity in any occupation.

Contents

Preface

The first glimmerings of my personal interest in Vietnam trace their origins to March 1970 and a kitchen table in Altoona, Pennsylvania. What had begun as a late-night snack with Jerry, my future brother-in-law, turned into a conversation about his recent experiences as an infantry soldier in Vietnam. The discussion stretched into the early morning hours. I was familiar with Vietnam only from the coverage on the evening news and the pictures I had seen in *Life* magazine; what I learned that night was something quite profound. I discovered that wars are fought at a personal level by very real human beings. I remember both Jerry's feelings of pride and his sense of grief and frustration. What I remember most was that one of his friends didn't die in cinematic glory during a vicious firefight while saving a wounded comrade; he suffocated while searching a dry well for enemy weapons.

My impressions of the entire Vietnam experience were altered by that first interview. From that point on, every other story about soldiers on the news or in magazines reminded me a little bit of the men who had been cast in stories I heard that night. I never forgot the story about the soldier who died in the well. Neither has Jerry. There was no mistaking the impact of the events he described. It was fifteen years before we spoke of it again.

Perhaps on that spring evening in 1970, and at the age of sixteen, I was not a threat. Perhaps at that moment the war needed to be talked about. But I think the reason a veteran shared his feelings and experiences with me that night was because he wanted to talk and *I* wanted to know—and I asked. As this study indicates, I am still asking.

Time casts long shadows over the memories of all events.

Still I believe that there is much to learn and everything to gain by allowing these Vietnam combat veterans to have a say in what history records about them. If collecting the thoughts of veterans and synthesizing their memories fails to provide us with a photographic sense of realism and detail, perhaps we are the more fortunate. What we do gain in these interviews is history from a distance—an impression that conveys feeling, mood, and a sense of perspective. Additionally, as Stanley Vestal noted, the most obvious advantage of interviews over all other types of sources lies in the fact that historians as well as casual readers of history are "altogether too apt to allow more authority to the printed page than it deserves. In an interview one has many opportunities to test the honesty, capacity, and knowledge of an informant. But when we read, we listen in the dark." [*Sitting Bull, Champion of the Sioux*, Boston, 1932. Reprinted in *The Past Before Us*, Michael Kemmen ed. (Ithaca, N.Y.: Cornell University Press, 1982), 392.]

During the course of this study I interviewed approximately fifty Vietnam combat veterans. I found my subjects to be thoughtful and careful of detail. While some of them at times got caught up in their reflections, most downplayed their experiences and strove to be honest and accurately understood. I verified their actual participation in Vietnam combat through offical records or through photographs and other documents, which left no doubt in my mind that they had served at the time and in the capacity they described. In those cases where I felt that information was exaggerated, I did my best to verify the material in secondary sources. Several of these veterans' units have been written up in Vietnam War literature. Sergeant Gerry Barker, for example, appears in *Bird: The Christmastide Battle,* by S. L. A. Marshall and David H. Hackworth, and Jerry Johnson's infantry company was the subject of the book *Charlie Company,* written by the staff of *Newsweek*. In only one case did I find reason to question a subject's overall truthfulness, and I have not used any material from that interview in this book.

None of the men I spoke with had been previously interviewed, nor had they, in most cases, discussed their military service in Vietnam in any formal manner since the war. About half of the interviewees believed this to be their first detailed discussion about Vietnam with anyone. Although some subjects expressed doubts about the importance of what they might recall, none of the combat veterans I contacted refused to be interviewed.

The reader should realize that although combat is certainly one of the most intense physical and emotional experiences a person can undergo, it is not without parallel in civilian life. Losing loved ones in a house fire or an automobile accident is certainly equivalent to the trauma of losing a friend in battle. What is different in the two experiences is that in civilian life such suffering is both uncommon and unanticipated. In battle, a soldier lives with the constant understanding that not only *might* such events occur, but they probably *will*—and if not to that soldier, then to someone close to him. That anticipation results in a pervasive undercurrent of fear that is all but absent in everyday civilian life.

Still, the prevalence of battle in military writing is an exaggeration in itself. Battle is relatively rare, yet its intensity tends to dominate men's memories—unless they have selectively excised those memories over the years. As Richard Holmes explains, "Memory tends to emphasize peaks and troughs at the expense of the great level plain between them." Thus battle—and the extremes of emotions, good or bad—is what soldiers tend to remember above the day-to-day tedium. History normally focuses on battle because that is where the excitement, drama, and decisiveness lie. Although battle is not necessarily the essence of soldiering, a majority of this work focuses on it. If this book were to reflect in length the actual incidence of battle in a year-long tour, I would estimate that only twenty-five of its pages should be devoted to combat, and the remainder to the tedium and exhaustion that make up the everyday life of soldiers.

This work examines the individual American infantry soldier's experiences in Vietnam: his emotions, frustrations, triumphs, failures, and, most of all, his remarkable ability to cope. In some cases it was difficult for soldiers to find the proper language to describe many of the sensations and experiences that made up their tours of duty in Vietnam. Many veterans struggled for the right words or analogies to convey

understanding. It was truly difficult, yet they succeeded. Any
wisdom or insight revealed in this work is theirs. If there is
misrepresentation or error in understanding, it is mine. Although I rely heavily on the words of the men who fought in
Vietnam, I alone am responsible for the interpretation of the
attitudes and opinions expressed herein. I have tried to be accurate in showing the reader a range of common attitudes or
experiences that most typified service in Vietnam. Not every
soldier or historian will agree with me.

There was no hidden agenda in this work, only a desire to
discover as much as I could about soldiering in Vietnam. In
the process, however, I came to respect these men not only for
having been in combat, but for enduring the more general and
universal discomforts—the fatigue and deprivation that were
so often their lot in life. I found after hours of interviews that
less and less came as a surprise to me, and more of what they
said made sense. The American infantry soldier was no different in Vietnam than his forebears were in any theater of
combat over the past two hundred years. If he is portrayed
differently it is not because he was cut from different cloth,
nor less toughened than his predecessors. He was simply a
participant in a war that was more widely and graphically reported. Vietnam was not so much different; it was simply
transmitted to the public uncensored and unfiltered.

Vietnam veterans have had to overcome one final obstacle
in their odyssey from military to civilian life—the stereotypes that society has placed upon them. Vietnam veterans
have had to deal with the image of being psychotic or drug
crazed, and they are often portrayed as crybabies seeking a
free handout. Such generalizations are unfortunate and, for
the most part, untrue. Most Vietnam veterans are victims of
movie hype and sensationalized primetime television, which
in the years following the war seemed to seek ratings at their
expense.

There is a great silent majority of Vietnam veterans who,
like their World War II and Korean War counterparts, put on
clothing other than worn fatigues and drive to work each day.
They are citizens, parents, voters, and human beings. They
hold jobs teaching school, selling shoes, managing busi-
nesses, and for the most part living quiet, everyday lives.

They are proud to have served their country and most have remained patriotic, but with one difference: Many of them were embittered because they were called upon to fight an unpopular war without much public support. They resented the loss of life and limb and the expenditure of their own efforts for what ultimately turned out to be little or nothing. Most combat veterans learned, as did marine Phil Yaeger, "It is not unpatriotic to question what your government is doing, it is unpatriotic not to." They did not see themselves as being particularly special, then or now. Theirs is a modesty typical of combat veterans. It was a sentiment eloquently expressed by Dan Krehbiel, who told me at the end of his interview:

> What I have just described sounds to me, as I am talking about it, like some unbelievable movie where you can put together dramatic pictures for all these incidents. But it reads better than it lives. It was just a matter of—I did it! I was just an average kid. I wasn't particularly brave. I wasn't super special in any way. I was just a regular, typical kid, and I did it! Anybody can do it. It is too bad anybody had to, but still, it can be blown way out of proportion.

> A chaplain who saw us off from Vietnam said, "As you leave on this plane there is one last piece of advice I want to give you to bear in mind and take with you always. There is only one difference between a fairy tale and a war story. A fairy tale starts out with 'Once upon a time' and a war story starts out with 'No shit! There I was.'" Those were his parting words and you have to watch out for exaggerating what you say. But no matter how you try to talk about it, it still sounds bigger, worse, more deadly, and more romantic than it actually was.

Acknowledgments

I would like to extend my thanks to the many people without whose help this book would have been impossible. Not only did they hold the ladder for me, but their encouragement on every rung made my climb enjoyable.

In particular, I am grateful to Thomas C. Magedanz of Pierre, South Dakota, who so generously shared with me his reflections on the Vietnam War—both written and remembered—together with letters, scrapbooks, and a vast array of statistical material. My sincere thanks also go to the South Dakota Vietnam Era Veterans Association and the South Dakota Vietnam Veterans Oral History Project for allowing me to quote from their excellent interview collection.

Special thanks are also due Mrs. Betty Ronke of Melrose, Wisconsin; Mr. and Mrs. Alvin and Pauline Austin of Granite, Oklahoma; Mrs. Corrine Hovre-Hill of Blair, Wisconsin; and Mrs. Dorthy Iwasko of Elmhurst, Illinois, for sharing with me personal letters and documents pertaining to their loved ones who served in Vietnam.

My expressions of gratitude must also include Stephen Fredrick, Vietnam veteran and friend, for his editorial and technical assistance, as well as his constant encouragement and unflagging enthusiasm. Also Earnest Brodsky, whose friendship and organizational skills helped keep both the manuscript and the author coherent.

I will never be able to thank adequately Dr. Richard Marcus of the University of Wisconsin-Eau Claire History Department. More than a thesis advisor, Professor Marcus was my mentor/confidant and, above all, a trusted voice of experience and good sense. His rigor was indispensable. Professors Maxwell Schoenfeld and Richard Coy, both from the

History Department, and Professor Richard Behling, Vietnam veteran and philosophy professor, also assisted me in this endeavor.

I offer a belated thank you to the faculty of Wartburg College—particularly Dr. Axel Schuessler, professor of history, and Professor Sam Mikkelson of the English Department, for planting the seeds that ultimately led to this work—and to my parents, Wayne and Margret Ebert, for imbuing me with a love of reading and for encouraging my curiosity.

More than fifty Vietnam veterans are represented in this study. They extended to me a trust that I hope I have not abused. They were tolerant beyond measure, and I am forever indebted to them. They have remained throughout the inspiration for this work.

I would also like to thank Dr. Dale Wilson of Presidio Press who, like so many others, worked diligently to make me better than I am. He made the chore of writing both pleasant and educational.

Lastly, my love and thanks to my wife Karen, who, like all war widows, took up the slack for the past four years and allowed me to devote my spare time to this project. Her love and support have been most crucial of all. And to my young daughter Kacie: Thanks for the smiles and hugs. You will never know how important they were.

CHAPTER 1

Induction

April 25, 1966

Dear Folks,

We had to work last Saturday night so we stayed in Janesville last weekend. We got a nice paycheck this week. I made $132.50. I am going down to the bank today and put in a hundred dollars. I'll have over $400.00 in the bank then.

I wish they'd call me into the Army pretty soon, I'd like to get in there and get it over with. I'm still hanging doors down at the plant, and I am starting to like the job pretty good. Chuck and I are going to Black River [Falls, Wisconsin] this weekend. I'll try to talk him into stopping down to the farm.

Your Youngest,
Len[1]

In October 1966, at the request of their "friends and countrymen," Leonard Dutcher and some thirty thousand other American males aged nineteen to twenty-five reported for induction into the armed forces as a result of escalating American involvement in the war in Vietnam.

Eleven million Americans served in uniform during the Vietnam era, yet only one in four made it to Southeast Asia. Of the 2.8 million who did, fewer than 10 percent served in the "bush" as line infantry soldiers engaged in seeking out the enemy. Yet it was on their shoulders and backs that most of the burden of the fighting fell in a war that left the vast majority of their peers, even those in uniform, untouched. Line infantry soldiers were the tip of the sword. It would be their lot as well to suffer much of the pain and the dying. Eighty-three percent of all U.S. casualties in Vietnam resulted from infantry combat operations. In a typical twelve-month tour, an infantry soldier stood a 3 percent chance of dying, a 10 percent chance of being seriously wounded, and a 25 percent chance of earning a Purple Heart. As in previous wars, so it was in Vietnam: Infantry soldiers were assessed much of the bitter cost of war so seldom considered when brave words are put to paper.[2]

The young men who became infantry soldiers, as in wars past, came mostly from the blue-collar industrial centers and rural back roads of the nation, where people lived in old neighborhoods and were paid by the hour. They were the sons and nephews of veterans. They played high school sports. Often they were from minorities and even more frequently they were poor. When recruiters put placards in front of post offices or visited high schools, these young men responded. It was their tradition. They had been raised to be patriotic, to believe in America. It was important that they did, for as sociologist Charles Moskos observed, a soldier must have an underlying commitment to the worth of the larger social system for which he is fighting.[3]

Although their trust in the country's leadership waned later in the war, they had been raised to believe in what Moskos referred to as the "legitimacy and superiority of the American way of life."[4] They saw a world polarized by "good guy-bad guy" imagery, and left it up to their government to distinguish who was whom. The eighteen year olds paid little attention to the larger world beyond their friends, their cars, and their Saturday nights. They viewed military service as, if not exciting, at least honorable. But what was most striking about many of the men who found themselves in uniform fighting in Vietnam was that so few ever envisioned themselves ending up there.[5]

Like the soldiers whom S. L. A. Marshall observed in World War II, the men who fought in Vietnam were "what their homes, their religions, their schooling, and their moral code and ideals of society had made them." As the 1960s gave rise to civil rights, youthful rebellion, and a substantial drug culture, the military in Vietnam mirrored each movement.

Neil Sheehan wrote of the American combat soldier in 1969: "He goes into combat with the disenchantment and developed sensitivity of his generation."[6] But if the American combat soldier had acquired the "sensitivity of his generation," he most likely did it *after* he was inducted into the military.

When eighteen-year-old James Raysor enlisted in the army in October 1965, he knew a lot about life in West Philadelphia but practically nothing about Vietnam. No one knew much about Vietnam then. As Raysor admitted, "To tell you the truth I was not into watching the news. I would rather watch 'Leave It to Beaver' or reruns of 'The Honeymooners.' I just wasn't involved with what was going on in Vietnam and didn't give it much of a thought."[7]

The war was not an issue for Donald Putnam, either—until he entered the army in 1968. Three years of carnage and a personal vulnerability to the draft at the very height of the war had made little impression on him. He doubted he even knew where Vietnam was. Nor did he much care; after all, he recalled, "I was eighteen years old, fresh out of high school and having a good time. I was making real good money working where I was, and the draft was something you always thought of. But you never thought about Vietnam. All you saw was a little bit on the news. Hell, when you are eighteen years old, who watches the news? You are more interested in going out and having a good time."[8]

A year later, in June 1969, Dan Krehbiel became concerned when he was drafted. By that time, he recalled, "Everybody had a pretty grim conclusion about the war. The general national feeling started to lean to 'Let's get out,' and that threw the soldier into a real sort of mind game."[9] Krehbiel was in college, however, where the issue of the war was frequently debated.

Most young men were simply unable to see themselves involved in a drama that had no more reality for them than the other programs they viewed on nightly television. Many thought that Vietnam was one of those things that it was best not to worry about. Typical of many graduating high school students, Ed Hoban was definitely aware in 1970 that there was a war going on, but Vietnam just wasn't a topic of conversation among his friends in Le Center, Minnesota.[10] Even after attending the funeral of a classmate who had been killed in Vietnam, Paul Boehm never considered the possibility of going to war. He remembers only that prior to entering the service he wasn't sure how to spell Vietnam.[11]

Arguably, few young men just out of high school had the maturity or experience to assign a value to their lives or to understand just how fleeting life could be. War is a concept that can be understood only after the fact, and such understanding seems impossible to impart to those who have not shared an equivalent experience. Phil Yaeger sensed as much in hindsight. When he enlisted in the Marine Corps in March 1966, he found himself questioning the war's validity but admitted, "I don't think I was intellectually mature enough to really spend that much time thinking about it."[12]

When Michael Jackson became eligible for the draft after graduating from Tennessee State College in June 1968, neither the draft nor the war consumed his thoughts. But being black and a bit more mature and better educated than many of his fellow draftees, his attention was drawn to issues of a more personal nature. "I guess like everybody else I watched TV news," Jackson recalled. "What was most meaningful to me before I went into the army was Muhammad Ali's stand against being drafted, and that had a lot of meaning to me and a lot of impact. It [Vietnam] was far, far away, so I didn't really give a lot of thought to it other than I knew I didn't want to be over there and be involved in it."[13]

Yet the distance of the war and the immediacy of personal lives were relative qualities that could be brought together through the most unexpected circumstances. For many who would serve there, Vietnam suddenly became much closer and more vivid than they could have ever imagined. The war would become the central experience of their lives.

Military service attracts young people in peacetime and time of war for reasons both personal and patriotic. The majority of men who were called to serve in Vietnam went dutifully. Some volunteered with the intention of serving in combat; others enlisted for precisely the opposite reason. But somewhere between the extremes of aggression and avoidance lay the personal motivations that attracted nearly eight million Americans to enlist during the Vietnam era. For some there was the allure of adventure or travel. Others saw the service as an avenue for social and economic advancement, attracting young minority members and the poor of all races with promises of education, technical training, and self-respect. For still others, the military was expected to provide direction and discipline.

Vietnam was not a concern to those who entered the service prior to the summer of 1965 largely because full-scale American participation had not yet begun. Theirs were peacetime reasons for joining the military. Consequently, when the first American infantry units deployed to Vietnam in 1965, the majority of the men in their ranks were volunteers. During the course of the Vietnam War, 90 percent of conscripts went into the army, but in 1965 less than one-third (395,292) of the army's 1,199,784 active-duty soldiers were draftees.[14]

The men who first deployed to Vietnam were, for the most part, professional, highly motivated, optimistic, and convinced of the legitimacy of their mission. The quality of those soldiers was equaled but never surpassed by the tens of thousands of troops who followed them there in subsequent years.

Gerry Barker was one of those early enlistees who seemed to gravitate easily toward the military. His father was a career army officer, so Barker grew up conditioned by war stories and martial trappings. He endured the transient existence of an army brat, rarely finishing a year in any one school. After high school he dropped out of the Richmond Polytechnical Institute and headed west to pursue a passion for rock climbing that led him to California Rock and the Yosemite Valley. Soon, however, the realities of making a living forced Barker to San Francisco, where, in 1962, while driving a delivery truck, "the bug hit me to try something different." He enlisted in the army. Infantry training, jump school, and a posting to the 82d Airborne Division followed in rapid succession. Barker liked it.[15]

The military served as a form of social welfare for some, a relief mechanism for those in need of opportunity. But it was not the stellar opportunity afforded by the military that drew the sons of America's poor and minorities into the ranks; rather, it was a lack of chances for employment elsewhere that channeled them into uniform, lending credence to the observation by Charles Moskos that the military is not so much a "pull" as an avenue of career mobility as society is a "push."[16]

Typical of many of the young African Americans pushed into military service was Willie Williams, who enlisted in the army in June 1962. According to Williams, "I grew up in a large, single-parent family and . . . to me [joining up] was the best thing to do because employment—there was nothing. So I joined the military in order to further myself and have money to help my sister through school."[17]

Native Americans also contributed a disproportionate share of soldiers to America's combat forces due in part to a tradition of honor connected with the warrior archetype, and, as was the case for many African Americans, because of economic disparity, prejudice, and limited job opportunities. Robert Emery, a Native American from near Valentine, Nebraska, was no stranger to difficult times. He recalled that, "It was kind of a struggle just to stay ahead. My Dad had a heart attack in 1960 and he was unable to work for a while, so my Mom went to work. In 1965 two of my brothers went into the service, and it wasn't long after that, that I went into the service."[18]

Many young men, minority members as well as whites, enlisted as a means of securing a better future and acquiring an education through the GI Bill. That was what drew Robert Moran, another Native American, into enlisting in November 1967.

> I had an older brother who was in the army and he had gone to Vietnam about two months before I joined, so I figured I would join up and help him. All I could see on the news releases was that a lot of them was dying. They needed more men, but I actually wasn't into just fighting; I was figuring there wasn't anything on the reservation for me to do. That was a way for me to start doing something. I started in the military and figured later on I would go to college, use my GI Bill.[19]

Although it is common to assume otherwise, the most serious inequities between those who served in combat in Vietnam and those who did not were based on social and economic distinctions rather than racial ones. Unfortunately, minorities in the United States were more likely to be poor; and the poor, as well as the poorly educated—regardless of race—found their way into the service and into combat at double the rate of their more affluent neighbors.[20]

During the Vietnam War, Rep. Alvin O'Konski took a random survey of one hundred inductees from his home district in northern Wisconsin and discovered that not one of them came from a family with an annual income of more than five thousand dollars. Postwar army records showed that an enlisted man with a college degree had only a 42 percent chance of ever going to Vietnam, let alone serving in combat there. High school graduates had a 64 percent chance of being sent to Vietnam, and dropouts stood a 70 percent chance. A Chicago survey conducted after the war by sociologists Gilbert Badillo and David Curry demonstrated that soldiers from low-income backgrounds were three times more likely to die in Vietnam than youths from high-income neighborhoods, whereas youths with low educational levels were four times more likely to die than were their better-educated peers.[21] General William C. Westmoreland pointed out that the highest percentage of men who served and died in relation to total state population came from states with generally lower average incomes. The highest such death rate was in West Virginia.[22]

Michael Jackson witnessed firsthand the reality of those who were economically and educationally deprived, and he found it difficult to discern the shading that prevented labels of racial bias from becoming statements of fact. There was no mistaking who got drafted in his neighborhood:

> In the area of Chicago where I lived, basically an all-black community, a lot of the people I had known in high school were being drafted and a lot of people in college, even before they graduated, were being drafted. So, I just had this overall sense that, yeah, black people and people of color—although I might have not been using that term back in '68—or people who could be classified as "have nots" were the ones

being drafted as opposed to people that I knew who
may have been white or people of means, money, [who]
were able to get into the National Guard or Reserves
knowing that things were happening in Vietnam and
this was a way not to be a part of that.

Without benefit of a college education, a young man was
more apt to enlist or be drafted. Jim Raysor, who was both
poor and white, signed on the dotted line because, "When it
came time to make a decision, there wasn't any money for
college." Nor was there money for Ed Hoban. Hoban was
from a small town, made All-Conference in three sports, and
was accustomed to living frugally. His father died when
Hoban was in the first grade, and Hoban and his six brothers
and sisters grew up on welfare.

I'd been accepted at a private college in Iowa, Westmar, on a little bit of an athletic scholarship from them,
not a whole lot. It didn't pay the whole way and I was
just real leery about how I was going to afford it.
Money was always kind of a big thing around our
house. If you didn't have it you could go without it. I
didn't have the money to really go to school, so I had a
friend that was going to go to Westmar with me and he
came up to the pool one day and told me he had enlisted in the marines. I said, "What the hell." So I went
down and volunteered for the draft and within two
weeks I was gone—that quick. I was debating all along
whether I could afford college or not and I evidently
decided that I couldn't. I had a low draft number. If I remember right it was sixty-seven. So I says, "If I don't
go to college they are going to get me anyway, so let's
get it over with." That is what made me decide to go in.

The military was also a place where a young man might
find some personal direction and self-discipline. For those
young men, enlistment did not always indicate volunteerism.
Some of these so-called volunteers were pressed into joining
by a magistrate or judge who saw military service as a way to

rehabilitate social misfits and petty criminals. One enlistee, Bruce Johnson, of Richland County, Wisconsin, recalled:

> The [judge] said I should probably go into the service for a few years and cool my heels a little bit—either that or sit in Green Bay [prison] for a while. I got into a lot of fights. I was pretty rowdy I guess, because I was small and I always got picked on. I happened to get into a fight and busted up some property and hit a cop and a little bit of this and that . . . that's what happened. It wasn't a matter really of choosing. The judge said that the army was the place for me, so I just went to La Crosse and enlisted up there with a buddy of mine.[23]

For Terry Musser, the motivation was an exasperated mother and high school principal who conspired with an accommodating recruiting sergeant. In early February 1965 Musser was in the principal's office of Melrose High School in Melrose, Wisconsin—again! The next day he was en route to Fort Leonard Wood, Missouri, for basic training—with the understanding that if he completed basic and passed the test for his Graduation Equivalency Diploma (GED) he would receive a diploma from his alma mater. The diploma arrived later that spring, but the road was not an easy one.[24]

For an unfortunate few, the military became a substitute for home because they had no place else to go. Vernon Janick didn't get many breaks in life. He left home at thirteen and traveled with a bean crew working Midwest farms until, in 1965, he turned seventeen and was able to live out a childhood fantasy. "[I] just had a love for the army," said Janick. "I mean, everything from real young on was army. [I] liked to play war games and bought all the army stuff, you know. [I] watched every army show. Dad was army. Grandpa was army. [I] just had a love for the army."[25]

James Stanton joined the Marine Corps in November 1967 when he ran out of other options. "My parents were split up and I was sort of just going on my own," he recalled. "I was living at home but doing anything I wanted. Then my mom moved in with my uncle. I couldn't live with them, so I moved in with my grandmother. That didn't work out. I ran out of places to live, so I joined the service. The only people that would take me was the Marine Corps because I never had a high school education."[26]

A number of men already serving in the armed forces prior to the Vietnam War saw the deployment of American infantry battalions to that country as a chance to really serve their country in wartime. There was an allure about the idea of combat that appealed to the adventurous side of many men, and more than a few soldiers requested transfers to units being deployed to Vietnam. Gerry Barker heard the "guardhouse rumor" that the 11th Air Assault Division at Fort Benning, Georgia, was preparing for Vietnam, and the army was seeking volunteers to fill it. The temptation was too great. Vietnam was where the action was and Barker wanted his share of the adventure.

> I think [the] Dom[inican] Rep[ublic] had just whetted my appetite because there was no real fighting when I was there. It was like kissing your sister or something. I had to give it one more try and I think I went solely for the adventure, with no real realization of what it meant. Everybody I had been around—I remember my father's buddies from World War II and Korea talking about the war and this sort of thing, and I had grown up with it. In 1965 I was terribly naive, but I always have been a risk taker.

Vietnam, at least before anyone knew better, seemed exotic. The allure of adventure and excitement was a siren song to Jerry Severson as well. He said that he and three other fellows "were bound and determined that we were going to fight this war. This was the only war available and, you know, you gotta go fight it. To have served in a good outfit and spent your whole tour in Fort Bragg, North Carolina, just wouldn't—well, from a personal standpoint I guess I looked at myself and thought, you didn't do what you should've done. So I requested orders to Vietnam."[27]

After Vernon Janick enlisted, he couldn't get enough of the military. For him, the chance to fight in Vietnam was like a dream come true. "I couldn't wait," Janick exclaimed. "I mean, I would have been really pissed if I couldn't have gone. I was young, gung ho, and volunteered for everything. In fact, I wanted to go airborne, Special Forces, the whole thing, but I was only seventeen when I went in. They had an age limit. On airborne or anything you had to be eighteen and a half and the best I could get was infantry, so that is what I took. I couldn't wait to go, you bet!"

More than a few men enlisted precisely because there was a war and they wanted a taste of it. Only later would Kenneth Korkow belatedly question his passion to experience war, but the knowledge came too late, and the lesson, as he recalled it, was painful.

> As a boy growing up we played cops and robbers, we played cowboys and Indians and I grew up around hunting. . . . I was making bombs when I was ten years old. . . . I just enjoyed making things go boom. So, as I got into college those first couple years, when we'd come back to the dormitory Huntley and Brinkley would be on and they'd be showing exotic footage of places like Con Thien and Phu Bai, the Rockpile. That seemed to be pretty exciting. I'd watched a lot of John Wayne movies and read a lot of GI Joe comic books, and there were some desires that I had to really see what action was—find out what the ultimate risk, supposedly, was. So that's the thing that compelled me and interested me in the Marine Corps. Frankly, I had never talked with anybody about combat experiences. I simply went by what I'd seen in John Wayne movies. I believed it all.[28]

Volunteering was a contagious affliction as the war heated up in 1965. The belief that it was America's mission to stop the spread of communism and defend the fledgling Republic of South Vietnam was widely accepted by most soldiers. Just as World War II had been their father's war, their sense of wanting to do something, of being involved with something important, lured many men in uniform into participating in what they felt was "their" war. And throughout their war, a majority of the men serving in Vietnam would be volunteers by choice or circumstance. Even in the middle years of American involvement, a sizable number of men in uniform not posted to Vietnam sought transfers there. In 1966–67 one in every five soldiers stationed in Europe submitted a request for transfer to Vietnam, either because they were bored, frustrated with the spit and polish, or just felt left out.[29]

Mike Meil was one of them. Meil was posted to Germany in early 1967 at a time when rumors about future troop levies to Vietnam were as common as deutsche marks. In the midst of all the rumors, Meil and a friend felt that it might be better to take control of their destinies, so they volunteered. As Mike recalled, "I had speculated about going over there [to Vietnam] anyhow, regardless of whether we volunteered or what. That was one of the reasons I went in the service. I guess I was pretty young and didn't understand exactly what the hell waving the flag and 'What to do for your country' meant. I guess I was one of those people that they call gung ho. Anyhow, it came about that we volunteered and were sent to Vietnam."[30]

David Carlisle volunteered for Vietnam in early 1968 while serving with the 1st Battalion, 70th Armor, in Augsburg, Germany. His request was as much an attempt to accelerate the inevitable, however, as it was to satiate his sense of curiosity about war.

> My battalion was getting so many levies each month for people to send to Vietnam and it was almost guaranteed that as soon as you made E-5 [sergeant] you would be gone to Vietnam within a couple of months or so, or at least within five to six months. I knew by March of 1968 or even before that I would probably be up for E-5 shortly and I was probably going to end up in Vietnam sooner or later. And by that time I was getting tired of the garrison environment. So one morning, I made up my mind I was going to volunteer and get it out of the way—and I did.[31]

That same sense of purpose or inevitability encouraged others to volunteer, not only from within the military ranks, but curious and patriotic civilians as well. One young enlistee, Phil Yaeger, admitted he didn't see the Communist presence in Vietnam as a very serious threat to America's national security, but he grew up in the conservative Midwest, in an environment where serving your country was taken for granted. "It was," he recalled emphatically, "your duty to serve." He took the oath in March 1966 and was quickly drawn into the vortex of Vietnam, but he was never able to identify the reasons why. "I had a high school friend killed in Vietnam. That possibly was on the periphery of it," he recalled. "I was bored. One semester at Indiana University and that didn't make much sense. I didn't have any direction at all. I didn't make grades, so I dropped out before I even had a hint of induction papers. I went ahead and enlisted in the marines."

Dave Carlisle chose to enlist in June 1966 after two somewhat lackluster years of college in South Dakota. It might have been curiosity. There were also some feelings about patriotism. But, even more than that, there was "the feeling that [Vietnam] was where the action was."

Throughout the war there would always be a flow of young men into the armed forces who enlisted for honorable reasons, albeit predicated on a somewhat innocent assessment of the realities of the war. As Tom Magedanz, himself a volunteer in 1969, reflected some twenty years later, "Many soldiers volunteered to go out of a sense of duty and many volunteered for more noble reasons than adventure, though the reality of those reasons was less than the perception. Most veterans' politics have changed—but not their pride in having served, nor their pride in having done their duty. Draftees as well felt, until very late in the war, that their cause was just; America was doing the right thing. But they would rather wait and be called than volunteer."[32]

The majority of Vietnam veterans are proud of what they did for their country, but their greatest pride is in what they endured for each other. While some now believe that they were victimized, those who volunteered can blame nothing more than their own innocence for their involvement in the war. They had not been duped or coerced by double-talking recruiters; they had simply trusted their government, believed the rhetoric, and stepped forward because, for whatever reason, that was the direction they wanted to go.

In describing his own circuitous route into the army in 1968, Randall Hoelzen may well have spoken for a generation of volunteers when he admitted, "Deep down I think I wanted to go. I was scared to go, but there was a couple of times I think I could have gotten out of it, and I chose not to for whatever reason. I went the other route towards Vietnam."[33]

There was a widespread belief in the country that even if the war were unjust or unwinnable, America could not simply turn tail and run. The war's goals were honorable. For some, the conviction still exists that while the war itself was militarily mismanaged and politically doomed from the start, the ideals for which they fought were the right ones all along.

Terry Shepardson believed Vietnam to be "his" war—at least he thought so back in 1969—and he figured that the fastest way to get there was to enlist in the Marine Corps.[34] John Merrell believed in what America was doing in Vietnam in 1967 and felt obligated to take part. He planned to take a year off after high school and then join the infantry and go to Vietnam. That was just what he did. There were no regrets in the aftermath of that service. John knew exactly why he was fighting. "I felt, and still believe it," he declared. "It sounds sort of weird to say it because I don't say it very often, but I was fighting communism."[35]

Tom Magedanz was just starting his junior year of high school in Yankton, South Dakota, in 1965 when the battle for the Ia Drang Valley, the first major ground action involving U.S. troops, took place. Vietnam was frequently discussed in his school, and Magedanz, like most young men from America's heartland, accepted the conservative values of patriotism and anticommunism that he had been exposed to throughout his childhood. "Our teachers told us that we were fighting communism and that was the thing we had to do. So all through high school I was in favor of the war," he reflected. "[In college] I read a lot about it and still thought the war was right and the United States should be fighting there and stopping communism. So prior to military service I was pretty much in favor of the war and believed and supported everything the government said."

In February 1969 Magedanz acted upon those beliefs and enlisted in the Marine Corps after he decided, "It was wrong for me to be in college taking a student deferment while there were other people being drafted. A lot of people who opposed the war were being drafted to go to Vietnam and I figured if I was gonna be in favor of the war, then I should be willing to go fight in it."[36]

Sitting out the war didn't suit Larry Hill, either. Hill was granted a IV-F physical deferment and legitimately escaped the draft calls that caught some of his classmates from Blair, Wisconsin. However, Hill believed that Americans should be "over there," and the untimely death of a hometown boy in 1967 decided the issue for him. "I started thinking I should do something too," he explained, "so I went and had surgery and then got reclassified I-A." He was drafted in March 1969.[37]

In the early stages of the war in Vietnam, America's involvement was popularized through the medium of books and movies, which no doubt inspired some enlistments. Certainly no military group was more sharply focused in the public eye than the Green Berets, who became, as Charles Moskos noted, something of a minor American industry. John Wayne starred in a movie titled *The Green Berets,* and there was a GI Joe children's doll complete with field manual. There were also comic books that reduced the complexity of the war to simple story lines illustrated with Del Ray dots and balloons filled with worn-out military clichés. The comics were very popular with adolescents, who were themselves only a few years younger than the soldiers whose lives were represented in the drawings and dialogue of the pulp adventures. Staff Sergeant Barry Sadler popularized the Special Forces with a hit record, "The Ballad of the Green Berets," and a book titled *I'm a Lucky One*. His was only one of more than a dozen novels and autobiographies extolling the mission and the men of the Special Forces.[38]

And though few would probably admit it, such images had a powerful effect. Paul Meringolo admitted being "caught up on the idea of maybe going into the service and maybe even be a war hero. There weren't a lot of demonstrations at that time or a lot of antiwar feelings, so you sort of knew that maybe there was a possibility of becoming a war hero like we were watching on TV."[39]

"You had John Wayne," Paul Boehm enumerated, ticking the motivators off one finger at a time, "and people were military minded and patriotic, and your father did it, so you were going to do it." The syllogism followed perfectly. "And the country wanted you to do it. So you did what you had to do." Doing less would have been shirking responsibility, and that was not a real alternative in Green Bay, Wisconsin, even in 1968.

The Marine Corps remained largely volunteer throughout the Vietnam conflict. Its traditions and reputation, along with a classy public relations program, created an elite image that attracted many young men. Some joined for studied and logical reasons, others were simply lured by the packaging. Phil Yaeger's motive was rational. "If I went in for two years, either draftee or enlisted, I would certainly without question go to Vietnam. And I felt I would be better prepared as a marine. I had other family members as marines and [I] knew a little bit about them."

Vince Olson chose the Marine Corps for similar reasons. A state champion wrestler, Olson was a person who accepted challenges. He saw the marines as being "just a little tougher, and I thought I could do a little better and better myself."[40] Richard Ogden, on the other hand, chose the Marine Corps because he liked their song,[41] and Robert Moran picked the marines, literally, from a hat. "Me and a friend of mine took army, marines, navy and air force and put them in a hat and drew out of it," Moran explained. "I drew the marines and he drew the army. . . . We picked, and then we debated on it. I said, 'If we are gonna wind up being in the war we might as well be well trained, so we'll go into the marines.' He still held out and went into the army because he didn't think he'd make it. From what I understood, the marines gave the best combat training, so that's what I decided to do."

Jeff Yushta decided, in retrospect, that he had fallen for the image. Yushta had always excelled in whatever he put his

mind to. He was motivated by challenge and held to the belief that if you are going to do it—do it well!

In Richfield, Minnesota, where I enlisted, all the recruiters were in the same office. . . . And me and a couple of friends went in one day. They said, "Let's all go
in the service together." So we stopped in and saw the
navy guy, the army guy, the air force guy. And the Marine Corps recruiter that we saw was a top sergeant,
which was unusual for a recruiter. He was the epitome
of a marine! I mean, everything was right on the numbers. A heck of an impressive guy. I just talked to him
for five minutes and you envision that they are all like
this. I said, "This is it, right here." And my buddy said,
"Yeah, that guy was really neat." So the next day I went
down and enlisted. They didn't.[42]

In retrospect, many veterans seem a bit saddened by the
exuberance and trust they felt. Jim Raysor, looking back,
thought his recruiter "must have had a degree in psychology,
because when I walked through the door, he said, 'Yep, this is
a perfect guy for the infantry. I can talk this kid into anything.' And he did. I enlisted for airborne right there, right on
the spot."
Few enlistees seem to have discussed their plans with returning servicemen who might otherwise have influenced
their decision. But one concerned former veteran did have
some influence on Deane Johnson. While attending technical
school in 1968, Johnson decided to join the army. When a
former helicopter crew chief in Johnson's drafting class heard
of his plans, "He took me aside and gave me a big brother talk
about the army and what I could be in for, and that essentially,
things weren't all that Sergeant Fury comic books cracked it
up to be—sort of like a Dutch uncle. His last advice to me
was 'Ride—don't walk.' I told the recruiter I wanted to be a
helicopter repairman. He asked me what kind, and I said I
didn't care, as long as I could ride and not walk."[43]
Johnson later became a crew chief and never had to walk.
But as part of his job he also became a door gunner. There
were some days he'd rather not have been riding, either.

Enlistees were able to choose the branch of service they joined, and they often had a guarantee of sorts to be trained in a specific military occupation. Guarantees did not ensure one would actually serve in the promised job, but even at the height of the Vietnam War, 88 percent of all servicemen were assigned to noncombat occupational specialities. Thus, enlisting offered better odds of avoiding combat as an infantryman than did being drafted. Enlistees with above-average aptitude test scores were often given jobs far away from the shooting, leaving the bloody part of the war to the less educated. Many men, rather than enlisting to fight, actually volunteered as a means of avoiding infantry service. One 1968 Defense Department survey indicated that 60 percent of college graduates who enlisted were draft motivated.[44]

By 1970 the Marine Corps had begun withdrawing from Vietnam. That same year, the government began the lottery system in an attempt to select draftees more equitably. Don Trimble's birthday ended up number thirteen in the lottery and he quickly reasoned that joining the marines made perfect sense. The marines' two-year enlistment program was the same as the army's draft, but going army included the near certainty of assignment to Vietnam. The Marine Corps's buildup was over, and he figured that the marines were only putting about 20 percent replacements back into Vietnam. Trimble took what he felt were the better odds and lost.[45]

Glenn Miller was almost a postscript to a war that had been going on since he was in the sixth grade. The war was winding down and many units had been brought home by the time he enlisted. But Miller had spent his young life immersed in the Vietnam War, watching the news and seeing the pictures in *Life* magazine. He wanted to see the place and take part in the action. He enlisted in the summer of 1971 and flew as a door gunner assisting Vietnamese troops in 1972. Miller was among the last of his countrymen to go, but he went for many of the same reasons that motivated those who preceded him. Ironically, just as the Vietnam War had begun with America employing a largely volunteer force, so it ended, with men like Miller who stepped forward and signed on the dotted line because, for them, it had been necessary to do so.[46]

National Guard and Reserve Service

One safe means by which a soldier could avoid Vietnam duty and still fulfill his military service obligation during the Vietnam era was to join the National Guard or the reserves. During the war, neither the guard nor the reserves were ever mobilized for deployment to Vietnam in great strength. Except for a brief scare in 1968 following the *Pueblo* incident, relatively few reserve component personnel were sent to Vietnam. There were notable exceptions, and some National Guard communications, artillery, and field support units did deploy overseas, but service in the National Guard and the reserve components of the various military branches carried a reasonable guarantee of remaining at home. Throughout the war, many thousands took advantage of the guard and reserves in order to minimize their obligation for military service or, at least, maximize the distance between them and Vietnam. Author Gloria Emerson observed that although America's "one million Vietnam era Guardsmen and reservists performed a measure of national service, as contrasted with those who avoided the military entirely, . . . they served in a way that involved much less personal hardship than did active military duty."[47]

A 1966 Pentagon study showed that 71 percent of the reservists questioned joined for reasons that were draft motivated. In 1968 there was a list of more than a hundred thousand men waiting for a spot in a guard or reserve unit— and all the units were full. By 1970, as draft quotas shrank, those waiting lists mysteriously vanished, and by late 1971 the National Guard found itself forty-five thousand people understrength.

Although such service in the reserve components did minimize the chances of becoming a casualty in Vietnam, it did not offer absolute safety. Seventy-two army National Guardsmen died in Vietnam, and reserve personnel accounted for nearly 9 percent of America's combat fatalities, most of them army.[48]

John Meyer admitted that he enlisted in the navy reserve specifically to avoid the draft and stay out of Vietnam. It was a plan that failed.

I started out my first year in the navy reserve going to meetings one night a month, two weeks of basic training at Great Lakes, Illinois, and after a year of service school you go on to two years active duty. [The war] didn't sound like anything I wanted to do! I can't say I had any strong political feelings, I just didn't want to get drafted into the army and know where I was going to end up. I guess I'd had as good a chance as it turned out taking my chances with the draft. The best laid plans of men and mice often go astray and this one sure did.[49]

Of the roughly one million men who enlisted in the reserves and National Guard during the Vietnam era, only fifteen thousand actually served there. John Meyer was right: His was an improbable statistical happenstance, but he was also a navy corpsman. The fine print specifies that navy corpsmen can be assigned to the marines.[50]

Conscription

Whereas many Americans voluntarily enlisted in the armed forces to seek or avoid service in Vietnam, the lion's share of the uncommitted draft-age men in America waited, in patience or in panic, for the government to come for them. The Vietnam War was not an issue of importance to them, or so it seems, until they were directly involved. In most cases that detachment vanished the moment their induction notices arrived in the mail.

"A notice for induction," wrote Willard Waller from the vantage point of 1944, "is for most young men a sentence to hard labor, and for some a sentence of death; for others it is a sentence to lose a limb or an eye: disfigurement that no civilized society can now impose as a punishment for crime."[51]

Although Waller's assertion might be slightly overstated, it is difficult to argue that for many draftees, orders to Vietnam were tantamount to a death sentence. For additional tens of thousands, the loss of limbs or other disfigurement constituted a sentence to a lesser life than they might otherwise have enjoyed. Still, although many of the men who were drafted as combat infantry soldiers exhibited a strong sense of duty to country, many others went unwillingly, angry about the war's disruption of their lives. Dwight Reiland's feelings in 1970 vacillated between the two extremes:

> It wasn't that I felt the war was unjust. Maybe unjust for our country's participation in it, but I felt there was something that needed to be done. But I wasn't sure that it was our job to do it. I wasn't convinced of that anyhow. But Jeez! We grew up and you always heard "Your country right or wrong" or whatever. A lot of guys were getting into the National Guard and a lot of them were enlisting in the navy or whatever to make sure that they didn't end up in the jungle someplace. And I thought I was kind of blessed anyway, and I felt I was going to get through this. And I didn't. But I had my mind made up that if they wanted me, they were going to have to draft me. I just didn't think it would happen. Well, it did. And nobody disliked it any more than I did, but I just thought, I got to do this.[52]

Some two million men were drafted during the Vietnam War. More importantly, as the war progressed, draftees continued to make up an ever-increasing percentage of combat casualties.[53] In 1965 draftees totaled 21 percent of America's combat force; as the marine battalions withdrew from Vietnam in 1970, the percentage of draftees increased eventually to 70 percent of the "foxhole strength" in the field. Not unpredictably, according to a study done by the Nader organization, draftees continued to represent more and more of the men killed in Vietnam. In 1965 draftees totaled only 16 percent of America's battle deaths. By the end of 1967 they made up 34 percent of all combat soldiers killed in action, a figure that rose to 43 percent by 1970.[54]

By the war's end, draftees accounted for approximately one-third of all combat deaths in all branches of service. They made up 48 percent of all U.S. Army fatalities and less than 5 percent of marines killed in action (KIA). Each year a greater share of combat was passed on to the draftees, resulting in the paradox, succinctly noted by Charles Moskos, that "those who are the least committed to the military as a career are the very ones who are the most military in the sense of getting killed or wounded in combat."[55]

The process of determining who would be drafted was left to the country's local draft boards, those "little groups of neighbors." The nation's 4,080 local draft boards formed the backbone of the Selective Service system and ranged in size from the twenty-eight registrants of Hinsdale County, Colorado, to the three largest of New York City's sixty-eight draft boards, which contained more than fifty thousand registrants each. Local boards were given monthly manpower quotas based on needs determined by the Defense Department. Each local board determined exactly who among its I-A (draft eligible) registrants would be drafted and in precisely what order.[56]

Each eighteen-year-old registrant received a I-A classification unless he was granted an exemption or deferment by his local draft board for a necessary occupation, hardship, schooling, or for obvious physical impairments. Petitions for exemption or deferment were supplied to the local draft board by the registrants themselves. Obtaining the deferment was the applicant's responsibility, and every man was expected to tell his local board, in writing, about his job, any family he was supporting, his schooling, or any other information that might affect his draft status. Local boards were accorded great leeway in determining deferments, but maintaining them was the registrants' responsibility.[57]

The process of selection, according to Lawrence Baskir and William Strauss, was inherently unfair and inequitable.

> The draft was not . . . an arbitrary and omnipotent force imposing itself like blind fate upon men who were powerless to resist. Instead, it worked as an instrument of Darwinian social policy. The "fittest"— those with background, wit, or money—managed to escape. Through an elaborate structure of deferments, exemptions, legal technicalities, and noncombat military alternatives, the draft rewarded those who manipulated the system to their advantage.[58]

Local boards began filling their quotas by drafting those the board deemed to be delinquent, that is, anyone the board believed had failed to meet Selective Service requirements. Regulations permitted a board to reclassify delinquents— such as those who refused to report for induction—as I-A, and draft them ahead of other eligibles. Any I-A registrants tired of waiting beneath the sword of Damocles for their notice to report could volunteer for the draft, and many chose to do so in order to get their obligation out of the way and get on with the rest of their lives.[59]

Doug Kurtz, who had been working on the Great Lakes until the winter of 1968, fell into the latter category. "I got tired of waiting for the draft," he recalled. "I was kind of between jobs. I was in the Merchant Marine and it was getting cold and they were shutting the lakes down, so I [figured] I might as well go get it done with. It was going to happen sooner or later."[60]

Next in line for selection were men who had lost their deferments: occupational, hardship, marital, or, most frequently, student deferments. The remaining I-As were taken on the basis of age, beginning with the twenty-five year olds and working down to those who were nineteen. The age sequence was revised by President Lyndon B. Johnson in June 1967, after which time selection was made in ascending order of age beginning with nineteen year olds.[61]

Predictably, enlistment rates varied from one draft board to another. Thus the additional registrants that a local board needed to fill its quota varied. Whereas one board might have needed to draft only 10 percent of its registrants to meet its monthly quota, a neighboring board with a lower enlistment rate might have had to draft 40 percent of its candidates. Married men might be drafted to meet a quota in one region of the country, whereas other local boards with higher enlistment rates found such measures unnecessary. Baskir and Strauss discovered that in the first five months of 1966, for example, 90 percent of the draft boards in Washington and Alabama drafted married men without children, whereas no boards in Connecticut were required to take that step.[62]

"Most of those who were drafted," wrote Loren Baritz, "thought of the draft as an event like measles, a graduation, the weather, something that happened to people."[63] Military service was a fact of life, an unhappy obligation that one accepted. Their teachers had told them so. Maintaining a free and democratic society depended upon it. When Jerry Severson was drafted into the army in December 1964, the Vietnam buildup had not yet begun. In spite of everything, Severson accepted the interruption of his life gracefully.

> When I went in the service I had this attitude to do your thing for God and country, and a little bit of the glory and stuff that goes along with it. So, if you're going to be there, you might just as well be in the best unit available, and that was with the Special Forces. I extended my tour so that I could get into the Special Forces. You had to be in three years in order to get into it, and being a draftee was only two [years]. At the time that I first went in I really thought I was going to be a twenty-year man. I liked the army. I liked the discipline of the army. I knew that. It was just probably my mental makeup that I could be a good soldier and I thought that this was the thing to do.

Paul Meringolo felt the same sense of obligation. "I think I was one of the last generation that anticipated that somewhere along the line we would have to serve some kind of military obligation," he said. "It wasn't really questioned, you just knew that. You registered for the draft when you turned eighteen and sooner or later you would be drafted and serve your two years' obligation, if you didn't enlist and get it over with, and come back to your civilian life."

In the ten years prior to direct American involvement in Vietnam, draft quotas had remained low and the I-A pool high. The Selective Service had been able to liberalize deferments and exemptions for the draft. Until 1966 special treatment was accorded to married men, who were given a special "low-priority" I-A status. By early 1966, however, deferments granted for hardships, parenting, or simply being married were twice as numerous as those given to students. But when President Johnson increased the call for troops from ten thousand to more than thirty thousand a month, sudden shortages began to crop up in the I-A pool. As they did, deferments and exemptions for fathers, married men, graduate students, and previously "safe" occupations dried up.

II-S student deferments became conditional, tied to academic performance or minimum scores on the Army Selective Service Qualifying Test. Many college freshmen were suddenly faced with the pressures of an "A, B, C, D, Nam" grading system, which only increased the pressure on students who had trouble enough adjusting to the rigors of academic life and social responsibility. The rule, of course, was well understood. Once a deferment was lost, it was gone for good.[64]

Meringolo, like many first-year college students, suffered just such a fate at Whister State College. Oddly, the immaturity that cost him his deferment was of no concern to those who would make him a soldier.

> I was no more prepared to go to college than I was to do anything else at that time but I did start. And I quickly realized that you are pretty much on your own to do your studying and take care of things and I didn't do much studying and didn't take care of much, so by the time the first semester was coming to a close I realized that if I did take my finals I would probably flunk half the classes. So what I ended up doing was dropping out before the first semester even ended to save this embarrassment upon myself.

By that time the army was drafting more than thirty thousand men a month. Meringolo had only to wait until the following September (1966) to get his call.

Dan Krehbiel was also fearful of the draft, which seemed to float overhead like a dark cloud when he entered college.

> I had feared it for a couple of years ever since I got out of high school in 1968, because early college was difficult for me and I had to make an adjustment that was hard for me to make . . . The II-S deferment was a big thing. The college I went to, if you had low grades they would make you sit out a semester before you

could return, and that happened to me. During that semester I lost my deferment. Without a deferment it was simply a matter of time.

Even though I returned to school, the deferment was still gone. I went back and settled down pretty well with a whole different character.

By then it was too late. When Krehbiel's draft notice finally arrived, it was met with a sense of resignation.

For some, it was not the academic rigor or the boredom and lack of purpose that brought their deferments to an end; it was beer by the pitcher, cards all night, and hormones that yodeled. William Harken blamed his slide down the ivy-covered walls on pinochle.[65] Tom Schultz and Steve Fredrick flunked out of college largely because of scheduling problems: Their social calendars allowed precious little time for academics. They were both unfettered by restraint or responsibility.[66] Fredrick remembers that being drafted in 1967 was disconcerting, but he was almost as fearful of his existing lifestyle. "I was scared, but I really didn't care because my life was at an end anyway," Fredrick said. "I had flunked out of college—this was the second time—and I'd been picked up going ninety-five miles per hour in a fifty-five-mile-per-hour zone and lost my license. I got picked up a month later for driving without a license. I was on my way to either jail or Vietnam, it really didn't make much difference. I really didn't care."[67]

Naturally, people who sat on draft boards took a particularly dim view of students abusing their academic privileges. Partying out, flunking out, or quitting were fast tracks to a I-A classification.

Later in the war there were limits to the number of semesters a student could remain in school and still stay eligible for a II-S deferment. Dwight Reiland said his draft complications stemmed not from poor grades but from his decision to switch universities and majors. He automatically became eligible for the draft in 1970 after completing his fourth year without graduating.

Deferments also ran out after graduation. As Michael Jackson discovered, "The fact that I was in college prevented me from getting drafted. So, after I graduated, I was thinking I had a fifty-fifty chance of not getting drafted. Had I gone into teaching or been a policeman I would not have been drafted."

Worries about the draft motivated some college students to change their course of study, so they would graduate with a degree such as engineering, law enforcement, or teaching— all fields that enjoyed nearly exempt draft status. Consequently, occupations that were almost invariably deferred were being flooded with graduating applicants. The state of New York, for example, reported in 1969 that 85 percent of students undergoing teacher training were draft-age men and some New York City universities reported as much as an 800 percent increase in the number of men taking education courses.[68]

But if the New York City draft boards publicly confirmed the inviolability of deferments for full-time teachers, those liberal policies had not reached the upper plains states, much to the chagrin of Tom Birhanzel.

At that time there was a teacher deferment available, but my draft board didn't honor that deferment. When I was out interviewing for jobs, the school districts would check with my draft board for a deferment and find out that I didn't have one. Therefore, I could never get a job. . . . After six or seven of these occasions, my wife and I sat down and had a long talk about my going into the service and getting it over with. We also considered moving out of the country in that situation, although that feeling wasn't very prevalent at the time.[69]

Most draftees viewed their notice to report for induction with resignation. There was no mistaking what that notice represented, but most men tried to remain as optimistic as possible as they tore open the envelope. Tom Schultz remembers the moment well: "I knew what it was prior to opening it, so I tried to think of all the places I could go besides Vietnam and what other military jobs there could be other than the infantry. After reading the letter telling me to report I felt empty."[70]

Jon Neely had been curious about Vietnam, and discussions with his friends had centered not so much on whether the war was right or wrong, but rather "What's it like over there?" In the end, Neely said that he and his friends were "basically pretty patriotic and figured this was our duty. The country called us to go and this is where we were going. The thought of either going to college or going out of the country to get out of the draft never really even entered my mind. I guess I just accepted it and figured, hey, let's go give it a shot—make the best of it."[71]

Although there were a few who looked forward to being drafted, the majority seemed to try either to forget that the draft existed or to wish it away. There was always a bit of shock among those who had done the wishing when the bitter reality arrived in the mail. Dwight Reiland remembered the feelings vividly:

> It was like, "Oh my God, it did! It happened!" I kind of suspected maybe. But God, I've always been kind of lucky at stuff and I honestly thought that probably they were going to miss me. I really did. I think it was the winter before when they had the lottery and drew the numbers . . . Mine was one hundred and sixty-nine. You always heard, "Hey! I hear they are going to one hundred and seventy-five," or, "I hear they are going to one hundred and fifty this year." You know. And the word was they were going to one hundred and eighty the year that I was a hundred and sixty-nine and I thought, Oh— I'll probably make it. I don't think it will happen. But it did!

Reiland entertained some brief fantasies of evading the draft, as nearly all draftees did, but they were only mental diversions.

> Canada seemed much more appealing then than it had been in previous conversations because the shot had been fired. You were drafted! But, by the same token, because you had been drafted, it wasn't like you headed to Canada and just hid out. I had been drafted,

so now if I took off I was running! And I didn't want to do that. But there were different people who said, "You know, I believe I'd run for it." And a person can't say that he didn't consider it. But at that time you didn't know [that] Carter was going to tell them, "That's okay, come on home." At that time, you thought, This is it. You go, you're gone! And I wasn't ready for that—for something that final. I thought, Well, I'm not running.

Donald Trimble was also a victim of the lottery that, in 1970, began determining the order in which men would be conscripted by drawing birth dates randomly. All draft-eligible registrants were selected in the order in which their birthdays were drawn. Trimble recalled that when the sequence was announced, "The paper carried the first twelve . . . and I wasn't on there, so I thought, Well, I'm probably way down at the end of the list, I'll never be drafted. The next day the paper ran the total 365 days and I started backwards and I got all the way down to the twentieth and I said, 'Well, what's going on here?' And my draft number was thirteen. So I knew then and there that I was gonna be drafted. That was a very low number."

In the end, war would expose the real meaning of the words spoken by those visionaries whom Willard Waller called "men of talk . . . who prattle of ideals and honor and fighting for the right." Americans by the thousands were called away to Vietnam because they were told it was necessary. Just like Leonard Dutcher, they were considered by their government to be the necessary human elements that personify written policy. They later returned home by the thousands, many questioning that necessity. And, like many World War II veterans, a significant number of Vietnam veterans came home bitter, disillusioned, and unable to articulate exactly why. Willard Waller spoke for all of them in 1944 when he wrote:

> The soldier has come to believe, and with considerable reasons, that those who talk about ideals do not fight for them, and that those who fight for them do not talk about them. The soldier knows that when the

nation fights for freedom and for justice in far-flung areas of the world, he must lose his freedom, his comfort, even his identity for the duration of the conflict. The ideals for which he is fighting can have little meaning for any soldier so long as the war lasts, while for those who die and for many of the wounded they can never have any meaning at all. He knows that those who speak so glibly of ideals have no conception of what the process of enforcing those ideals means in terms of pain and starvation and death and horror.[72]

Those who would later see combat in Vietnam knew nothing of the things Waller described. But then, they had yet to receive their real education. That would come—*after* training. As they entered adulthood they were simply young men on their first real adventure; they did not realize it would change them forever.

"Jesus Christ," Vernon Janick said years later to the floorboards beneath his feet. "It just about changed my whole life 'cause before I was just a young kid. Didn't really do anything in life. That was my first—going in the army was my first go-out-adventure other than work, so I really never had a chance to . . ."

He never finished. What he had never had a chance to do was too broad and inclusive a statement to complete. But what the war would weave into the fabric of his future was easier for Janick to summarize: "Whatever I learned was during them times."

CHAPTER 2

Basic Training

October 7, 1966

Dear Folks,

Well, we made it to Texas this morning and it's colder than hell down here. We left Minn[esota] at 10:00 last night and got here at 3:00. As soon as we got here we were marching all over signing in. They finally let us go to bed at 7:00 this morning. They let us have three hours of sleep and now we are going to get our hair cut and a lot of other junk.

I'd better close for now.

Len[1]

In order to exorcise the civilian from the new recruit, military service begins with all new men passing through a course of basic instruction and indoctrination. This "basic training" or "boot camp" begins molding civilians into something resembling soldiers or marines in roughly eight weeks. It is a process that is not without accompanying pain.

This sudden immersion in military life often came as a shock to the new trainees. It was the first genuine good-bye for most inductees, the first time they would be away from home for more days than they had clean underwear. The separation from home represented a great unknown for which there was little in their civilian lives to prepare them. The speed with which recruits were swallowed up was a hidden blessing, because, like pulling teeth, there was less pain in a rapid and purposeful procedure than in one that prolonged the agony. Their training began, then as now, with a sudden feeling of shock, separation, and disorientation. Recruits found themselves in a very competitive and masculine environment in which much of the impetus for the training came through peer pressure, negative reinforcement, and carefully applied increments of stress. What was most unsettling to the new recruit, however, was his total lack of control. The new recruit was compelled to depend on the military for every necessity. He thought and felt as part of a group and, in most cases, he came to believe then, and will still maintain, that he is better for having endured the experience. He may well be correct.

Every subsequent step in the training program was orchestrated to mold the recruit's thoughts and actions into those of a soldier. During the Vietnam War, the army, constrained by manpower problems imposed by the one-year rotation policy, sought to make boys into soldiers in forty-four working days—a total of 352 hours of instruction.[2] The official time allotment, however, was misleading. In reality, recruits seldom experienced a training day of less than twelve hours, and eighteen-hour days were frequent.

During this intense training regimen, recruits were taught the proper attitude and basic skills of soldiering. In addition, the program was designed to suppress individuality and condition each man to react in a predictable way to stressful situations so that later, in combat, a man's actions would be synchronized with those of his fellow soldiers.

That such predictable behavior was necessary in combat later became obvious to Ed Hoban, who observed, "Their whole purpose was to teach you to react without asking why, because you can always ask why later. . . . You don't have time to think, Why is this right or wrong? You need to react to the situation first and then, if you need to think about it or want to think about it, you can take the time when it is all over."

Although basic training provided soldiers with the fundamentals of military discipline, protocol, drill, and tradition, Gwynne Dyer saw its primary purpose as something entirely different. "Basic training," he wrote, "is not really about teaching people skills; it's about changing them, so that they can do things they wouldn't have dreamt of otherwise. It works by applying enormous physical and mental pressure to men who have been isolated from their normal civilian environment and placed in one where the only right way to think and behave is the way the Marine Corps wants them to."[3]

The alchemy of turning civilians into soldiers was the responsibility of the noncommissioned officer (NCO) instructors. To this end, the army borrowed the drill sergeant concept from the Marine Corps and tried to glamorize the position to attract the best personnel. However, the same top-quality, highly motivated officers and NCOs so necessary for effective training in both services were also desperately needed in Vietnam. Experienced sergeants, especially in the early days of the war, often viewed training assignments as undesirable postings that could not compete with the allure of adventure and accelerated promotion available in the combat units deploying to Vietnam. But, as the war progressed, veterans provided an ever-increasing percentage of the training staff. Their experiences helped instill a confidence and purpose in the training regime.

For Donald Putnam, listening to these combat veterans was a preeminent part of his training.

> I think probably the biggest thing in looking back on that is not so much the attitude of the recruit going in, but of the people handling the recruit at that time. I think those people had a whole lot to do with whether you were gung ho or not, because they could tell you about things that happened there [in combat] and you had to believe them. Some of these guys were wearing Purple Hearts. Every one of them naturally had a CIB [Combat Infantry Badge] and you learned what that meant right away. All of a sudden you knew you were probably going to end up there, so maybe you should listen to these guys. Maybe they could tell you something that would help you survive. And they would tell it the way it was.

The most enduring test men faced throughout their training was constantly dealing with the unknown. They entered a labyrinth of physical and mental challenges that were tolerable to most and abusive to a few. The training provided an avenue for adventure and excitement to the majority of trainees, along with a regimented discipline, the necessity of which became obvious to those who later saw combat. But for most recruits, first impressions were not encouraging.

Troops arrived for processing and training amidst everything from snow flurries to sand fleas. Even the weather sometimes seemed to conspire in establishing appropriately somber tones to accompany the start of military life. The drill sergeants took the recruits in tow as soon as the bus doors opened. Paul Meringolo vividly remembers assuming the "front-leaning rest position," a euphemistic term belying a sinister purpose with which all men entering training became intimately accustomed. Palms firmly set in the soil, body rigid, toes straight—each trainee got an earthy feel for his respective training site as the drill instructors counted out the first of what seemed like tens of thousands of push-ups.

The new arrivals made the acquaintance of their trainers, who quickly defined the terms of their relationship. Donald Putnam said that his drill sergeant, a Sergeant First Class Acuna, patiently explained exactly why Putnam and the others were there and exactly what they could expect. Acuna displayed obvious relish as he further described their status: trainees—lower than anything else on earth, although he used somewhat more pejorative language. Most soldiers, for varied reasons, never forget their drill instructors. Donald Putnam didn't either.

Vince Olson's first day in the Marine Corps was a bit confusing. He arrived at the Marine Corps Recruit Depot in San Diego where, he said,

> they took us through a kind of an assembly line deal and got us tennis shoes and jogging shorts, T-shirts or whatever. We threw everything in a sack and had a haircut. From there they marched us to the tin huts and we kind of threw our bags in the huts and they told us to get outside and make it rain. We got out in the sand and started throwing sand up in the air and making it "rain." I don't know how long we did that, but we were pretty well exhausted. We never took our clothes off or any-

thing. [At the end of the day] they just said, "Get in the barracks and go to bed."

From the moment processing began, all aspects of the recruits' daily existence were rigidly controlled. Marine "boot" Tom Magedanz was allocated five minutes for each meal and his group of eighty men was allotted seven minutes to shower and shave. Even latrine breaks were scheduled and of uniform duration.[4]

The emphasis during initial processing was on getting men equipped and evaluated. At the same time, the recruits began to learn the importance of putting collective needs ahead of individual desires. Once in uniform, each man surrendered his individuality and began the long process of learning to soldier—either willingly or through the coercion of his instructor and the dynamics of his training group.

The removal of one's identity was not a surgical process. It was more a steady application of pressure, like squeezing the contents out of a sausage casing and then restuffing it with the substance of the training. Civilian identities, along with civilian clothing, were folded and stored away or shipped home for use in an unforeseeable future when, it was hoped, both might still be found to fit.

Through an endless succession of lines and waiting in tiled hallways, each recruit proceeded down an assembly line that included sixty-second hair styling, inoculations, and the poking and probing of physical examinations covering everything from teeth to toes with predictably discomforting intrusions into those regions in between. The processing continued with clothing issue, barracks assignments, and an endless flow of paperwork and questionnaires. Recruits were given a pay advance, the so-called flying twenty-five, with which they purchased toilet articles and brass and shoe polish. There were psychological screenings, biographical data sheets, aptitude tests, and a lecture on the soundness of investment in America by buying bonds through the payroll savings plan.

Most trainees dutifully signed up to purchase savings bonds, a deduction that, like most decisions in the military, was never completely voluntary. But every unit had those who resisted the system. Refusing to buy savings bonds was one of the little things that identified these men to their instructors. James Raysor was one such person. He fancied himself a tough guy at the time and challenged the system. Later, he recalled, "Our DI said, 'Everybody will buy a savings bond.' I was making about sixty-two dollars a month. . . . So I said, 'No way. I'm not buying any savings bonds.' I did ungodly amounts of extra duty for weeks and weeks."

The endless frustration and irritation of processing days quickly gave way to the routine of aches and pains and lack of sleep that marked the actual training cycle. The initial phases of basic training seemed to resemble nothing more than pointless harassment and mindless physical stress. But there was method to the madness, and the army and Marine Corps were not prone to waste precious hours. A letter to Steve Fredrick's father from the lieutenant in charge of Steve's training at Fort Lewis, Washington, assured the following to Fredrick's family:

> His training will emphasize the development of disciplined precision in thought and action, physical fitness, self-reliance, patriotism, and individual responsibility. . . . To this end the finest and most experienced Non-Commissioned Officers in the Army have been selected and given special training to act as his Drill Instructors and Drill Sergeants.[5]

The "most experienced Non-Commissioned Officers in the Army" initially began by conditioning each recruit to accept being trained. The physical training toughened the mind and body and slowly built confidence. Jeffrey Beatty's first letter to his mother from Fort Hood, Texas, described a week of running, marching, and exercising that he confessed had actually passed rather quickly and wasn't as bad as he had anticipated.[6]

Harassment and regimentation gradually increased over the first four weeks of training, but this was calculated to expose the men to tolerable levels of stress and later served as a foundation for building up unit pride and a sense of purpose. According to a ten-year-long study conducted at Fort Ord, California, stress levels among recruits reached their peak after three weeks of training, and revealed anxiety and anger levels in training that approximated the levels experienced by men awaiting actual combat.[7]

And those days of training, as Steve Fredrick remembered them, were filled with things to do:

> We get up about 4:30 every morning and get dressed, make our beds, clean the barracks and fall out for breakfast about 5:30. After that, we clean barracks and training areas. We have a company formation about 7:00 and then the classes begin. We march at least a mile between classes. We have had classes in bayonet, first aid, military justice, guard duty, etc. We have about an hour of scheduled PT every day and on top of that we usually have to do some running. We get back to the company area about 5:00 every day for supper. After supper we usually have to run or march until 8 or 9 o'clock, then we come in and clean the barracks again and shower and shave if we have time. Lights are out and we have to be in bed—no talking—at 9:30. That is a typical day and they are the busiest days I have ever seen in my life. I just don't have time to do anything.[8]

Training days in the Marine Corps were very similar, beginning at 0430, according to one marine, and continuing until about 2100 hours. Just as with the army, the day was divided into periods of drill, classroom instruction, physical training, and the seemingly endless barracks cleaning, interspersed with meals, mail call, and the occasional free minute or two just prior to lights-out to scribble a few lines about it to someone at home.[9]

Life in a basic training platoon acquired a unique sense of institutional blandness. To the ear, training was noise in unison, and even the snoring that permeated the barracks at night seemed to be a collective enterprise. Smells ran the gamut from disinfectant and abrasive cleanser to floor wax, boot polish, and gun oil. The eyes, however, were deprived the most. Training occurred in an ocean of olive drab and khaki, from uniforms to bunk beds to latrine stalls. Ultimately, even the mood of the soldiers seemed to mirror the drabness.

Training continued in hurry-ups and waits, fits and starts—an often morose experiment in social engineering and industrial efficiency where nothing was left to chance or done alone. Within days a recruit was no longer an individual; he became part of a platoon. As such, he began to accept this association and identify with his surrogate family. His connection with the past slowly began to fade as his new military identity took over. Each man lost by degrees his familiarity with the face he shaved each morning. Jon Neely recalled:

> After probably a week of getting into the program, we pretty much all accepted the fact that we all looked the same. We all acted the same basically. No more making fun of each other; it was time to get in shape, and drill instructors have a way of getting you into shape. I wouldn't say that it was the roughest eight weeks of my life, it was just a totally new experience, learning to do things in a strict fashion constantly, day after day after day. The training was, of course, every day. Not much time for personal things. A lot of the guys would sit around after lights-out in the evening and do their letter writing. There were no phone privileges for the first few weeks and [it was] just something that you had to accept and make the best of.

Steve Fredrick explained that what he was experiencing was "a lot like a prison camp," and the regimentation and lack of freedom to which he was introduced became "like an invisible noose around my neck which doesn't tighten or isn't noticed unless I try to move."[10] Conformity became the adhesive that bound the trainees together so that, in thought and action, young men from every walk of life and every part of the country could act in concert. To this end recruits were motivated, indoctrinated, cajoled, and disciplined—both individually and in groups. They would acquire, each in their own measure, pride, aggression, discipline, physical stamina, and soldier skills. It would never be enough, not for what lay ahead, but these were necessary qualities that would provide them a fighting chance. And the nation, having called these men into service, owed them that much.

The physical training was structured so that the majority of recruits succeeded, although that was not apparent to the participants. Few trainees were unable to meet the physical tasks. Those few who did fall short were singled out for their failure and threatened with repeating the training cycle. For most, this was incentive enough to bring about an improved second effort. There were special training groups for the overweight or unfit. But because every man was expected to successfully complete his basic training, as Gwynne Dyer observed, the training was by nature truly basic.

The men who run the machine think and talk in terms of the stress they are placing on the recruits: "We take so many c.c.'s of stress and we administer it to each man—they should be a little bit scared and they should be unsure, but they're adjusting." The aim is to keep the training arduous but just within most of the recruits' capability to withstand. One of the most striking achievements of the drill instructors is to create and maintain the illusion that basic training is an extraordinary challenge, one that will set those who graduate apart from others, when in fact almost everyone can succeed.[11]

Malingerers and slackers, those who "shammed," were quickly singled out by their peers. Punishing the group, usually with push-ups or extra one-mile runs, was a common method of ensuring conformity and maximum performance. Marine boot Larry Iwasko, for example, wrote his mother that a fellow recruit "got caught taking a leak out of the back door of one of the huts by an officer. He's in jail now for bringing discredit upon the Marine Corps. However, we all had to pay for his mistake. We did about 75 pushups, 100 straddle hops, 100 sit-ups, and 100 squat thrusts. A lot of the guys were so stinking sweaty when we were through, you could wring the sweat from their clothes."[12]

Doug Kurtz recalled that while he was in basic training at Fort Campbell, Kentucky, "we low crawled more than anybody in our battalion. . . . We were always on our belly. We never smoked. They wouldn't let us smoke when everybody else was because we were always last in our inspections and stuff. We used to have to sneak over to the other barracks and have a cigarette. We were always digging six-by-sixes [holes] under our barracks. We would have to go underneath if we screwed up. If one guy did, we all had to dig [a hole] six-by-six-by-six by morning. So we would just take shifts doing it. Low crawling and digging holes was quite a bit of it, and Fort Campbell had a lot of clay."

The majority being punished soon lost their tolerance for those whose lax attitude or performance cost the platoon points during an inspection or a qualification, or brought down the wrath of the drill instructors. Those who brought on punishment were ostracized and verbally humiliated or bullied into conducting themselves properly. Much more rarely, group frustrations toward a recalcitrant "screw-up" resulted in acts of violence, such as "blanket parties" in which the target of the group's wrath was beaten. It is difficult to appreciate the destruction of self-esteem and the feeling of being utterly forsaken that failure in training could engender; it should be sufficient to note that years later, veterans could still recall the fate of those who failed—and they were mightily pleased that such a fate had not befallen them.

Jeff Yushta recalled that Marine Corps boots learned early that if they did what was asked and did so quickly, they could make it through training without drawing attention to themselves. Anonymity was the key to avoiding punishment. Yushta said that he worked hard and "squared myself away and I didn't have a problem in boot camp. Once you adjusted to the lack of privacy, the lack of free thought in anything, boot camp was kind of easy."

The army and Marine Corps both hammered home the idea that whatever a person had been in civilian life was meaningless, and both were inclined to emphasize one's ineptitude, although the army appears to have been a bit more subtle. Both services also preached that survival meant separation from one's old self and total concentration on working toward a new and improved one. Ed Hoban recalled that his army instructors "tried to put the fear of death into you." He also remembered there being "a lot of Vietnam talk about 'If you don't do this, Charlie will get you.'"

Equally as persuasive were the drill instructors whom Tom

Magedanz encountered in boot at San Diego. The three in charge of his platoon seemed somehow stereotypical of the common personalities possessed by training cadre through-out the military. The ranking NCO was Staff Sergeant Villoria, who was unspeakably mean and sinister. The men believed him to be on the verge of insanity. After boot camp, however, Magedanz realized that Villoria had been extremely competent. The second, Sergeant Johnson, had never been to Vietnam and seemed to be mediocre. He was lazy, petty in his discipline, and generally not well liked. Johnson's exact opposite was Sergeant Stewart, who, Magedanz recalled, "had already spent thirty-one months in Vietnam and had two Bronze Stars and three Purple Hearts. He used to tell us about Vietnam and he had the ability to tell it in an emotional and inspiring way. He wasn't boastful—he didn't need to be—and we had tremendous respect for him. He told us simply not to expect to live out our enlistment; we were genuinely moved by that. He made us feel proud to be marines and we were ready to go and die if need be."[13]

If Sergeant Stewart raised the fledgling marines' morale, another NCO whom Magedanz saw in San Diego gave him and his fellow trainees serious second thoughts. Magedanz encountered the man at Edson Range in March 1969:

> We were still new, scared, and wide-eyed. There was a guy there, apparently back from Vietnam, and he had almost no face. His face and head had been burned and scarred beyond recognition. His ears were just stubs and his mouth and nose were more or less gone. His eyes were still OK. We couldn't help but stare and wonder how it happened. We were in awe of guys who had come back from Vietnam, but seeing him jarred us. And you could tell by his eyes that he knew we were watching him.[14]

The use of profanity was prevalent during training, and verbal assaults on the trainees' masculinity were routine. Basic training techniques were particularly aimed at motivating adolescents to establish a strong masculine self-image. Failure in any facet of training was immediately and unmistakably

brought to a recruit's attention. The implication was that those
who failed were less than men. Drill sergeants frequently referred to their charges as girls, faggots, pansies, fairies,
pussies, queers, Shirlies, or dollies, as well as other more colorful terms not found in *Webster's*. The monosyllabic military
jargon also served as a leveling device, establishing a pattern
of communication to which many recruits were unaccus-
tomed. In addition to questioning the masculinity of those
who fell below expectations, drill instructors launched
equally imaginative verbal attacks on their intelligence. These
recruits were given such sobriquets as moron, idiot, or Gomer
(after the television marine Gomer Pyle). There were constant
comparisons between wayward recruits and animals or veg-
etables. The DIs' emotive outpourings were calculated to add
pressure in challenging but tolerable amounts. Such eloquence usually inspired the recruits to greater effort, particularly when it was used to compare them with slime, maggots,
pigs, germs, turds, and other varieties of feces. In the marines,
one who reached the epitome of ineptitude became known as
a "shitbird."

Such treatment bruised the psyche and reinforced a feeling that if the trainees were to become something useful in
the service of their country, it would be only as a result of
military training. No recruit was spared a fair share of this
verbal abuse. "It didn't matter if you were thin or tall," Vince
Olson recalled, "everybody got the same treatment. But it
seemed like when they were chewing somebody else out, you
just chuckled to yourself."

Dwight Reiland figured that the army wanted to create
anger in the recruits and then channel that anger in the desired direction. To Reiland, the goal was to morally or psychologically defeat a trainee's personality and then build it
back up into something militarily useful. Reiland, like most
recruits, said that he went through training with the attitude,
"If this is what they want, we'll give it to them. We can
scream and holler and act like we are ripping somebody's giz-
zard out with a bayonet or something. And if that makes them
happy . . . fine! We'll growl and roar for them and stuff. Let's
just get our nine weeks or whatever it was in and beat it—
move on to something else."

The intellectual portion of the training was scaled down to the lowest common denominator. During the heavy draft calls of 1967 through 1969, this scale went very low indeed.[15] Tests that the marine recruits took were always available to the drill instructors. Jeff Yushta recalled spending evenings with other recruits sitting around the Quonset huts in their skivvies while the drill instructor would read the test questions and then the correct answers. This repetition of questions and answers continued throughout training. It amazed Yushta that on test day there were still men who failed miserably.

Academic standards were no better in the army. Glen Olstad was taught everything three times and then was quickly tested so that, as he put it, no one could flunk. Under such scholastic rigor, classes could become incredibly boring. Mike Roberts was one of many who simply dozed off and was made to stand up to stay awake when caught.[16]

Jeff Yushta saw the marine ideal of intellect and regimentation carried to humorous extremes. One day his platoon was told to write letters home. After everybody had gotten out a pen and paper, the DI told them to write "Dear" and the name of the person they were writing to. When that was accomplished, the DI dictated what each man should write. Every letter was the same except for the salutation and closing.

But the demands for conformity were sometimes anything but comical—especially in the Marine Corps, where drill instructors apparently had more leeway to physically correct recruits. Such abuse by the cadre was a sobering and humiliating experience, and for those who suffered the shame and anger of such treatment the memory often survived as the central experience of their training, frequently acquiring an emphasis out of all proportion to its severity.

Training in 1965 was a bit rougher in what Phil Yaeger called the "Old Corps," although he admitted that every marine who ever stood on the yellow footprints at receiving barracks had to listen to the guy in front talk about the Old Corps because he'd been there ten minutes longer. But there was a degree of physical abuse in mid-1960s and earlier training that, although acceptable in World War II, was often viewed as shocking to parents and to those opposed to the military on principle. Throughout the Vietnam War the question of legitimacy concerning America's role in the fight made it easy for critics both in and out of uniform to oppose not only the war, but the methods by which troops were being trained to fight it. War is a dirty business and there is truth in the old military adage, "The harder the training, the easier the fight." Whatever the men suffered in training, or so the reasoning went, would pale in comparison to what awaited them in the jungles of Vietnam. Still, no one who received a beating ever seemed to feel better for it, though it certainly made for conformity.

Yaeger said that some degree of corporal punishment was the norm. "It happened to everybody. I only screwed up once in boot camp. I was a pretty squared-away marine, but I lost my temper and went after somebody with my pugil stick. One of my DIs picked me up by the face mask of the football helmet and my feet were hanging off the ground . . . He weighed, I don't know, probably two-sixty, and slapped me pretty good. The classic screw-up in the platoon was constantly . . . they were constantly in his face. But, almost universally, they punished the whole platoon if anyone screwed up. It was part of the psychological training. They brainwashed us."

James Stanton agreed that the training was hard. His first breach of Marine Corps decorum occurred during a formation at Parris Island.

There is no doubt about it. They say it is the toughest of the services, but they make you live up to a standard. Otherwise, sometimes there is a mental punishment and sometimes there is physical punishment: constantly yelling at you, brow-beating I guess you would call it. And that is every day from five o'clock in the morning until ten o'clock at night.

On Parris Island they have sand fleas and there are nine million of them and one was in my ear one time and I slapped my ear and we had to dig a six-foot hole for the sand flea and this was in ninety-five-degree weather. The discipline was stringent. There is no doubt there was a fine line. Either you adhered to it or you broke it. So it taught you. One way or the other, you were going to learn.

I was hit once the whole time I was there. So to

me that was negligible. The rest was brow-beating—
screaming at you constantly from sunup 'til sundown.
But after a couple of weeks they started to soften up a
little. They stopped yelling quite so much. By then you
were starting to listen to what they had to say. And they
taught you everything they knew about killing a person—whether it was with a rifle or a bayonet, a knife, a
piece of rope, anything—they instilled in you that you
were going to have to do it.

Stanton's most lasting impression of boot camp was the
night a drill sergeant made each man in the barracks drink a
capful of Wisk laundry detergent after someone was caught
talking past lights-out. Such was life in the Marine Corps.

Punishment was also more severe for those in positions of
responsibility within the recruit platoons. Jeff Yushta's proficiency and enthusiasm made him one of the top recruits in his
training cycle, which had some unforeseen and negative side
effects.

There was a lot of physical correction and the discipline and correction grew more intense as you rose in
seniority within the training unit. There was an equal
number of guys in each squad in training and they
were arranged behind the squad leader in perfect pecking order. The squad leader was the top man in the
squad, the most proficient; then the next guy, and the
next. The guys marching at the end were real characters
and typically they seemed to come from the cities and
coastal areas. I was the guide of my platoon of seventy-
five recruits. There was a chain of command and the
drill instructor was at the top of it. I was the next man
in line. Every morning at five o'clock I would go into
the drill instructor's hootch and stand at attention.
There were three drill instructors who worked on a rotating basis and they would hit me and knock me down
and I would have to get up and assume the position of
attention and another one would hit me—never to hurt
me, but they were always saying, "You make sure that
everything goes well today. We are not going to deal

with the individual peons out there. Anything that goes wrong we are taking care of right now, so when it does go wrong it is your job to straighten it out."

If somebody wasn't pulling their weight, it was my job to make sure they did. And below me were four squad leaders, so very seldom would I correct a recruit. I would go to the squad leader and say "So-and-so is not pulling his weight—get on his case. . . . We are doing extra push-ups because of this guy. You correct him. And if you can't handle it, I'll correct him. If I can't handle it we are in trouble, because that means they've got to handle it and we are going to get it in the end."

Though physical punishment was often communal and paid off in sweat, veterans maintain that, in general, gross abuses were very rare. There was some attempt by the army to control physical abuse. William Harken's basic training unit was one of several participating in a 1968 program at Fort Lewis designed to stop the physical abuse of trainees. His drill sergeants' power to make them drop and do push-ups or other "stupid things" was restricted. Athletic exercises were to be done "on the PT field and on the PT field only." It didn't put an end to push-ups and other physical exercise as a form of punishment, but Harken's experience with punitive physical exertion at the whim of the training cadre was limited and certainly better than that experienced by many recruits.

Even the most recalcitrant recruit understood the need to train, but he didn't have to like it. And, as the war continued and the number of draftees increased, the attitude of many recruits deteriorated. When Terry Tople entered basic training in March 1968, "people had the feeling that they didn't care what anybody told them. I think they'd just as soon be thrown into the stockade. They figured, 'Well, what the hell can you do with me? I'm going to Vietnam anyway.' "[17]

Real anger generally occurred only when the men felt that they had been subjected to correction or abuse that was uncalled for. Typically, this was a result of someone exercising his authority over a helpless recruit in a petty or demeaning way. At other times it was resentment born from a lack of tact rather than physical punishment. Dwight Reiland recalled one such case:

> I realized that you had to train. You had to be in physical condition and all that and they had to adjust the way you think. But there was a lot of it that was just some jerk-ass having some fun with authority, somebody that probably for the first time in his life was in a position of authority over someone else. And they were just living it out—that kind of crap. Our drill sergeant—the thing that sticks in my mind from him, and I hated the man—was that a guy in our platoon had gotten word in the morning that his mother had died. He'd gotten a phone call from the Red Cross or whatever. I don't know what the procedure was, but anyhow after lunch you had an afternoon formation to get organized for training, and he wasn't there and the drill sergeant says, "Where is so-and-so?"
>
> And somebody said, "Well, he is in the barracks."
>
> "Go get him."
>
> "Well he's not feeling well; he just got word his mother died and he is trying to get organized because he is leaving or whatever."
>
> And the comment of the drill sergeant was, "I don't give a goddamn if Jesus Christ himself died he will make my formations."
>
> From that day on I thought, You detestable son of a bitch. . . . Everybody in our platoon, if they could have cut his throat and got away with it, would probably have done it. To me that didn't serve any purpose. Sure you've got to toughen people up, but that served no purpose whatsoever.

The repetition and drill worked toward a specific end: immediate and instinctive response to orders. For Jeff Yushta and his fellow marines, responses did become automatic, although Yushta initially resented the techniques the DIs employed. Nevertheless, when he got to Vietnam he realized that there was a reason for what they did.

You take seventy-five people off the street and present them with a situation and you are going to get, if not seventy-five different responses, you are going to get quite a few. Well, I feel somewhat safe in saying that if you take seventy-five recruits just out of boot camp at the time that I went through and present them with this situation, you would probably only get one or two responses. They are all going to do the same thing. And in a combat situation—say you're pinned down someplace and you got another group over here, it is kind of nice to know that you know what they are going to do. And in that way, I think the brainwashing was necessary: to condition a response to a particular situation. Regrettably, the situations they conditioned us for weren't in tune with the kind of action that we were going to be involved with.

Eventually, the harassment subsided and confidence levels increased as training began to focus on the technical skills of soldiering. When Michael Jackson finished training he thought he was in the best physical shape of his life. He remembered some of the drill sergeants at Fort Polk, Louisiana, saying, "When you leave us you will have muscle in your shit." It seemed to him that they were right. "Fat boys generally got thinner," he recalled, "and small skinny people generally got muscular." But being able to do the training, especially if one could do it with ease, boosted self-confidence. That was no accident. Like everything in training, increasing confidence was a prescribed part of the diet, and it was carefully programmed into the training schedule.

Almost every recruit gained confidence as the training cycle progressed. Steve Fredrick wrote home during his second week of basic, "I don't like it. I feel as if I don't belong to myself." A week later he wrote, "I can't really explain what they do to you here but they kind of try to make a machine out of you and I don't like it at all."[18]

By the third week there was a hint of change. Marksmanship instruction had begun with the M14 rifle and there was suddenly more apparent purpose to the training. Fredrick wrote with some pride of his ability to run three miles. A week later it was a thirteen-mile march with full pack. He "pulled it out." There was even more positive reinforcement when the army selected him to go to a leadership preparatory course. Later, he ran a mile in seven and a half minutes and his whole platoon made a twelve-mile march in three hours. Hand-to-hand combat and night infiltration exercises further increased Fredrick's interest. He was genuinely proud of his boxing and pugil stick abilities, and he slowly bonded with more of his fellow recruits, which led him to write at the end of the fourth week, "I am beginning to take pride in being in my country's armed forces and in the best army in the world."[19] That same week he was awarded a sharpshooter's badge.

A week later Fredrick wrote his parents in Iowa, "We won the award for the best barracks. When the lieutenant announced we had won the award it made all the sweating and slaving worth it." But this last letter written from basic also included a definite air of despondence concerning the senselessness of killing, as though he had suddenly realized the purpose to which the knowledge he'd gained would some day be directed. Yet the letter ended on a note of confidence: "I am beginning to acquire a different attitude toward things. I don't give up on a difficult challenge."[20] Through Advanced Individual Training (AIT), NCO school, and in Vietnam with the 101st Airborne Division, Fredrick's confidence might have faltered, but never his acceptance of the challenge.

As surely as the first month of training tore the men down, the second rebuilt them as soldiers. Training at the rifle and grenade ranges drove home the purpose for the humiliation and physical punishment. The recruits were given a chance to prove themselves by qualifying in assorted combat skills. The aggressive, sometimes violent nature of these activities served as an outlet for the frustrations that had built up in the men over the past weeks. Every emotion and pent-up frustration was channeled to some purpose; even games of touch football or "pig-in-a-pit" encouraged conflict and aggression.

Ed Austin had considered going into missionary work before joining the Marine Corps. A very gentle man according to those who knew him, Austin began a diary near the end of his training. Along with his opening dedication, which left no doubt as to his "unfailing faith in God and a love for his Son and mankind," Austin's first entry included a testimony to the effectiveness of marine training. "I almost got into a fight with a guy today," he wrote. "Fortunately, he was all mouth and no guts. On the outside I would take his mouth and leave him alone, but here things seem different. I don't give anyone a bad time, but I don't take one either."[21]

Peter Barnes, in his book *Pawns,* writes that beginning around the fourth week of basic training there was a transition period during which the recruits began to sense purpose and gain confidence as their physical abilities improved. The men could do the push-ups and run long distances without falling out. Each man tested himself against the other trainees and accepted the training as a positive challenge. They developed a new self-respect as drill instructors began to award praise and address them by name. The NCOs began to impart some of their wisdom and experience, and the recruits listened with purpose and intent. As confidence grew, so too did the desire to test newfound skills. Like Ed Austin, the men didn't look for a fight, but they no longer backed down from one either.

The easing up was a welcome relief for trainees. They were allowed more time for writing letters home or to use the phone. Sundays turned out to be free days most of the time. There wasn't much to do, but it was relaxing just being left alone for a few hours to dream about the world outside the fence and wonder if it had changed—or about how much they had.

During the final weeks the trainees prepared for qualification testing. Most of all, though, the men looked forward to their upcoming graduation and the resulting increase in status that would accompany it. Graduation meant a change of scenery with their next posting and it brought them one step closer to the trip home each would receive after finishing Advanced Individual Training. Aspiring marines, having been more deprived of creature comforts in boot camp than their army counterparts in basic training, looked forward as well to such simple privileges as enjoying a candy bar. As one marine wrote during the final week of boot camp, "Here it's like the day before Christmas vacation in school. Everyone is jumping around and can't keep quiet."[22] Graduation itself did not evoke such spirit, it was thoughts of leave and the knowledge that basic training would soon be over.

Although the soldiers retained many aspects of their former civilian identities, their erect posture and improved physique were unmistakable and hinted at other changes beneath the surface. The men were linked to a collective group with collective values and symbols that could not be understood by the uninitiated. They perceived themselves as different: bigger, stronger, and certainly more confident. They felt, too, that they understood something of the mission and their responsibility toward that mission. They were proud.

When Jeff Beatty entered training, his commander at Fort Hood, Maj. Gen. John E. Kelly, wrote in a form letter to Jeff's mother, "Upon completion of this eight weeks of training, your son will have become a capable, rugged soldier and a better American citizen."[23] Although this was undoubtedly a bit of hyperbole, many of the graduating soldiers probably agreed with the general. The future would demonstrate that they were not yet rugged and capable soldiers, but to this day, most of those men would agree that the experience had somehow made them better Americans.

Only one thing could cast a shadow over the jubilation of graduation: The fate of each soldier and marine was posted on the barracks bulletin board before they returned from the ceremony. The rosters were brief and of portentous significance. Beside each man's name was listed a school assignment and a cryptic alphanumeric combination indicating the military occupational specialty (MOS) that bureaucratic fate had bestowed upon him. The lists indicated who would most likely be headed to Vietnam. Many feared that they would be assigned to the infantry, and their apprehension was well founded. Soldiers awarded an 11B MOS (for marines 0311) got orders for infantry training—and that almost certainly meant Vietnam. Yet no matter how expected the bad news was, actually meeting one's fate came as a shock.

Paul Gerrits had worked in his father's shop repairing cars and doing body work since he was thirteen. He was certain that he would be sent off to some sort of vehicle maintenance training. He was wrong. He was ordered to report to Fort Sam

Houston, Texas, for training as a medic. It was not the kind of body work he had hoped for.[24]

Michael Jackson felt equally bitter about his posting. Upon entering the service at the reception station, recruits filled out what were appropriately referred to as "dream sheets." Jackson, a twenty-three-year-old black recruit with a four-year college degree in recreation, was naive enough to think it would matter.

> This guy looked at my dream sheet and said, "Oh man, you got a degree in recreation! Shit, you got it dicked. You'll be a recreation specialist and all you'll have to do is go to the gym and throw out the balls, hold the towels for the officers, and things like that."
>
> So, as a result of that, I was pretty motivated in basic . . . because I figured I was going to be like the people who were in the reserves. I knew I wasn't going home, but I wasn't going to be like these other poor saps who were going to Vietnam. After graduation from basic training they called out the MOSs and they were calling names of white boys who I knew had an eighth-grade education—certainly not a college diploma. For them it was "missile school, cook, clerk, truck driver." For me it was "Jackson: Eleven-Bravo [infantry]!"

CHAPTER 3

_____

Advanced Individual Training

January 17, 1967

Dear Mom and Dad,
 Received your nice letter today and was glad to
hear from you. Sorry I haven't been writing more
often but they've been keeping me pretty busy lately.
Tomorrow we go out to the field and learn how to
shoot the 50 cal. machine gun. That should be fun.
Well, the lights will be going out in about five minutes
so I'd better close for now. I'll write later on this
week.

Your Son,
Leonard[1]

During the Vietnam era, twenty-six training schools provided
instruction in more than 350 military occupations in the army
alone, with programs varying in length from two months to a
year. Whereas draftees were simply told what training they
would receive, volunteers were given choices that hinged on
"eligibility" for training in a particular MOS. This eligibility
was established through aptitude tests taken at the time they
entered the service. Some disappointed enlistees, despite a
recruiter's assurances to the contrary, had their hopes of attending electronics or computer training dashed when they
were switched to some alternate military occupation at the
whim of a Pentagon computer that matched MOS training
slots with whatever personnel were available.[2]
 There were many desirable military occupations, but the
threat of Vietnam duty did little to make the job of "infantryman" an attractive prospect, for an assignment to that MOS

had much to do with determining whether a recruit's war stories would be firsthand or not.

As with most aspects of military life, there was no explanation of how or why an individual was singled out for infantry training. Many soldiers tried to fathom the reasoning behind the decision, believing that their assignment to the infantry had something to do with their answers to questions about whether they liked to hunt or go camping. Most, however, resigned themselves to the fact that they were simply unlucky.

In any event, Tom Magedanz was certainly not alone in marveling at the perplexities of the selection process when he wrote to a friend, "I don't quite know what to think of the good ol' USMC. They looked at my college calculus, chemistry, and physics and said I'd make a good infantryman."[3]

The stigma attached to the 11B infantry MOS was so rooted in the minds of some soldiers awaiting school assignments that many of them overlooked the fact that there were other, equally dangerous and unsavory infantry occupations such as 11C (mortars) or 11H (antitank). Assignment to these training schools also meant a future tour of duty with an infantry company and the likelihood of exposure to battle and physical adversity that was no different than what was to be anticipated by the men who had been selected to serve as "light weapons infantrymen."

Only a few MOSs carried the guarantee of hardship and the potential for injury and death that was the lot of the men assigned to be trained as line infantry soldiers. Their mission was to go outside the base camps and protected rear-area enclaves of Vietnam on a day-to-day basis, seeking out the enemy and attempting to destroy him. It went without saying that the enemy would be engaged in much the same activity. The men who would fill the infantry platoons were the ones who would be exposed to the greatest dangers. Their advanced training therefore consisted of learning the skills involved with light weapons and infantry tactics. In plain language, they were taught to kill close up and would witness firsthand the results of having done so. Thus soldiers bound for AIT tended to undergo an accompanying shift in mood, which Tim O'Brien readily sensed:

On the outside, AIT looks like basic training. Lots of push-ups, lots of shoe-shining and firing ranges and midnight marches. But AIT is not basic training. The difference is inside the new soldier's skull, locked to his brain, the certainty of being in a war. . . .

The soldier in advanced infantry training is doomed, and he knows it and thinks about it. War is real. The drill sergeant said it when we formed up for our first inspection: every swinging dick in the company was now a foot soldier, a grunt in the United States Army, the infantry, Queen of Battle. Not a cook in the lot, not a clerk or mechanic among us.[4]

The Marine Corps prided itself on making every marine a rifleman. Consequently, after boot camp, every marine received two weeks of infantry training. Those marines destined to become garden-variety riflemen (0311s) went on to eight weeks or more of intensive infantry training and the near-certainty of a trip to an exotic Southeast Asian locale upon graduation. When the "Remington Raiders" and "Office Commandos," as the grunts called them, left for their respective training schools, the infantry remained behind to complete five additional weeks of training with their Infantry Training Regiment (ITR) followed by three more weeks of training at Basic Infantry Training School (BITS). When that was finished, the mortarmen and machine gunners were shipped off for additional specialized training.

The army's light weapons infantrymen, although officially designated "11-Bravo," referred to themselves sardonically as "11-Bushes," "11-Bang-Bangs," or "11-Bulletstoppers." It was well understood by the infantry trainees that there was little need for riflemen outside of Vietnam. That knowledge made their training seem a little more purposeful than it had in basic. At Fort Polk, Louisiana, a billboard welcomed trainees with the message: "Infantry Replacements for Vietnam." That erased all doubt from Paul Boehm's mind. "You knew you were going to Vietnam when you walked in the door and everything was geared toward that," he recalled later.

Infantry training was devoted to teaching soldiers the tools of the trade, and that trade was killing. Much of life is spent learning and obeying society's rules. Infantry training attempted to override basic sensitivities and bring to the surface a more primitive instinct necessary for survival in wartime. Author Gwynne Dyer has suggested that there exists in every man "... the inherited values and postures, more or less dimly recalled, of the tribal warriors who were once the model for every boy to emulate."[5]

What the military sought to do in eight additional weeks was to break down the psychological and social barriers against violence that society had spent a lifetime constructing, and reacquaint the trainee with his tribal past. Three themes were stressed: kill or be killed, do one's patriotic duty, and, to a lesser extent, hate the enemy. Separately or in concert, each of these ideas, it was hoped, would imbue each man with a fighting spirit. But whether some people were meant to be killers at all might be wondered by anyone looking at the photos of those very young and often forlorn-looking men standing in their fatigues before signs such as the one at Fort Polk that proclaimed, "Every man a Tiger." Certainly, most men taking infantry training did not see themselves as such. Most, like Jon Neely, tried to avoid thinking seriously about why they were there. According to Neely, "When the guys got together and were talking there was still no real urgency to talk about Vietnam, although the drill instructors and the cadre—they pounded it into your head daily, 'Hey, get yourself ready, get yourself psyched up and geared here. You are going to 'Nam and this is what you are going to do. You are going to fight.' But when you hit your free time, that's probably the last thing you wanted to talk about."

When Tom Magedanz had his official Marine Corps photo taken, he was surprised to learn that he would not be photographed wearing real dress blues. Instead, he was handed a hat with a heavily polished bill and the front section of a dress uniform, a vest-type affair that looked real from the front only and had elastic clasps in the back to hold it on for the camera. The same false front traded hands as quickly as the flashbulbs popped. Like those dress blues, most soldiers and marines seemed to wear their training loosely around their shoulders as a facade—giving the appearance of fierceness, but belying the truth.[6]

Although the training curriculum taught survival through applied violence, some troops wrote their parents, wives, or girlfriends on military stationery, such as "Home of the Infantry" writing paper that bore the image of a charging soldier with bayonet in subdued blue. Marine Corps stationery portrayed the flag-raising on Iwo Jima. There was also cute stationery sold in the PX that might give to parents or loved ones the impression that their "soldier" was away at summer camp rather than in the military. There was a "Precious Moments" type of GI with limpid eyes peeling potatoes. Another innocuous card showed a figurine in fatigues strapped to a missile, looking for all the world like a Hummel porcelain. One card depicted a caricature of a uniformed man wearing a helmet with plumbing fixtures sticking out of it. The clever caption read, "We even wash our clothes and take a bath in our helmets." It was a strange counterpoint to the nature of the training and the words written on the stationery describing it.[7]

Soldiers were taught the most effective ways to kill. They were no longer simply trying to qualify with their weapons; they were focusing on the function for which those weapons were intended. Paul Boehm recalled that his instructors tried to make the idea of killing more palatable by telling soldiers that "a gook was just like a deer or something. If you killed one, who cared? It was no big deal." But, Boehm added, the reality became apparent as training progressed. On the rifle range they shot at silhouettes shaped like men. "Even the police fire at silhouettes," he said, "they don't fire at little round dots—[they shoot at] people figures. We were shooting at people."

Survival was a strong motivation for human action, and training often followed the simple reasoning that if you did not kill your enemy, he would certainly kill you. To kill was the central theme of training; it was the occupation of the infantry soldier. Tom Magedanz remembered his indoctrination: "War is our business—business is very good," and "*Semper Fi,* do or die. Kill, kill, kill."[8] The trainees learned the purpose of the bayonet: "To kill—without mercy." Shouting

"Kill!" accompanied almost all activities intended to bring about that specific goal. As the training continued, Don Putnam noticed, "After awhile, when the men hollered 'Kill' they began to mean it."

Putnam said that he was amazed at how simple the methodology really was. He explained that the instructors sought "to instill the kill idea in your head. Constantly, whether you were marching or singing or whatever, you were being repetitiously reminded to kill, kill, kill. You were introduced to your enemy and his methods. Most of the time the focus was on the VC—they were always your enemy. It was a way of making you believe the army's way."

Marine Jeff Yushta remembered his most blatant encounter with the "kill mystique." Church was mandatory in his marine training unit, and while marching there the members of his platoon would shout "Kill!" every time their left foot hit the ground.

Wherever trainees went they chanted songs as they double-timed. The songs had what Yushta described as a "subliminal message" degrading the Vietnamese people. The chants had other messages as well. The lyrics promoted masculinity and degraded women. Drill instructors referred to the men's girlfriends with nicknames suggesting they were sexually promiscuous. A rifle was a rifle, a penis was a gun; one was for killing, the other for fun. The litany was endless. Yushta said that attempts were also made to degrade the antiwar movement and peace activists. Sergeants told recruits that they were going over to Vietnam to do the fighting for the cowards and the peace marchers. They were doing their dirty work. It helped them build anger.

But not everyone remembered the kill message as being quite so blatant. According to marine Phil Yaeger, "It wasn't like they locked you in a padded cell and showed you blood and guts and sensory deprivation. It wasn't that at all. It was more 'You better be prepared to kill or die! You have two choices. Eighty-three percent of the Marine Corps is infantry. You *are* going to Vietnam. All marines sooner or later will go to Vietnam. You better be prepared to kill.' "

Many former soldiers used the term "brainwashing" in reference to their training. In hindsight, Michael Jackson could look back and see the mental manipulation in the songs they sang, calling the cadence, running the morning mile singing, "I want to go to Vietnam, I want to kill a Viet Cong." They were being programmed.

Most of the men adapted psychologically to the game, but a few trainees were stressed beyond their tolerance. Terry Tople witnessed one such instance at Fort Lewis in the spring of 1968:

> To me it was all a brain game. I just couldn't believe it. We did push-ups; they'd say, "Kill, kill, kill." You went through the monkey bars, you know—
> "What's the word?"
> "Kill, kill, kill."
> In the chow line the drill sergeant would be standing there and grab you, "What's the word?"
> "Kill, kill, kill."
> We had a couple of guys who went berserk; it just drove them to that point. I think maybe that's what they were getting at, to see what a person could take under stress. One guy . . . just broke down in the chow line. He had his steel helmet on and just smacked the drill sergeant right in the face. Just went berserk. I think . . . he got out with an undesirable discharge; couldn't adapt to military life.

There was so much emphasis on killing and so many different methods and weapons being introduced to the trainees to accomplish that purpose that Jon Neely and the other men at Fort McClellan, Alabama, began to refer to the training sarcastically as "one thousand and one ways to easily kill your mother-in-law."

It was nearly impossible for the men to go through all of that training without harboring at least some curiosity about the activity for which they were being trained. Most men thought that weapons training was fun; firearms were more fascinating than fearful. And although the men did not generally relish the idea of combat, their youth denied the fledgling warriors the experience and, perhaps, the good sense to fear

it as they should. Stephen Fredrick seemed cautiously curious
when he wrote from AIT at Fort Polk in 1967:

> I have learned a tremendous amount about warfare
> and survival since I got in. I am actually kind of anx-
> ious for some practical application. I don't really want
> to go, but I won't feel cheated or something if I have to.
> Maybe I have been well indoctrinated, but I see things
> in a different light now. However, from what I hear, the
> Viet Cong is one of the toughest fighting men the U.S.
> Army has ever faced. They say if a Cong gets fifteen
> rounds in a clip he will get fifteen hits right between the
> eyes.[9]

Most of the men took the training with a mixture of seri-
ousness and acquiescence. For those who described themselves as "*gungi*," or "gung ho," such as Vernon Janick,
training became something more akin to religion.

"We were always told that sweat on the training field saves
blood on the battlefield, and I definitely agree. So I used it
good and wisely. I didn't try to get out of things. When you
hit it, you hit it—just like the real thing. But a lot of guys
wouldn't take cover or anything, [they were] just playing. But
I took it really serious. I was just gung ho and wanted to learn
all I could. It was worth it."

Training proceeded at a busy pace, acquiring a "for my
own good" kind of validity. In the jungle, the soldiers were
told, their lives depended on their training. Survival meant
immediate response, and that was conditioned through repetition and drill. British military historian Richard Holmes observed: "Part of the stress of battle stems from its puzzling
and capricious manner; battle drills help to minimize the randomness of battle, and give the soldier familiar points of contact in an uncertain environment."[10] Though few trainees
could really imagine themselves in life-or-death situations,
later events would often demonstrate that survival truly depended on appropriate behaviors for which there would be no
time for thought, no second chance.

Through indoctrination and unofficial dialogue, the
trainees were also exposed to racist ideas that would help

make the concept of killing easier to accept. The apparent message in training was not to trust any Vietnamese. Ed Hoban recalled: "The army just gave you the opinion that *all* Vietnamese were bad. I never, ever heard anything about a friendly Vietnam person when I was in AIT."

Bryan Good agreed. He could recall nothing being said about America's Vietnamese allies in training, only that it seemed that all Vietnamese were "Charlie, VC, gooks. If he had slant eyes he also had an AK-47. If it was a woman, she would have a hand grenade stuck up under her dress someplace."[11]

Inevitably, the enemy was often characterized as a subhuman species—parasitic and evil. The manner in which the Viet Cong were portrayed by the cadre left some recruits with the perception that the enemy was little different from rodents or other vermin. For a few, training only aggravated preexisting racial attitudes. Vernon Janick, for example, recalled:

> The way we were trained was that they were more animal than anything. You just didn't trust any of them. We were always told that kids or women were just as much your enemy as anybody else. We always kept that in mind. We just never trusted any of them for damned sure.
>
> I already [hated them] before I went over there. Pretty much anything with slanted eyes was the way I was. You always thought they were snakes—sneaky, which they are. I had that in me. Slant-eyed people . . . [you] couldn't trust 'em.

Killing such creatures was not only acceptable but admirable when it was justified in the historical context of duty. It had been done previously by generations of Americans, and Vietnam-bound recruits were simply there to do it again.

Norman Cousins suggested that killing is internalized even more readily by the young because of the influence of the modern mass media:

> Long before children learn to read, they learn how to turn on a television set. They are quickly introduced to

a world of howling drunks; pampered idiots; wild-swinging trigger-happy bullies, and con artists. Whether you saw on TV the Indians, Nazis, Japs, Commies, or any other genetically predetermined thugs, there are bad guys in the world. Color them evil. America, on the other hand, held a special place in the world order. Possessed of more strength and intelligence, morally superior and chosen, we are the good guys. Color us God blessed. The message regarding the requirements of manhood was that to be a man in America you had to be against more than just bad guys. To be a man in America you had to kill bad guys.[12]

Patriotism sometimes obscures other sensibilities, and in training it could, on occasion, even inspire racial hatred. Internalizing disdain for the Vietnamese was a subtle process, and one that many Vietnam veterans may not have recognized as having taken place within themselves. But because more and more of the men who were in charge of the training had served in Vietnam, had been witness to acts that convinced them that the Vietnamese enemy was not an altogether admirable specimen of humanity, the dehumanizing process took on a dynamic of its own. Being trained by Vietnam veterans made it easier for trainees to assimilate the prejudicial attitudes that would be expected of them once they arrived in Vietnam. A callous attitude toward the enemy was easily cultivated, whereas the lack of cultural education kept the soldiers ignorant of the Vietnamese people and their society as a whole.

Homilies given in the shade near the training sites included stories of a deceitful and treacherous civilian population. This racial component of Vietnam training became evident to parents when their sons began to write home of "gooks," "dinks," or "slopes"—indication that a mental realignment had begun to take effect. It not only influenced the soldier's perception of the morality of his fight, but allowed him to excuse in his own mind the consequences of subsequent actions in combat.

Michael Jackson was deeply sensitive to racial prejudice before he entered the service, so the process of racial motivation and indoctrination was effective, and obvious to him. He later recalled:

> Most of your cadre in basic, AIT, NCO school, and Ranger school were people who had already been to Vietnam. Whenever they talked about Charlie or VC, they would refer to them as gooks. And we had these films and/or slides from time to time. I think this came in NCO school and Ranger school as I went up the ladder in terms of training. They would show real gross films of what Vietnamese had done to Americans and how they were animals, et cetera, et cetera.
>
> I remember one thing that had an impact on me was . . . they were talking about how the enemy was being worn down and that they were resorting to eight-, nine-, ten-year-old boys and girls for combat troops. And when I got to Vietnam I found that wasn't quite true.

Jack Freitag attested to the thorough nature of his Marine Corps instructors, noting:

> We didn't look at the Vietnamese as human beings. They were subhuman. To kill them would be easy for you. If you continued with this process, you could stack them up like cordwood and you didn't have any bad feelings about it because they were a subhuman species. That was how they prepared us for it.
>
> They used the terms "gooks" and "zipperheads" and we had to kill different insects every day and they would say, "There's a gook, step on it and squash it," and similar things like that. Every day you had to kill something. And they kept putting that in your mind. These were gooks and you had to kill them.[13]

Trainees were fed a constant diet of anecdotes about the sneaky Vietnamese, reminiscent of stories told about the Japanese in the Pacific during World War II. Men in training were warned not to be overconfident when dealing with the Vietnamese. At the same time they were cautioned to never trust a "gook." There were plenty of stories illustrating the danger. Bottles of pop, they were assured, would be contaminated with poison, urine, or shards of glass. There were stories of grenades hidden in the shoeshine boxes or styrofoam coolers carried by children. Old women hid land mines and old men paced off the distance to American positions for Viet Cong mortar crews. There were elements of truth in such stories, to be sure, but there was also disaffection so that, after arriving in Vietnam, the American combat soldier might more easily convince himself of the veracity of those rumors.

Sociologist Wayne R. Eisenhart wrote that the term "gook" or "slope" was overused in training and may have had subtle negative effects on the troops. It may have increased black-white tensions when minority trainees heard such phrases as "Kill the Yellow bastards," or "You can't trust any gook." Nonwhites tended to be more "color conscious," especially when African Americans, Native Americans, or Asian Americans translated somewhat differently the training jargon that alluded to white superiority.

Because schedules were rigid, very little effort was made to teach soldiers about Vietnamese culture during their preparation for war. No regular infantry soldiers received a sympathetic alternative view or insight into the lives of the people they were supposed to be assisting in the democratic fight for freedom. Eisenhart viewed the racial aspects of the men's training as counterproductive, because racial prejudice against the Vietnamese was being inculcated into troops whose success depended not on the conquest of the land, but on obtaining the allegiance and support of the indigenous people.[14]

Gaining the confidence of the Vietnamese peasants was referred to in training as "winning hearts and minds." Its ironic acronym, WHAM, was perhaps more indicative of the military's true feelings concerning this imperative. Drill instructors were fond of crudely reminding their charges that winning hearts and minds was easy: One needed only to grab people by the balls and their hearts and minds would follow.

Whereas racial hatred for the Vietnamese enemy may have motivated a small percentage of troops, a far larger portion of the men in training were motivated by the anticommunist aspects of the struggle in Vietnam. Marine Jeff Yushta, like most recruits, downplayed the role of the psychological and racial trappings of killing and hatred.

> I don't think the songs and the slogans allowed you to kill without remorse or thought. I think they helped build a barrier that made it easier. I think you could have taken out all the songs and slogans and just stressed the history of the Marine Corps, the pride of the marines in World War I and World War II, Iwo Jima, Chosin Reservoir—all those guys that gave their lives fighting for their country. Now here are the Vietnamese—I should say North Vietnamese or Viet Cong. Here is another enemy that has to be fought and you guys are the best the country's got. Here is a job that has to be done. Now be men and do it!
>
> Your classes were filled with the glowing exploits of Chesty Puller and other marines. So, we kept comparing ourselves. "Gee! Wouldn't it be nice if they talked about me like that someday?"

Yushta and others were far more motivated by appeals to their sense of honor and patriotism. In keeping with this idea, the army and marines easily incorporated this third motivational tactic into the training programs.

Like the heroes of Homer's *Iliad* centuries earlier, John Wayne and a host of Hollywood heroes provided the young men of the 1950s and 1960s with models of heroism and conduct to which they might aspire. Their fathers won World War II. These young men had been weaned during a cold war in the Stalinist fifties and schooled in the imperative of protecting America. No child growing up with *Sergeant Rock* comic books or movies such as *The Sands of Iwo Jima* ever doubted that his own moral responsibility, like Superman's, was to defend "Truth, Justice, and the American Way." Training films, including *Your Tour in Vietnam* and *Know Your Enemy: Viet Cong,* utilized the talents of Hollywood patriots such as Glenn Ford, Charlton Heston, Jack Webb, and others. Duty and patriotism were major themes in these films, just as they were in the training regimen itself.[15]

Military service was an occupation in which many soldiers took some degree of pride. For some this was little more than generic "mom-and-apple-pie" patriotism. For others it took on the significance of a mystic bonding with the past: There was an enemy to be fought and it would be best to fight him over there, rather than on American soil. As Rick Atkinson explained, "The army was much given to such apothegms; they provided a vehicle for transporting the wisdom of the ages and, less generously, a substitute for reflective thought."[16]

Along with motivating soldiers and trying to give them sound reasons for killing, the military continued to instruct them in the practical use of weapons and tactics. The men saw firepower demonstrations by tanks, armored personnel carriers, and attack helicopters. They also received in-depth training with all the basic infantry weapons: the M60 light and M2 .50-caliber heavy machine guns, the M79 grenade launcher, the light antitank weapon (LAW), and the M1911A1 .45-caliber pistol, as well as the standard infantry rifle, the M16.

Hours of classroom instruction were devoted to each weapon, but practical experience firing the larger, more expensive weapons was especially limited. Training on a .50-caliber machine gun might consist of only five to ten seconds of live firing. Each man fired only one or two LAWs, unless he became an antitank specialist. Hand grenades were thrown with the utmost economy, with each trainee tossing only a handful of live grenades. Rigid safety rules were also enforced. With all these constraints, each man got a feel for the weaponry and little else. Training on some specialized weapons was often limited to only one or two men in a platoon. Jeff Beatty, for example, wrote home with obvious enthusiasm that he had been singled out to be trained on flamethrowers.[17]

Soldiers did spend a lot of time on the rifle range, however. Marksmanship, especially in the Marine Corps, was an important facet of training. In 1967 the army began experimenting with a new shooting technique in a few select training companies. It was a type of quick reaction or instinctive shooting, called "Quick Kill," developed by a Georgia tobacco salesman. In Quick Kill, soldiers were taught not to aim. The rifle became an extension of the eye, locked to the shoulder, stock flush with the jawbone, left arm fully extended. Both eyes were kept open and focused above the target. Troops learned the technique with modified Daisy Model 199 air rifles, with heavy stocks added so that they would feel more like their actual weapons. The men began by shooting BBs at can lids or aluminum disks tossed into the air in front of the weapon's barrel. Within ten minutes most soldiers could hit the lids at will. Troops then began shooting BBs at silhouettes set fifteen yards away. After a few hours and the expenditure of about eight hundred BBs, many recruits could hit coins tossed in the air, so it was claimed. The technique was then applied with M16s. Although the quick-kill technique was not intended to replace standard marksmanship practices, it did help soldiers react instinctively to an enemy that they would often engage in dense jungle at ranges of thirty feet or less. Under such conditions soldiers would glimpse enemy troops only rarely, and seldom, if ever, have time to sight and fire properly. Survival depended instead on shooting first and shooting accurately.[18]

Soldiers spent more and more time in the field and were introduced to ever-increasing degrees of stress and lack of sleep. As the training neared its climax, the exercises became more complex and increasingly realistic. Steve Fredrick described one such training exercise in a letter to his family:

> For two nights we had mock battle training. The first night Bob Newsum and I skipped out of the training and snuck back to our tents and spent the rest of the night in our sleeping bags. It was really great to have those four extra hours of sleep and also pull one over on the army. The second night we were put out in foxholes in a big circle called a perimeter. This ended up to be almost like a real battle. Harken and I were in a foxhole together with machine guns and rifles firing blanks at us. We also had blanks for our weapons. They had TNT planted various places that went off once in a while. Before the whole thing started we were having a cigarette when the calm was broken by a loud voice with a

foreign accent. It was Vietnamese propaganda. The voice asked us to surrender because we were surrounded and it was hopeless to fight. The voice spoke of our homes and told us the war was not our war. Sitting in our cold, wet holes it sounded pretty good. I can imagine how a troop would feel 10,000 miles from home fighting a war he doesn't understand and wants no part of anyway. You can see it was a realistic evening.[19]

Before his last field exercise in AIT Leonard Dutcher wrote, "The way it sounds it's going to be pretty rough out there. This time they are going to have real air strikes and artillery coming in all around us. I sure hope those fly-boys know what they're doing. The air force is out there tonight practicing. I don't know if they are any good or not but they sure make a lot of noise."[20]

Two months previously, Dutcher's platoon got its first ride in helicopters, practicing airmobile operations. His twenty-mile flight in the UH-1 "Huey" provided little more than a basic familiarization with the aircraft, but the ride was enjoyable.[21] In similar fashion, marine Tom Magedanz's helicopter training consisted of a few short flights into open areas about a week before the end of his infantry training.[22] Layne Anderson's helicopter assault training was even more primitive. "What it amounted to," he remembered, "was wooden benches raised up like a helicopter and that was it. Load up and jump off; you're trained."[23]

But no matter how much "blade time" a soldier received in training, it would never prepare him for a helicopter assault under actual combat conditions. Terry Musser received more helicopter training than most infantrymen after joining the 11th Air Assault Division, which was later deployed to Vietnam as the 1st Air Cavalry Division. He recalled that his training "may not have been that bad except that we weren't ready for air assaulting into hot LZs. You can read about them in a book and they can tell you about it, but until you actually have been to a hot LZ there is no conception of what it is. Nobody was ready for it."

Villages and the people who lived in them were other

facets of Vietnam that were hard to simulate. As early as 1966, trainees went through mock Viet Cong (VC) villages. The troops who did so at places such as Fort Lewis and Fort Dix, New Jersey, found the winter snows a bit unrealistic. Of course there were no Vietnamese civilians living in the simulated villages, so the confusion and clamor of hysterical mothers or their screaming, frightened children were notably absent. There were no foreign smells, no noisy pigs and chickens. The chaos that resulted from language barriers, heat and fatigue, frayed nerves, and fear were all factors that defied simulation. None of the young trainees entering those villages had lost his best friend the week before. Their clothing was not spattered with blood from a booby-trap victim evacuated earlier that morning. But most of all, the trainees moving methodically through the make-believe villages were not scared and pumped up with adrenaline. Jeff Yushta acknowledged later:

> All the time you were in the States you knew it was a game. [In combat] it totally changes. Like the guy standing in at batting practice hitting home run after home run. Well, then there is the last game of the World Series and you are down three to two and a man on and you are the last man up. There's all that pressure. The big putt on the eighteenth green at the Masters. You have made that putt ten thousand times in practice. Well, this is a little different now. There is no way to prepare for that. The training they gave you just didn't function under those conditions. . . .

Many critics have suggested that there were significant shortcomings in the training for Vietnam. Soldiers received no culture or language training, and only a select few were given jungle training in Panama. As the war progressed, more instructional time was given to booby traps and the settings where they would most likely be encountered, but the subject was never dealt with completely. The major shortcomings of the training stemmed from the fact that the average infantryman serving a two-year hitch simply didn't have the time to be trained beyond the necessities of Basic and AIT, and, unfortunately, the core curriculum in those training programs was not well suited to Vietnam.

A case can certainly be made for the fact that throughout the war unit tactics and training curricula mandated that American soldiers use conventional tactics against an unconventional enemy, rather than adopt methods and tactics more suited to low-intensity counterinsurgency warfare. However, the army was also required to retain a large presence in Germany and Korea, which meant that soldiers had to be trained for those missions as well. Given such diverse and conflicting roles, and considering the constraints of time and money being imposed, it was simply impossible to do more. Additional specialized and in-depth training would have also required highly motivated men of above-average aptitude, and such men were always in short supply.

Colonel Andrew Krepinevich, Jr., studied at great length his service's reluctance to deviate from its basic concept of conventional war, a term that implied the type of war that the army wished to fight. Since the military's basic philosophy ignored low-intensity guerrilla warfare, there was little deviation from the belief that what had brought victory in World War II would be equally successful in Vietnam. The American "concept," as Krepinevich refers to it, was based on large units with limited ground mobility carrying tremendous firepower. The military relied on technology to provide the edge needed in combat and gladly traded dollars and materiel to spare the blood of American soldiers. Considering the protracted nature of the war, one might wonder how much blood was ultimately spared as a result of this line of thinking. At any rate, the road to promotion in the modern, corporate-thinking military hierarchy of the 1960s and 1970s lay in decisive command in combat, and that meant the destruction of the enemy's battalions. Promotion was much less likely to be found in baby-sitting some rural hamlet and defending a rice crop.[24]

The United States exhausted much of its manpower and resources deep in the interior of Vietnam trying to "find, fix, fight, and finish" the enemy. When U.S. troops did get close to civilians, it was usually just long enough to damage relations, but seldom long enough to develop them. There were precious few times when Vietnamese civilians saw Americans in the role that most GIs fancied for themselves: protectors and defenders of democracy in Vietnam.

In retrospect, many soldiers who served in Vietnam were displeased with that lack of specialized training. Randall Hoelzen, for example, noted, "The types of things you used in Vietnam—the Claymore, M16—were introduced in AIT but they weren't any more important than some other thing that you would never see in Vietnam. They had their routine. You went through this—qualified on this, this, and this. It was Korea[n War]-based or even before. There was some toughening physical work, but as far as skills that you needed in Vietnam, no. I won't say nothing, but it wasn't what it should have been—no way."

Many ordinary riflemen began to sense that something was wrong after a month or two in Vietnam. Terry Musser observed that he and his comrades "were nowhere near adequately trained for the job that we had to do once we got there."

Gerry Barker, who spent four tours in Vietnam, the last two with the 5th Special Forces Group, was a new NCO with the 1st Battalion, 8th Cavalry, during the battles in the Ia Drang Valley in November 1965. It seemed to Barker that when his unit first went over there, "we really made every mistake in the book. We were not trained for it. We were trained to fight World War II, and we were bad. I remember night patrols—getting a mission of going three and four kilometers in a night out of An Khe in September and October of 1965. Just totally unrealistic missions. And we didn't know that. We went out and couldn't do it and thought there was something wrong with us."

Nor were soldiers emotionally prepared for the battles awaiting them. Apart from making the most obvious observation that everyone in battle is scared, American combat soldiers were not taught how to cope with fear, or what feelings they could expect to experience prior to and during combat.

Lieutenant Bruce Heim of the 101st Airborne Division wrote to the cadets of his alma mater, "There is nothing the army or West Point has in its training program that will prepare you to see your first dead GI, your first wounded child, your first crying widow. Military Art and Tactics never told you of the butterflies and near nausea that are continually with you as bullets fly over your head."[25]

The end of infantry training triggered the first reactions of genuine fear that most men experienced regarding their impending futures. Soldiers and marines realized the destructive potential of the weapons with which they had been trained. Even their M16 rifles were fearful weapons.

"The M16," wrote Tom Magedanz, "is pretty nice. It weighs about six pounds and is easy to shoot. It doesn't jam like the stories you hear. The instructors call it 'Matty Mattel' because it feels like a toy. I have seen toy guns that look more realistic, but you don't want to be on the wrong end of an M16. We had a demonstration where they shot at an ammunition can full of water which made it pretty heavy and the bullet had such a high velocity that the box full of water just flew when the bullet hit and tore a great big hole in it and crumpled the box. It is nothing to mess around with."[26]

Trainees were becoming more aware than ever that combat was serious. They identified with their mission in terms of kill or be killed, and they accepted the logic that told them that halfway around the world others were training to kill them. Most were replacements, after all, and they were each aware to some degree that many of the men they would replace had not completed a full combat tour. Every man finishing his infantry training harbored suspicions as to where he would be going next; for most, that realization brought serious reflections concerning life and death.

In NCO school at Fort Benning, future sergeant Stephen Fredrick's unit spent a couple of hours on patrol in the woods with BB guns and special face masks. "It was really fun and yet in a way it was deadly serious," he wrote, "because when you got hit with a BB, it made you stop and think."[27]

By the end of AIT, soldiers could operate their weapons with some proficiency and they were acquainted with squad tactics. Most of them had been motivated and indoctrinated to some degree and a few were eager for a fight—or at least to test their skills. Many secretly felt pride upon graduating from AIT and receiving orders for Vietnam.

"It might sound weird," said Terry Tople, "but I figured,

well, I'm going to really go fight for my country. [I was] scared, nervous, but also proud. I don't know why—maybe it was just bred into me."

Some adventurous GIs longed for the excitement of combat, but the majority were apprehensive to varying degrees, mostly fearing the unknown. Most troops were also bored. They were fed up with training and tired of playing army and they knew, whether they looked forward to it or dreaded it, that their next year or thirteen months (depending on whether they were soldiers or marines) would most likely be spent in Vietnam. At the end of their training, most soldiers and marines expressed a strong desire to simply "get on with it," although many of the men felt a secret desperation accompanying the sentiment.

Death could intensify that desperation as well as bring the war uncomfortably close. The loss of a friend or acquaintance in Vietnam could instill both a desire for revenge and a fear of one's own death. More than anything else, it made each soldier face up to *why* he was putting his life on the line. Patriotism and duty are noble concepts when war is weeks away and over a distant horizon; when the time draws nigh, these concepts are less comforting. Steve Fredrick was given pause to reflect on death after he was notified of the loss of a friend, Paul Striepe, during the final phases of his training. At the end of his AIT in January 1968, Fredrick may have been thinking as much about the possibility of his own death as that of his friend when he wrote, "I would like to think he died for something, but I just can't make myself believe it."[28] That, too, was a deficiency carried into combat by many soldiers heading for Vietnam after 1966. Sadly, it was something no amount of training could correct.

Phil Yaeger's first battle in Vietnam would be the assault on Mutter's Ridge. He defended his Marine Corps training but believed that the real learning didn't occur until a man arrived "in country." Yaeger never criticized his trainers because he believed that their mission was impossible. "How do you prepare somebody for that type of carnage? You don't! . . . I learned way more my first two months in Vietnam about war than they could [ever] have taught me in boot camp."

Dwight Reiland espoused a similar view, admitting that although he could try to teach someone to swim on the living room rug, there was no way of knowing how good the instruction was until his pupil was thrown into the water.

Infantry training was probably less physically demanding during the Vietnam War than it was during the Korean War or World War II, but it was designed to be every bit as stressful. Some critics, such as author Mark Lane, collected horror stories of abuse, terror, suicide, and humiliation during training, which, if true, were hardly representative of the experiences of the vast majority of men who underwent it.[29] An equally scathing indictment could be made against high school football programs, by choosing selectively. Although many men resented the way they were treated during infantry training, much of this resentment was, as Charles Moskos noted, nothing more than middle-class youth—often with some college experience—feeling superior to their training instructors and being angry at the fact that for the first time in their lives they were subordinated to people who they felt were inferior to themselves.[30]

No one was critical of the need for physical conditioning, nor did most who served in combat in Vietnam mention their training as being unreasonably harsh or abusive. To a few, perhaps, training was more difficult than they thought necessary, but that was not a common sentiment. Most soldiers who served in the bush found their training to have been soft compared to what awaited them.

Former marine Eugene B. Sledge, writing of his experiences in World War II, suggested:

The technology that developed the rifled barrel, the machine gun, and high-explosive shells has turned war into a prolonged, subhuman slaughter. Men must be trained realistically if they are to survive it without breaking mentally and physically.

I griped as loudly as anyone about our living conditions and discipline. In retrospect, however, I doubt seriously whether I could have coped with the psychological and physical shock and stress encountered on Peleliu and Okinawa had it been otherwise. The Japanese fought to win. It was a savage, brutal, inhumane, exhausting, and dirty business. Our commanders knew that if we were to win and survive, we must be trained realistically for it whether we liked it or not.[31]

In Vietnam, soldiers would fight in the same conditions and against an equally dedicated enemy. But to suggest that those in charge of preparing soldiers for Vietnam were any less understanding of the realities of war than the men who had trained Corporal Sledge would be a great injustice. Although Vietnam-era trainers have been criticized for being heartless and lacking proper understanding, perhaps their actions were, in the final analysis, proof that they truly cared.

CHAPTER 4

Going

October 3, 1967

Dear Mom,

   This ship sure isn't very pleasant as it is overly loaded with men. During the day there isn't hardly standing room up on deck. In the compartments where we sleep there isn't any room at all. Sure will be glad to see land again even if it is Vietnam.

   One thing about this ship, they have services every morning at 9:00 o'clock and have communion every Sunday. It sure seems to help make this trip more bearable. The first few days out, there were a lot of guys seasick, which didn't make the trip any more pleasant as you might guess. I never did get sick though, but [I] didn't feel just perfect the first two or three days.

   Sure will be glad the day I get out of this man's army and be a free man again. It will probably take a few weeks to get used to being back home after I get out. Well, I've got to close for now as the lights are going out in a few minutes. Don't ever worry about me as I have the whole United States Army on my side.

   P.S. See you in 349 days or less.

Love and luck,
Your Son, Leonard[1]

Prior to embarking for overseas duty, soldiers bound for Vietnam received leave, and with it a chance to live as civilians for a few days, sleeping late and enjoying some home-cooked meals. Leave provided a welcome distraction from each soldier's increasing preoccupation with the war. Not surprisingly, the apprehensions soldiers experienced were mostly about the unknown. Soldiers embarking for Vietnam later in the war usually had some contact, however brief, with veterans who had returned, providing a degree of focus for their concerns. But the first American combat units deploying in 1965 were largely in the dark as to what lay ahead. When Terry Musser got ready to ship out with the 1st Cavalry Division in August 1965, neither he nor his parents had much inkling about what a war in Vietnam would mean.

> Probably eighty percent of the people couldn't find it [Vietnam] on a map and I was one of them. Coming home of course, your parents are always worried, but outside of that there probably wasn't a great deal of concern simply because the war really hadn't started and the body count and the guys coming home dead hadn't occurred. It was more anticipation. You were always nervous about something, but you really had no idea what to be nervous about. You were indestructible. It was always going to happen to somebody else.

Only after the weekly body count tallies began to appear in newspapers and combat footage became part of the television news ritual did soldiers departing for the war find a concrete basis for their fears. Men deploying later knew the score—literally—and were more inclined to be fatalistic. Although the dangers were downplayed by both friends and relatives, the act of saying farewell made each parting significant and potentially absolute.

How each man filled his days on leave between training and deployment depended on his individual nature and needs, but for a lot of soldiers and marines the pattern was the same. Leave promised a last fling, a frenzied schedule of good times interspersed with periods of quiet and closeness to family and friends, wives or sweethearts—a time when they might draw more closely together or simply catch their breath. In any case, the behavior of men on leave was often predicated on the vague sense that the future was unforeseeable and its duration unknown.

Directly influencing the conduct of many young soldiers on leave was a profound self-confidence and machismo, side effects of their training, which encouraged thousands of young soldiers to take to the streets of their hometowns feeling lean and mean and ready to take on the world—or at least as many of its experiences as they thought they might reasonably get away with.

Tom Roubideaux returned to South Dakota with the attitude and élan that infects most young paratroopers after completing training. Roubideaux recalls feeling, "I could whip any six marines or ten gooks or North Vietnamese. Soaking wet I weighed a hundred and ten pounds. On my leave I was strutting and everything else. I went out and saw my girlfriend and did what every young man did."[2] Jon Neely's experience on leave was probably typical of most:

> The first thing we did was go and change and put "civvies" on. Then we went out and hit the streets to see what the gang was up to and see if anything had changed around there. Ironically, nothing had changed. Everything was exactly the same at home. The only change was in me. During the next two weeks at home, well, I guess it was starting to sink in that I had to, at least in my mind, [do] a lot of living in two weeks. I had heard plenty of stories of guys that had gone over and really been messed up—guys that had gotten killed. A few friends of mine from Altoona [Pennsylvania] had gotten killed already in Vietnam and it was starting to be a reality in my mind that something could happen. So those next two weeks were party time. And that was basically what I did . . . go out with the guys, get about half blitzed every night—out with the girls and see what I could get. I just tried to live everything I could in that time period.

The final evening of Layne Anderson's "thirty-day party" began at a local bar, evolved into a road race, and ended up at the Trempleau County Jail in Whitehall, Wisconsin. His father had to intervene so that Anderson could make his flight to Oakland, California, the following day. Anderson's experience was unique only in that he was actually taken into custody, albeit briefly. "He's going to Vietnam" was an excuse that served to exonerate a lot of adolescent behavior, as well as some behavior that was definitely not adolescent and that would most certainly have been, in any other circumstance, less likely tolerated by local magistrates or parents.

War's background presence provided a melodramatic atmosphere that encouraged sexual maneuvering, although intent far outpaced accomplishment. Young women during wartime have always felt great pressure to "prove" their love—or simply to provide it. Later, antiwar movement literature and posters included a sort of modern "Lysistrata" approach to encourage men to avoid military service by suggesting that girls "Say Yes to Boys Who Say No."[3]

But the pleasure most commonly pursued to excess by Vietnam-bound GIs was the consumption of truly prodigious quantities of alcohol. The age of most servicemen made this an illegal pastime in most states, but under the circumstances, many drinking establishments and parents and most local constabularies chose to ignore the law. A nineteen-year-old soldier was not legally an adult until the Voting Rights Act of 1970 was ratified as the Twenty-sixth Amendment the following year. The amendment lowered the voting age to eighteen for all state and federal elections; subsequently, many states amended other age restrictions in order to bring them in line with the new voting age. Prior to that time, there was truth in the popular phrase "Old enough to die, but not old enough to buy." Ironically, most soldiers and marines went to Vietnam "underage" for nearly everything, or so it seemed to them, except to die. It was certainly perplexing to Stephen Banko, who noted in a Veteran's Day address to high school students in Buffalo, New York:

> The average age of the Vietnam soldier was 19.7 years. When I went to Vietnam, we weren't allowed to vote—most of us couldn't drive a car at night legally— and most of the troops weren't trusted to buy alcoholic beverages in their home states.

But these same boys . . . were not only allowed—
they were required—to use deadly force on a daily basis.

Not only that, but these same young men, too young
to enjoy most of the responsibilities of domestic citi-
zenship, were required to use such force with judicious
restraint.[4]

But going for the gusto, to borrow a line from a popular
1960s beer ad, was not really based on the fear that a soldier
might never get another chance. Few servicemen went to war
convinced of their impending doom. Only after they had been
exposed to combat did they begin to realize just how delicate
the threads of their mortality were. Rather than fearing death,
many men went to Vietnam convinced of their immortality.
Bill Harken refused to believe that anything would happen to
him in Vietnam. "Before I went overseas I just went out and
saw my friends, my lady friends, and drank beer and had a
good time," said Harken. "I knew I was going and I knew I
was coming back—alive! I just knew it. I can't explain it but
that was the way I felt."

Feelings of dread did creep into the mind, but they seemed
to come and go in response to one's general mood. Donald
Putnam remembered:

One day you knew there was no problem, you would
make it. The next day there was a lingering doubt all
the time. You didn't really know for sure. So it changed.
It was day to day. Emotionally, however you felt that
day was really how you felt about it. I guess on the
flight over—that was probably when the realization
came home, especially the closer we got to Vietnam.
"Hey! I might not make it back from here." And there
was self-doubt at that time, but prior to that it was one
day, "Yeah, I'll be coming back, no problem." And the
next day you might think, Maybe I won't be. So it was
kind of back and forth at that point.

Faced with the unknown, men who would soon be separated from home by half a world tended to place a much

higher value on family relationships. Many of these reappraisals of family significance were the result of changing beliefs concerning life's permanency, which they had previously taken for granted. For many, these final gatherings with parents and friends seemed desperately important. Dwight Reiland remembered wanting to tell people "all those important things" in case he didn't come back. He wanted to say the words; but like most soldiers, he never did. The perfect opportunity for such expressions rarely presented itself, and those to whom soldiers wished to be closest were, in the end, seldom embraced, nor the important words exchanged. Still, volumes were spoken in awkward silences, and most soldiers and marines went off to war understanding their loved ones a little better.

Leave often created new beginnings and endings. Ed Hoban broke up with his girlfriend because he knew he was going to Vietnam and he wasn't sure if he would be coming back. There was very little else about the visit he remembered. Bryan Good got married during his leave, making his final farewell from the airport in Madison, Wisconsin, all the more difficult.

Kenneth Korkow didn't consider himself a very sensitive person when he went home to say his farewells in December 1967, but the young marine recalled one important moment with his father at the family ranch.

We happened to be in a spot there, just dad and myself, and I said, "Dad, you must feel pretty good. As far as you can see it's all your land and all the livestock is yours." We happened to be on a place that his folks lost for taxes during the Depression, and he'd added a couple other ranches to it, you know. And he said, "You know, that's not how I measure life." He said, "When I die, what's really important to me is they won't be able to put all my friends in one church." That was interesting because dad and I would talk work, but we never talked politics. Sports, but we didn't talk neighbors and we didn't talk philosophy. But that's one of the conversations that I recall.

Sometimes departures and good-byes seemed terribly anticlimactic. Jon Neely's departure was, in retrospect, "kind of dry," almost as though he were "going out of town for a little while and would be right back." If there was any worry on his family's part, they didn't show it. Maybe, he reasoned, that was good psychology. Anyway, he had anticipated more parental concern and was disappointed when he didn't see it.

Tom Schultz experienced much the same thing with his parting. It seemed to Schultz that his parents were ignoring the war's reality or else addressing it unrealistically. "I knew the day I got my draft notice where I was going," he said, "but nobody else wanted to face that reality. When I was in training I would call home or get a letter or something and it would be like, 'Well maybe you'll go to Germany or Korea or some place like that!' Well, the orders came down, and then it was, 'Well it's only a year and we know you'll be all right,' and all that . . . mom and dad stuff."

Some parents had experienced sacrifice and suffering during previous conflicts. They knew what their sons going off to war could only imagine. When Tom Roubideaux returned to Rosebud, South Dakota, en route to Vietnam in 1965, his mother met him with tears. She had lost her first husband in Italy in World War II. Her second husband, Tommy's father, had lost his legs in the war and had gone through some delayed stress resulting in an eventual divorce. She understood the suffering that war could visit upon a home. But Roubideaux's most memorable experience came on the day he left. One of his grandfathers "came over to the house and sang a traditional going away song. This song essentially said, 'Be strong, you're a man now.' In Lakota it means that you're seeking a black face, because killing is a thing God doesn't appreciate, so you wear a black face to hide. You see this with traditional dancers at powwows. His song said, 'Be strong, you're representing the people now, your grandfather [referring to the president of the United States] has asked you to go. Walk with pride. Reveal the Lakota braveness.' "

Most soldiers were not honored with songs by their grandfathers, but they did feel an instinctive pride and purpose in going off to war, in attending church with the family, or sharing dinner with friends. Whether or not they would later admit it, many soldiers were proud—at the time they left. But many of them would soon discover that they, too, did not appreciate the killing, and they would put on a black face of their own when they returned.

Fathers who had experienced combat in World War II or Korea understood all too well what lay ahead for their sons, but they were seldom able to express a warning. Some, however, found themselves inadvertently supplanting a lifetime of patriotic rhetoric with a moment of involuntary fear at the eleventh hour. All of his life, Terry Tople remembered that his father had "pushed the idea of the Midwest soldier" on him.

> He was a prisoner of war of the Japanese for four years and he said you should be proud to fight for your country and all this. We just weren't too close. But the day I went to get on the plane, my dad came up to me and said, "You know, Son, you can go to Canada. I wouldn't mind a bit."
>
> That really surprised me because I heard all my life that you should go into the army and serve your country, and to hear that from him . . . I guess maybe he thought that he could lose a son. It brought tears to my eyes. I mean, here's a man who preached all his life that you should fight for your country, and he was proud right up to the moment he died. I was still proud that I was going but when he said that, it floored me. He actually pointed to another plane. I doubt if it was going to Canada, but he said, "There's a plane over there; if you want to go to Canada, go." It shocked me.

As the war progressed, many departing servicemen had to contend with friends or relatives who were fiercely opposed to the war. This situation put many of them in a dilemma because they had harbored similar thoughts. When Dan Krehbiel went home on leave, he discovered that his mother was really scared and that his father, a World War II veteran, was proud. One of his sisters, however, was dismayed.

> She was really a peace activist at the time [1969]. She was really involved in it and she kept telling me I

should desert and go to Canada because it was an unjust war and I would be branded a criminal and everything else for my involvement in it. And my mother
couldn't stand it. We didn't know it, but she was in the
pantry working and listening and she came out just fu-
rious, in an absolute rage, in tears and all this and she
screamed at my sister, "Leave him alone! What do you
want him to do? What are you asking him to do? He is
stuck. Why don't you support him?"

And then, after a while, . . . we talked and [my sis-
ter] said she was really sorry. She hadn't considered it.
And that was how I felt too—just how I felt. I thought,
What do you want me to do? I can't [go to Canada]. I
don't have the courage or the guts for it.

After returning from their furloughs, many soldiers experienced a post-leave depression that was often intense, although normally short lived. Paul Meringolo felt it on his
return to Fort Hood and the 1st Armored Cavalry in August
1967. He remembered that when he got back to the barracks
area he flopped down on his cot and just lay there realizing,
"from here on it was Vietnam and the unknown of the war
and maybe coming home and not knowing what to expect—
knowing it was going to be a long time and a lot of experiences before I was ever going to get home to see my family.
It was a pretty depressing moment. But you started getting
caught up in the packing and the getting ready to move out after awhile, so you quickly got over that."

Prior to a unit's initial deployment, there was usually time
for some final training and organization, but not always.
Haste often undermined a unit's readiness. The 1st Cavalry
Division deployed with a serious shortage of key personnel
because of expiring terms of service. These could only have
been extended by a presidential declaration of national emergency. The division thus found itself with twenty-seven hundred men who could not be deployed, and a critical shortage
of some five hundred pilots, mechanics, and aircrew. After arriving in Vietnam in September 1965, the division was further
reduced by a malaria outbreak. Although the 1st Cavalry had
been training for two years as the 11th Air Assault Division

at Fort Benning, its members had received no jungle training and the division was issued M16 rifles only ten days prior to its departure, resulting in a hurried familiarization program.[5]

Similarly, the 9th Infantry Division assembled and packed off to war from Fort Riley, Kansas, in a hurry. The division pulled enlisted troops from ten different reception stations to fill out its three brigades. "The Old Reliables," as the unit was known, lacked critical equipment, such as night vision devices and communications gear; M60 machine guns had to be borrowed from the local National Guard; there was a chronic shortage of officers; and, finally, the division's training schedule was shortened twelve weeks in order to deploy the unit by its December 1966 deadline. The men who stepped ashore in Vietnam were new and possibly eager, but their enlisted leaders were also unfamiliar with their subordinates, and precious few men had any actual combat experience.[6]

The 11th Light Infantry Brigade went to Vietnam as part of Task Force Oregon, which later became the Americal Division. The brigade was plagued with problems that began with its initial deployment in December 1967 and lasted until it returned home in 1971. The battalions were neither fully trained nor equipped when they were ordered to the combat zone. Some thirteen hundred men were deemed incapable of being deployed with the unit, presumably because of insufficient time left on their terms of service, and their slots were quickly filled with whatever personnel were available. The confusion and last-minute adjustments did nothing to improve the unit's combat readiness and cohesion when it arrived in Vietnam.[7]

These units were not the only ones to suffer deployment problems, but their difficulties were indicative of those experienced, in varying degrees, by all units that deployed en masse halfway around the world. Soldiers with only a few weeks remaining on their enlistments were not shipped overseas, and all personnel with more than a year remaining would rotate home from Vietnam en masse a year after their unit's arrival because of the policy of one-year combat tours. When the return date arrived, sizable portions of any unit's strength, that is, its survivors, departed—taking with them the valuable experience they had gained. Naturally, there was some attrition caused by combat, accidents, and sickness, which brought a steady trickle of replacements into every unit, but the way in which the army tried to avoid the exodus of troops from units originally deployed en masse was to trade a portion of its soldiers after a period of several months with men from other units with different DEROS (date of expected return from overseas) dates.

This "infusion" resolved the problem of a mass rotation, but it was costly in terms of unit cohesion for both elements involved in the trade. The situation improved after 1967, however, when the major unit deployments were completed. Eighty-one army infantry battalions deployed to Vietnam during the course of the war, two-thirds of them (fifty-four) prior to January 1967. By 1968, only eighteen battalions experienced infusion problems, and this was reduced to only two battalions by the second half of 1969. All marine regiments except the 27th were deployed before 1968. The 27th arrived in February 1968 and withdrew seven months later.[8]

The withdrawal of combat units later in the war created a similar problem. Units packing their colors and returning to the United States did not keep their unit integrity; instead both army and marine units sent home only those men who had completed eight or nine months of their tours. Those who had the lion's share of their tours yet to complete were transferred into units remaining behind. This policy significantly diminished unit integrity. In other cases, units were simply not given replacements. When the strength of these battalions was sufficiently reduced, their personnel were combined into a single unit and the colors of the others were cased and sent home with a small detachment to accompany them.[9]

The majority of Vietnam combat soldiers, however, were shipped over as individual replacements, each with his own separate DEROS date and little else in common with his planeload of companions except the knowledge that the fortunate ones would be riding together in the opposite direction a year later. Replacement personnel often encountered one or two men with whom they had become acquainted during their earlier training, so the journey was not always made in friendless isolation.

Marines, prior to shipping out for "WestPac," returned from leave to a staging battalion. Staging provided a final bit of pre-Vietnam refresher training and was a catchall for shots and paperwork before departure. Even marines who had previously been to Vietnam went through a staging battalion before returning for another tour.

Phil Yaeger's staging in July 1966 was simple enough. He remembered being assigned to a captain, and when about five hundred marines had been assembled, they were taken over to the air base at Twenty-nine Palms, where they boarded planes for the trip over. In 1969, Tom Magedanz and his fellow marine replacements went through a staging regime that included three weeks of refresher infantry training, instruction in topics relating to Vietnam—such as booby traps—and the bureaucratic paper-pushing that accompanies all military moves. He and his fellow marines were allowed passes into Oceanside, California, a community he remembers as overflowing with two classes of people: marines and those trying to make money from marines.

There were "millions" of places in Oceanside where one could buy all types of military equipment, from uniforms to jungle boots. Magedanz's letters revealed the contempt he held for the commercialism and high-pressure sales tactics of the town. He found particularly peccant the jewelry stores ("Buy your gal a ring to remember you by") and the Bible business ("If you buy now you also receive absolutely free this beautiful reproduction of Our Lord's Last Supper complete with attached frame and night-light for your mother"). "Oceanside," he was convinced, would "shrivel up and die without marines to gyp."[10] Men bound for Vietnam made those necessary, last-minute purchases of personal military equipment at places such as Ranger Joe's near Fort Benning. The purchase of choice was a "boonie knife," an accoutrement included on the belt of many a well-dressed combat soldier. The oversized knives were seldom used for anything more lethal than opening a recalcitrant can of C rations, and many of these pieces of cutlery, like Vernon Janick's, simply got lost.

Shipping Out

Units leaving en masse were kept busy with preparations for the ocean voyage. The busywork of logistics and the presence of familiar faces helped bolster a man's spirits. Scuttlebutt was rampant as men anticipated possible assignments to Vietnam. In some cases the "word," as is common with rumors, reached the ear of the lowly infantryman before the commanders were officially notified. Major General Arthur S. Collins didn't receive formal notice that his 4th Infantry Division was going to Vietnam until April 1966,[11] but one of the division's privates, Jeff Beatty, wrote his mother the month before that he had heard that he would "be going where it is hotter than hell and there is a lot of rain. That's all I can tell you about it for security reasons. Don't mention it to anyone. The report is we have within 90 to 120 days."[12]

Some troops conducted deployment exercises prior to embarking. Sergeant Willie Williams's unit, the 2d Battalion, 27th Infantry of the 25th Infantry Division, had several practice alerts. When the time finally came, he was uncertain whether or not they were actually being deployed.

"No one was sure because they played games," Williams said. "You would go out on a boat and train, go through your alert procedure where you fill out all the documentation for your family to be brought back to the States, the allotment forms. . . . They did that twice with me between September and the time we actually left [December 1965] and that is why . . . it didn't dawn on me that we were actually going when we did."

Once under way, there were advantages to traveling by sea. The voyage acted as a buffer between "The World" and Vietnam. Soldiers traveled in the company of men with whom they had trained. The trip also allowed for gradual acclimation to the increasing temperature and humidity. But as home gradually slipped behind, so did their connections to it.

Troops aboard ship could measure their progress toward Vietnam in several ways. Every day or two they set their clocks back an hour until they had performed the task thirteen times. In addition, the voyage took the troops across the international date line and ever deeper into the tropics. The trip also included stops at some less-than-exotic ports of call, such as Subic Bay in the Philippines, or the island of Guam, where the ships were refueled and the sea-weary soldiers were given a chance to go ashore to stretch their legs and get a soda or a few beers. As the voyage progressed, the weather got hotter and the humidity rose with the temperature.

Accommodations for the infantry at sea have never been first class, and the crowded conditions below deck, along with the unfamiliar rhythms of the sea and the motions of the ship, made the voyage a thing of which most soldiers would retain vivid memories. Infantrymen have always felt a certain enmity for ocean travel, and the cruise to Vietnam, especially during the first days at sea, was not always a pleasant experience. Paul Meringolo recalled:

> I don't think I would want to go across the ocean by cargo ship again. First three days I remember it was very difficult to get my sea legs. I spent most of my time just lying in my rack because that was the only way I really could feel comfortable. If I stood up I seemed to get seasick, so I just sort of lay there and fought the nausea. We were sort of up in the front of the boat I guess, because you could feel the bouncing of the boat from the waves. And when you had to go into the shower area or use the latrine you could see the actual shape of the boat curving up front and it was far from accommodating when you have lots of guys using the same shower area, same john, same sinks, and living basically in the same area. You quickly lose any sense of privacy—if you had any in the first place. But we all managed to get by.

Terry Musser shipped out of Savannah, Georgia, with the 1st Cavalry Division on the USNS *Geiger,* a converted ocean liner stacked with bunks so that as many personnel as possible could be packed into the ship's tiny compartments. It reminded him of scenes in old World War II movies. Considering the length of the voyage and the cramped conditions, Musser was amazed that the army was able to keep the 753 officers and men of his battalion from killing each other during their thirty-two days at sea. He could not remember any big fights aboard ship, a fact that left him bemused twenty years later.[13]

Not all voyages were without incident, however. Willie Williams's voyage in January 1966 as part of the 25th Infantry Division was marred by the death of a soldier in a gambling dispute. Jerry Vetterkind remembered that in October 1967, when his shipload of troops from the 198th Light Infantry Brigade was about a thousand miles out of San Francisco, a soldier jumped overboard. In spite of the crew's almost instant reaction and a thorough search of the area, the man's body was never recovered.[14]

The time in transit aboard ship varied with the port of embarkation and the general age and condition of the vessel. Vernon Janick's voyage from Fort Lewis to Tuy Hoa in August 1966 took twenty-one days. It was a relatively brief journey, but his sentiments most likely reflected those of the entire 4th Infantry Division when he later said of the trip, "The last week we didn't care if they [the enemy] were sitting on shore waiting for us with machine guns. You were just so glad to get off [the ship] and go at her."

One saving grace, which compensated in part for the misery the men experienced at sea, was the knowledge that every day spent aboard ship was subtracted from the total days allocated for each soldier's tour of duty in Vietnam.

The men spent their time aboard ship in various ways. Jerry Vetterkind had very little to do during his voyage, but other soldiers and marines recall taking part in physical training, cleaning weapons, and receiving refresher courses on a myriad of topics. On the *Geiger,* Terry Musser and Gerry Barker took physical training on the sun deck—175 soldiers at a time going through the calisthenic ritual of the "Daily Dozen." This was followed by a twenty-minute run in place.[15]

Sergeant Barker recalled spending much of his time aboard the *Geiger* readying equipment. The men of the 1st Cavalry Division still wore their regular cotton twill fatigue uniforms, but they dyed them a darker green either prior to leaving or while aboard ship. They also dyed their white T-shirts. Barker had the distinct impression that everyone and everything seemed to have a greenish tint on that voyage.

Terry Musser got his first glimpse of a real M16 while en route to Vietnam with the 1st Cavalry. The men were told to take their new rifles up on deck to strip and clean them. The rifles began to corrode immediately in the fresh salt air. As long as Musser kept his original weapon, it was plagued with rust.

Before arriving off the coast of Vietnam, members of Jeff Beatty's 2d Battalion, 8th Infantry, put on a talent show. He was surprised at the caliber of the performances. His letter describing it also mentioned that he would be based at Pleiku, and he took care to write out the pronunciation carefully for his mother. The letter's closing contained less than reassuring news. During the previous week, Pleiku had been the site of one of the worst battles of the war up to that time. Perhaps that was why Beatty took communion aboard ship the day he arrived off the Vietnamese coast. The sermon was on "The Equality of Men."[16]

Leonard Dutcher was impressed with the little things the navy crewmen did for the soldiers under their care. Their last meal aboard his ship was turkey with all the trimmings. They were even fed "Christmas cookies," which he said were delicious but made him feel homesick. While in Subic Bay two days earlier, Dutcher wrote, "Everyone got off the ship and got drunk. It was a good time—our last one for a long time."[17]

Thoughts turned to home and the year ahead as the troop-ships arrived at ports such as Cam Ranh Bay or Da Nang and the men waited for the tide and the barges that would allow them to be off-loaded. Most expected hostile fire and were disappointed when they encountered none. There was the usual "hurry up and wait," giving them an opportunity to write a letter home. For some, such as Paul Meringolo, there was time for a bit of final reflection about the unknown and perhaps some foreshadowing of things to come.

I can recall that evening looking at the landscape of Vietnam, the contours of the hills against the dark sky, and you could hear the booming noise of exploding shells from artillery or whatever. I could see a destroyer coming up the coastline shooting off rounds from their big guns into the hills. It was an eerie feeling for all of us. I recall just looking out there, listening to these muffled sounds of explosions and not being able to see land itself, just the shadows and the darkness. I guess it was almost like a metaphor for what the actual war was like, because most of the war seemed to be fought in the darkness and in shadow and shapes; not really seeing your enemy, not really knowing but anticipating them . . . feeling them all around you. It was anticipation most of the time in Vietnam that something was going to happen, and anticipation can really be worse than the actual experience—sometimes.

Ship travel minimized many of the physiological, emotional, and climatic changes soldiers underwent. Perhaps most importantly, traveling in the company of good comrades took some of the sting out of going to war, with all of its unknowns. Such was not the case for the majority of Vietnam-bound servicemen who traveled to war at about five hundred miles per hour in comfortable, quiet, climate-controlled Boeing 707s and Douglas DC-8s.

A Flying Leap

Most soldiers went to Vietnam as replacement troops and, although they flew in crowded commercial airliners, they were essentially traveling alone. Soldiers received their travel orders prior to going home on leave. These orders specified that they report to either Oakland Army Base or Fort Lewis. There they were processed for shipment overseas on flights originating at either Travis Air Force Base near Oakland, or McChord Air Force Base, located between Seattle and Tacoma.

Second thoughts about going to Vietnam seemed to multiply exponentially at that point in the process, as did the desire to get the show on the road. While awaiting his flight to depart for Vietnam from McChord Air Force Base in November 1968, Steve Fredrick wrote:

I am not sure what I am doing here yet. On top of this I am not sure if I will be here much longer, as I have been called on by my country to fight a war that I do not understand and which I doubt the leaders of this country understand. . . .

I feel I am compelled to go and fight because of all the men who went before. I don't think the war is right; but I must go. If the time comes and I must die, I have made up my mind that I will die proud. It is a big challenge and I have to meet it, in fact, I am anxious to meet it. I am ready to go.[18]

"If you showed up at Oakland or at Fort Lewis," Dwight Reiland noted, "you had already answered the question as to whether you were going to do it or not—you went!" From his vantage point in February 1971, Reiland decided that the Vietnam War wasn't going to end for him until it started, and it wasn't going to start until he got on that airplane.

Many critics of the Vietnam War point to epidemic numbers of AWOLs (absence without leave) and desertions as proof of an overwhelming opposition to the war among men in uniform. Richard Holmes points out, however, that the Marine Corps's desertion and AWOL rate was highest in 1975, *after* the United States completed its withdrawal from Vietnam. Holmes cites statistics showing that boredom in peacetime actually makes soldiers more inclined to desert than in time of war.[19] Guenter Lewy noted that of the thousands of deserters during the Vietnam era, almost all were stationed in the United States. Far from being politically motivated, he says, soldiers separated themselves from the military for more practical reasons, such as personal problems, financial difficulties stemming from the low pay they received, or an inability to adjust to military life.[20]

Fear also made it easier for some servicemen to search for arguments, excuses really, upon which they might make a philosophical stand and justify avoiding the war or deserting. According to Lawrence Baskir and William Strauss who gathered data for President Ford's clemency board, a hundred thousand military personnel were punished for going AWOL or deserting during the Vietnam War, yet only about seven thousand Americans absented themselves *after* receiving orders to go to Vietnam. Only when confronted with orders for duty in the combat zone did "late-blooming Conscientious Objectors" realize just how much they opposed the war. Baskir and Strauss suggest: "Since these men did not seem to be opposed to the war in Vietnam until they had to go there, it is safe to assume that they were motivated by fear for their own life rather than opposition to the war. It was a question of survival; they might get killed there."[21]

That was precisely what Larry Gates concluded when he went AWOL in 1970.

> I got home and had fifteen days leave and two days travel time. I was still more or less a pacifist, at least to my own mind I was, and I didn't know if I wanted to go to Vietnam at all at that point. I went AWOL and spent about fifteen days making up my mind whether I wanted to go and shoot people. Finally the question popped into my mind whether I was really that altruistic. Was I really worried about whether to shoot people or was I worried about getting shot myself? Between not knowing that and not wanting to look over my shoulder the rest of my life I decided to go, so I reported into Oakland, where I shipped out from there.[22]

Tim O'Brien found, after making all the necessary preparations to go AWOL from Seattle, he simply couldn't do it. He burned the letters he had written to his family that would have explained his actions. What it came down to was a feeling of shame. "It was over," he wrote later. "I simply couldn't bring myself to flee. Family, the hometown, friends, history, tradition, fear, confusion, exile: I could not run. I was a coward. I was sick."[23]

Thoughts about desertion and fleeing to Canada were relatively common by the height of the war. Thomas Birhanzel recalled friends of his from the West Coast discussing the merits of going AWOL toward the end of Advanced Individual Training in 1969. By the time he took his final stateside leave, the notion of going to Canada began to grow in him as well. Birhanzel's wife was due to give birth while he was home on thirty-days' leave, but the baby was late. Birhanzel called everyone he could think of, from the authorities at Fort Lewis to the Red Cross, but could get no definite answer to his request to remain for the birth. He was told simply to show up for the flight. At that point he came close to deserting, not for political reasons, but for paternal ones: He feared that he might get killed and would never be able to see his child.

Many soldiers considered desertion, but a very small number actually planned such a move, and only a few carried out their plans. Soldiers did, however, seek ways within the military to avoid duty in Vietnam or to avoid serving as combat infantrymen. Such attempts were usually doomed to fail. Soldiers might reenlist for a longer period and receive training in another MOS, but that meant a longer service commitment. Others tried pulling whatever strings were available.

Although Jeff Beatty made no mention of it in any of his previous correspondence, when the rumor began to circulate concerning the impending deployment of the 4th Infantry Division, Beatty wrote to his mother that he was angry with the army. He had enlisted on the promise that he would be a cook and he was trained as an infantry soldier instead. His platoon sergeant agreed to check his records to see if he had been guaranteed that schooling, but he was unable to get an answer. Beatty's last letter before he shipped out in July 1966 included the phone number of the 4th Division's casualty desk. Next of kin, he informed his mother, could call collect. There would be no need. The telegram bearing the news of his death was delivered directly to her door.[24]

Processing for overseas flights from the West Coast was a universally frustrating procedure. Dan Krehbiel's description is typical, though perhaps more detailed than most.

> I reported to Oakland by noon on a certain day and they checked me in and they said all you have to do is go to these barracks and find a bunk and sit down. Every morning and every afternoon you have to fall out with a thousand other guys on this big huge company street and then some guy with a loudspeaker up there calls out names and when your name comes up you fall

out and fall back in over there and get ready to go. By then your orders had been cut. For four days I . . . waited. Every morning I went out there and listened for my name and it hadn't come up yet.

Meanwhile, the place was flooding. There was this massive amount of soldiers thrown into the service at that time [summer 1969] so it was [very] overcrowded. A place that was supposed to hold 350 or 375 had 700 men in it on top of each other. Periodically, a whole batch of them would leave and a new batch would come in the door. It was interesting. It was this mass of humanity. So you just listened for your name and kept out of trouble. At least I did. And that is pretty much it.

Eventually, they called my name. And then they took us to another warehouse where we had all of our stuff together and they locked us up! That is pretty much what it came down to. We were under lock and key in this big huge airplane hangar with bunks, telephones, snack bar, and all kinds of junk inside. We were stuck there. After an interminable amount of time they finally got our flight manifest put together and we were broken down into groups. They took us by bus to Travis Air Force Base and loaded us on a plane. This was all a couple of days after we got locked up—about six days—and we went overseas.

Knowing the effects that too much idle time could have on morale, the military tried to keep the men occupied. Dwight Reiland recalled: "They would call out some names and for the rest of the day you were supposed to do this and supposed to do that, but nobody did. Everybody just kind of found a spot to hide until the evening formation, when they would call out some more names. If they needed somebody for KP they would grab somebody. So you soon learned to send somebody else to the formation." Reiland said that he and his buddies took turns going to the roll calls and answering up for each other. In that way, he explained, "only one guy was out there exposing himself to KP. The rest of them were hiding out, peeking out the windows or whatever in case they called their names. If they called you up to the front for some reason or another, you had to be ready to haul ass up there and make it look like you had truly been in formation."

The waiting was not to anyone's liking, and Reiland said that he felt relieved when his name was finally called. Oakland, he remembered, was "the pits" in February—cold and rainy—and the accommodations were nothing more than a warehouse full of cots. It was an experience that made four or five days seem like months.

Stephen Fredrick found some diversion in watching the men with whom he was deploying as they prepared to depart for Vietnam. He recorded his observations in a letter home while sitting on the bus at McChord Air Force Base. "Even if they aren't talking," he wrote, "you can almost guess what is on their minds. A lot of them are going over for the second time and it is great to watch them and listen to them as they talk to the first-timers. A lot of men are loud and joking and laughing all the time. You wonder if they are just trying to cover up their own nervousness. Many men are quiet and speak hardly a word. I suppose that, for a lot of us, this will be the last day we ever spend in the States. I wonder which men or what type of man will die in Vietnam. I guess war does not care what kind of man it kills."[25]

Private carriers were contracted to fly troops to Vietnam: United, Air Canada, World Airways, Continental, TWA, National, Flying Tigers. Boarding was by rank; officers and civilians first, then senior NCOs, and finally the rest of the enlisted personnel. The Boeing 707s or Douglas DC-8s were stripped of all the amenities and filled to capacity. The act of boarding the jet finally convinced Ed Hoban that he was really headed for Vietnam. He remembered hearing the Peter, Paul, and Mary song "Leaving on a Jet Plane" while getting ready to board the aircraft, and the song's lyrics, which seemed so appropriate at the time, stuck in his mind.

Aircraft cabins quickly filled with nervous laughter and conversation. Looking around the cabin gave a passenger the sense that he was in a clone factory. Men nervously adjusted the little turret-shaped air spigots above them, directing the flow of air onto their military haircuts, and waited. Flight attendants moved down the aisles as the engines warmed up. It was then that it dawned on Tom Schultz and approximately two million others that they were actually going to Vietnam. Schultz wondered if anybody really believed it before the jet was pressurized.

A young man sat across the aisle from Schultz looking at a picture of his wife. She had just given birth to their first child, a girl. The army had denied his request to stay a few days and see her. Schultz was not surprised. His own experience demonstrated that the army was sympathetic to death, but not to a new life.[26]

Once the plane was airborne and began the northern portion of its great-circle route across the Pacific, the flight became a mosaic of individual feelings and perceptions. Phil Yaeger barely remembered his flight at all—only that, like Ed Hoban's, it seemed long and tiring. There was a stopover for fuel in Tokyo, but Yaeger and the others on board were not allowed to leave the plane.

Jack Freitag passed the time playing cards when he went over in 1966. "We were playing 'Guts,' " he recalled, "and money didn't mean too much to any of us. Guys would bet on nothing and you had to match the pot. We had some big pots there. It was very boisterous and the stewardesses were there giving us drinks. It was a fun time going over."

Flight attendants were a memorable part of everyone's flight, as Paul Boehm remembered. "We had stewardesses and they took a hell of a beating on the plane—all these guys were talking about going over and not coming back," he said. "One guy would drop a pillow and she would bend over and another guy would take a picture under her skirt. We had a good time."

Micki Voisard was one of those flight attendants, and she remembered the beatings far better than the soldiers. Voisard dealt with a wide range of difficult situations. She saw men masturbating on the flights, a frequent enough activity that new stewardesses were warned to "never take a blanket off a sleeping GI." There was also considerable sexual abuse, although that term was not one she would have used back in the 1960s. The men played jokes with catsup and sanitary napkins or asked for help with their seat belts while the others laughed. Bending over for anything ran the risk of a roving hand underneath a dress. She also saw, on occasion, soldiers who would jerk open the door of the lavatory after a flight attendant had gone inside to use the toilet. Such things seemed incredible in retrospect, but she remembered them as being routine. Despite all the "bad apples" on the flights, Voisard also recalled:

> There were also guys who would let you know that they didn't approve of what they saw going on. A lot of them would come up and say, "I'm really sorry that happened to you." They weren't all older guys either; some were just young kids. You saw where respect came from. . . .
>
> Fortunately, I came out of it not hating them. I knew a lot of girls that ended up that way. They were having difficulty dealing with the men on the flights. I was able to function and talk with the GIs the whole time; it's just that I found myself giving commands all the time. In order to survive, I had to challenge them. They would challenge you, and if you could speak louder and be more authoritarian, then they would buckle under to you.[27]

For many a melancholy soldier, the mere presence of flight attendants made a profound difference. Many Vietnam-bound soldiers remembered the genuine smiles and kindness of those women, and the men's desire to touch them was not meant to be obscene or indecent. Randy Hoelzen recalled how beautiful the stewardesses looked on his flight. "I remember sticking my arm out or hanging it over the side so I could get a slight feel of a stewardess going back and forth, knowing that was probably the last American woman I was going to see in a long time."

Dan Krehbiel found little joy on the way to Vietnam in the summer of 1969. His memories were more woeful than most.

> The flight was just full of despair for me and most of the other guys. There was a cloud of gloom in the whole airplane, and this was a big huge 707 with everything first class ripped out. There were just a lot of seats and they were all full. I don't know how many soldiers

there were on that plane. They had films for us—you know, all this good stuff. It was a commercial flight. It wasn't like going by [military] air transport.

We stopped at Hawaii. The only time I've seen Hawaii. We were there about a half an hour, which we spent in the snack bar. No, I take that back, it was the bar! And we took off from there and landed at Guam, refueled there, and then flew into Bien Hoa.

Those who claimed that flying to Vietnam was going to war "first class" never spent twenty hours in an airline seat. In jump school, those qualifying for airborne status learn there are seven points of contact during a parachute landing roll. On the flight to Vietnam, the fourth point of contact—the one on the seat bottom—died first. The other six soon followed suit. Slowly the body began to settle into a dull ache that was immune to any efforts spent to correct it. As the flight progressed, the conversations and the card games quietly died out. Paul Boehm noticed that while "at first everybody was joking around, . . . from Japan on it got a little quieter."

Likewise, Jack Freitag remembered that as soon as they neared the coast of Vietnam, there was a hush. "You could hear a pin drop," he said. "Everybody was just staring out the plane, even the guys on the [aisle] seats were standing up trying to look out the windows. It was just a lush green canopy. I guess it was all curiosity at first. I think that is what hit most of us . . . if there was a war going on down there. Nobody really knew for sure. It was a different feeling."

Michael Jackson displayed his naivete as they arrived in the evening skies over Vietnam and began to descend for landing. Seeing flashes of light in the deepening dusk, Jackson prodded the man next to him and remarked, " 'Jesus Christ! Look at all that lightning—and I don't see any rain.' The guy looked at me kind of dumbfounded and said, 'That's not lightning, that's artillery.' And then, after the artillery, I started seeing tracers and I thought, Holy shit! What is this I'm getting into?"

Marines landed at Kadena Air Base on Okinawa en route to Vietnam. There they stored excess gear and exchanged stateside uniforms for jungle fatigues. Orders and travel documents were checked and the men were given malaria pills. Some marines remembered receiving a painful "GG" shot, which they were told would help their blood clot more quickly. It was just one more stab in the arm that rounded out the innoculations for typhoid, typhus, tetanus, yellow fever, cholera, plague, and whatever else the military felt duty bound to protect servicemen against. There was no strain of penicillin known to man, however, that could combat the dreaded "Black Syph," a supposedly incurable and much-heralded venereal disease against which most personnel bound for Vietnam recall being solemnly warned.

False rumors hinted that infection with the lethal disease would result in a victim's family being notified that he was killed in action. Meanwhile, those suffering the deadly contagion would be spirited away to a special facility on Guam, or the Philippines, or some other island or hidden corner of the world where the colony of unfortunates died in agony and shame. The purpose of the rumor, which seems to have been officially sanctioned, was to help give abstinence a boost. It apparently worked. William Harken was adamant that he wasn't about to "touch any women in Vietnam," although he acknowledged that, had he been in Vietnam long enough, his "resolve might have gone away. But," Harken added, "the rumors [of venereal disease] scared me."

Finally, the marines on Okinawa were given liberty. When journalist Charles Anderson made the flight in 1969 he noted the details of the briefing given to the incoming marines right down to the final item: the VD rate on "Oki" was 97 percent.[28]

Vietnam-bound marines saw their first returning "grunts" on "Oki" and discovered, as Anderson put it, the tenacity with which Asian bar girls can separate a marine from his money. They learned lessons from both.

Phil Yaeger's time on Okinawa paralleled the experiences of thousands of marines:

> We were in a casual status, which means you just fill the day with barracks cleaning and PT and you are sort of in limbo. And then you have an inspection and liberty call and you go get drunk. Then you come back the

next morning and strip the floor again and do PT and clean rifles. At that point they were sending us over in small groups. We really didn't realize that, but after awhile we did. They would come in and read off twenty to thirty names.

We stored one seabag there, which was basically stateside uniforms—tropicals, greens, things we weren't taking to Vietnam—and we boarded the plane for Da Nang.

While on Okinawa, marines were also given their Vietnam unit assignments. Terry Shepardson remembered waiting in a line before a sergeant and a clerk who were stamping orders. He looked at the clerk and, as their eyes met—BANG! The stamp hit his papers: 3d Battalion, 5th Marines. He recalled looking at the clerk in disbelief. "I had trained for the last four or five months," Shepardson reflected, almost as though the memory were freshly minted, "and all of a sudden, it hits you: You are going there."

CHAPTER 5

Arrival and Processing

October 26, 1967

Dear Mom and Dad,

Well, I've made it through my first day in hell. Right now we are bedded down in a town called Chu Lai, if you want to call it a town. I guess we will be moving out into the boondocks tomorrow or the next day. I'm sure not looking forward to going out there.

The way I heard it today, we will be moving a long ways into the interior and building our own base camp. It will probably take about six months to complete it, so we have a lot of work staring us in the face.

Right now I could think of a thousand places I'd rather be than here. People in the States don't know how good they have it till they see a stinking hole like this. I miss you folks a lot and I will be writing again soon.

Your Son,
Leonard[1]

No single experience was more common amongst Americans serving in Vietnam than the impact of the first gamy concentrations of heat and odor that welcomed them. David Carlisle arrived in the middle of a typical day in April 1968. The air conditioner on his plane was kept running, but as he got closer to the door it got hotter and hotter. When he finally stepped through the door and out onto the portable stairway, the heat struck him in the face like a blast furnace.

It didn't seem to matter when a serviceman arrived, the

temperature was always hot compared to what he had left behind in the States. Jon Neely arrived in November and likened the heat to someone holding a hair dryer up to his nose. Phil Yaeger described the shock in July as being almost physical, like a slap in the face, whereas a sauna was the most fitting comparison that came to Dwight Reiland's mind. It was little better at night, but dawn brought forth the heat as surely as the light. Francis Whitebird arrived at midnight and guessed that by sunrise the temperature at Cam Ranh Bay that March morning was already over eighty-five degrees.

Even the gradual acclimation to Vietnam afforded by an ocean cruise did little to diminish the shock of those first blistering days in country. While waiting to disembark from his ship in October 1967, Leonard Dutcher wrote, "Last night it got pretty cold, cold enough so you couldn't sleep without a cover. But today is the other way around as it is hotter than hell. It must be 110 degrees or so." He warned his parents that they would have a hard time reading his letter because he was sweating all over the paper. The sweat stains and smudged fingerprints conveyed his point more clearly than words.[2]

Although the heat was universal and could be described through any number of appropriate metaphors or similes, the odor that accompanied it seemed to defy every attempt at description. It was a smell unlike anything most Americans have ever experienced: seminauseating and often likened to dead fish. But it was more, much more. It had its origins in rotting vegetation and a lack of sewers, according to Terry Musser, whose first unforgettable moment in his personal catalog of Vietnam experiences was the stench hitting him in the face like a wet towel.

Tom Schultz found it ironic that despite the billions of dollars spent for the war effort he never saw one flush toilet. The privies were fifty-five-gallon drums cut in half and set under wooden planks inside flimsy walls and a makeshift roof. When the barrels were filled, they were removed, soaked with diesel fuel or kerosene, and given to some luckless GI, or, more frequently in the rear areas, a Vietnamese "mamasan" who ignited the concoction and stirred it until the entire olfactory abomination had been consumed by the oily flames. It was an all-day task that left a thick, sour stench of fuel and feces draped across each firebase and outpost. The apparent permanence of that odor convinced Schultz that there was never a moment when there wasn't a smoldering pot somewhere nearby.

Phil Yaeger isolated other basic smells on that pallet of offensive odors that permeated the country. There was napalm and the human excrement used to fertilize rice paddies, as well as the *n'uoc mam* and garlic sauces that spiced up Vietnamese cuisine. Together these smells combined to create an element that was as alien as it was malodorous.

The troops waded into the stench and heat of Vietnam carrying their duffel bags as well as an assortment of preconceived notions about what they believed would greet them. Many presumed that their arrival in a combat theater would be fraught with danger at every turn, but the apparent safety of their surroundings failed to mesh with their nervous expectations. They had been exposed to war stories and embellished tales of horror that invariably ended with a sardonic, "You'll find out when you get to Vietnam." Now they were there, and their arrival, whether by sea or air, seemed somewhat anticlimactic.

Jerry Johnson was a little surprised not to be wearing jungle fatigues on the flight over. He had been under the impression that "we would low crawl off the plane, grab our weapons, and low crawl into the jungle." Instead, he recalled, "We went over there in khakis and [when] we landed, Bien Hoa looked like a stateside air force base."

The presence of civilian airliners was more suggestive of Chicago's O'Hare Field than Vietnam. But a few men, such as Terry Tople, had their fears realized within moments of touching terra firma. Saigon was under attack when his plane arrived above Ton Son Nhut Air Base, so it circled for a while. The attack continued after they landed, and Tople recalled: "Rockets were coming in while we were running to the bunkers. We were still in our khakis, and I was saying, 'By golly, this is it.' "

Randy Hoelzen's arrival at Cam Ranh Bay was uneventful, but when he flew to Bien Hoa on an air force C-130 transport, things grew uncomfortable. As they approached the huge U.S. air base, the plane began weaving around. Hoelzen remembered looking out the cargo door in the back of the plane and thinking, "What in the hell is going on? I saw green tracer rounds. I thought, I've never seen green tracer rounds before. I asked the guy next to me, 'What's with the green tracer rounds?' He told me, 'Those aren't ours.' "

Most arrivals, however, were uneventful. Ed Hoban was pleasantly surprised when he arrived in Bien Hoa: "I remember looking out of the hootch [barracks] and there was a restaurant called Alice's Restaurant. I think we spent the first night in Bien Hoa in some temporary barracks and they put us on the bus the next day. I remember thinking, Wow, they have restaurants here? This wasn't my anticipation of war. Boy! You could go buy pop and candy—it was, 'Hey! This ain't going to be too bad.' "

Replacements arriving in Vietnam were shuttled as quickly as possible from their arrival points to a replacement depot, where in-processing was completed and the men were assigned to a unit. Bus transportation to the "Repo-Depots" ran only during daylight hours, so that men arriving late in the day were kept overnight in air force transient barracks. In the morning they were taken to the replacement center and, in the process, got their first real glimpse of Vietnam. Jerry Johnson was curious about the heavy wire-mesh screens on the buses. He was told that the screens prevented grenades from being tossed inside. It was Johnson's first tangible evidence that someone might really want to kill him. Terry Tople's first day in country continued in the spirit with which he had been welcomed. After being rocketed at Ton Son Nhut Air Base, he and his traveling companions were taken to the 90th Replacement Battalion in three or four buses. All went smoothly until one of the buses hit a mine. Several men were killed. "They were only in the country an hour," Tople reflected. "They hit a mine. . . . We'd gone over the same road and the tire must have just hit the right spot."

There were armed vehicles everywhere patrolling the highways, but the sight of them soon lost its novelty and the soldiers succumbed to the heat and humidity and the monotonous drone of the helicopters overhead. Occasionally, the sound of the rotor blades was masked momentarily by the crescendo of thundering jets, whose dark shapes huddled against the landscape as they moved off toward the war that always seemed to be just over the horizon. In all, the journey took on a surrealistic feel.

Along with those first hints of war, men were exposed to Vietnamese civilians and a degree of poverty endemic to most Third World countries but totally alien to most Americans. It was a brief glimpse really, but enough to convince many of the new arrivals that Vietnam was not the mysterious and exotic locale they had imagined. The roads to Long Binh, Da Nang, Cam Ranh Bay, and other key bases were lined with shanties and half-naked children. Most Vietnamese seemed to live in squalor and filth. In rural areas, and even in the cities' poorer sections, livestock shared living quarters with people. There was no apparent public sanitation. Charles Gadd was particularly interested in the way people would "take empty pop and beer cans, cut out the ends, flatten them and make aluminum shingles for their rooftops."[3]

Lieutenant Gary McKay's Australian unit always passed through the villages of Ben Cay and Phouc Thanh on the way to the Vung Tau Rest and Recreation (R & R) Center. The villages had a stench that "literally jerked your head back," he recalled, "and [the stench] often caused men returning from R & R with fragile heads and bellies to surrender the contents of their stomachs."[4]

Nothing in Ed Hoban's experience in rural Minnesota prepared him for the culture shock of Vietnam, and much about the land surprised him. "I was awed that there were so many of them, that it was so crowded. There were people everywhere!" he exclaimed. "They had to move to make room for the bus to go through. This was a war zone and I was surprised there were this many people running around with no guns over them."

Jon Neely and other new arrivals were also intrigued by the local economy, which apparently relied entirely on the spending power of American servicemen. It was Neely's first encounter with merchants who were apparently as intent on selling their sisters as they were cheap souvenirs. And Lieutenant McKay discovered that trips past the hovels that made up a village instantly produced hordes of children who would wave and flash the V sign and beg for cigarettes or candy. One of McKay's men threw a particularly unappealing Australian luncheon meat ration to a youngster, who immediately recognized what it was and hurled it back, making an obscene gesture and screaming, "Number fucking ten Cheap Charlie."[5]

Although some Americans felt a natural aversion toward this poverty and were appalled at the begging, they quickly became inured to it. Terry Musser recalled how in 1965 he

> got off the boat in 'Nam and the kids were there begging for chocolate and stuff. I think that put us off on the wrong foot because we were the American saviors of a country and we weren't accustomed to all these people begging for food. We weren't prepared for that—how horrendous living conditions were.
>
> I think, at least in my case, it was such a frustrating place to be because there was nothing you could do to help those people. Anytime people have a problem and you can't help them I think you turn inward and you shut them out. They were in such a frustrating squalor of conditions, and you couldn't do anything about it. So, you either let that work on you, and there is always some of that, or you shut it out. And once you shut it out you became that much more hardened, or drained, or whatever term you want to use. You couldn't do anything about the problem. So you turned it around and didn't let it work on you mentally with everything else you had to do.

Not only was the poverty discouraging, but the customs of the people and their Asian appearance were difficult adjustments for young Americans whose own material culture collided headfirst with that of their hosts. Army adviser Stuart A. Herrington noted that "Americans loved dogs, had no respect for the elderly or for ancient things, and insulted everyone with boisterous, intemperate conduct and ungracious displays of wealth."[6]

Marine Josh Cruze remembered the Vietnamese as equally unsavory.

When you first arrive you see them sitting around in that squatting position and talking and you think, What an odd way to just hang out, squatting like this. And you see the women with betel nut in their mouths and their teeth are all black and you think, Ooo, they don't take care of their teeth. Then you see men holding hands, and you think, They're all faggots. But it's a custom.[7]

Many Vietnamese resented their rich American allies as well, which was disconcerting to those newly arrived troops who expected a welcome more in line with what they had seen in World War II film clips. On occasion, Vietnamese demonstrated outright hostility toward American servicemen. Marine John Meyer recalled arriving in Da Nang in 1970, and discovered on the way from the airport to 3d Marine Amphibious Force headquarters that "people would line the street, shake their fists, flip you the bird, throw things at you. There was not a friendly face in the crowd. Not one. Not in Da Nang!"

GIs had not been properly prepared for the shock. The main thrust of their "formal indoctrination," as Charles Moskos noted, "stresses the need to maintain friendly relations with local peoples and the necessity for American servicemen to fulfill the obligations of 'ambassadors in uniform.'"[8] Servicemen were thus given no real sense of the culture or history of the people for whom they were fighting. They had no realistic expectations of what they would find when they arrived. Training films such as *Your Tour in Vietnam*, narrated by Jack Webb, did nothing to educate them about the country or its people. Rather, the films emphasized World War II-style images of soldiers sharing candy bars with children, conducting civic action medical projects in villages, or building schoolhouses—all activities that American troops actually took part in, but generally with less than satisfying results.[9]

The poverty and squalor of Vietnamese life and an ever-increasing hostility by rural Vietnamese toward American soldiers were not evident in training. Those conditions remained hidden under a Hollywood-like optimism. Soldiers sometimes found reality a bit confusing, and it may have convinced some men that the images they had seen, like much they had been told about Vietnam, were projections of fantasy.

American concern with material goods and the value placed on them generated feelings of superiority, frustration, and disgust. As a result, some GIs would patronize or victimize their hosts as they saw fit, and many more Americans never found anything in Vietnamese society that they deemed worth saving, let alone sacrificing their lives for. But the majority of American soldiers, whether as a result of chance or inclination, simply never got to know the Vietnamese people. The soldiers neither hurt nor helped the locals, but kept their heads down and their minds on their own affairs, and sought to complete their tours. The disparity in background between even the poorest Americans and the agrarian peasant society into which they had been cast surely made understanding difficult to achieve. Romantic concepts that many servicemen entertained about their mission prior to arriving in Vietnam—that of assisting a quaint and appreciative peasantry held hostage by Communist hooligans—was supplanted over a period of months by feelings of aversion, shock, and disgust. Jerry Severson recalled that in June 1966, he didn't think, "Boy! I'm gonna get over here and win this war for these people. It was more a reaction of—Boy! I wouldn't want to live here."

But there was little time for arriving soldiers to dwell on the social aspects of Vietnamese life when their own fates were of far more immediate and personal concern. Men were funneled into one of three general replacement depots. The 22d Replacement Battalion at Cam Ranh Bay was responsible for assignments to the I and II corps tactical zones in the north. Farther south, the 90th Replacement Battalion at Long Binh handled the administrative tasks of troops throughout the remainder of Vietnam. Marines, who were almost exclusively posted to I Corps, went through a reception station of their own at Da Nang.[10] After listening to a welcoming speech, often in the form of a tape-recorded message from Gen. William C. Westmoreland, the commander of American forces in Vietnam from 1964 to 1968, personnel exchanged their stateside money for military payment certificates (MPC), filled out more paperwork, and were sent to a holding area to await their orders. Most men spent the time trying to adjust to the thirteen-hour time differential and the suffocating heat and humidity. A few went exploring.

The large base camps were like cities, and they were as safe as it got in Vietnam. The army base at Long Binh, for example, did not typify the image of a wartime military outpost. By 1969, the base covered twenty-five square miles and included movie theaters, swimming pools, a "Steam & Cream" combination steam bath and massage parlor, and a host of facilities for food and drink, such as the giant Chinese restaurant complex known as the Loon Foon. Air-conditioned buildings housed the headquarters facilities. More than twenty thousand Vietnamese were employed on the base. The aristocracy of staff officers lived in air-conditioned billets and kept small lawns and flower beds. Many had access to a wide range of consumer goods and services, including prostitutes brought to the base every afternoon.[11]

If the bases seemed secure, however, the sounds of the night did not. They were foreign and distantly dangerous sounds. Those first nights were difficult ones in a strange country. Few men slept well. No man could have slept where Phil Yaeger ended up—next to the airstrip in Da Nang. Each jet fighter taking off all night long, as Yaeger put it, "just felt like it was sucking the eyeballs out of your head when they would come down the runway." There was often outgoing harassment fire from American artillery and the clatter of smaller-caliber weapons that blended with no particular pattern into a backdrop of unfamiliar sounds. Sometimes flares would freeze the distant landscape in their icy glare, lengthening the shadows in sinister light. On other occasions, incoming rocket rounds would add their particular terror to the atmosphere.

Steve Fredrick, remembering his first calling card from "Charlie," said, "Second night I was in country we got shelled by 177mm rockets. That was scary as heck, boy. Then I found out that these guys [veterans] would help me quite a bit because I was a cherry, and they all told me what to do and we jumped on the floor and put our mattresses over us. We were in a building and you could hear these things coming in going—[whistling sounds]—*Ka Boom!* One landed about fifty feet outside our barracks, I think. We went out the next morning and looked at it. I was pretty damned scared."

Layne Anderson heard incoming enemy rockets at Chu Lai his first night in the reception area.

> Not one round landed in my area, although I think we had fifty casualties from broken legs and cuts. We were new in country and they were telling us all this stuff and when they started getting rocketed we started running. . . . They had a big culvert sandbagged over the top and we ran down in there with the rats and the other stuff. There were guys falling down breaking their arms, breaking legs, running into the culvert with their foreheads. . . . I don't know how you would describe it. You just woke up and said, "Oh Shit! They're shooting at us." There were people trying to kill you. I guess you were sitting in that bunker thinking, they're after us.
>
> I went back there after I was in country for a while to attend leadership school and by then I knew what was going on and could just watch these guys going nuts. We had been the same way, I'm sure—just scared. But it was kind of comical after a person had been there for six or seven months to watch these guys go through it. But it wasn't that funny when you first went through it.

As the new men were processed, there was limited contact with other soldiers rotating home. They were men who had survived their tours, and reached their DEROS date. Usually, such contact was limited to a few catcalls and callous remarks about the number of days that the new men had left to serve on their tours. The new arrivals felt those barbs keenly, with a despair only men with 360 or so days to go in country could appreciate. Most of the departing troops, however, said nothing.

Some marines heading home shared the transient barracks beside the airstrip with Phil Yaeger, and he was haunted by their silence. "The look in their eyes said it all," Yaeger remembered vividly. "They didn't have to say anything. I think we kind of wanted them to say something. We wanted to hear any little bit that would improve our chances of survival. There was nothing they could have said. They weren't in very good shape and I understood that much later. I didn't understand that then."

Just what most servicemen thought about their presence in Vietnam once they had arrived is difficult to ascertain. It is the type of question that can be answered only by trying to recall one's thoughts at the time, and that is a precarious basis for truth. Most soldiers probably had no concrete justification for being in Vietnam except that it was where the road they had started down so many months before had led them. Some insight into those initial feelings is offered by an impromptu study conducted by Pvt. Carl D. Rogers, who arrived at Cam Ranh Bay in March 1966. He believed that men "should have some thoughts to express about what their feelings were, leaving their wives and girlfriends and their home life and going to a foreign country to fight a war."

Rogers questioned some one hundred new arrivals about their feelings and recorded their candid thoughts on tape. Their responses amazed Rogers, who obviously opposed the war and his participation in it, at least at that time. Almost all of the men responded rhetorically at first: "What do you think I feel?" What surprised Rogers, however, was that his subjects' frustrations about being in Vietnam were based on personal matters rather than on what Private Rogers believed to be the really important issues regarding the validity of the war. According to Rogers, the men's personal concerns were mostly sexual. "At no point during the four days that I looked and listened and talked with these fellows did I hear anyone talking about anything relevant to the concerns, the complexities of the whole war situation."[12]

Draftees began arriving in greater numbers by 1967, and they were, as Charles Moskos discovered, "profoundly skeptical of political and ideological appeals." Some of them were patriotic and believed that they were in Vietnam ultimately to protect the United States. Practically none of them believed that they were defending democracy in South Vietnam. The majority of soldiers whom Moskos interviewed were draftees who simply saw their service in terms of personal misfortune.[13] Whether they approved of the war or not, there was no provision for them to change their minds and turn around and go back. The only path open to them was a difficult one, with few shortcuts, most of which involved injury or worse. Where each man stepped onto that path to begin his personal, and somewhat solitary, journey, and whom he would meet and travel with along the way, were matters left to chance, or God—or the whim and pen stroke of a clerk who sometimes seemed able to overrule both.

Decisions concerning the unit in which a man would serve were made at the replacement depots. At Cam Ranh Bay, Da Nang, or Long Binh, the "powers that be" divided up the supply of incoming troops and shuffled them into units like letters at a post office.

Tom Schultz's Iowa farm background afforded him a colorful and no less accurate description of the process: "They cut orders. If you can picture loading a cattle truck: we need ten cattle for steaks; we need ten for hamburger; we need ten for roasts. And the first ten in this line went to the 82d, the ten in this line went to the 1st Cav, and that's how you were cut."

Waiting in temporary barracks for orders and making formations was by then a familiar process. In fact, it was a process that many World War II veterans would have recognized.[14] Dwight Reiland found this replacement processing surprisingly pleasant compared to his previous experiences with military procedure. "I thought they were pretty nice to us, really," he noted, quickly adding, "Always through basic and everything we were just a bunch of dumb cattle. We had to be told everything. But here it seemed like they were halfway decent. But it was just guys like us that were doing their job. Their job was to get the cherries organized and head them in the right direction. They weren't drill sergeant types or anything."

Dan Krehbiel continued the description of the replacement system in even more detail:

> When we landed, we went to Long Binh to a replacement depot—the "Repo-Depot"—and there were

a lot of people there. Everywhere I went in the service [it] was overcrowded. My whole tour was that way, just like everybody else was going at the same time. The first day all we did was try to stay out of each others' way and not bump into each other. We made formations when they were called and it worked on that same principle all the way through until we finally got down to our final unit. We would go out there and stand. When you heard your name you moved. If you didn't hear your name you'd come back that afternoon or the next day. The rest of the time was yours to go to the EM [enlisted men's] club or whatever.

How long each man awaited his assignment depended on the supply of arriving troops and the shortages that existed in the field. The wait seemed to be about three or four days at Long Binh and about the same at Cam Ranh Bay.[15] John Merrell spent only one night at Cam Ranh Bay before being sent to the 4th Infantry Division, but he remembered hearing something about a desperate need for replacements at the time.

The war's appetite could work in strange ways. Bob Keeling recalled that when he got to Vietnam, "we had a situation where they needed some people in the mortar platoons. They had a lot of Eleven-Bush people, Eleven-Bravos, and if you were curious and wanted to learn to run an 81mm [mortar] or the 'Deuces' [4.2-inch mortars] you could go to a two-week school which was a cram course to familiarize you with the guns. I took that because I wanted to get as much 'sham time' as possible. That's why I was reassigned. The unit I was going to got hit hard and they needed a lot of men."[16]

One could speed up processing by filling one of the ever-present slots, although most soldiers were immediately skeptical of such opportunities. However, Dave Carlisle learned that the old truism about never volunteering wasn't always valid. He volunteered for a position requiring someone who could drive a jeep and operate a machine gun, radio, and typewriter. He had volunteered to go to Vietnam from Germany, and this time raising his hand got him a job driving for a liaison officer with the 26th Support Group stationed at

Quang Tri, north of Da Nang. He wasn't told the job's specifics when he volunteered for it, but it definitely sounded better than driving a tank. It was. The work was interesting and kept him out of direct combat.

At each step of the replacement process there was a chance of being assigned away from combat, although if a soldier was already trained in a combat MOS, the chances were very slim indeed. Still, it didn't hurt to tell everyone of any importance about a special qualification or skill. Many men touted their typing and office skills. Steve Fredrick made a point of telling anyone he thought might have some influence about his ability to operate heavy construction equipment. Jon Neely likewise saw the amount of construction going on at his division's base camp and tried to parlay his carpentry skills into a rear job. The strategy failed in both cases.

Down the line there were additional sortings at division, brigade, and battalion, and thus further chances to be interviewed for a noncombat slot. A replacement never lost hope.

There was no apparent pattern to the system of supplying troops to the field except the demand of the combat units, the never-ending parade of incoming flights, and the alphabetical sequence of each man's last name. The lists of names read off at each formation were alphabetized, and Layne Anderson drew an assignment to the same battalion in the 198th Light Infantry Brigade with men named Akirs, Akridge, another Anderson, Ambort, and Boehm.

Most men knew nothing more about the units that would become their homes than the numbers designating them. Jon Neely was assigned to the 9th Infantry Division, which he had never heard of before. Ed Hoban drew F Troop, 8th Cavalry, and all he could think of was the television comedy series called "F Troop," which portrayed an inept cavalry outpost in the Old West. Assignments ranged from the 1st Infantry Division to the 199th Light Infantry Brigade, and each unit was based in a place with a name that meant nothing to the uninitiated. Dwight Reiland had heard of the 101st Airborne but he wondered, Where the hell is Phu Bai? Men lined up to search the map adjacent to the posting boards, subconsciously beginning at the bottom in the Delta region and working gradually northward. Privates Akirs through Boehm looked at the map next to the bulletin board and were more than a little anxious to discover just how far north Chu Lai was.

Randy Hoelzen remembers being given a bit of indoctrination prior to joining his unit.

> A certain group of us were going to go to the 1st Cavalry Division. They had an unenclosed building . . . with benches in there and a stage in the front and the group that was going into the 1st Cav went in there and General [Maj. Gen. Elvy B.] Roberts, the commanding general, came in. He thought he was General Patton. He had two .45s on his hips with pearl handles—the whole "shmeer"—the spit-and-polish look with the helmet and everything. He marched up there and gave us a pep talk: "And they only killed so many of ours and we killed so many of theirs. We killed hundreds of theirs. We have this war in hand. Dah, da-dah, da-dah. You should be proud you are in the cav."

After the inspirational speech, the fifty-odd soldiers in the audience were dispersed in all directions. Hoelzen ended up on a C-130 headed for Quan Loi, the battalion base camp for the 2d Battalion, 7th Cavalry.

"Destiny," wrote James McDonough, "is not born of decision, it is born of uncontrollable circumstances. As you move mindlessly through the replacement system, the whim of an unseen clerk sends you to a unit in a quiet sector—or to a unit that will take its men like lambs to the slaughter."[17]

Men returning for a second tour in Vietnam usually hoped to return to their previous units. Gerry Barker wanted to rejoin the 1st Battalion, 8th Cavalry. But when he got there, they were filling the 2d Battalion and he wasn't given a choice. "That was all right," he explained. "I'd have taken anywhere in the 1st Cav. I was better off. I ended up in a real good company with an old twenty-year captain who had been a company commander in the Korean War. But that was just dumb luck."

Kenneth Korkow was the last man assigned out of his

marine staging group in Da Nang on 1 January 1968. He waited and hoped to get someplace where there was a whole lot of action. His orders finally came down for the 26th Marine Regiment, located at a place called Khe Sanh. A marine who looked knowledgeable assured Korkow that "things up there were building fast." Korkow remembers thinking, Fantastic, let's go get the show on the road. The fight for the hilltop outposts leading to the siege of Khe Sanh was just three weeks away.

Most new replacements assumed that the farther north their unit was located, the more combat and casualties they would experience. Marines generally anticipated more action if they were assigned to the 3rd Marine Division operating along the DMZ than if they were posted to the 1st Marine Division in the Da Nang area. Tom Magedanz recalled hearing a rumor during his staging that married marines would go to the 1st Marine Division and single men would be sent north to the 3rd. Though untrue, the existence of the rumor served as evidence of the men's apprehensions about going "north."[18]

These geographical fears did have some truth behind them. During ground combat operations in Vietnam between 1965 and 1973, the most intense fighting, based on American casualty figures, took place in I Corps (redesignated Military Region 1 in 1970), where most marines operated. Historian Guenter Lewy pointed out, however, that it was Quang Nam Province, *southwest* of Da Nang, that exacted the most marine casualties. Between 1965 and 1969 the 1st Marine Division, responsible for operations in this province, suffered more than six thousand combat-related deaths, which accounted for nearly half of all marine fatalities during the war.[19]

Thomas Thayer, a Defense Department analyst, compared American combat deaths from all branches of service in the various provinces and found statistically that 53 percent of American combat deaths occurred in Military Region 1 (I Corps) between 1967 and 1972 and only three of that region's five provinces—Quang Tri, Quang Nam, and Thua Thien—accounted for 40 percent of all American deaths. The other two provinces in Military Region 1—Quang Tin and Quang Ngai—and the two northernmost provinces in Military Region 2—Kontum and Binh Dinh—also had high casualty rates. Overall, 77 percent of American combat deaths occurred in only ten provinces in South Vietnam.[20]

Army personnel, like their marine counterparts, also feared postings in the north. But casualty statistics demonstrated that there were dangers in the south as well. Three of the ten provinces accounting for the highest army casualties—Tay Ninh, Binh Duong, and Hau Nghia—were located in Military Region 3 near Saigon.[21]

Stephen Fredrick felt lucky in November 1968 to be assigned initially to the 101st Airborne in the Cu Chi area near Saigon and just east of Tay Ninh Province. Later, he felt that the dangers he had experienced in the south would be nothing compared to what awaited him when his unit was sent north to Camp Evans near Phu Bai in 1969. As it turned out, there was less activity and fewer casualties in the north during his tour, although the margin was drastically reduced when his company went into the A Shau Valley.

Apart from the geographical location to which a soldier was assigned, two other elements influenced the likelihood of his experiencing a high level of combat intensity. The most obvious of the two was the year in which he served his tour of duty. A steady increase in contact, though by smaller-sized enemy units, occurred from mid-1965 through the middle of 1969, after which ground combat action declined steadily until the final American withdrawals in 1972. There was also an annual cycle of combat that correlated to South Vietnam's climatic patterns. In the northern part of South Vietnam the rainy season extended from September through January. In the southern part of the country, where the infiltration routes entered from Laos and Cambodia, the rains extended approximately from May through September. Thus, the best time for the enemy to launch offensive operations was between February and April, when all of Vietnam was dry.[22]

Beginning in February, the number and intensity of enemy contacts usually increased until the third week of June. A lull in the fighting generally lasted through July, while the south was inundated; then activity rose again in mid-August, culminating with a brief period of offensive operations lasting into early September. The rains reached the northern part of South Vietnam in late September and, by October, troops and materiel were depleted and enemy activity reached its lowest annual level. In November, as the rains shifted northward and away from the infiltration routes in the south, supplies began moving down the Ho Chi Minh Trail in preparation for the next spring offensive. Infiltration and resupply continued until the offensive cycle started over again the following year. In this manner, *where and when* often determined the amount of enemy contact an American soldier was likely to experience in Vietnam.[23]

After their orders were cut, the new men were moved by truck or by air to the headquarters of the division or brigade to which they had been assigned. It was the second step down the path leading into the bush. Transport to distant locations was by air. Francis Whitebird went by cargo plane to Chu Lai. The aircraft had the seats pulled out, and he and a dozen other men sat on the floor and pulled a cargo strap over their collective waists as though they were on a giant carnival ride.[24]

Dwight Reiland plopped down on his duffel bag in the back of another C-130 and, after an hour of nearly freezing temperatures at altitude, was deposited in the northern city of Phu Bai. Doug Kurtz flew in the opposite direction to the 9th Infantry Division at Dong Tam in a twin-engined Caribou and touched down on the airstrip's perforated steel planking (PSP) in the middle of a rocket attack. Jerry Johnson and Jon Neely both headed for their respective units by truck. Neely's deuce-and-a-half ended up with a flat tire and the men, not having been issued ammunition for their M16s, stood guard with one magazine apiece, courtesy of the driver, who loaned them the ammunition while he fixed the tire. Dave Carlisle flew to Da Nang and then boarded an LST (Landing Ship Tank) sailing up the coast to a place called Wonder Beach. From there it was a short truck ride to Quang Tri. By air, sea, and land—whatever was available—the men were dispersed.

Headquarters areas were in larger base camps that resembled small cities. On his way up to the demilitarized zone (DMZ), marine Tom Magedanz processed through III Marine Amphibious Force headquarters in Da Nang, and he assured his parents that the base there was 100 percent safe, explaining that he would be in no more danger than they were at home in Yankton, South Dakota.[25]

Dan Krehbiel arrived at the 25th Infantry Division's head-quarters in June 1969 and found Cu Chi equally secure. He described such base camps as "huge—like big cities with big berms and six million strands of concertina wire and booby traps and mines. You couldn't overrun that thing if the bunkers were manned at all, and they hadn't been overrun. The place was too big—too many people there. But [there were] a lot of sapper attacks. Anyway, they were secure, so I didn't even really know that there was actual combat going on. I kept looking for it but I couldn't see it. There were no signs of it the whole time I was there at Cu Chi."

Just how quickly Americans had transplanted a piece of America and secured it behind the defenses of Cu Chi was evident. Krehbiel arrived there just three years after Willie Williams and the rest of the 25th Division dug the first bunkers and strung wire for the first perimeter in 1966. At that time, Cu Chi was a small rural hamlet and the biggest problem in defending the newly established base was the fact that it was built on top of a huge Viet Cong tunnel complex. Sergeant Williams remembered that his men were often ha-rassed by Viet Cong from tunnels inside the perimeter itself. But by 1969, Cu Chi was as safe as any property could be in Vietnam. Although most division base camps were less lavish than Cu Chi, they were considerably more secure than the battalion firebases and smaller outposts that the infantry sol-diers who operated in the field considered "rear areas."[26]

Upon reaching a division or separate brigade, soldiers were again processed in, issued field equipment, and given some form of refresher training before being assigned to a company. This training allowed the newbies a week or so to adjust to the climate and be exposed to some additional in-struction prior to their first field operations. It seemed that the cardinal rule of in-country training was the ever-present ad-monition for the newly arrived: "Forget everything you learned back in the States. This is the 'Nam and we're going to teach you how it *really* is."

During the initial deployment into Vietnam, entire units went through a break-in period that included some in-country training after their arrival. Willie Williams and the rest of the 25th Division's "Wolfhounds" were based in Vung Tau for two weeks and given some helpful hints from the 101st Airborne, whose soldiers manned the perimeter while Williams and his comrades played war games and learned what to expect in the weeks to come. Sergeant Williams was unimpressed. "I think the two weeks we did were really less useful . . . than the training that we got in Hawaii where we actually went through jungle warfare training," he said. "Hawaii is where we actually saw the different types of booby traps that the Cong used and we were also taught to make our own. In Vietnam it was orientation."

Sometimes unit familiarization training included actual operations, but in a quiet sector. Upon arrival, the 4th Infantry Division's battalions were briefed by members of the 101st Airborne and, after three days, they deployed and began conducting patrols outside of Tuy Hoa. Vernon Janick remembered his company making sweeps through rice paddies and villages that the 101st had obviously already cleared. But several weeks later, when he and his comrades were flown into a new area on CH-47 Chinook helicopters, the operations became decidedly more serious.

In-country training with the 1st Infantry Division lasted a week. Jerry Johnson's classes in late 1968 were conducted at Lai Khe. Tom Magedanz received three days of orientation at Dong Ha in the summer of 1969 when he joined the 3d Marine Division. There was no apparent consistency in these schools, apart from an attempt to instill in each new man respect for the enemy and teach him to listen to experienced people. Most of these unit orientations were five days long and covered basic survival skills. In 1966, Sgt. Gerry Barker found that the 1st Cavalry Division had started a "charm school" for new people. Classes were conducted outdoors near Hong Kong Mountain at An Khe. Although Barker had fought with the division a year earlier in the Ia Drang Valley campaign, he was still required to attend the week-long course.

Doug Kurtz's week of training was courtesy of the 9th Infantry Division at Dong Tam. He remembered that they roped off a little training area in a swamp near the base and ran the new people through the area looking for trip wires while their instructors "popped some rounds" at them. Kurtz was most

impressed with the sudden presence of real bugs and snakes
that "stirred you on your way."

Steve Fredrick went through his in-country orientation
with the 101st Airborne in 1968. Perhaps because Fredrick
had completed NCO school before arriving in Vietnam, his
training was slightly different.

> In the 101st rear base camp they had what they
> called a combat leader's school where they took guys
> who had been in combat already as privates and taught
> them how to be leaders. They also took guys like me
> who were already E-5s and sent us to that school, too,
> so that we could mix with those guys and actually learn
> something about Vietnam. So I went to that for a week.
> Actually it was two days in the classroom learning a
> bunch of language and stuff, and the rest was live stuff.
> We went on some live ambushes. I went on two am-
> bushes with those guys. It was pretty strange because
> here I was with all these guys that had been in country
> for six months. I didn't know that at the time.
>   The third day I was there we went out on a night
> ambush and the funny thing about that was I kept
> smelling this funny smell all night long and I couldn't
> figure out what it was. We didn't see anything that
> night. Hell, we could see the lights of Saigon. I mean,
> it wasn't any big ambush. The next morning we had our
> debriefing. Boy, the captain was really pissed. Seems
> that all these guys who had been out in the bush for a
> long time knew [that] if they could see the lights of
> Saigon they weren't going to get in any firefights, so
> they were all smoking dope. I couldn't believe it. That
> was the first time I'd ever smelled marijuana and I never
> forgot what it smelled like after that.

Gary Thorson was given a week of training at Camp Ray
with the 101st Airborne near Bien Hoa. He described the activities as "Vietnam and Jungle Training School" complete
with lots of harassment. Each day, he wrote, they were required to "exercise and run several miles before dawn, lots of
long marches with full packs, et cetera. [It] gets you used to

the climate. Classes [are] all Vietnam-oriented on M16, M60, M79, Claymores, grenades, mines, mortars, booby traps, ambushes, patrolling. Practical work. Not just classroom sessions. Valuable stuff for one in Vietnam."[27]

Several things about in-country training at Chu Lai with the 198th Light Infantry Brigade stayed with Paul Boehm. He was given instruction in practical matters such as calling in artillery, packing a rucksack, and escape and evasion, but the class on packing a rucksack stood out in his mind. The instructor wore a varnished human ear on a chain around his neck. Boehm thought that was kind of novel. An ear implied much about the man who wore it, but, as the soldiers would discover with time, such a trinket in the rear meant little. It could easily have been purchased from a soldier coming out of the bush, or at a Vietnamese flea market.

Layne Anderson went through the classes with Boehm. Anderson's most vivid recollection of the week of refresher training was a Hawaiian sergeant who taught escape and evasion techniques. The men gathered on a hillside with seats arranged like a large amphitheater. From their seats they watched a self-defense demonstration. Anderson was impressed and still remembers the sergeant's last piece of advice: "He told us not to trust anybody, and we believed him."

John Meyer and Donald Trimble both entered Vietnam as part of a marine Combined Action Platoon with the 2d Combined Action Group. Combined action units worked closely with Vietnamese militia and remained in a specific locality living among the villagers. Because of the nature of their mission and the proximity in which they worked with the indigenous people, their in-country training was usually more culture and language based. Meyer, a navy corpsman, entered Vietnam in April 1970 and received two weeks of training in Da Nang. Trimble arrived the following year and was given a six-day orientation. Both were taught some Vietnamese, though by American and not indigenous instructors. Both men also received lectures on conduct in the field as well as in the villages.

Trimble was impressed by a demonstration that was a popular part of many in-country training programs: having a former VC or NVA sapper walk outside the perimeter and then infiltrate back in through the concertina wire and booby traps. It was truly amazing to see a man clad only in a loincloth snake his way so quickly through the razor-sharp barbs of concertina wire and trip wires attached to flares and Claymore mines, which had, up to that moment, inspired such a sense of security. One tip offered to Trimble's class by a former Viet Cong was to "shoot low and to the right of a target." The sapper told them that VC and NVA soldiers believed that the M16's recoil moved the muzzle upward and to the left when fired on automatic.

Glen Olstad was assigned to the 4th Battalion, 23d Infantry (Mechanized) of the 25th Division. As an armored personnel carrier (APC) mechanic, he expected such a posting. He did not anticipate what happened upon his arrival at Cu Chi, however. He and five or six other replacements were sent down to see the first sergeant, who

> told us we had a five-day, in-country school to go to before we went out to the field. I told him that I was a mechanic—I wouldn't have to go through it, and he said, "You *were* a mechanic! Your MOS has just been changed!" I said something about, "Hey you can't do this. My congressman will get in touch with you." He said, "When your congressman stands in front of my desk and says 'no,' then you won't [have to go through it]—until then, you will!"

Olstad discovered later that the 1st Platoon of Company B from the battalion had been hit hard prior to his arrival and, because of the heavy casualties, he had been made an infantry soldier.[28]

Shortages of men for the field did occur, although there never seemed to be a shortage of men in Vietnam sweating out the war in the rear areas. An MOS could easily be switched and, at times, expediency in the field required it. The problem with specialists suddenly transferred to the infantry was their lack of infantry training. For all the criticism about infantry AIT's ineffectiveness, it might be worth reevaluating the training in light of the comparison between those who had it and those who did not.

Sergeant Gerry Barker was troubled by the fact that "the 1st Cavalry Division was really understrength by early '67 because we had been hotly engaged for months. They sent us everything that came into the replacement units regardless of MOS. I took in eight replacements, none of them infantry. They were truck drivers, clerk typists, you name it. I lost all eight to booby traps in the An Lao Valley. And that is all I lost. They hadn't been on the ground a month. They were dangerous to themselves."

Army specialists transferred into an infantry MOS were often lost souls. The Marine Corps, however, takes great pride in the fact that every marine is a rifleman first and receives some infantry training after boot camp. James Stanton's initial posting was to a teletype facility within sight of the R & R center and near the giant PX in Da Nang. That was before fate intervened. Upon reporting for duty he was told that the marines needed radio operators in the field. Stanton remembered vividly that the NCO with whom he was speaking pointed to a nearby helipad and said, " 'There's your helicopter—go get on it.' I was supposed to be stationed at the headquarters place right there in Da Nang," he lamented. . . . "It was plush. And I didn't make it. I went out to the bush."

At the end of the men's in-country training they were assigned to battalions. Tom Schultz found himself deposited on the doorstep of the 7th Cavalry at Camp Evans. Evans, he decided, was "a desolate place surrounded by barbed wire and no trees or ground cover, just sand and dirt and lots of army green." He was taken by a sergeant to a holding area and further assigned to Company C, 2d Battalion. It was a company that he would soon discover spent very few days in a camp of any size.[29]

Marines bound for infantry units were treated similarly. Tom Magedanz described Dong Ha near the DMZ as mostly barbed wire and sandbags, with a bunker for every building. On the positive side, the young marine found that the beer at Dong Ha was fifteen cents a can at the enlisted men's club, and there were outdoor movies. All in all, he decided, Dong Ha would be a pretty good place to spend the war if it wasn't quite so windy, dry, and dusty. Unfortunately, Dong Ha was a hub for patrolling marine units. For most of the leathernecks sent there, Dong Ha was little more than a place to come back to. Magedanz would spend most of his time humping the bush for weeks on end.[30]

Medics, officers, and forward observers were usually assigned to a headquarters company, which would then parcel them out to the line companies as the need arose. Riflemen were assigned directly to the line companies to replace casualties or personnel rotating home. And so, like orphans, the new soldiers waited expectantly to be claimed and taken to their new homes. It was a strange, lonely feeling as Jeff Yushta remembered it.

> The company was out on an operation. There was nothing for me to do with nearly everybody gone. Typical service situation. Your company is out. "We don't have anything for you to do. They are going to be back in a couple of days. We are not going to send you out there."
>
> I had no place to sleep. I started sleeping in a maintenance shed on top of some seabags. They didn't issue me a weapon. I thought that was strange. The country was at war and I was walking around there without a weapon.

There were usually menial duties to keep the newbies occupied. Such tasks also helped keep their minds from dwelling on the apprehensions of the immediate future. Layne Anderson burned human waste. Jon Neely filled sandbags for bunkers. Robert Keeling, with his penchant for finding ways to sham, ended up on KP in the officers' mess at Pleiku, cleaning the tables and pouring the residual alcohol from the glasses into a tumbler for himself.

Phil Yaeger arrived at 3d Marine Division headquarters at Phu Bai on his way north and recalled, "The second we touched down a gunny [gunnery sergeant] came out and grabbed us for a detail and we unloaded body bags off of helicopters and put them in six-bys to go to Graves Registration. Then it really hit me. The stench of death was unbelievable."

The working and waiting caused one to ponder all sorts of imponderables. There were trivial things, such as Michael

Jackson's curiosity about why his company was referred to as "Dying Delta." Others were more serious, the traditional fears of men about to go into combat: Am I a coward? How will I react under fire? Will I disgrace myself? What does a dead person look like?

Perhaps, most of all, each new man thought about the unit he would be joining. What would the other soldiers be like; would they accept him? Those questions would be answered soon. The rest would all be answered in due time.

CHAPTER 6

Being New

October 30, 1967

Dear Mom and Dad,

Just a few lines to let you know that I am fine and well. Have been in Viet Nam six days now and so far the only wound I have got is a bad sunburn. Since we got here we've killed about six or seven Cong that were trying to get into our base camp.

Yesterday was the first day since I've been in 'Nam that it hasn't rained, but it sure was hot. We are just about done with our base camp now and will be going out on operations by the end of the week. I will be kind of glad to go out as there is a lot of work to do building a base camp.

Your Son,
Len[1]

New troops arrived at their units in the field feeling as self-conscious and out of place as anyone showing up for their first day at a new job. Much of a replacement's time on that first day was spent simply trying to blend in. It was an impossible task, considering the million-and-one things that distinguished new soldiers from the veterans around them. New people *looked* new, a condition made obvious when they were first introduced. Comparisons were impossible to avoid. Larry Gates recalled that the experienced men in his unit looked like seasoned veterans when you put the two side by side. "Anybody could pick out which one was which, even if you put them in the same uniforms," he said. "You'd just know who was the veteran and who was the rookie."

Tom Schultz felt totally out of place in his brand-new clothing, boots, and pack. Tom Magedanz arrived in Vietnam in August 1969 just as the marines were being issued new camouflage utility uniforms. The old-timers in his unit were still in olive drab, and Magedanz remembers sticking out like a sore thumb.

This newness was not only apparent in the physical appearance of a man's uniform and equipment, it was equally evident in the way new soldiers wore it. To the seasoned eyes of Charles Gadd, a replacement and his accoutrements seemed more representative of a disorganized one-man band than a combat soldier.

> Every piece of equipment the army had issued was hanging from their pistol belts and rucksacks; it looked as though it would all fall off the first time they had to run for cover or dive behind a thicket of bamboo. We referred to them as "cherries," the common term for those who had not yet lost their virginity to combat. After a few minutes of awkward introductions, we took them inside the tent and helped them rearrange their equipment in a more practical fashion and discard some things that only added extra weight.[2]

There were other, more basic symptoms of newness as well. When Gadd joined his unit, he felt betrayed by the paleness of his skin in a land where everyone else was deeply tanned. Predictably, a new man's pale epidermis was subject to severe sunburn, a particularly ignoble condition that proved as painful to the ego as to the touch. Jon Neely was badly sunburned while helping to build new bunkers at Dong Tam as he awaited assignment to a line company. Dwight Reiland removed his shirt for the first time while digging trenches and foxholes around the perimeter at Firebase Birmingham in I Corps. His miscalculation caused him to suffer more than simple indignation:

> I didn't have my shirt off more than an hour or two and, Oh my God! I got the worst sunburn. . . . I never had a sunburn itch like that. I got to itching and I

thought I was going to go crazy. I went to the medics and they were upset that I got sunburned in the first place. . . . Of course they didn't have anything for it. Jeeze, I can remember lying on the ground wiggling around trying to scratch my back because it itched so bad. It was driving me nuts. I spent a miserable night that night and the next day. It seemed like the second night it tapered off.

Jerry Johnson's light complexion never adjusted to the intensity of the tropical sun, and he described himself as "looking like a lobster" during his entire tour. His ruddy face, accented by bleached hair and eyebrows, earned him the nickname "Red" throughout his tour.

Sunburned or not, new recruits looked, in the words of Johnnie Clark, like "fat, happy kids"—perhaps because of their clean-shaven faces or white-sidewall haircuts.[3]

Dan Krehbiel remembers coming in at the end of an operation "grubby and full of mud and whatever. You are just an absolute mess but you are back," he said. "The operation is over with. God! You pull the magazine out of the rifle, clear the chamber, and just walk over and drop your stuff. Shower coming up. A clean uniform and a beer—wow! And then you notice five guys that are lily white. I mean they got no tan at all. And here you are after being in the tropics for all this time. Everybody is bronze as hell. You could always spot the FNGs [fucking new guys]."

Veterans were always conscious of replacements—looking them over with the practiced eye of seasoned horse traders. Some of the new men, such as marine Terry Shepardson, remembered those looks as being almost hostile. He recalled feeling "like [a] piece of shit," an assessment of his relative value to the group that was probably consistent with that of most newbies. He interpreted the veterans' glances to be a silent but subtle warning: Hey, you better get your act together quick. Shepardson remembered those veterans well. "[They] wanted to get out of there at any price," he said. "And then we come in there all spitshined. We were lower than a goddamned turd."

Tom Magedanz recalled being awed by the men he

encountered when he joined the 3d Marine Division near the DMZ:

> In Da Nang you saw a few [veterans], but in Dong Ha these guys were just coming down off the DMZ, and they had big packs and ragged, ripped clothes. Their jungle boots were a mess: the black leather part was all tan like the soil and the green canvas part was all tan like the soil and often times the boots would be ripped. Their toes would be sticking out and the canvas would be ripped and worn and just shredded. And they all had a bunch of sores and bandages on their arms. I thought they had all been wounded or something, but it was just jungle rot. They all had about three or four days' growth of beard and kind of shaggy hair. It wasn't long hair, but it wasn't like what we had back in boot camp. I thought that they must have been in the biggest combat of all time.

Climate and terrain conspired with the C-ration diet and heavy packs to give veterans a half-starved appearance, sharply contrasting with the generally healthy look of the well-fed replacements. Although there was no ignoring the external differences, outward appearances were superficial—scratched and battered war paint that cloaked soldiers from the scrutiny of others. The real difference between the new arrivals and the combat veterans was internal.

During the Civil War, men who had been in combat referred to the experience as "seeing the elephant." For them, war was no longer a great unknown. Experiencing battle did nothing to make the prospect of future combat less fearful, but it did give veterans a degree of reassurance that they would not disgrace themselves under fire. That sense of self-confidence was impossible for new men to imitate. But seeing the elephant left its mark in the eyes of the veterans, an afterimage impressed upon the memory, a gaze that betrayed them in unguarded moments, the proverbial "thousand-yard stare." When corpsman John Meyer joined his Combined Action Platoon in 1970, there were a lot of experienced hands in the unit. For Meyer, looking into their eyes was like looking "right down into hell." He knew that they were marines who had "been there and seen it."

Bryan Good found the eyes of veterans equally enigmatic. "They looked so old," he said, searching in vain for the words to describe twenty-year-old mental images. "They just had that look to them."

Marine Jeff Yushta also remembered the strange look in the eyes and faces of the veterans, as well as the mood they projected:

> You just had a strange sensation when they looked at you and you looked at them—when you made eye contact. It was kind of like they were looking through you. This was usually in unguarded moments. There was a macho game most of the time. "This doesn't affect me. This is a blast. I can't wait 'til we go out again"—that type of thing. There are some pictures in some of those *Time-Life* books and some of the other books that show the faces of the guys when they are kind of off guard and that is what it was.
>
> They were real rude. You were new meat coming in. They would say, "Wait 'til Charlie gets a hold of you!" They weren't much different than the drill instructors in boot camp as far as relationships go. You were the low man on the totem pole. "Don't ever mess with me," you know, or, "In a couple weeks if you fit in then . . ." It took you awhile to become just like them, but you did. Then you were a part of the game, too.

Veterans protected themselves with a thin veneer of bravado and a nearly impenetrable aura of mutual trust and brotherhood. Access to that brotherhood was almost always denied to replacements. Standing in the dust of a firebase or waist deep in elephant grass thousands of miles from home, it became evident to the new arrivals that they were separated from the battle-hardened men facing them by experiences that seemingly spanned light years.

Dwight Reiland recalled how, when he reached his unit, "They were standing there looking at you and you were standing there looking at them wondering, Are they nuts yet?

And they were wondering, What's this new guy, this cherry, going to be like? It was just kind of comical the way everybody sized up everybody else trying to get acquainted."

It took replacements weeks to earn a measure of confidence and a share of the comradeship that signified acceptance as a viable member of the group. Larry Gates, for example, found the men of his platoon in the 198th Light Infantry Brigade to be very standoffish toward new people, an attitude that he felt derived from their lack of trust in the abilities of new soldiers. "They didn't know what to expect out of you," he surmised, "so rather than expect anything . . . they stayed away from you. It took a little bit of getting used to for them."

Trooper Ed Hoban found that when he was new, the men in his aerorifle platoon were nice, but no one trusted him. There was always a period of close scrutiny before any new soldier earned the trust of his comrades. Glen Olstad defined new as meaning: "You were the guy nobody wanted for a partner. You were the guy nobody would trust. And you were the guy that could talk all day long and nobody would hear you. That only changed," he added, "after a couple of fights if you did a couple things right. Only then did trust begin to develop."

Until that time, as Phil Yaeger discovered, life could be very lonely. "What you expected was to be accepted as a marine, and on some levels you were," Yaeger explained. "They were glad to have replacements. But you weren't trusted at all. It was just an overriding attitude [like] Come back and see me in a couple of months if you are still alive—maybe we can make something out of you. It wasn't a conscious, callous kind of thing, but that was the way it felt. In hindsight, and having been on the other side of that equation later, it was more a sense of being dwarfed by the sense of brotherhood that was there, and not being able to penetrate that immediately."

The future would demonstrate a new man's usefulness to the rest of the group, but, until proven, replacements were seldom relied upon. In Ed Hoban's platoon, as in most, new guys were simply kept "out of the way."

A new man's reception depended in part on where he

joined his unit, how many new replacements came in with him at the same time, and how long the rest of the unit had been together. Treatment could be brusque for men who arrived in the field when a unit was in combat. Contact often necessitated replacements, but in a unit under fire there was little time for niceties. Phil Yaeger and approximately ten other marine replacements discovered this when they flew into "Helicopter Valley" (Ngan Valley) through heavy enemy fire in July 1966:

> They threw off some ammo and water cans on top of us and we dragged them away from the chopper. We hit the deck and worked our way to the edge of the landing zone, dropped again, and started firing like everybody else.
>
> It was hours before we actually had an NCO come up and ask what unit we'd been assigned to. That happened toward evening, after contact had been broken. I was with Kilo Company that day and the next, before I finally caught up to Mike Company. Everybody was taking casualties, so they just sort of split up the nine or ten of us that were sent out, a couple to each company.

Many units operated in the bush for weeks on end, requiring replacements to join their respective companies in the field. It was not the best place to begin a soldier's assimilation. In the bush, men were usually preoccupied with concerns other than making someone feel welcome, and new people were received by their platoons with about as much zeal as the last-picked, least-skilled players grudgingly chosen by sandlot baseball teams. Dennis Foell's initiation into the 196th Light Infantry Brigade's 3d Battalion, 21st Infantry, hardly inspired self-confidence. "When I went to Delta Company as a new replacement the company happened to be on LZ Center, which was in our area of operations," said Foell. "There were sixteen of us replacements that day. The platoon leaders [looked us over] and said, 'You, you, you—come with me.' We got [to our platoons] and the squad leaders did the same thing. You were kind of a number there, like being drawn out of a hat."[4]

Units back in the rear for a day or two were more relaxed; there was time for veterans to acquaint themselves with the new people. Jon Neely reached the 9th Infantry Division while his unit was guarding a small base camp. The light duty they were performing gave Neely and the men in his unit a chance to get to know each other:

> We set up in an area and finally got ourselves straightened around so we could sit down and talk for a while and I found out where these guys were from. First thing I did was look for guys from Pennsylvania, and we had a couple in our unit. My squad leader was from Elyria, Ohio, and we called him the Ohio Bomber. I'm not sure why but . . . that is what we called him all the time. Some of the other guys in the squad were relatively new. They had been there a little bit longer than I had, but these were the guys I was going to spend at least a year with, hopefully.
>
> Luckily, there was not really much action going on. I got to learn a lot about the people, about the unit itself, what operations were decent and what operations were extremely tough. They told me I was going to spend a lot of time on the APCs [armored personnel carriers] but we would also spend a lot of time actually humping through the boonies. They also told me things would seem very barbaric, but this was jungle warfare.
>
> I am glad that I got a chance to kind of take it easy for a few days before we got into anything. [At] least I had an idea of what to expect.

Naturally, it was more difficult for new people to break into units that had a solid core of troops who had deployed together. Phil Yaeger joined the 3d Battalion, 4th Marines, during Operation Hastings in 1966. Most of his battalion's personnel had been in country for some time. Despite his arrival during the initial assaults on "Mutter's Ridge" and the high casualties his company sustained, acceptance was slow in coming. Yaeger remembered:

Everybody was pretty much a hard ass. I think they were good. I broke into the platoon with three or four other people, maybe as many as six over about a week's period, as best as I can recall. But it seemed like everybody had been there for a long time. There was a big gap. The unit went over together in 1965. The ones who survived their tour left and another whole group took over. Well, I joined that second group. Most of them were well into their tour—five, six months. And then here were the peons of which I was one. Even after a few more people came in, there was always that gap until those older veterans left.

Coming into a unit with a group of other replacements offered a degree of safety and obscurity in numbers. At least it seemed that way to Mike Roberts, who observed, "With eight guys it wasn't so bad. You didn't have just one guy to look out for or chum around with. There were eight of us and it was easy to go with another new guy to chow or whatever. But, as far as the usual name calling: FNG, Greenie, Cherry, it was about the same old stuff."

Part of the assimilation problem concerned unit survival and the relatively insignificant value of a new replacement in helping the group realize that goal. Equally important, servicemen's attitudes concerning the war and America's role in it varied, as did individual motivation and enthusiasm for the fight. Rifleman Randy Hoelzen, although admitting to overgeneralization, identified within his unit in the 1st Cavalry Division three basic types of soldiers when he joined it in the summer of 1969:

There were people over there that were just putting their time in, and I was one of them. We did what we had to do, but we weren't out to be John Wayne. There were "John Waynes" who loved what they were doing and would re-up [reenlist for another term in the field]. And then there were some that were there because they had to be there and weren't doing what they had to do.

The ones that thought they were John Wayne would get to you eventually [with their war stories]: "Well,

Kid, stick close to me and you'll be all right. I'll show you how to survive here." I don't want to be cynical. There were some who were saying that and really meant it. I met some good people over there. But there were some that were crazy and loved it and I considered them crazy then and I consider them crazy now.

How a new man reacted under fire was the all-important question, the only one that mattered. When Tom Schultz joined Company C, 2d Battalion, 7th Cavalry, he was told, "You're either a shooter or a shaker." Schultz found that being a shooter was something that did not come automatically with the uniform. A man had to "build into it," and until the first several enemy contacts, it was impossible to tell whether a replacement would shoot or shake. Most soldiers found, as Terry Shepardson did, that the majority of new guys handled things well and eventually blended in.

First impressions about replacements could be erroneous, however, and the crucible of combat often provided some surprises. Mike Meil remembered one new addition to his cavalry unit whom nobody wanted anything to do with:

He was an older guy that was in National Guard and he was missing his meetings, so they put him on active duty. He was a family man. Everybody was scared to be with him because it always seemed like he was talking to himself whenever he had the chance to be alone. He had a tape recorder and he would tape shit and send it to his wife. And it really got to be tear-jerking. He would be back there crying. Jesus, nobody wanted to be tied up with him because they were scared of his thoughts of being back home, and of his wife, and of his being family oriented . . . and the fact that he would sit there and be able to openly show emotion in front of all those guys. I guess it kind of overwhelmed us and we shied away.

But boy was he a firecracker! They had his ass up against the wall one night and he fought like a son of a bitch. We got hit with rockets and small-arms fire and a lot of guys were assholes and elbows looking for a place to hide with that shit coming in. They expected him to crack and he didn't. He got out there and he fought like there was no goddamned tomorrow.

The reception given to newly arrived personnel was also based upon how "short" an individual was. "Cherries" who had arrived during the previous thirty days looked upon faces newer than theirs with relief. New men always stood at the end of the pecking order, so that earlier replacements relished being bumped up a notch. The former boots were thus spared the continued uncomfortable scrutiny of their comrades and the so-called shit details that were passed down to the newer replacements. These included unloading ammo, humping water, digging latrines, and other onerous tasks. In Phil Yaeger's platoon it also meant having the "absolute and total last pick of the C rations," which, he recalled with a smile, "were pretty bleak to begin with."

Short-timers still in the field were overly cautious by nature and sought to avoid any condition that might lessen by the smallest fraction their chances of completing their tours intact. Thus, Tom Schultz soon learned that short-timers didn't want to be near a new guy; it was paranoia or bad luck, he thought.[5] Mike Meil sensed the same attitude among the "gray beards" of his unit. "Guys were scared to take new guys underneath their arm to try to teach them stuff," he said. "Sometimes new guys would scare the shit out of them. New guys were taboo because they were inexperienced. You expected them to screw up because of that lack of experience. They probably should have gotten them closer, jammed them in between two old vets or something. But there were so many reasons why I think you didn't want to have contact with new guys; they always seemed like they got their asses in trouble."

For the majority—those soldiers somewhere in the middle portion of their tours and in the prime of their combat efficiency curves—new replacements were just one more burden to bear, but a necessary one. Units that were undermanned tended to welcome replacements of any kind. Men with special jobs in the platoon would train the new people as quickly as possible so that, as the veterans got shorter, they would have suitable replacements. Over time, dangerous or unpleasant tasks in the field devolved to newer personnel through a combination of seniority and performance. Until that time, cherries led an inconsequential existence within their units. On the unit ledger of relative worth, a new man's value was generally registered as a debit.

Soldiers in the field never really came to know much about the majority of the men they served with apart from the things that servicemen deemed important, such as trustworthiness under fire, hometown or state, and nicknames. The use of nicknames flourished during the Vietnam War, and Tim O'Brien found it interesting that a soldier could "go through a year in Vietnam and live with a platoon of sixty or seventy people, some going, some coming, and [yet] leave without knowing more than a dozen complete names."[6]

According to veteran Roger Hoffman, nicknames were bestowed as an indication of acceptance as a new man moved up the infantryman's social ladder. Most nicknames derived from a personal characteristic, physical quality, place of origin, or whim. Hoffman, for instance, was known as Rib Cage because he was skinny. A particularly poor card player in his unit was known as Ace. Other men with whom Hoffman served were nicknamed Smoke, Blade, Sly, Iceman, and No-bones.[7]

One particularly memorable individual in Tom Schultz's outfit earned the well-deserved nickname Pig Pen. Schultz explained that the man refused to change field uniforms because "he believed that new fatigues were an omen that he was going home in a box. He even went on R & R and came back dressed in his dirty fatigues. The same boots—same clothes. He'd change socks, but not his clothes."

Hometowns or states were also a good source for nicknames. Jon Neely's squad leader was the Ohio Bomber; the point man in Randy Hoelzen's platoon was called Minnesota. A man in Jeff Yushta's platoon was known as An Hoa because that was where he joined the unit.

Size also helped establish identity. Terry Tople served with a black soldier named Honey Bear who was six foot five and "gentle as a lamb." Generic references to size, such as Pee Wee or Moose, were equally common monikers. John Merrell soldiered with Larry "Beaucoup" Ekinrode, from Pennsylvania. *Beaucoup* is a French word used as slang in Vietnam for anything big or in large amounts. Ekinrode was known as Beaucoup because he was. Another marine in Jeff Yushta's platoon was called Shorty, although, in Yushta's opinion, Shorty could just as easily have been nicknamed Crazy.

Nicknames just seemed to fall into place. Medics were universally referred to as Doc, although a man in John Merrell's platoon earned the appellation because of his fondness for codeine.

Jeff Yushta became Jake because, as he explained, "a guy in our group was a good singer. His name was Ron Youngblood but he was called Hillbilly, and he named me Jake because there was an old song by Jimmy Dean called 'I Won't Go Hunting with You, Jake, but I'll Go Chasing Women.' He said, 'You look like the type of guy I would like to go chasing women with.' So I became Jake."

White Southerners, particularly from poor rural backgrounds, were often saddled with the name Hillbilly. In recalling Hillbilly's real name, Yushta noted that the man was a lance corporal and "one of the dependable guys." Over the years, the quality of a soldier somehow became inseparable from his nickname.

Other names were ethnically derived. Native Americans were habitually known as Chief. Tom Magedanz recalled that the Chief in his platoon was from the Southwest and carried a machine gun. Similarly, soldiers of Hawaiian or Polynesian descent were often known as Pineapple. One of Tom Schultz's close friends was a Hawaiian from Seattle, Washington. Schultz remembered him as short in stature and always jolly and good-natured. Pineapple's death was a staggering blow to Schultz and the rest of his platoon.

The names of African-American servicemen in Vietnam were usually prefaced by Brother. Tom Magedanz, recalling several of the brothers in his marine outfit, noted that Brother Snout (Willy Holder) was quiet and confident in the bush, always hardworking and courteous. Brother Snout got along with everyone. Brother Hardtimes, on the other hand, was quite militant, but had obvious good points. Magedanz recalled hearing that one night Brother Hardtimes caught some marines in a mortar platoon putting cigarettes out on the skin of a prisoner they were assigned to guard. Brother Hardtimes allegedly told the mortarmen that he would "Kick every one of their asses off the hill if they didn't stop."[8] The threat apparently brought an immediate end to the activity.

Later in the war practically everybody was called Bro—a shortened form of brother—and phrases such as "How's it going, Bro?" transcended all ethnic lines.

Hispanic soldiers also were given nicknames relating to their ethnic origins or associated stereotypes. Though not Hispanic, Terry Tople was nicknamed Chico because he carried his machine-gun ammunition crisscrossed over his chest like a Mexican bandit.

All replacements were assigned tasks in keeping with their status. Carrying extra ammunition for the machine gun was a typical entry-level job assigned to new men in an infantry unit. Responsibility for the weapon itself was seldom delegated to new people, however. Humping the M60 was hazardous and fatiguing duty. It was hazardous because the gun drew a lot of enemy attention in a firefight. It was fatiguing because the gun's barrel and folding bipod became readily entangled in the dense undergrowth. In addition, a machine gun was heavy. The standard M16 infantry rifle weighs 8.2 pounds with a loaded magazine, but the M60 machine gun weighs in at 23 pounds empty, and considerably more with a hundred-round belt of ammunition loaded into the feed tray.[9] But, heavy and cumbersome as it was, giving the machine gun to a new man was not advisable if the unit anticipated having to use it. Every man in the field depended on the M60's firepower, and the gunner's job, though not necessarily desirable, was critical. The Marine Corps had a specialized training program for the job, whereas army machine gunners were not assigned the job until after they arrived in Vietnam. Not surprisingly, the job often fell to men of large stature.

Platoon Sergeant Donald Putnam explained the process of cultivating a machine gunner in his 9th Infantry Division platoon:

I used to put [a new guy] right next to the gunner so the guy ended up helping that gunner feed ammo if we got in a firefight . . . and he would learn about the gun. I would tell the gunner, "This guy is going to be your replacement—I want him to be as good as you are unless you can make him better." And they would do it. Those gunners didn't want to carry the machine gun the whole time they were there. Once in awhile you got one that did because he liked the machine gun; the firepower felt good. Most of them didn't [want to carry the machine gun] because it was a big load. So when you told them, "I got this guy here and I want to make him a gunner. He will take your gun but you got to make sure he is as good or better than you are," they would do it. They knew if they did a real good job with the guy, in two weeks they could be back to carrying an M16 again.

By 1970–71, in units where there was little likelihood of contact, rather than being viewed as a piece of critical equipment, the machine gun became little more than twenty-three pounds of extra metal. Such a situation resulted in the weapon often being given to a new man so that a veteran wouldn't have to carry it. Mike Roberts inherited an M60 when he reached his company in the summer of 1970. "A lot of times you would give it off to a new guy," he explained. But Roberts kept his M60 throughout his tour because, as he put it, "I always felt more comfortable when I slept right next to the gun. To me, that felt good. Security blanket, I guess."

Carrying a radio was perhaps the least desired job, and those who labored with the twenty-five-pound box, telltale antennas, and spare batteries often sought new guys to free them from their burden. The radiomen, who were known in the field as RTOs, had a job that was crucial, as well as dangerous, carrying radios for the company commanders, platoon leaders, and artillery forward observers. As one army author noted with a hint of hyperbole, "The operator was the link with civilization that kept fear and isolation at bay. . . . He was the bond that held the command together; to the enemy, the soldier with the radio was the man to be cut down in

the first volley."[10] Because they were unavoidably tethered to
their radios by the umbilical cord of its transmitting handset,
leaders and RTOs thus shared the dubious status of being priority targets. To lessen the danger, some radiomen began
wearing their PRC-25 radios upside down to better conceal
the antennas, which served as signposts for the enemy.[11]

There were two types, a three-foot flexible "tape" antenna
and a six-foot "whip" antenna. The longer antenna was used
for long-distance communication, whereas the shorter one
was used during normal patrolling. Marine RTO Jim Stanton
was convinced that the most crucial part of his job was simply "keeping the antenna down unless you were going to
transmit." To make his antenna even less conspicuous, Stanton removed the tape antenna from his radio and wrapped it
inside his shirt when he left the helicopter during an assault.
He would reattach it once he was safely under cover.

Being an RTO went hand in hand with being new. Larry
Gates drew the radio on his first combat operation when the
regular RTO complained that his knee hurt and he couldn't
carry it anymore. "Why they [entrusted] it to a new guy,"
Gates wondered aloud, "I don't know. I didn't know squat
about running it other than what I had been taught at school.
I got it mainly because no one else wanted to carry the load."

Most jobs in a platoon devolved through a sort of human
entropy that gradually sifted people into niches that suited
them. In the same way that each platoon harbored some human oddity that relished eating the culinary abomination
C-ration ham and lima beans meal, so too would someone become the RTO and like it. Dan Krehbiel was one such person.

> It's kind of funny how sometimes what you really
> need out of life shows up for you. . . . I couldn't get out
> of being in the infantry and I couldn't get out of Viet-
> nam. I just had nowhere to go but forward. I knew I had
> to do this. And then I discovered the radio because
> somebody had got hurt.
>
> They said, "Here—Krehbiel, you, new guy! Here,
> put this on." And I said, "I don't want to carry the ra-
> dio." And they said, "We're not asking!"
>
> There were two [radios] to every platoon and one

goes with the platoon leader (the officer) and the other one goes with the platoon sergeant, usually one at the front and one in the rear, because we always marched in column because of booby traps. So there I was carrying the back radio and trying to pick up on everything real fast and learn how not to be nervous when it came time to talk and how to keep my mouth shut when it was time to. And it was a long learning process.

It got you out of a lot when you had the radio. I was never very brave. I wasn't your real gung-ho troop. I just went through it. But [I] didn't have to be with the radio. My responsibility was simply to know how to get hold of somebody. Also, I was an infantryman. You would go out with a rifle and shoot when it was time to shoot and do what you were supposed to do. But I never had to walk point. I never had to be a machine gunner, and that was just a dirty, hard job. I never had to pull much KP or stuff like that.

But by the same token, when we were up in strength, there would be a guy or two who would be able to be left back each time off of the operation and that would give him one or two or three days off where he could write letters or whatever and then it would be somebody else's turn. Only the RTO never got to do that. The RTO always went out. You always had to have the radio and it was a rather specialized thing. So I never had to pull a lot of cruddy details, but I never got a break off from going out in the field either. I liked it, though. I really did. I felt important to the group. I felt like it was really a necessary job.

Layne Anderson's temperament was less suited to the radio than to the machine gun. When he first joined his company, Anderson was told to carry the radio. Not liking the assignment, he said he asked a veteran of the platoon, " 'How in the hell can I get out of carrying the radio?' The veteran replied, 'Just don't answer it.' "

"So," Layne continued, "I didn't. Lieutenant Porter came up and asked me, 'Don't you want to carry the radio?' And I said, 'No, sir, I'd just as soon carry a machine gun or something if I have to carry something heavy.' So I got to carry the machine gun."

Most men carried M16 rifles, although a variety of other weapons, ranging from twelve-gauge pump-action shotguns to LAWs to foreign-made pistols and rifles, might also be found. Personal weaponry was sometimes a matter of choice and sometimes a matter of availability.

Marines remained particularly suspicious of the M16 after numerous problems occurred with the weapons jamming in the field when they were first issued to the leathernecks in 1967. Rumors of marines dying with a broken-down rifle cradled in their arms because they were unable to clear them of jammed rounds inspired many more marines to retain a firm grip on their much heavier but more familiar M14s. Marine sniper Robert Bonesteel, who later did many of the range tests on modifications for the M16, arrived in Vietnam just after his regiment had been issued the new rifles. The results in his company lived up to the rumors, as Bonesteel explained:

> There were people dying because they didn't know how to clear their weapons or how to take care of them. The M16 was good, it was just that we didn't have time to train with them. Our actual training was, "Here's your rifle, I'm taking the old one." And that cost us.
>
> We had a couple of guys killed with cleaning rods stuck down the bore trying to get them cleared. That happened within my company. It was a different platoon than I was assigned to, but it happened. I was out policing up American bodies at the point of contact and I could tell that the guys weren't ready to shoot. They were trying to clear their rifles. That was demoralizing. So the word started that the M16 was a piece of trash and a lot of people who could—staff and senior people—would get M14s or the old Thompson submachine gun. There were all sorts of weapons around, but the "smuckatella" in the trench got last choice.[12]

At other times assignment to a weapon was based on competency. Such was usually the case with grenadiers. Most platoons had several men who carried 40mm M79 grenade launchers. They were called thump guns or bloopers because of the sound the projectile made when it left the barrel: a sound similar to the removal of a tight cork from a large, empty bottle.

While waiting to go out on his first operation, Jon Neely was given a chance to find a weapon with which he was comfortable. His choice was the grenade launcher, which looked much like a sawed-off shotgun with an oversized barrel large enough in diameter to accept a silver dollar. After working with different weapons, Neely found: "It just seemed like I had the knack for shooting it and I hit what I was aiming at."

But by far the most critical job in every platoon was that of point man, a specialty upon which every unit depended for its survival. Most platoons had an experienced man walk point when the situation required. At other times, replacements—at least in their own minds—were used as a sort of human mine detector to locate trouble. Sergeant Steve Fredrick remembered how, shortly after coming to the 101st Airborne Division, he was ordered by his company commander to lead the company into a Viet Cong base camp. Fredrick was certain that he was selected simply because he was new and no one else wanted to do it.

On occasion, new men were assigned to walk point to gain experience. Within days of his arrival in the 1st Infantry Division, Jerry Johnson was asked whether he had ever walked point. His reply was negative and the following day he found himself out in front of his platoon as it provided flank security for a company sweep into an enemy bunker complex. His tutoring was a bit primitive:

For me it was OJT [on-the-job training]. The column would be twenty or thirty meters behind, and [Lieutenant] Foxwell would give me an azimuth to follow if I had a compass. If I didn't, he would just tell me to go this way or that way. I remember the first day I walked point, I did it John Wayne style. I let the flaps [of my bush hat] hang down. I'd look this way and hear something over there, then look that way and hear something over there. It was just the damned flaps on the bush hat rubbing on my shoulders. No more Vic Morrow and

"Combat." I just played it straight. They told me what to watch for as far as booby traps. If I came up on something, [Foxwell] explained it to me. But I really didn't walk with anybody.

In some units, the point position was rotated, with new men taking their turns. Point men got their feet wet gradually in most cases, or through quick and total immersion in others. Most units, however, stayed with one or two experienced men who were good at walking point, or preferred to do the job themselves rather than trust their lives to someone else.

Platoon Sergeant Gerry Barker found keeping good men on point to be an unhappy part of his job. "It was unfair as hell in my platoon. Everybody did not walk point because some guys were good at it and some guys were never going to be good at it and you couldn't take two chances on a guy. You gave him one chance. Once! I watched him closely. If he wasn't any good at it you didn't use him again, which meant some guys got kissed a whole bunch more than others. But I didn't have a better answer. I never heard of anybody else that did either. Nobody was ever expendable in a rifle platoon."

Old point men trained new ones as their rotation date drew near. There was an unavoidable decline in competency during the interim. Every attempt was made to ensure that the transfer and training of new point men corresponded with quiet periods when contact with the enemy was light. The role of apprentice usually fell upon whoever happened to look trustworthy at the time that the existing point man chose to reevaluate his situation and preserve his remaining store of luck. That was how Paul Boehm landed in the position while with the 198th Light Infantry Brigade in 1968. "A black guy, I don't remember his name, kind of took me under his wing . . . and taught me what he knew," Boehm recalled. "He'd walk point and I would walk second and watch him. I probably started walking point myself maybe a month or less after I was there."

Whatever their jobs, new arrivals usually felt lonely, a bit scared, and eager to find friends. Slowly they began to work their way into positions of trust and, at an individual level, began to develop cohesion. Replacements were also frequently mentored by an experienced hand and, over time, developed a trust that spread through their four- and five-man fire teams into the squads, where additional layers of respect and reliance ensured that each soldier received the moral, physical, and technical support necessary for his survival—so long as he reciprocated in kind.

Dwight Reiland described his squad as like a small clique. "Your platoon was a close-knit group, but your squad was tighter yet. It stayed that way. And fortunately—God, I don't know that we could have got a better mix of personalities if we had been handpicked—we just got along great."

An essential part of an infantry unit's subculture, according to Richard Holmes, was its norms—the communal concept of what proper behavior within that group should be. Each new man was expected to conform to and internalize those standards of behavior and perform at an acceptable level.[13] This translated into doing one's fair share, remaining alert, and being reliable. It also meant, as Glen Olstad discovered, that there was very little emphasis on spit and polish and the traditional pettiness so often associated with the peacetime military. In the field, Olstad found that his leaders were "tough on things that were important, but as far as military appearance or military discipline, they could give a rat's ass. But you kept your weapon clean and you knew who was on your right and on your left. You knew which way to point your gun. You knew what to carry. You didn't have things rattling. You didn't light a cigarette at night. They were tougher than hell about the things that would save your ass."

Thinking in terms of group survival was a necessary prerequisite to gaining the support and assistance of the others. Survival in combat depends on everyone doing the right things. Competent and safe behavior by the other squad members was as important for survival as one's own behavior. A careless footstep could trigger a booby trap, an action as detrimental to the people ahead or behind as to the man who actually hit the trip wire. Jerry Johnson knew from walking point that "you not only had your own life to worry about, but the lives of everybody behind you." The force of that statement came back to Johnson toward the end of his tour when a new man took his place on point. Johnson quickly

reclaimed the job after watching his replacement pass by a
booby trap. "I yelled for everybody to stop and I told [Lieu-
tenant] Foxwell I wouldn't bitch about walking point again,"
said Johnson. "If I had killed myself, that was one thing, but
having someone else kill me . . . So I went back to walking
point."

Punishments meted out to marines for slapping at sand
fleas during basic training may have seemed harsh and inane,
but combat provided a rationale for those measures. Johnnie
Clark recounted an evening when a large group of North
Vietnamese soldiers, much larger than his own small ambush
team, walked through their position in the darkness. "Flash-
backs of boot camp blended with fear," he later wrote. "One
slap of a mosquito and my life was over. One sneeze. One ill-
timed twitch. I remembered when Private Allen slapped that
sand flea in front of me. The DI kicked him in the shins and
knocked him down. Then he made the whole platoon lie
down and he screamed at the top of his lungs, 'Private, you
have just killed your entire platoon!' "[14]

One almost universal standard among American units in
Vietnam was that you took care of your own people and *never*
left anyone behind. That meant a lot to Sgt. Steve Fredrick.
"The 101st was pretty neat that way," he said with obvious
pride. "We had an unwritten law that we never left the dead
or wounded, no matter what happened. You never got left.
That gave you a lot of—not incentive, but if you were under
heavy fire or heavy attack and you were stuck out somewhere,
you knew that you didn't have to worry. They weren't going
to leave you. I saw guys and I did it myself, went out under
fire to bring back a dead guy. And that doesn't make much
sense. But it makes sense if you are out there fighting."

The knowledge that men could absolutely count on each
other was one of the few things that enabled a soldier to walk
out of the perimeter and into the hazards of the bush. No man
relished the thought of going to the field if he could not reasonably entrust his life to his comrades. These were responsibilities unparalleled in civilian life.

Phil Yaeger, recalling the trust within his unit, Company
M, 3d Battalion, 4th Marines, with which he served during
1966–67, said, "You were proud of putting your own ass at

risk for somebody else. You were proud of just knowing that somebody could count on you—that we counted on each other. And nothing, nothing is more important than that. I've managed forty-million-dollar construction projects and they are dwarfed by that experience. They are just nothing compared to another marine relying on you to cover his ass and vice versa."

Past experience and tradition could influence a unit's priorities and values to some extent, but it was the makeup of the personnel in a unit that gave it character. Because of the one-year tour policy and the rapid personnel turnover it caused, unit character was subject to constant change. Not surprisingly, replacements reflected the evolving values and attitudes of the society from which they were drawn. As attitudes about the war changed at home, those changes became evident in the men donning uniforms. The constant turnover in personnel altered unit identities, which changed to fit the current consensus. Just how widespread the changes were over time can be seen by their effect on the Marine Corps. During six years of large-scale involvement in Vietnam—from 1965 to 1971—the Marine Corps turned over an average of half its personnel each year.[15] Men in both the army and marines who served two tours were something of a rarity, so that every unit experienced a high turnover—whether or not it experienced substantial combat casualties.

By the end of their tours, most servicemen found that they had little in common with the replacements who made up their units. Ed Hoban found it difficult to maintain friendships during his tour in 1971. "They sent everybody to Vietnam one at a time and so everybody's experiences were different. You didn't trust just any GI. You trusted the people you were with. But your friends shifted. Your best friend could leave three months after you got there and you would have to find a new best friend. And then he would leave and you would have to find another best friend. . . ."

Veterans were also quick to squelch the enthusiasm of overzealous replacements. New men were expected to use good sense and restraint, conducting themselves in a manner that would not expose the group to needless risk or excessive danger. Veterans were quick to recognize and to acknowledge

genuine acts of courage and selflessness—of which there
were many—but they loathed false bravado and bold talk. In
the bush, experience spoke more forcefully than rank. "It
didn't matter what your rank was," observed former machine
gunner Vince Olson. "You could be a private or a sergeant,
but you usually listened to the marine who had been there
awhile—whether he was a private or whatever. Otherwise,
you didn't last very long. If you tried to act gung ho or something it didn't work out. If you didn't get along with the squad
or the platoon you became an outcast."

The word "hero" acquired the same negative connotation
in Vietnam that it had during World War II. In talking to Vietnam combat veterans, Charles Moskos found that the term
was most often perceived to denote a person who jeopardized
the safety of his unit. A John Wayne attitude, as noted earlier,
was commonly held to be one that resulted in casualties because of carelessness.[16]

Squad leader Vernon Janick was forcefully reminded that
the enthusiasm and comradeship in the field, which typified
the 4th Infantry Division's first year in Vietnam, were not
shared by the men who joined his unit as replacements in late
1968 near the end of his second tour. Although constant patrols were necessary to protect units from mortar fire and enemy attack, volunteering for them was deemed overzealous
and excessive. Janick, irreverently known as Sergeant Hard-
core, began to lose faith in the military he loved when his enthusiasm and esprit ran headlong into the reluctant warriors
in his unit. Janick recalled with great emotion:

> I did go out one time with a squad and they said that
> was pretty well it. They all sat down. I said, "Well, what
> are you doing?" See, I had volunteered for a patrol
> again. I just liked patrols. But they said, "We're not go-
> ing any farther."
>
> "Well," I told them, "you guys can't just stop—we
> got to go."
>
> Then they all kind of pulled the hammers back on
> their weapons and locked and loaded on me like, If we
> move, you've had 'er. I figured one of two things: I
> could either shoot them myself, or turn them in when I

got back. But that wouldn't have done any good. I'm sure they would have got me for it later anyway. So we waited there awhile and then went back and told the company commander we had made our sweep, which we hadn't. After that I just kind of backed off of everything.

The desirable middle ground for a combat unit was to avoid being sloppy or careless in operations and to get the job done without looking for extra trouble. It was a concept that soldiers in the field clearly understood. Sensible units left the determination of what was reasonable and what was excessive to those with the most experience, regardless of rank.

The philosophy of Dwight Reiland's unit was typical. "We didn't specifically avoid contact," he explained. "If we were reasonably sure there were some gooks up this creek bottom or whatever, and if that was where we were supposed to patrol, we did. But, by the same token, if we felt there were gooks up this creek bottom and our job was to patrol that ridge, we patrolled that ridge. If it was something that was necessary—you did it. If it wasn't necessary you didn't. We did what we were told to do. We weren't out to get any extra credit."

As in any social organization, maintaining group standards was the responsibility not just of the leadership, but of all the members. Thus, infractions of group norms were usually corrected by collective group pressure.

Sergeant William Harken's recollections illustrate that point succinctly: "We had this one character. We went on ambush and . . . he carried his poncho liner out there. He was not supposed to have it in the first place. He carried it out there and stood up and was shaking out his poncho liner on an ambush! I didn't have to do anything [laughter]. The guys around him took care of that real quick."

Replacements, despite being closely watched, made errors or lapsed in concentration. New people had a tendency to bunch together—a condition known as "cluster fucking"—which often attracted sniper fire. Moreover, men who were bunched up had a tendency to talk, and, in the process, let their minds wander from the dangerous task at hand. Being lax was known in the jargon of the bush as "diddy bopping," and it was heartily discouraged by the veterans, who knew what could result from such behavior. Jerry Johnson remembered some new people in neighboring squads who could not maintain noise discipline. He didn't know what became of them—they joined his unit just before he left the field—but their behavior would never have been tolerated in his own squad.

Dwight Reiland also witnessed the group dynamics involved in keeping unit standards from lagging:

> Somebody fell asleep on guard. That happened a lot. In this particular situation it was a black man that did. It was hard for me to distinguish if they were jumping on him because he had done that or whether there was a little racism involved. But man they came down on him hard. They just read his ass up one side and down the other in less than kind names. But it was anger, and by the same token, it was fear that brought that on too, because nobody was pulling guard on that sector of the perimeter. Everybody knows if somebody scares the shit out of you, it makes you mad. And part of your anger is the fact that he scared you. The guys said, "Hey, if you are sleepy, then wake somebody up and tell them. Don't just go to sleep."

In most cases, humiliation and a good chewing out were sufficient to correct deficiencies. However, if replacements continued to demonstrate carelessness in their actions, steps were taken to have the offender removed from the unit before his ineptitude resulted in fatal consequences. Platoon Sergeant Gerry Barker explained the process:

> I had two soldiers that I left in garrison because they didn't work out when they were in the woods. I just gave them to the first sergeant and said, "Do as you please with them—I can't have them out there." One of them actually ended up helping us because he took good care of our stuff in garrison. He was just dumb as dirt. But the platoon liked him. I hated to do it because

of the morale of the other guys, and I got into a conversation with the guys one time about it.

We were sitting on our rucksacks on a PSP airstrip talking about how we couldn't all come out in the woods, and the platoon actually seemed to understand that. They were not against it at all. In fact, they made a couple of recommendations of others that should go to the rear. I never had a problem as severely as some other people. I heard stories of platoon sergeants who shot one of their privates.

Marine units also trimmed themselves to a functional level through a natural weeding out process that placed untrustworthy people back in the rear. Jeff Yushta got to Vietnam in the summer of 1969 and found that in Company B, 1st Battalion, 5th Marines, there were men who didn't pan out. "Most of those were people that didn't want to be out there anyway and you just let them pull themselves to the side," he said. "It was a lot easier on the psyche being out there with a group of people you could work with rather than having higher numbers but being less effective. If you can't trust a guy you become much more selective about what you will be willing to do."

The frustration felt by one young NCO as he tried to keep his experienced personnel together is indicative of a problem that was endemic throughout the war. In early February 1968, Sgt. Leonard Dutcher wrote his parents that his squad was up to twelve men and, in spite of all the replacements, he was still the only squad leader in the company who could boast of not having lost a single man.

The next day he received bad news and wrote his parents again: "We just got the word that we are going on another long operation into the hills. I also got the word that I will be losing two of my best men to another company that is short of guys. They took the best guys that I have so [I] will have to find someone to fill their jobs."[17]

Two days later the platoon received fifteen replacements, and some additional experienced personnel were transferred to another platoon. "I have all new men now," Dutcher lamented. "We are getting a new platoon leader and platoon sergeant; sure hope we get better ones than we had."[18]

By the end of March the unit had been in heavy contact and more replacements arrived. Dutcher's anguish was apparent when he wrote, "All our new replacements that we get have only been in the army about three months and then they ship them over. A lot of them haven't had enough training to know which end of the rifle the round comes out. I always hate to see them come as they are getting zapped faster than we can get them or else they get someone killed who knows what is happening. I better close now as there will be a chopper coming any time."[19]

Such frustrations were grounded upon the sad truth that, as in any war, new men could be a very real danger to themselves. Statistics of American combat deaths in Vietnam compiled by military analyst Thomas Thayer revealed that 43 percent of all army deaths during the period 1967–72 occurred while the soldier was in his first three months in country. Marine deaths were more difficult to assess because 3,110 of the marines who were killed (28.5 percent) did not have their time in country recorded. With this omission in mind, 33.8 percent of all marines died in the first quarter of their tours, a figure that would undoubtedly be higher if the missing data were available.

The correlation between combat deaths and experience continued through all four quarters of a serviceman's one-year tour of duty in Vietnam. Twice as many American troops died during the first half of their tours as they did in the second half. Combining the figures for the first two quarters accounts for 71 percent of all army and 51 percent of all Marine Corps combat deaths. The third quarter accounted for 19 percent of soldiers and 12 percent of marines killed in action. Combat fatalities occurring in the final quarter included only 6.5 percent of the army total and just 5.2 percent of marines.[20]

Noncombat deaths followed a similar pattern. Of all noncombat deaths, 31 percent occurred in the first three months of a tour, and the percentages declined as the year progressed. Only 10 percent of noncombat deaths occurred in the final quarter of a tour.[21]

Fortunately, most mistakes made by green replacements

were corrected before they had serious ramifications on the welfare of the men or their units. Tragically, a new man's ineptitude posed a lethal danger to others as well as himself.

This cold fact is much more horrific in human terms when considering the nature of these tragedies and the preventable circumstances that often surrounded them. John Merrell remembered an instance while operating in the Central Highlands with the 4th Infantry Division, in which a combination of inexperience and fear became fatal. A young replacement in the unit was accidently shot outside the perimeter by one of the men in the company. "I had talked to him earlier that day," Merrell recalled. "Well, he was scared. I just told him, 'Hey man, ya got to cool it. Don't worry about it. We're all here.' Then he got his ass blown away because he went outside the perimeter. You just didn't do that at night."

At other times, as Phil Yaeger recalled sadly, "new people simply malfunctioned." One such incident resulted in the loss of an experienced squad leader from Yaeger's platoon who was shot in the face by a new man while on ambush.

> A guy flipped out. We were operating out of Camp Carroll. He was a new guy that just freaked out and started screaming in the middle of the night. The squad leader tried to get to him and shut him up and calm him down and the guy shot him. He just totally lost it.
>
> The man's screaming had blown the ambush, so they pulled back. But they couldn't come all the way back in. They pulled back to the last checkpoint, which was pretty risky in itself, but not as risky as staying where they were. And they spent the night out there. Fortunately, all the fire team leaders were experienced, so it wasn't like it was one squad leader with a new squad out there. There were other good hands out there.

Michael Jackson found it difficult to accept a tragic accident that had similar catastrophic results:

> We were in light contact and the CO [commanding officer] sent maybe a squad of people down to recon, to check it out. And this real goofy dude who hadn't been

in country very long didn't have his M16 safety on. They were coming up a little knoll that was real steep and muddy, and this guy's M16 discharged accidentally and shot another guy in the foot. The M16 round tumbles. It isn't a clean round, it is a messy round. It went in his foot and came out in his leg and he died of shock. He died and he had something like two weeks to go. He didn't even have to be there—and being killed by this stupid asshole. That was frustrating.

Government statistics concerning nonhostile deaths include listings for "accidental self-destruction" and "accidental homicide." These two categories account for 1,784 casualties, or about 16.5 percent of all nonhostile deaths in Vietnam. Excluding vehicle and aircraft crashes, accidents and self-destruction accounted for 28 percent of all nonhostile casualties. Interviews with veterans indicate that accidents involving personal weaponry or friendly fire were predominant. It may also be safe to assume that numerous victims of firearms accidents were listed as combat deaths because the incidents occurred in the field under combat conditions. Casualty reports from the Vietnam War also contain an interesting category titled "Misadventure," which is included under the listing of death by "Hostile" causes. Just what is included in this category is not explained in the casualty tables, but of the 46,397 men killed in action in Vietnam, 1,326 were listed as Misadventures.[22]

Vietnam era soldiers were no more accident prone than their predecessors who fought in Korea or World War II. No army likes to advertise such tragic and preventable losses, so in many such cases, comrades in the field probably concealed facts concerning the death from parents and family who would find acceptance of a loved one's loss easier to deal with if attributed to enemy action. Korean War statistics list 112 American soldiers killed and 1,377 wounded due to "Accidents in the Use of Own Weapons," and certainly many more men died of accidents caused by the weapons of their fellow soldiers.[23]

Three days after arriving in Vietnam with the first detachments of the 4th Infantry Division, Jeff Beatty wrote from

Pleiku in 1966, "Our brigade has seen no action so far but over in the 1st Battalion, 12th Infantry, three men have been killed by carelessness—the old habit of pointing a loaded weapon at somebody and not knowing the weapon was loaded."[24]

A similar tragic accident cost Gerry Barker's company one of its best-loved members.

Every company has a clown that keeps everybody else's spirits up. We had a company clown that was just outstanding. He was black and could do Jodie cadences like nobody's business. We got the first new replacements that came into the company—first new replacements after getting into Vietnam. And they unloaded them off the Huey and they were sitting on their rucksacks out in the field and this clown walks up to them playing the role. . . .

"Let me see that rifle! Damn replacement."

The replacement was sitting on his rucksack with a round chambered, weapon selector set on "fire," and his finger on the trigger. When he pulled up on that gun the thing went off and shot the company clown through both eyes. Boy that was terrible. Some really fine people went down the tubes there.

It is not enough to bury the mistakes of carelessness and inexperience. The memories of those moments remain with the living, who were as frustrated by their occurrence as they were powerless to prevent them. Sergeant Steve Fredrick vividly remembers holding in his arms a dying black machine gunner who had been with the unit for only a few days. "I don't even know his name," Fredrick confessed. "He was about six or eight guys behind me and I heard 'duh-duh-dit.' I thought we were under fire. I ran back there as fast as I could and he was lying there. He had spread out the two legs of the bipod and leaned over with his arms splayed out over the bipod and sunk his body down over the barrel. Something on his web gear or something must have caught the trigger. . . . It went off and he got three rounds right through his chest. He died right there, too."

Arranging for veterans to look over the shoulders of the new men helped prevent accidents. Most soldiers recalled these mentors with genuine fondness as friends who in great measure preserved their lives. Mike Meil's guardian angel was an NCO named Smitty who "really knew his shit. . . . He just had all the goddamned savvy in the world when it came to combat. I took pride in knowing him and I learned a lot. He instilled something in me as far as being real careful and not to make mistakes."

Ed Hoban credited much of his survival to Tony DeTevis, who took him under his wing during his first few weeks with the unit. Robert Keeling's helping hand came from his platoon's medic. Larry Gates claimed that he had hardly ever seen any blacks in his life before B. T. Dunbar took him under his wing and showed him "the ways of the bush." Dunbar became his first and best friend in Vietnam.

Not everyone had a mentor—or wanted one. The old-timers showed John Merrell how to pack up his gear and a few other practical skills, but that was it. "Nobody said anything earthshaking to me; I think I could see as much as anyone else," said Merrell. "When it was time to be scared, everybody was scared. When it wasn't time to be scared, nobody was. I found out after being there awhile that you could sense when you were going to do something that had more risk to it even though they wouldn't tell you."

Real closeness and camaraderie, however, came very slowly for most. It was something that Tom Schultz really didn't understand until after he'd been there awhile. "It was a matter of not getting too close to somebody," Schultz said. "I think everybody took an interest in you initially to help you get started. Then, after a period of time, you developed small relationships with people, and if that worked you went on from there."

One of the first things that Jon Neely said he was told when he got to Vietnam was not to get too close to anybody because there was a very good chance of losing them. "Probably the most fortunate thing that happened while I was there," Neely reasoned, "was that, of the original six guys that I started out with on that APC, every one of us made it. We were all injured at one time or another, but we all made it back. We put our year in and came home. Some of the other squads weren't near as lucky."

Such warnings were well-founded. Losing friends was devastating, and many soldiers later claimed that they resolved never to allow themselves to build such friendships in combat again. It is doubtful that they actually followed through on that decision. Close bonds are necessary in a combat environment, and most veterans speak of their bonds and friendships with their fellow soldiers as being among the strongest and most intense they ever made. The decision to avoid friendships was more an emotional overreaction to tragedy than a coherent and logical rationalization.

Sergeant Willie Williams, for example, saw heavy fighting and a lot of new faces in his battalion of the 25th Infantry Division. Each new man replaced an old friend who had come with him from Hawaii. Such losses made him claim ambivalence toward new friendships. Still, the sergeant's parental instincts made it impossible for him to resist becoming close to his men.

> My heart was open to a lot of the younger guys that came over, and I could sense the fear in them. I really felt for them. One in particular was a kid named Simmons from Florida. He was fresh out of high school. He had a lot of fear. He respected me a lot and I kind of took him under my wing and he got killed after I transferred.
>
> Seeing Simmons get killed the way he was has been tearing at me even now and I think it is because Simmons and I had something special. I looked at him more or less as a son. He had written his parents and told them a lot about me and how he respected me and they corresponded with me. I even had the chance to escort his body back, but I couldn't. I couldn't face his family. I broke communications with them because they were asking me questions that I knew I couldn't answer, and I didn't want to face them.

New men were not inordinately abused or shunned, nor were they usually left to fend for themselves, although full admission into their combat units had to be earned over time. But most soldiers remembered being treated quite decently. After joining the 101st Airborne Division, Tommy Roubideaux was pleasantly surprised to find that "there was none of this FNG stuff. You were airborne and you were part of a group. Our first sergeant made sure of that."

Tom Schultz found that the veterans in his platoon "pretty much mother-henned you for the first month or so if you lasted that long. There wasn't any of this 'Give it to the FNG' or anything like that," he said adamantly. "It was more 'Let's get this guy started right.' And that was the way we treated everybody that came in. When it was time to smoke and joke, why, you laughed about the new guys and gave them a hard time but it wasn't vicious or malicious kind of stuff."

Men who had been in the bush could still identify with new people and accept the fact that only a few months earlier they had been just like them. Each new face became a point of reference, and in looking at the new men, veterans were casting a backward glance.

Nervousness was a way of life in Vietnam, just as it is in any war. Unlike most previous wars, however, soldiers in Vietnam seldom had the opportunity to gird themselves for an upcoming invasion or offensive. Combat in Vietnam was often impossible to anticipate. A man did not "go into combat" in Vietnam so much as he gingerly stumbled around battling the climate and the jungle while waiting for combat to find him. The initiative was often with the enemy. Accordingly, new replacements simply took their place in the column and moved out, watching and waiting and—most of all—worrying about what combat was really like.

Some men served their entire tours in the bush and never saw the enemy. Most saw him infrequently, and then usually as a corpse. But the proof of his living presence was costly, and first experiences with the enemy generally changed each soldier's perceptions about what war was really like. War was not what they had envisioned it to be. But then, war probably never is.

CHAPTER 7

First Combat

November 7, 1967

Dear Mom and Dad,

We are getting ready to be airlifted out to our landing zone by chopper. We're going out about ten miles north of our base camp and search and clear a mountain. The mountain is supposed to be a hiding place for the Viet Cong in the area so maybe we'll see some action today.

I wish that someone had a camera here so I could have a picture taken of me to send home to you folks. I've got more equipment on that I don't think I could use it all in a month of Sundays. I have over six hundred rounds of M16 ammo, six frag grenades, three white phosphorous grenades and four smoke grenades. I've also got on a bayonet, entrenching tool, helmet, rifle and web gear. In my field pack there is enough C rations to last for three days, foot powder, extra socks, flares, and cigarettes. On my web gear there is four canteens of water, first aid kit, ammo pouches, and field glasses. I think that is about it. I don't think Dad's pickup could haul all this gear. (ha ha) Oh! I forgot the compass and maps. I don't know how I am supposed to fight when I can't hardly move. Well, so much about the army.

How is everything back home? I suppose you have a foot of snow on the ground now. Oops! Here come the helicopters. I have got to close. Will have to give

this to one of the crew on the chopper to mail for me.
Will write again soon.

10,000 miles from home,
Leonard[1]

Most Americans who fought in Vietnam had no previous
firsthand experience with war. Their knowledge of battle was
in most cases limited to the myths about combat to which
they had been exposed at the Saturday matinees or in their
Sergeant Fury comic books. Many new soldiers and marines
expected their first combat to conform in part to those images. It was not to be.

After his first major engagement with the enemy, infantryman Terry Musser was able to sum up his feelings in terms of
a definitive change in perspective. "When you first got there
you were still used to remembering the John Wayne movies,"
he said. "I mean, you wanted to do good and go back home a
big wartime hero. Probably after the battle of the Ia Drang
Valley I just figured, first, I want to go home. And then, after
that, everything else was second—way down the line in
second."

If actual combat was not like the movies, neither was it
like training. Training rarely succeeded in conveying the stark
reality of life and death in a firefight. Nor could it duplicate
the fear and apprehensions that often influence the dynamics
of battle. Training was never more than pretend war, no matter how sophisticated the charade. Many soldiers thus went
into battle ignorant of what awaited them, anticipating that
their war would conform to whatever images they could draw
upon.

Soldiers waiting for their baptism of fire often found
themselves less concerned with lethality than with appearances, however, so rather than harboring any real fears about
their own mortality, most men were concerned primarily with
how their more experienced comrades would judge their performance. A study of three hundred American volunteers
who fought in the Abraham Lincoln Brigade during the Spanish Civil War led John Dollard to conclude that what a soldier
feared most was dependent upon whether or not he had previously experienced combat.

Fear of being a coward was the most strongly felt sensation on the part of troops going into action for the first time. Other major fears—of being crippled, killed, captured, and tortured, or painfully wounded—were markedly less common. Yet, on the other hand, only a very small proportion of veteran soldiers were concerned at the possibility of being a coward: for them, the fear of being crippled was infinitely more serious.[2]

Vietnam was no different. Men who had yet to experience combat were aware of the dangers and were scared that they might truly end up dead, maimed, or crippled. But these concerns were overridden by the fear of failing to perform acceptably. Their nearly universal concern was whether or not they would be able to act properly under fire, or instead reveal some flaw of character or honor that would depreciate or destroy them in the eyes of their fellow soldiers.

During World War II, marine Eugene Sledge was plagued by a fear of showing cowardice even during his training days in San Diego. Sledge later admitted, "The fact that our lives might end violently or that we might be crippled while we were still boys didn't seem to register. The only thing that we seemed to be truly concerned about was that we might be too afraid to do our jobs under fire. An apprehension nagged at each of us that he might appear to be 'yellow' if he were afraid."[3]

Likewise, Tom Magedanz also traced his apprehensions back to boot camp. "When I was still in training," he recalled, "the troop handlers told us stories about how in Vietnam squad leaders would shoot shitbirds (new guys who were always fucking up—incompetents). They said they had seen it happen more than once and I think that scared me more than anything else before I went to Vietnam. I was afraid that I would not be able to perform in Vietnam and that my own squad leader would shoot me for it."[4]

Terry Musser agreed that overcoming fear was necessary in order to avoid being seen as a failure by other members of his unit—not only on one's first combat operation, but in subsequent actions as well. It was, in his words, "the only reason

you kept doing it. That was damned important! The respect of
your peers was the most motivating factor."

Surprisingly, first combat was often far less traumatic than
most untried soldiers anticipated it would be. British military
historian Richard Holmes observed: "A soldier who is unfamiliar with battle may invest combat with far more alarming
characteristics than it turns out to possess." In fact, Holmes
noted, quite often a soldier is "surprised to discover how well
he copes with it."[5]

Francis Whitebird, a medic with the 196th Light Infantry
Brigade, experienced his first contact with the enemy in
March 1969, and the event seemed to him nothing but noise
and total confusion.

"This guy told me to get down," Whitebird recalled. "I was
scrambling around and I got behind this little burnt kind of
thing. They were shooting. I couldn't figure out where the
shooting was coming from. Somebody was saying, 'There's
some AKs over there,' but I couldn't differentiate the sound.
All I could hear was a lot of racket on our side and racket
coming from over there."

Marine Ed Austin seemed to express both relief and surprise following his baptism of fire when he confided to his
diary:

> Went on patrol from this hill today. A guy named
> Russell was shot in the head and killed. There was a lot
> of VC and a gigantic firefight. We only had one [man]
> hit but that was enough. There is something exciting
> about a firefight and being shot at.[6]

As a soldier gained experience, the nature of his fears
changed, but few men grew accustomed to battle and even
fewer were able to claim they lost their fear of it. Nevertheless, experience provided a more accurate yardstick for measuring the dangers of combat. Vince Olson discovered after his
first experience with enemy fire that every time he heard a
round he was scared. "I don't know if there was any time I
was scared more than others," he said, "but it seemed like
later you knew what would happen." Then he added quietly,
"There were nights you were in contact—combat situa-

tions—that you did quite a bit of praying. It would help out a little bit I guess."

Journalist John Sack's account of a first fight suggests that respect for death was a learned trait and knowing what to be afraid of was a skill developed over time.

> The celebrated effects of a baptism of fire, a cold sweat, a heart like a kettledrum, an unreliable sphincter, a shrinking-in of the nerves like a jellyfish pulling up its tentacles—the legendary symptoms were all surprisingly mild. The truth is that [they] had never quite had the imagination to see themselves dead, a deficit of imagery that one more month in Vietnam was to partially redress.[7]

The legendary symptoms Sack described are well known to combat soldiers. Symptoms of prebattle stress such as wetting one's pants or defecating, John Dollard noted in his Spanish Civil War study, were certainly the most unwelcome and were themselves sources of further anxiety.[8] Vietnam combat veterans vividly recalled experiencing these same unwelcome symptoms. Dwight Reiland described indirectly how even his fear of death was supplanted by a preeminent concern over having his terror inadvertently revealed to his fellow soldiers:

> We had walked into an ambush. The rate of fire was pretty intense for a short period of time. Anyhow, it came raking down through the jungle there and branches were falling off and everything, and I dove behind a log. And God! The rounds were hitting that log just "Thunk-thunk, thunk-thunk!" And the bark and chips were flying, and I was scared to even raise my head to shoot because I was convinced the little bastard was shooting at me. By that time our guns started working . . . but that log was still getting hit pretty regularly and I thought, son of a bitch, he is going to keep sawing until he gets through this log and gets me.
>
> Oh God! I was so damn scared! My stomach was turning. I suspected I was going to vomit and also have

a bowel movement at the same time. I remember thinking I would rather throw up because that wouldn't show, but I can also remember—and why a person would think about that at a time like that—but I thought, God I don't want to shit my pants. If they find me and see that I've shit my pants they are going to know how scared I was.

That most soldiers experienced similar physiological symptoms while under fire is evidenced in part by terms such as "pucker factor." Paul Boehm, for instance, recalled that after hearing the distinctive *crack* of an AK-47 being fired, "your ass is so tight you couldn't pull a needle out of it." In reality, far from tightening anything, terrifying situations generally had the opposite effect on soldiers, loosening their sphincter muscles and giving special meaning to the phrase "scared shitless."

The spontaneity of small-unit actions in Vietnam made them difficult to predict and orchestrate. There were few clues that would enable a soldier to assess his risk on any given day. Vietnam was a war without front lines. There were no beaches with a dug-in enemy to assault. Nor were there unit training periods followed by redeployment to the front line for the next "big push." In Vietnam, most of the time grunts found themselves on a nervous walk in the sun, patrolling the bush and peeking through the foliage.

Jerry Johnson was deeply troubled in the aftermath of his first enemy contact, wondering how he was going to fight a war when we couldn't see the enemy. His first fight had been

mass hysteria and all I could do was hear them. No one knew what was going on. I didn't know what we were supposed to do. I just dropped down and gave supporting fire. We fired out with everything we had and just mowed down the jungle all around us. I emptied four or five magazines right away. I remember looking around and seeing the first sergeant get it right in the head. Pfoooh; dead!

Then we picked up our casualties and called in fire support. We had walked through triple-canopy jungle right into an enemy bunker complex. It was so thick you could walk right up on a bunker and not see it. I remembered thinking afterwards, Jeez, it's going to be a year of this and you don't even know what you are running into.

There was very little accurate information about Viet Cong or NVA locations, strength, or plans. What little intelligence there was concerning enemy activity seldom trickled down past the platoon leader, unless a radio operator intercepted "the word" and passed it on to the troops. Soldiers were usually ignorant of where they were going, what they were looking for, and what their chances were of finding it.

According to John Merrell, a former rifleman still active in the army reserve in 1989, "The army didn't inform the troops very much as far as our operations and so forth. Today we are taught to break down an operations order right down the line so everybody knows what is going on. Over there, of course, it was a lot different. When you were out in the bush you couldn't all gather up and say, Let's have a little meeting."

Over time, many soldiers believed that they began to develop a nose for trouble that was attuned to the smallest clues and alerted them to impending danger. At times there was no mistaking that danger. If there had been a recent contact or if a unit was returning to a location that had the reputation of being a "bad AO [area of operation]," then everyone in the unit felt a sense of apprehension. New people themselves were a clue to impending operations. Jerry Severson remembered that "you could almost tell when something big was gonna happen because all of a sudden you would end up with a bunch of new guys coming in."

Relatively few contacts with enemy forces in Vietnam occurred at battalion level or above. Although the press often reported American units chasing after this or that NVA division or regiment, contact, when it came, was almost entirely fought by small units from the company level down. Military analyst Thomas Thayer discovered the following in his studies:

Most of their actions took the form of standoff attacks, harassment and terrorism, which did not involve direct contact between their ground forces and those of the allies. The communist ground assaults where their troops came in contact with allied forces accounted for less than 5 percent of the total actions during 1965–1972. More than 95 percent of those actions were attacks by communist units smaller than a battalion. Incessant small-unit actions truly was the name of their game.[9]

Precisely because most attacks were small, there was usually little forewarning. The best a new man could do was to pay attention, watch the veterans, and imitate their behavior. "Nobody was telling me what to look for," recalled Jeff Yushta. "I just watched the guy in front of me. Where he stepped, I stepped. And everything you did—you didn't know what the result was going to be. Every single thing! You didn't know how you were going to eat, how you were going to keep your weapon clean; you didn't know if you were going to be able to pull the trigger. You didn't know a thing. But with every day that went by, you learned a little more."

The longer soldiers waited, the more intense their apprehension became. Waiting was especially difficult while standing guard during a soldier's first few nights in the bush. Yushta recalled some vivid impressions from his first few nights in the field:

It was black. The air was oppressive and everything just moved right into you. I remember standing watch that first night for a couple of hours, sitting alone in a shallow depression so if we took rockets or something I could lie down and be out of the shrapnel area. I was trying to figure out how in the heck I was supposed to do anything because I couldn't see anything. Those other guys didn't realize how endangered they were. I was nervous. It was pretty tense.

Randy Hoelzen's company dug bunkers during his first night in the field, an activity that made him particularly nervous because no one seemed to complain about doing it. Later that night, while standing his first turn at guard, he heard a high-pitched voice call softly: "Fuck you! Fuck you!"

Hoelzen's first thought was, That has got to be only twenty feet away from me. He nudged the man next to him and asked, "What's that?" The veteran listened as the call was repeated in the inky darkness.

"NVA," the man whispered.

"Oh, Jesus!" Hoelzen gasped.

Later, members of Hoelzen's squad explained to the shaken soldier that he had heard the nocturnal call of a "fuck-you lizard."

Each day the new men anticipated enemy rounds from every tree line or hamlet and imagined every black-clad peasant to be a Viet Cong. But when the bullets finally did fly, the contact was often so sudden and unexpected that it seemed, in hindsight, to have been anticlimactic. Firefights served as important milestones in a new man's educational process, yet very few contacts allowed a soldier the opportunity to actually see his enemy. In view of America's overwhelming fire superiority in Vietnam, the enemy generally employed hit-and-run tactics that negated this advantage.[10]

In many respects, the danger passed before it was perceived. But no matter how brief the exchange, every firefight held the potential for tragedy. Tom Schultz discovered just how close death could be when the helicopter taking him out to the field for the first time began its descent over the sands south of Camp Evans.

> We were ten feet off the ground in the helicopter just sitting there shivering we were so scared. All of a sudden the helicopter snapped back into the sky as if it had been attached to a tether line. Below, men were running and falling to the earth. The other two [new] guys and myself looked at each other. Nobody knew what was going on. The door gunner finally leaned over and yelled over the noise of the chopper that as we had started to land, the Viet Cong had thrown some mortars at the NDP [night defensive position].
>
> After about five minutes we circled and came back

down, this time at a faster rate of descent. As we touched down there was a scramble of soldiers removing the food and water from the chopper. I stepped off the helicopter and saw four men carry two ponchos to the chopper and put them on board. Two men had been killed by incoming mortar rounds. They threw the bodies—GIs in ponchos—on the helicopter and they told me, "Get your gun and go over there." Yeah! I didn't hardly even have my feet on the ground.[11]

On his first operation in the field from LZ Gator, Layne Anderson's company was mortared after a civilian paced off the distance to the unit's position. Incoming mortar fire was simply one of many experiences that Anderson and the other new personnel had not yet encountered, and their reactions were slow. Anderson and four of his fellow newcomers were wounded, although none were hurt seriously. He recalled being confused by the sudden *ploop, ploop, ploop* sound that the mortars made when they were fired. "Then it dawned on us that we better get in a hole," Anderson said. "I was about the last one in. They always say cover your ass," he added with a smile. "I didn't get mine covered. I had a bunch of shrapnel in my rear end."

"War is hell," GIs in Vietnam were fond of writing on the cloth covers of their helmets and latrine walls, "but actual combat is a motherfucker." Combat in this instance meant a firefight—an exchange of small-arms fire between enemies for periods lasting from several seconds to, on rare occasions, several hours.

Randy Hoelzen's response to being under fire the first time was probably typical:

I remember being absolutely scared shitless. I wasn't much help that time. I was eating dirt that very first firefight. It didn't last long, but I remember thinking, What kind of a pathetic person are you? All you did was hug the ground. That is not what you are supposed to be doing. I felt pretty incompetent and wondered what kind of training I got.

All I heard was bullets, guns, ammo going off. And

here is this guy, he has got blood all over him and they are calling in a medevac. I think it was a feeling of what the hell is going on? Are we out of control here?

Even as the enemy bullets whistled past their ears, men found it difficult to believe that someone was trying to kill them. The shock of hearing those first rounds of incoming fire often made new soldiers forget the lethal nature of the projectiles. Vince Olson said that his first contact with a sniper left him "kinda looking around trying to see where they were shooting from. I remember a guy who had been there awhile telling me, 'Get your head down, get down.' Those rounds were just coming around. I looked to see where the rounds were coming from or to see the flash of the muzzle or something, because that is what they trained us to do in basic, but we never did see where the fire was coming from."

Don Putnam's initial reaction to enemy fire was anything but instantaneous or reflex driven. Fortunately, the soldier with him had already supplanted his curiosity with instinctive good sense. Sergeant Putnam explained:

The first night we were out in the field on bridge security and we were sitting by the bridge about ten o'clock at night. There were two of us sitting up on top of the track [armored personnel carrier], and we had both the main hatch and the fifty [caliber machine-gun] hatch open so you could drop down inside. I was sitting right alongside the fifty gunner and we were talking when somebody let go with one round. When I think about it now it's funny, but at the time it scared the hell out of me. The round went zinging right past my head and I heard the crack as it went by, but I didn't react to it. I just sat there. And one of the other guys dropped inside and reached up and grabbed me by the shoulders and pulled me down. He said to get the hell inside before I got myself killed.

Men in contact the first time often found it difficult to know just what to do or exactly how to do it. On Larry Gates's first day in the field, his unit encountered a dug-in position that their Kit Carson scout, a former enemy soldier, said held "beaucoup VC." Gates said that everyone

> hit the deck and a couple of guys started shooting. It is easier for me to talk about this now because I sound like I know what was going on, but I really had no goddamn idea then.
>
> The gooks were down in the damn bunker and everyone was shooting in the holes. We were lying there and some guys were shooting and I wondered what the hell I should do. A guy next to me got a grenade out, so I followed his lead and I got a grenade out and pulled the pin. I had the pin pulled and asked, "What should I do?" He said, "Throw the damn thing!" So I threw it. Then I saw how close I was to the hole and I pitched another grenade down in there and we killed some gooks. Two or three grenades and a bunch of M16 bullets later, the Kit Carson scout must have heard something in Vietnamese, because he stopped shooting and they started coming up out of the bunker.

Overreaction during one's first firefight was just as common among new men as was little or no reaction at all. The mixture of fear and the overpowering desire to suppress whatever it was that caused that fear could produce intense reactions that did much to prolong the duration of firefights. Robert Keeling explained that anxious GIs often continued to shoot long after those who had initiated an ambush had withdrawn. But, he confided, "once you had the hell scared out of you, you wanted to make damn sure that you got things under control. Sometimes it would take us ten minutes to wind down [the firing]."

Jerry Severson saw considerable action with E Troop, 17th Cavalry, and came to believe that what he once thought of as overreaction was simply good sense. He was amazed at the volume of bullets that he and his fellow troopers fired during a contact. "You'd just throw a blast of fire out there, much of it ineffective," said Severson. "Actually, the firefight probably lasted longer on our account than because of what they did. They might fire just one round and . . . you'd get behind a tree and go through a clip and then get another one. Then, pretty soon it would dawn on everyone that, 'Hey, there ain't nobody out there shooting at us anymore.' But there was so much racket that it took awhile for that to happen."

After returning home from Vietnam, Severson read a book about a soldier who claimed he never fired on full automatic because he couldn't sight in properly. With his own heart accelerating at upwards of "two hundred and twenty miles an hour" each time he was in combat, Severson knew the author of that book was a lot different than he and possibly a little less truthful.

Pulling the trigger was a natural reaction, and the lightweight, fully automatic M16 rifles issued to soldiers and marines through all but the earliest days of the war in Vietnam made the volume of fire prodigious. Glen Olstad recalled:

My first actual enemy contact all I saw were a couple of flashes. It was at night. I was told where to run to if we got hit that night. I ran there and fired back. I fired at the muzzle flashes. The fight might have lasted fifteen minutes, maybe twenty. It seemed like hours, but it wasn't more than fifteen or twenty minutes. I was scared to death.

You have to put out fire and still keep your head down. I just prayed to God I wouldn't get hit. It happened so fast. All of a sudden you don't have time to think. And then it's over. I did what came naturally, I guess. And I couldn't see who was shooting at me. I just shot back at the flashes and knew damn well that they were shooting at flashes too. I had two or three bandoliers of clips, and in that fifteen minutes I emptied all of them. I got my ass chewed because the sergeant said all I was doing was spraying. He said I should pick my targets and shoot.

Sergeant Michael Jackson's attitude toward economy of fire probably reflected that of most soldiers in Vietnam, although most did not put it as succinctly. "I wasn't a good shot," he admitted with a broad smile, "but wasn't nobody going to fire more rounds than I fired."

Taking those first rounds of enemy fire was like nothing else Vince Olson had ever experienced. "It triggered something in your brain so you got right in the mood of things," he said. "Once you came under fire, or got shot, or saw somebody else get shot, you understood that you were in a completely different situation. You weren't in training anymore, you were in actual war—combat."

Once one awakened to the reality of combat, fear grew in proportion to the volume and intensity of enemy fire. Terry Tople recalled walking down a rice paddy dike at night and hearing the voices of Viet Cong on each side of him. When Tople told the men with him to get down, "they opened up on us. Man, fire was just—it was just mad. It seemed like hours, but I think it was only a few minutes. I was getting scared and I said to myself, This is no game. You had these things whizzing over your head. And the AK-47, you'll never forget that sound. We kind of lay still face down in the mud until the sun came up. Boy was I scared."

Soldiers would quickly discover that fear could emanate from any number of sources. Booby traps planted by the Viet Cong or the NVA were terrifying to American soldiers in Vietnam. They were frustrating as well, for when the mines claimed their victims, there was seldom an enemy against whom to react. Marines and GIs simply absorbed the losses, registered the experience, cleaned up the mess, and moved on. During Dan Krehbiel's war with the 25th Infantry Division, enemy soldiers were seldom seen. Krehbiel could count the firefights he experienced on one hand. His was "a different nature of war, a war of booby traps, mines, watching where you walk, and having nobody to shoot back at when somebody gets hurt or blown up." But the fear of booby traps and the nearly continuous casualties they exacted from his unit came to typify his daily struggle in Tay Ninh Province.

Booby traps were a menace to which Krehbiel was introduced on his second day in the bush:

> We started . . . a search-and-destroy type mission and we walked right into a huge, booby-trapped area.

There were no enemy soldiers, no shooting. The guy in front of me stepped into a *punji* pit and his leg slid down the side right before the stakes. He didn't get stuck, but I saw the stakes—the discoloration—at the tip of each stake: cow dung and stuff like that. At the same time, three ARVN soldiers walked into a white phosphorous artillery booby trap, a big 155mm shell, and it went off and threw white phosphorous all over them and they burned—they just cooked. All three of them died. Everybody got down. Nobody else moved. Then somebody set off a hand grenade behind us that wounded someone. Anyway, the whole area was just plagued with booby traps and I didn't know what I was doing. I was all set to put my gun on automatic and wait for something to move in the bushes. I figured we were going to get overrun or something, but that was it.

A guy came by and rapped me on the helmet and said, "Keep an eye out that way and if you see anything at all, holler." That was all I had to do. Then he said, "Welcome to the war," and he went on his way. That was my first enemy contact—if you want to, call it contact by indirect method. The three guys died. The guy wounded with the hand grenade was okay. The guy in the *punji* pit didn't get hurt at all. There was also a tilt rod with a wire attached to it going underground in the middle of the *punji* pit, and they dug into a grave, because this was also the edge of a cemetery, and there was this big huge bomb. It must have been a B-52 bomb or something. It would have killed us all. But he didn't step on the tilt rod; he missed that.

I didn't realize what a degree that luck played and we were playing the game day in and day out. It was just luck. We learned how to keep our eyes open and how to spot things that weren't supposed to be there. Our reflexes got real fast.

But no matter how intense, unexpected, or frequent the contact, nothing drove home the serious nature of combat as rapidly as seeing maimed or killed Americans. According to Paul Boehm, "The first GI you see get it is the worst I think, because he is one of your own. This is a good person here—one of the guys in the white hats getting shot. It isn't a pretty sight. And that really tears you up—at least it did me."

Forward observer Jack Freitag came to that same realization when he witnessed a fellow marine shot by a sniper on one of his first operations.

"He got shot and I wanted to see it," said Freitag. "You know how curiosity is? And then everybody opened up, and I heard all this noise for the first time—it was a real firefight. That was the first guy I saw hit. He got shot in the leg. Nothing serious. But I wanted to go over there and see it. I just had to see it. It was all kind of like a make-believe thing until that first actual event. Then I said to myself, There really is a war going on here."

Tom Roubideaux's first action as a medic with the 101st Airborne Division was a milestone in his life, one that shattered the myths he grew up with:

I heard people say "Contact, contact!" Then the sergeants were moving men, and I heard someone yelling out for a medic. So I came running forward and grabbed this guy and pulled him behind this bush and started working on him. The next thing I knew, the sergeant major was yelling, "Get your ass down." I looked up and what was a bush before didn't have a leaf on it. It was a miracle that I didn't get hit. I guess I was so busy doing my thing. I was trying to patch this guy up.

I got him squared away and got him back to the CP area there and I went after another guy. I was pulling him back and his head popped and just kinda misted, you know. All this junk, gray matter, came out all over and he was lying there with the left side of his head gone. Then I realized it wasn't like "Combat" or your John Wayne movies. This was for real and it was slow motion after that.

It was raining pretty good there, but my mouth was dry. I couldn't spit or anything. I was trying to get everybody back, keep people from getting too shocky and stuff, pushing in IVs and all that stuff.

After we got them all medevac'd, I was sitting there

and the first sergeant came up and said, "You want a cigarette?" I never smoked before in my life, but I was smoking like a champ then. I remember I couldn't keep the damn cigarette dry, even though I was cupping that poncho over me, because I was slobbering so much. I'm not kidding, just slobbering.

The presence of American casualties could also change a soldier in more subtle ways. Some felt a sudden sense of vulnerability; others were left unnerved by death's random nature. Still others, such as Larry Gates, found out that dead Americans sometimes inspired a desire for revenge and feelings of hatred for the enemy. Gates recalled that in his first fight several enemy soldiers were killed, which left him feeling badly about it. "I was half sick to my stomach and pretty teary eyed, and then we got some GIs hurt not too long after that," he said. "What my comrades told me in the bush was, 'You'll get over it the first time you see a GI fucked up, Larry.' And by God I did. Then we got a little bit of the revenge factor involved and we got pretty gung ho wanting to inflict great pain on these people. You just came to hate them—to fear them and hate them all at the same time."

The aftermath of battle erased some of the confusion and reduced battle to its horrifying refuse of broken equipment and broken men. In the period following contact, proof often remained that the events that had so recently transpired were real. Certainly the dead were testimony to the fact that there was nothing that made one man's life more valuable than that of another. Looking back on his experience, Jeff Yushta surmised that "at nineteen years of age you felt you had an indestructible body. Most males do. I still had that belief at that time, but I think that night was the first time I realized that the bullets were real. They do damage when they hit. I knew then that I had as good a chance as anybody of not going home. I didn't sit and dwell on it. It was just something that all of a sudden I knew."

Although soldiers realized that they were likely to come into contact with death, their first confrontations with it almost always came as an unexpected shock. Death seems to rob a human being of some inexplicable quality. It makes the dead strangers—and thus uncomfortable to be near. Decomposition further disguises corpses. Soldiers making their first acquaintance with death outwardly kept a mask of bravado, but inside they were unnerved.

"When you see a person who has been dead for only ten minutes or so, it is hard to fathom," recalled Tom Magedanz. "They lie there so still and start to look like plastic dolls if they are not too shot up. The bodies had to be checked for weapons and papers and it is hard to touch them at first—you don't want to startle them. But everyone is standing around watching you, and they might have doubts about you if you don't go through with it."[12]

Searching the dead was a part of the job that sniper Robert Bonesteel never got used to. "I didn't do a good job of searching the bodies," he confessed. "I should have, because they taught that in training, but there was something about actually killing a guy where once that was done I wanted it to be over."

Sometimes, as Paul Meringolo discovered, it could be difficult to recognize the dead for what they really were until one became accustomed to seeing them. The first time he recalled seeing a body, Meringolo was riding in his APC through a deserted village that had been previously occupied by the Viet Cong. "We saw what looked at first to be almost like a slaughtered pig on the ground," he said. "It didn't have a defined shape to it, but you could see the white skin like the coloration of a pig. Upon closer scrutinization, we realized that it was a piece of a human body; I assume a villager. We later found out that when the North Vietnamese would come into a village, they would quite often decapitate or use various other methods of killing some of the villagers just to put the fear of God in them [for] cooperating with the Americans, as opposed to helping the VC. But it was strange when you realized that this piece of flesh you were looking at was once a living, vibrant person."

When Sgt. Gerry Barker and his men got their first glimpse of the effects of war in the tidal backwash of a battle that had preceded them, they were struck by the delicate appearance and youthfulness of their enemy. As the sergeant pointed out, however, while investigating their enemy his men were oblivious to their own youth. "We had nothing to do with the fight there," said Barker. "They had killed a couple hundred VC in the area, none of which were buried. They were small. In fact, I can remember a couple of my guys saying, 'God—they are just kids!' But *we* were just kids! I was an old man there at twenty-one. We spent that night there and the smell was already getting to us. We moved out and started walking towards what was going to end up being the battle in the Ia Drang Valley."

If the new men were shocked by the sight of death, their more experienced comrades seldom seemed to be, at least outwardly. Lieutenant Robert Steenlage's first two weeks with the 4th Infantry Division's 124th Signal Battalion were spent helping arrange the 1968 Bob Hope Christmas Show at Pleiku. On 1 January, however, the West Point graduate was sent to an isolated relay and monitering station in the jungle near Kontum. That night the little base was attacked by Viet Cong sappers who broke through the wire and nearly destroyed the site. The following morning Steenlage found himself shocked as much by the callousness of his fellow survivors as by the carnage left from the battle. "It was death on a mass scale," he remembered, his voice trailing off at the memory of it. "One Viet Cong had been hit right above the eye with an M16 on automatic and it just literally took the top of his head off." Steenlage shook his head, then added: "Some of the American soldiers were running around with cameras taking pictures to send home, just like they were at a picnic. The whole thing was sickening."[13]

Robert Keeling's encounter with the residue of battle introduced him to the same fact, that men become rapidly desensitized to death and many reached a point where the dead hardly warranted a second glance or a second thought.

The second day I was out we got into a contact. The NVA were the ones that hit us and they hit us hard. The thing I'll never forget was when we went out to see how many bodies we had the next morning, we couldn't find anything. I mean, we knew we killed a bunch of them, but all we could find were naked bodies—no clothing, no weapons, no anything. I saw what a fifty-caliber machine gun would do, which is amazing. If a man gets hit in the shoulder, he is a dead man just from the shock of it because it would just rip his arm off. And I guess what I really couldn't believe was [that] our captain told one of the tank drivers to take the bodies out and bury them. We never thought anything of it. The driver hauled them out somewhere and all of a sudden you heard the tank's engine rev up and then it came back. A guy had a big old chisel bar—a big old pry bar—and I went over and asked him what he was doing.

"Ah, the damn gook. His arm fell off and I got it caught in the track and it went through the sprockets and I got to get his bones out of there."

What they would do is take the bodies out and lay them out on the road and run over them with the tank and do one of those spin-around jobs and just grind them into the ground. I couldn't believe that anybody could be that inhumane. But you learn after awhile. It is kind of sad, because you really do become very callous.

A macabre fascination with death drew soldiers to their first corpse with more than professional interest. A "kill" is tangible proof of military success. It is also degrading—a break with one of the most fundamental laws by which a man clings to civilized existence. But, for better or ill, killing was a rite of passage for the soldier that marked his most intense first experience in war, save perhaps for the death of a close companion. Most soldiers in reaching that milestone found little joy or sense of triumph, however. James Stanton, twenty years after the fact, still believed that if he could undo a single event from his past, it would be the moment when he was forced to shoot his first enemy soldier. After that fateful burst from his M16, Stanton admitted feeling ill for two days.

"It was in a firefight and he started running away and he run right into me," Stanton recalled. "He was about fifteen feet away and he was at a full run. If I wouldn't have got him he would have run over me, so I shot him. Threw up right afterwards."

The former marine shook his head after a moment and added quietly, "It is one thing to shoot a deer. It is something else to shoot a person. I will never forget it as long as I live. I can see it as well today as I did then, and that is something you can't get rid of. The only thing that keeps you sane is what if you didn't—what would he have done? I stopped him, so I don't know what he would have done. He didn't have his rifle aimed at me."

If James Stanton saw a distinction between killing a deer and a human being, not everyone did. Paul Boehm claimed, whether true or not, that he was aloof to the killing. Such a belief assuaged the conscience; it relieved the soldier of guilt, and shifted responsibility for his actions to the army and the government that had hired and trained him.

Deane Johnson was quite surprised by the lack of remorse he felt following his first kill, but Johnson was a helicopter door gunner and never got any closer to his first victim than the range of the shot that killed him. "I really thought that would be a horrifying experience," said Johnson. "I thought I'd have dreams and nightmares. We went in on an insertion and a dink jumped up from behind a rice-paddy like about thirty-five yards away. I just sawed the son of a bitch in half with an M60. I went home that night and went right to sleep. He had an AK, but I blew the guy away."

After a time, soldiers were often able to kill without compunction, but for new men, killing required some consideration. While on his first operation in the Delta, machine gunner Terry Tople and his party ambushed three Vietnamese in a sampan.

I hesitated, you know. I said "Jeez I don't know." I was kind of scared. I shot in the boat. They tell you six-round bursts—man, I must've gone through a thousand rounds just like that, just firing into the boat. I think it was kind of a small miracle in itself—there were two VC in there with a civilian kid. They'd taken him out of their village and were using him like a hostage. And for some reason he never got a scratch. He was just screaming and I was right on him. I thought about killing him and then I thought, Something's wrong here. The other two—the VC—were dead. We found out later through our Kit Carson that the kid was

fourteen years old and that these two VC had taken him
out of the village while they were escaping.

I admit it, I was scared. I froze. I just couldn't do it,
but I did it. I did do it. God, you know, they were about
ready to take the machine gun out of my hands. I froze.
I just couldn't. They knew it, too, and we talked about
it later. It just had to be. That's what we had to say; it
just had to be.

Sergeant Steve Fredrick also hesitated before shooting at
the first enemy he encountered. His rationale was interesting:

I was probably in country about ten days. You hardly
ever saw them. You'd get fire from them and you knew
they were out there, but you never saw them. I did see
two one time running across a field and, unfortunately,
I screwed it up because I was a rookie. But I was also
the sergeant. Two of my men wanted to shoot them
right away. But God! Y'know, I'm just not used to seeing people killing. They both had their guns up to shoot
and I said, "Don't shoot. I want to look at them."

And God! I looked at them and they were wearing
black pajamas. They were carrying AK-47s. One had
an RPG. They were gooks! Bad ones! Unfortunately,
we began shooting too late and they both got away. That
was strange. That was the first time I ever saw one and
they were running right across a field and we were
looking through a hedgerow at them. They couldn't see
us. It was pretty strange.

Later that same day, however, Sergeant Fredrick squeezed
the trigger.

The platoon sergeant told me to take my men and go
out on a sweep five hundred yards out and then come
back. There was all kinds of VC activity there, so I took
my men and we went out. This was one of the scariest
times I ever had in Vietnam. I had one guy on point and
I walked behind him. We were going right through the
jungle and all of a sudden he got down and motioned

for us to get down. I crawled up to him and here came two VC walking right down a road we were crouched on the edge of. The road came right towards us and turned [to the right] and they were coming right towards us. We were back about ten yards and it was impossible for them to see us.

I told the point man to take the one on the right and I'd take the one on the left. We waited. God, they couldn't have been more than eight feet away. I shot once and I got the guy right through the center of the forehead. The point man put his M16 on automatic and missed. He didn't get his guy. The guy went running down the road and I missed him, too. He got away. But the other one was deader than a doornail. And . . . it's hard to explain this.

We walked out to the road and we were pretty scared. I got my men out there, all of them, and I put them in a circle. We set up a perimeter because every time you killed somebody you had strict orders to search them and take everything they had. While they sat around, we searched him and we got a bunch of money off him. This other guy, I let him have the watch. The dead VC had a beautiful Seiko watch. I shouldn't say things like this, but it was plunder. That is what it was. I got about eighty bucks from him.

He didn't look bad at all, but there was a big pool of blood under him. All he had was this little tiny blue hole in the center of his forehead, but then I turned him over and the whole back of his head was gone—just blown right off. One round from an M16. It was unbelievable. When I turned that guy over I threw up. I got pretty sick.

Grenadier Jon Neely also discovered that nothing in his past experience had prepared him for killing, nor did he suspect at the time that the event would stick with him the rest of his life.

A small base camp had gotten hit pretty hard by Viet Cong and we were called in to support them. We drove in on our APCs. The VC were taking off as fast as we were getting there. . . . The platoon leader told us to get off the APCs and we had to sweep through the jungle. The first thing they told us was . . . no civilians should be out there. Anything that is out there shouldn't be there. If it moves kill it.

Well, we were sweeping through a section of the jungle and I was probably fifteen to twenty steps behind my squad leader when I saw a guy come out from behind a tree and point his weapon at my squad leader. I guess it was just instinct. I pulled up and fired first. I was carrying a grenade launcher and—well, I hit the guy dead center and there wasn't much left of him. It was all over. That turned out to be my first kill. Although we had to continue sweeping through the jungle, I started getting the feeling that I wasn't going to make it too far. When my squad leader and I went over to the dead gook, I took one look and I just puked my guts out.

I had been in several fights back on the block as a kid and although I got beat a few times I won a couple of fights and it just didn't seem to bother me to be in a fight. But to physically kill someone—it really got to me and it took me a few days to get over that. . . . Of course, some of the guys made fun of the fact that I really got sick over the deal, but I guess that is the way they pick on the new guys.

No matter how good their training was, soldiers and marines were rarely prepared for the confusion and noise, the chaos and disorder, or the death and suffering encountered in battle. Nor were they prepared for the lack of decisiveness. Men fought and died. Men were horribly injured. They suffered ringworm and malaria and heat stroke, and their efforts exhausted them. Yet there was nothing to show for the effort except a tally of enemy dead in the weekly *Stars and Stripes*. There were very few signs of a population wanting to be liberated—no flag-waving throngs along the roadside, and no changing lines on maps to mark the rollback of communism. Instead of a front there was only the jungle or the hamlets and villages that pressed in on all sides and seemed to swallow the soldiers as they passed through. Living and operating every day in that void, infantrymen had little sense of progress and no means for measuring it. There was no road to Hanoi, just one day less to serve before they could finally go home.

Miraculously, the men began to adapt. Paul Meringolo wondered at his own adaptability. "I always anticipated the possibility of something happening, but I couldn't function if I had continued to feel that way," he confessed. "So through some metamorphosis I learned to live with the fear. It didn't go away, but it wasn't as overpowering as it was in my first days. I adjusted to the reality of seeing dead bodies, the possibility of being ambushed, or the possibility of hitting booby traps and mines."

Soldiers developed numerous ways to cope with the war, and as they did their newness faded. With each passing week their knowledge and combat efficiency increased.

Killing was the function of a military unit, and soldiers carried out that task to the best of their ability. It got easier as the men became desensitized, but they had to give up something of themselves in order to do so. The fact that soldiers and marines hardened themselves to the killing did not mean that they lacked compassion or morals—it was simply the process by which a soldier programmed himself to do his job while retaining as much of his sanity as possible. They hardly noticed the changes in themselves, but every now and then they were made aware that they were different from what they had once been, and what had once been incomprehensible was now commonplace.

Steve Fredrick became aware of the change one afternoon while eating a C ration next to an enemy corpse. Jeff Yushta first noticed it after helping to load a wounded marine on a helicopter. "That could have been me lying there," he realized. "But at the same time there was something in me saying, Well, it was him, it wasn't you. It was one of those steps in the hardening process. And you felt a little loss. I look back now and realize I lost a little bit of humanity every time something like that happened."

CHAPTER 8

Humping the Bush

December 5, 1967

Dear Mom and Dad,

Received your letter yesterday and was glad to hear from you again. Sure wish that I had more time to write, but they have been pushing us pretty hard lately. I would give a thousand dollars for a good night's sleep as I haven't had much since I got here. We've been doing a lot of moving around looking for the Viet Cong. So far they have been finding us first. We were hit last night just as we were moving back into base camp by sniper fire so we were up all night chasing them all over the hills. We moved into base camp about two this morning. About seven we had to come back out here and do some more looking.

I haven't been inside a PX since I got to Viet Nam so [I] am running out of a lot of things. One thing I need is socks. My last pair rotted off the other day so my feet are getting in a state. When you get my next money order would you take some of it and send me some socks. I just ran out of ink in my pen so I could use some pens also. We haven't had our pay given to us yet this month and it is two days past payday. Everything is messed up over here.

Tell everyone that I'd appreciate them writing me some letters. I'd be glad to write them back when I find the time. You wouldn't believe how much a letter will help when a guy is over [here]. In fact, that's the only thing a soldier has to look forward to is mail call. I know I sound depressed but I can't think of anything that has went right for the last month. I've got to close now as we are going to be moving out again. I'm writing this letter on a chow break sitting on a rice paddy dike.

Your Son,
Leonard[1]

Vietnam is a beautiful country, but it proved to be almost impervious to American technology and it was particularly adept at sapping the physical endurance of American soldiers. The climate and terrain exemplified an observation made a century earlier by Ambrose Bierce: "No country is so wild and difficult but men will make it a theatre of war."[2] The reality that typified the existence of the field soldier in Vietnam was not so much combat with enemy forces as it was the day-to-day hardships, fatigue, and frustration of living and coping in that harsh and hostile environment.

Soldiering meant living in filth, eating tasteless food, enduring leeches and mosquitoes, getting little sleep, and feeling minimal accomplishment, despite exertion that drew the last reserves of physical and emotional strength from each man. While serving in Vietnam, Larry Gates came across a description of the life of a World War II infantryman that had been reprinted in *Pacific Stars and Stripes*. The passage, written by Ernie Pyle, described with simple eloquence a reality that Larry had been unable to fit into words himself.

It's the perpetual choking dust. The muscle rocking, hard ground. The snatched food sitting ill on the stomach. The heat and the flies and dirty feet and the constant roar of engines and the perpetual moving and near settling down and the go, go, go, night and day and on through the night again. Eventually, it works itself into an emotional tapestry of one dull dead pattern. Yesterday is tomorrow, and one area of operation is another area of operations, and God, I am so tired. They were and always have been frontline infantrymen.[3]

Though his own description was less eloquent, Sgt. Michael Jackson lived the experience and conveyed its realities: "Living out in the field, sleeping on the ground, digging your toilet with an entrenching tool, and carrying everything you own on your back is a fact of life that is not really publicized because it is dull and boring. But that as much as anything remains with me. Combat only lasted a matter of minutes. The rest of your time was spent living like an animal outdoors under real deplorable conditions."

Life in an infantry company was neither glamorous nor gallant, and it was certainly not romantic. Each day was different, yet delineated by the same patterns of exertion and scarcity, roughness and fatigue. For a rifle company in the field, many days began just before first light when the listening posts and ambush patrols out beyond the perimeter were brought in, and the men not standing watch were roused from what sleep they had been able to muster. Most units kept their night ambush patrols outside the company's perimeter until dawn so that there would be less chance of an accident as the men approached their own lines. Then, according to Sgt. Gerry Barker, "everybody stands to, everybody is awake looking out. It has been basically watch-on-watch all night—one man on guard and one man sleeping, except for the ambush patrols, which may not even get that. After standing to, you let the guys eat, check all the weapons, and clean them if they need to be. Usually, you have gotten your mission during the night, which is usually just to move to a new location. Then you start putting the platoon together."

Sleep in the field was usually broken by several hours of guard duty during the night. The rest of the night was spent on the ground with knees doubled up in a fetal position, wrapped in a poncho or a poncho liner. Evenings seemed always to be damp, or wet, or flooded depending on the season. And no matter what the time of year or terrain, soldiers seemed to be plagued by mosquitoes that rose in clouds from the elephant grass and paddies to feast upon them.

Stephen Fredrick recalled how once, while trying to "sleep on the edge of a rice paddy, the mosquitoes got so bad I eventually ended up sleeping with everything but my face under the water. I put the gas mask bag over my face and that is how I spent the night. I just couldn't stand it. You put that insect repellent on and it was real good stuff. It would last for three or four hours. But in the middle of the night it would wear off. And my God! You would wake up and your face would be covered with mosquitoes."

Soldiers seldom awoke refreshed. There were too many stiff muscles and joints. There were also disturbing thoughts to keep men company during the seemingly endless hours of darkness. Jerry Severson often found it impossible to sleep. "You'd doze in fits and spells and you'd hear something," he explained, "and you would be awake again thinking, those dirty sons-of-guns are coming after you again!"

Sergeant Fredrick found the lack of sleep nearly intolerable. "I was tired all the time," he said. "We never got any sleep in Vietnam. I just wasn't prepared for that. I could fall asleep leaning against a tree when I was over there the first three or four months. I was awake—honest to God, I would say I was awake between nineteen and twenty-one hours every day. I averaged three or four hours of sleep a day for the first three months I was there. That was incredible. You can't be an effective fighter when you're half conscious all the time."

Sergeant Barker believed that lack of sleep was the only thing that kept infantrymen sane in combat. "They are so damn tired they don't give a shit anymore," he said simply.

Lack of sleep affected physical performance and contributed to a decline in each soldier's coordination, endurance, and mental acuity. Fatigue decreased levels of concentration and lowered vigilance. It built up fluctuating emotions of anger, elation, or gloom. But, worst of all, sleep loss was dangerous. Under normal combat conditions in Vietnam, soldiers such as Vernon Janick found that:

A day seemed like a week. You walked all day and slept part of the night. You were dragged out. You were amazed that all day you humped the hills with those packs and only a little to eat. Then, if you only had a couple guys in a hole, you would be on two [hours' watch], and he would be on for two—two on, two off; two on, two off—all night. You would get half a night's sleep. Right away in the morning you were back humping again. Same thing every night. Many times everybody just dozed off. You just couldn't help it. You took a hell of a chance, but you could only put up with so much. After awhile you were just in such a daze. You were tired. I don't know how in the hell we did it except that we had to!

Four hours of sleep a night was about average for most Vietnam combat veterans, about equal to what American soldiers who saw action in World War II experienced.[4] The accompanying overall feeling of weariness was often the most common condition a soldier in Vietnam experienced. Such exhaustion is one thing that never comes across in war films, but it is indelibly impressed into the memory of every infantry soldier.

The combat soldier must lay his life on the line each day and he depends upon his wits and his alertness to protect him. The enemy's possible presence dictates that soldiers remain awake and vigilant as much as possible, but remaining that way for long periods creates conditions under which the soldier is least capable of functioning.

The utter exhaustion that soldiers in Vietnam experienced was perhaps best revealed in episodes that even the infantrymen themselves found amazing. Terry Tople, for example, recalled how, while operating in a swampy area in the Mekong Delta, "we were so tired that we set up alongside something like a channel. We were just lying there, and in the meantime the tide came in. God's truth, I woke up and the water was right up to my neck. I was lying on the ground and had my helmet in back of my head and the water came in. We were all lying in the water."

Soldiers gradually came to terms with their schedules, however. After a few months, Ron Flesch's biological clock had rearranged itself so well to the two-hours-on, two-off watch cycle that he would awaken almost automatically. Humans are wonderfully adaptable.[5]

The days in Vietnam always seemed incredibly long, but every day was different. Tom Schultz found that, "You didn't think about how long they were because you were constantly doing something." Schultz's company was up and moving by 6:30 A.M. getting breakfast, packing up: "Everybody would be milling around cooking their coffee." But a certain bleakness accompanied most activities around which they lived, and breakfast was no exception.

Breakfast always posed a unique challenge. There was only one breakfast entree available among the dozen or so varieties of C-ration meals.[6] And to the soldier's discerning palate, scrambled eggs and ham ranked just above the ham and lima beans meal—an abomination with a flavor that earned it the sobriquet "ham and motherfuckers." William Harken, however, ranked the breakfast entree even below ham and lima beans. The grayish color and coiled appearance of eggs lying in the can did nothing to make them more appealing. Donald Putnam said that he could eat them only if he doused them with Tabasco sauce. Paul Gerrits, a medic, avoided the eggs entirely because they reminded him of brains.

Cooking a ration for breakfast was also bothersome. Most soldiers preferred to eat light. Larry Gates usually started his morning with some instant coffee or a C-ration packet of hot cocoa mix. Some soldiers combined the two in a mixture known as "mocha." Gates topped off his morning coffee with a tin of pound cake—if he was lucky enough to have one. Pound cake was as valuable a commodity as one could possess in the bush. It became pure ambrosia when mixed with peaches and powdered cream.

In some units, the morning field routine was periodically made more interesting with a ritual known as a "mad minute," during which every soldier fired his weapon out into the area surrounding the company's night defensive position.[7] The purpose of this extraordinary exercise was to foil a possible enemy attack, but in many instances, according to Gerry Barker, it merely served as a means of disposing of ammunition that might have gone bad in the tropical climate.

Such displays of firepower were impressive. They were good for the morale and confidence of soldiers who often lived with the feeling that they were being watched or even stalked. Usually conducted at dawn or dusk, mad minutes generally passed without incident. On rare occasions the barrage of fire would dislodge snipers from the trees or prematurely spring an attack. More often they raised havoc with the foliage and little else.

In a few tragic cases, however, the casualties were neither the enemy nor the foliage. Michael Jackson vividly recalled how, after one of his unit's mad minutes, when "everybody stopped firing their weapons, you could hear this person saying, 'War—war.' A real bone-chilling, soulful declaration. 'War, war—Oh God!' And Captain Seversen said, 'Stop firing! Be quiet! I think we got one of ours.' We had two people killed that morning. One of them was shot in the head. What happened was, they never got the word there was going to be a mad minute."

With breakfast finished, such as it was, the soggy poncho liners that had served as bedding were stuffed back into packs where they would never dry out, alongside spare clothing that was also wet and mildewed and destined to remain so. There was the ritual of pulling old wet socks on after having tried to dry one's feet out a bit—an experience that made dry socks a luxury in the infantry. But in Vietnam, dry socks usually became wet three seconds after a soldier put them on anyway.

What a soldier carried depended as much on personal choice as military policy. In 1965 and 1966 the equipment, like the tactics, was adapted from existing stocks. Nothing had been specifically designed for Vietnam and its unique conditions. But, as the war progressed, equipment went through an evolutionary process. In those early days, however, according to Gerry Barker, the equipment was sometimes a liability:

> The old fatigues [uniforms] were a shiny bright iridescent green after they had been starched a number of times, which was no camouflage in the jungle at all. It was okay if you were in light grasses somewhere. But they still needed dying. We still had the old seat-pack. In neither of my tours in the 1st Cavalry Division did I see the stuff that was used later on.
>
> Boots rotted off us, especially the old Corcoran jump boot that we all went into country wearing. A lot of a soldier's money in the prewar days went into keeping his uniform up because he was rewarded for it. That

was how you got promotions, "Colonel's Orderly," and that sort of thing. In an airborne unit, much of a private's hundred and forty-five dollars or a buck sergeant's two hundred and nine—counting jump pay—went to uniforms. But it was all the wrong stuff to take into country.

The boots rotted right off in two to three weeks. The heavy cotton fatigues were just eaten through with the sweat and the rot of the jungle. Even in the dry season you were wet. In the wet season you just bathed. You were always wet, particularly in an infantry company, and you were always dirty.

The amount of equipment carried by the "grunt" in Vietnam was staggering—literally. Each unit learned from experience what was necessary and what was not. Vernon Janick remembered:

We weren't aware that we would be carrying all that we were. We thought we had a lot in the States with just our regular pack and stuff. We couldn't believe that we were actually going to carry all that. Like I said, at least a hundred pounds with all the ammo and stuff they had you carry: poncho, poncho liner, three or four canteens, entrenching tool, first-aid kit, ammo magazines, extra knives or guns. You could take anything like that you wanted. Grenades, smoke grenades. Just an unreal amount of ammo. I was a grenadier at first, I had the M79. And the minimum you had to take was thirty-five rounds, which was a heck of a lot of extra weight and took up a lot of room.

C-rations. We were given enough for five days to seven days at a crack. Three meals a day. That is fifteen to twenty meals at one time. And there just wasn't enough room for all that, so you just kept what you thought you were going to make it on till the next drop and threw the rest away. If you ran out, well, if your buddies had a little extra they shared. Otherwise . . . the next time, if your drop was a little late, you were out. We had the same problem with water at times.

Nothing much as far as clothes. We had extra socks but everything else was just for eating, drinking, and ammo. That was pretty well it. Guys took cameras and stuff like that but you crossed so many rivers and creeks and it rained so much that the stuff would get soaked. There were places you would go up to your neck. Your pack would flood. It would just wreck everything. There was just no way anything could stay dry.

Men quickly wised up. Unnecessary equipment was left behind. When John Merrell joined the 4th Infantry Division he was issued a pile of equipment, much of which never left the supply shed. "The supply sergeant was right. We didn't need most of it," recalled Merrell. "I needed a poncho liner, my rucksack, canteens. I didn't have enough canteens. I only had two to start with. My ammo pouches. Yeah, I'd use those. And the clothes I had on my back. That was it. That is what I needed. That is what I found out I needed. I had no regrets because I had to carry everything I had, so I didn't wish for anything."

Upon arriving in Da Nang in June 1967, Vince Olson received the normal marine issue "782 gear" pack and gas mask, flak jacket, tent poles, shelter half, and so forth. He left it all back with the company supply except for a poncho, flak jacket, ammo, weapon, canteen, helmet, and an entrenching tool. Jungle boots were not part of the equipment that Olson was issued. The lightweight jungle boot had nylon mesh uppers and drain holes in the side that helped the boot dry out quickly. There was a protective mesh in the sole designed to prevent *punji* sticks from penetrating into the soldier's foot. The boots were more resistant to rotting, and were more comfortable to wear, but they had not yet been issued to the Marine Corps. If jungle boots were not yet part of the leatherneck inventory, they were a part of the public relations campaign of the Goodyear Chemicals Company, which advertised in magazines during the same month Olson arrived: "Boots with Chemivic synthetic rubber vinyl soling compound outlast old boots by 300 percent in Vietnam."[8]

If some equipment was not well matched to Vietnam's climate and terrain, other standard gear was equally ill-suited to the small-unit counterinsurgency style of warfare. Soldiers throughout the Vietnam era discarded gear ranging from the older bazooka-type antitank weapons to telephone switch-boards and shelter halves, and they passed on the wisdom of their actions to those who followed.

Alterations to existing equipment began almost as soon as the first troops arrived in country. Uniforms, T-shirts, underwear, and towels were dyed green when the 1st Cavalry Division departed Fort Benning.[9] Canteen covers became ammunition or grenade pouches by tearing out their lining. Extra socks were stuffed full of C-ration cans and tied to the belt, or tied together and worn over the pack or around the neck. There were several types of army butt packs early in the war, and everyone wanted the ones with the rubberized sleeve designed for storing ponchos because the sleeve could be overloaded. Later, in 1967, the army's Quartermaster Corps began issuing soldiers the new ALICE pack, a large nylon rucksack with an external aluminum frame far superior to earlier army equipment. Marine haversacks never did improve and never got good reviews from their users. Johnnie Clark thought that the Marine Corps's packs weren't "worth crap," an opinion that fostered a tendency in marines to exchange their packs for those used by the NVA, which were bigger and made of softer canvas.[10] "The Marine Corps haversack is too small and unnecessarily uncomfortable to carry," Tom Magedanz explained. "The NVA have bigger packs with wider straps that don't cut into your shoulders and three separate pouches on the outside so you can organize your stuff and know where it's at. One good thing about killing a gook was that you could get his pack; it worked a lot better."[11]

Perhaps of equal importance was the fact that possession of such a pack was a status symbol implying that the new owner had done serious time in the bush.

Squeamish soldiers found the use of materiel liberated from the dead somewhat ghoulish, but most accepted the utility of the practice. NVA jungle hammocks, belts, and weapons—even their small rations of canned mackerel in tomato sauce—were seldom ignored when bodies were searched. As American uniforms came apart during operations in the jungle, it was not unheard of for GIs to wear

North Vietnamese fatigue pants, especially in the early days before American fatigue uniforms made of rip-stop material got to units in the field. When new equipment *was* issued, it seemed that those who got it first were the ones who needed it least. Typically, the first set of jungle fatigues and the first jungle boots that Gerry Barker saw in Vietnam were on a supply sergeant. "He came out in the field and there he was in all this jungle stuff," Barker recalled, "and we were out there with clothes hanging off our asses in rags and tatters and our boots held together with communications wire."

If there was any area of supply that fell drastically behind demand throughout the Vietnam War it was footwear and clothing. Serviceable jungle boots were always scarce. According to Jon Neely, "The guys came down with an awful lot of jungle rot and stuff on their feet and you did your best to keep your feet dry. But it just seemed like every time you got back to the base camp and tried to get a new set of jungle boots, you couldn't get them."

Tom Magedanz was keenly aware of the same shortage in his marine outfit. The men's boots were always "all scuffed up and some guys had their toes sticking out of their boots." Magedanz admitted, however, that the marines were "kind of proud of it, too, because we always said the army had it easier than us." Jon Neely would have argued otherwise.

Fatigue uniforms were equally deplorable; the constant dampness rotted the seams and weakened the threads and the jungle constantly clutched and tore at the clothing, making short work of the hardiest material. Vince Olson's recollections were that jungle fatigues would be "pretty near ripped clean off you." When his marine unit received clean clothes after two or three weeks they were always used, "but they weren't ripped or anything. They'd last awhile until you got them torn again, but it didn't matter if you tore them or not—you didn't get a new set until you went back to the rear." Most fatigues ripped around pockets or through the crotch, the latter causing a unique problem. Because most soldiers in the bush did not wear underwear, in an effort to prevent "crotch rot," the result of torn trousers and the GIs' aversion to underwear left many a soldier, as Tom Magedanz succinctly put it, "with their asses hanging out."

Helicopter pilot David Hansen often saw American troops who had been in the bush for weeks, indeed, even months at a time. He described one such group that he observed during a resupply mission:

> I can remember resupplying an outfit in pretty jagged country, and it was cold that day. We hovered down in the triple-canopy jungle and weaved our way down in there to get to them. They were coming down the side of a hill into a ravine where the stream was. Now, we were kicking C rats out to them in cases and I was watching these guys as we were hovering there and kicking stuff out. Their jungle fatigues—some didn't have any legs on them. They were torn off. Shirtsleeves were torn off, and I mean it was about forty-seven degrees and was raining. I would have had pneumonia for a year and those guys were out there doing that. I had a lot of respect for them just putting up with that kind of crap.[12]

Besides boots and clothing, some other pieces of American equipment remained strangely scarce in Vietnam. Bandoliers for ammunition were particularly rare in the early days. Gerry Barker remembers soldiers coming to blows over them. Later in the war the problem was solved when new M16 ammunition came prepackaged in cloth bandoliers, with enough ammunition for seven magazines in each. Canteens also seemed to always be at a premium. In general, equipment that was useful always seemed to be scarce, and new equipment always seemed to appear in the rear areas first. Only slowly did things like the more practical two-quart water bladders make their way to the field.

Important items such as canteens were passed on to friends when the old-timers rotated home or when a man was medically evacuated. John Merrell ended up with six of them before he finally had enough. "They gave us the one-quart type to begin with, but the prize was the two-quart," he said. "When people went back to the rear, I suppose, they stopped in and begged one off the supply sergeant. Eventually they got to us. Nobody ever came out and said, Here—everybody can have one."

Soldiers balanced what they felt they needed to carry with what they could get. Point men such as Jerry Johnson usually needed very little. Johnson carried a Claymore bag with twenty magazines of M16 ammunition and wore web gear, a harness affair consisting of wide suspenders attached to a pistol belt. He swapped his two one-quart canteens for the larger water bladders. Breaking trail was arduous work and water was something he needed. At the back of his web gear was a Claymore antipersonnel mine, and around his waist he tied a poncho liner for sleeping. His towel went around his neck, and, at night, it folded over the magazine bag to make a pillow. Food and his M16 completed his combat load.

Tom Schultz, a rifleman with the 1st Cavalry Division, described his load as

> a pair of boots, two pairs of socks—one on your feet and one in your pack—fatigues on your back, steel pot, and an ammunition belt that you put water jugs on. Then, we had the regular canteens and two-quart blivets to carry extra water. I carried a rucksack with C-rations. Poncho and poncho liner. One of those little fold-down spades. Grenades . . . You might have three to five pounds of C-4 (plastic explosive) in your pack. A little bag of your personal stuff like pencils and paper in a plastic bag, mosquito repellent, oil for the gun, bullets. . . . We never carried gas masks or machetes, and we traveled relatively light.

Units such as Jerry Johnson's 2d Battalion, 28th Infantry in the 1st Infantry Division, often operated on short patrols out of remote firebases that lasted several days and required less equipment. Other maneuvering units such as Tom Schultz's might operate anywhere from a week to ninety days in the bush without returning to a rear area. Those units were resupplied in the field every three or four days by helicopter—if the resupply birds could get through.

Soldiers divided up and carried unit equipment such as mortar shells, machine-gun ammunition, Claymore mines, and starlight scopes. They also humped a variety of personal gear reflecting the individuality of the man who carried it. Metal ammo boxes were desirable for personal possessions. The boxes were heavy, but they were waterproof and, when placed at the bottom of a pack, they made a flat surface that allowed the pack to stand by itself. Paul Gerrits carried a Kodak Instamatic camera in his box, along with writing paper, a Zippo lighter, and a hunting knife. He also carried a .38-caliber revolver he bought from a helicopter pilot. Cameras such as Gerrits's were common with new guys, but few veterans humped them. They had already seen enough to remember, and the film often deteriorated in the dampness. Larry Gates carried a comb and some French's mustard. Tom Schultz remembered people in his unit who carried pictures of real food, such as steak. Leonard Dutcher carried Hoppes #9 gun-cleaning solvent and novelty postcards of giant ears of corn the size of tree trunks being cut on a portable sawmill. The caption read, "Grown by Len Dutcher of Melrose, Wisconsin." He gave the postcards to friends or mailed them home.

Jeff Yushta carried a wallet with nothing in it. He also carried James Michener novels in Zip-Loc bags. Steve Fredrick read the poems of Robert Service while resting along the trail or waiting for a helicopter. Everyone carried letters if they received any, or hid their disappointment if they didn't.

Towels were another indispensable piece of personal field gear. Worn around the neck, towels were handy for wiping away sweat even though they were always sopping wet. Layne Anderson wore two towels, one around his neck and one around his machine gun to pad the weapon against his shoulder. Dwight Reiland positioned the tails of his towel to let the pack straps ride on them, preventing the straps from cutting into the forward part of his shoulder.

The burden of the radiomen (RTOs), however, was probably worst of all. In addition to their personal gear and weapons, they shouldered the radio and its accompanying paraphernalia. Dan Krehbiel cringed at the memory.

> The radio was twenty-one pounds with the battery in place, which you had to have. It was twenty-four

pounds for the radio and the handset. That usually went on a solid backpack that we wore. Then, I had to have a bedroll. I only carried nine magazines of ammunition. I had to carry that and the rifle. Also, as an RTO, you had to carry smoke grenades for identification and location, to bring in helicopters and things like that. So you had to take out eight or nine or a dozen smoke grenades depending on how long the operation was. You had to have star clusters and flares at night. These were in long tubes. You took the top off, put it on the other end, and it acted as a little detonator. You popped it on the ground on its butt and it fired off a parachute flare or a star cluster for night illumination. I usually went out with about ten of those things. So all that weight added in, too.

I had it all put in one backpack and it seemed like a tremendous amount of weight to carry on your upper back, which is where it all tied up tight. And everybody used to say, "Krehbiel! How can you do that? You're going to break your back." They had all their weight distributed. And then I would lean up against a low tree limb or a rock or something, and I would let that rock take the full weight of all my gear and I could sit there and be so comfortable. I didn't have to unload six million things to relax.

Krehbiel remembered men in his unit carrying anywhere from fourteen to twenty-one magazines for their M16s. Some went out with up to forty magazines strapped on them.

Terry Shepardson was one of those who took as much ammunition as he could carry. "They always said ten magazines for your M16," he said. "Well, I always took twenty. There was no way I was going to get caught without ammunition. I paid the consequences because I grunted and was tired every day from marching, but I never ran out of ammo. Matter of fact, I'd always have a few rounds to spare. There was no way I was going to go hand-to-hand with nobody. No way! I wanted plenty of rounds with me. I had a fear: some gook running at me with a three-foot blade, sticking me in the guts because I didn't have any ammo. I didn't want that."

Where equipment was carried was also a matter of choice and expediency. In 1965 and 1966, when the old senior NCOs were still in the field, equipment was carried by the book. While Gerry Barker was with the 1st Cavalry Division, they never carried machine-gun ammo slung over the body like Pancho Villa.

> That was just always a no-no. I know that I have seen lots of pictures in *Life* magazine of that sort of thing being done all over Vietnam but it was not one of those things we did. It screws up the ammo. And can you figure out how to camouflage a guy with brass dangling all over his body? It is a noisemaker, a dead give-away.
> We carried it inside the little green bag that it came in, or in the box. Not many ammo boxes ever went out. Usually it was taken out in the hundred-round containers and guys stuffed them in their ruck-sacks, or the machine gunners themselves slung it over their bodies, but it was never out in belts. Later on I saw a lot of sloppiness, but at that time in the war we were good. We made lots of other errors, but the care of the gear was pretty good.

Grenades were dangerous pieces of equipment often worn on the outside of a soldier's gear. Marine Jeff Yushta found them hard to attach to his equipment and harder still to put where "they wouldn't get in your way when you were doing something." Most men stored grenades in a pocket or a Claymore bag. Of all the equipment he carried, Michael Jackson was most afraid of grenades "because we carried them on our front pack straps so we could get to them quickly if we needed them. But going through jungle and stuff, if a twig released the safety pin, that was it! We crimped the pins over but I was always anxious about that."

Respect for hand grenades was worth cultivating. Vernon Janick saw a fellow soldier die in the Central Highlands when the pin on a grenade attached to the man's gear somehow got pulled and the grenade exploded. Leonard Dutcher experienced a similar but more disastrous incident at his unit's base camp near Chu Lai. During his first month in Vietnam he wrote:

> We had another bad accident in our company. It happened in the chow line the other night here at base camp. Everyone was in the line when somebody accidentally pulled the pin on a grenade and it went off. The thing wounded twenty-six men and killed two. I was standing about twenty feet from it so I'm real lucky. I guess the Lord was on my side this time.[13]

One of the most adaptable and serviceable pieces of equipment was the GI steel helmet and liner. Designed for head protection, it also served at various times as a washbasin, cooking pot, chair, or "butt armor" when riding in a helicopter. Sergeant Steve Fredrick used his helmet for a stove in a frigid downpour during the monsoon in the Central Highlands. He and a buddy crawled under two ponchos, lit some C-4 plastic explosive, and covered it with a steel helmet. The "stove" worked well.

The helmet's cloth camouflage cover reduced the shine from the helmet at night and blended into the foilage in the daytime. The cloth cover also provided a handy billboard on which a man might profess his religion, his politics, or his longings.

Antimilitary slogans became common later in the war: "Re up?—Throw up" or "F.T.A." (fuck the army). Peace symbols were literally everywhere. Home states and the names of girlfriends or wives were prevalent. Some soldiers, such as Jim Stanton, believed that the ace of spades was a bad omen to the Vietnamese, so he and many others decorated their helmet covers with them, or stuck a playing card in the heavy rubber band that secured the cloth cover to the helmet. Men penciled in "God is my Pointman" or expressed the wish that President Johnson himself was serving in that capacity. Photographs of soldiers taken in Vietnam reveal helmets with sentiments such as "Home is where you dig it" or "God Bless Du Pont Chemicals' Defoliant and Napalm." Other soldiers remembered "Just You and Me Lord" or "If You Can Read This You're Too Close." "Don't Shoot, I'm Short!" was another popular slogan. Many men kept track of their days remaining in country with a short-timer's calendar inscribed on the liner of their helmets.

Helmets were handy storage racks for an assortment of items. Cigarets were stored inside the webbing of the liner; so were matches, pictures, letters, anything precious or perishable. The helmet webbing was the only dry, easily accessible place a soldier had. Tucked under the large rubber bands outside the helmet were items a soldier would either need quickly, such as sterile bandages or gun oil, or use routinely, such as insect repellent or a plastic C-ration spoon. Stephen Fredrick even saw a man carry blasting caps under his helmet band. Helmets revealed a lot about their owners.

Sometimes soldiers wore helmets and sometimes they didn't. Helmets with nearly completed calendars seemed to be worn all the time. They were heavy and, when exposed to the tropical sun, made one's head feel as though it was inside a Dutch oven. But helmets offered protection to their owners, so the decision to wear one was not taken lightly.

"Boonie hats" or "bush covers," on the other hand, were made of cloth and were much more comfortable. But a boonie hat wouldn't stop a round from an AK-47, whereas one might glance off a helmet.

Paul Gerrits hated wearing helmets. His entire company did. But Gerrits's new company commander required their use. On the unit's first assault after the new captain took over, the men rebelled and "threw the sons of bitches out of the helicopters when we were flying in," said Gerrits. "He made us wait right there on the LZ until he flew out another helicopter full of steel pots. The next time anybody got caught without [a helmet], it was an Article 15 right there on the spot. [We] hated his ass right away, but come to find out that when the shit hit the fan, he was the best [commander] to have around."

Men donned their equipment carefully, layering it over their bodies. First the web gear was strapped on, then bandoliers or belts of ammunition were slung over the shoulder, followed by Claymore bags. Next the pack was strapped on so that one could drop it quickly in an emergency. Putting on the helmet or bush hat was the last act in preparation for a "hump." After a soldier struggled into his pack, usually a two-man job, the head gear was set atop the heap of flesh, blood, and army or marine issue, and the weight was shifted into as comfortable a position as possible, with a visceral grunt from the heavily laden infantryman. Many soldiers believed that the little grunt was the origin of their nickname, a 1960s euphemism eloquently attesting to their status and exhaustive workload. That vocalized grunt was a point of pride, earthy and indicative of the life the soldiers lived. Grunting the load onto their backs also signified a readiness or acquiescence to spend another day as an infantry soldier. Tom Magedanz wasn't sure exactly how much his rucksack weighed, but, he said, "It was heavy enough so that in order to put on your pack, you'd have to pick it up first, get the strap in your elbow and then kind of jerk it and bounce it up so you could get the one strap on your shoulder. Then you'd take the other strap and do the same thing."

Equally as important as arranging equipment and readying weapons for action was the act of mental preparation. It was a process that Rick Atkinson described as "somewhat akin to the one followed by a professional athlete putting on his game face in the locker room." According to Atkinson, "Emotions ranging from arrogance to raw fear were stowed as carefully as the ammo clips in the rucksack, ready for deployment as needed; . . . everything not directly relative to the prospective fight sloughed away in a little heap of superfluities."[14]

Tim O'Brien noted that soldiers carried, among other things, "the mental baggage of men who might die," and the most cumbersome of those emotional burdens was "the common burden of cowardice barely restrained, the instinct to run or freeze or hide." O'Brien added that it was a burden that could "never be put down."[15]

So the men's emotions, reputations, fears, and aspirations all went into the packs that they grunted up into place, and the column formed up behind the point man.

Military operations, even patrolling patterns, were given a variety of code names alternating between the grandiose and the euphemistic, but to the troops, it was all humping. A hump could be good if the day was cool, the duration brief, or the day netted some enemy kills. Humps could be bad if they were long, hot, or costly in American casualties. In Vietnam, a patrol that covered a few thousand meters could mean progress measured by the swing of a machete and a day spent leaning back against the elephant grass or passing the mortars and machine guns from hand to hand up slopes on which a soldier could barely crawl. If there was a purpose in these movements—these humps—few soldiers ever knew it, for few of them ever had their missions explained.

Humps were usually easiest at the start of the day. The sun had not reached its zenith, and the initial movement was usually downhill, moving off the previous night's NDP (night defensive position, or "pos" in Marine Corps terminology). If a resupply helicopter had come in, packs would be heavier than normal, but morale would be correspondingly higher. Food and mail often came in with the resupply birds and that meant letters and edible goodies from home.

Troops left the previous night's position and patrolled according to directives from above. They searched thousand-meter grid squares that appeared on the maps carried by leaders and artillery observers. In the south, the squares were filled with symbols indicating rice paddies or jungles. Farther north, the map's grid squares were crammed with squiggly brown contour lines—so close together that they could hardly be resolved by the naked eye—depicting rugged, jungle-covered mountains. The word "destroyed" appeared in parentheses near scores of villages.

Columns of troops undulated along their routes of march like great human Slinkies, stretching as they moved up the steep hillsides or compressing together as the men crossed streams and rivers. After the sweep of an area was completed, the maneuvering unit would retire to another hilltop toward evening and, in its own fashion, set up a new NDP.

Dwight Reiland remembered the moves as sheer drudgery. "You got up and got organized and started off to patrol your sector of the area," he explained. "You walked an hour and sweated, took your breaks. Maybe break for lunch and send out a couple of X-ray [local] patrols in different directions to see if they would find any indication of enemy activity. They would come back and off you went. Lots of days that is all that happened."

Each day the process repeated itself from one NDP to the next. The pack, the climate, and the terrain made it a challenging physical effort.

"After a while," said Tom Magedanz, "the circulation in your shoulders would be cut off from the [pull of the] straps. You had to be careful, too. You had to be alert for the enemy. We'd move frequently to a new spot so that we wouldn't get pinpointed. Every half hour or so on those humps they'd say 'take five,' and you'd sit down and take a break and have a cigaret, then get up and move out again."

Steve Fredrick's first letter from the bush explained, "We are so busy it's amazing. All we do is walk thru the rice paddies and jungles all day and half the night."[16]

There were numerous rest stops, but their value seemed minimal to Gerry Barker. "You took a lot of breaks, but you never got to really rest," he recalled. "You'd stop moving and everybody would just squat. Well, you get a guy with ninety pounds on his back squatting up and down every quarter mile; that takes a hell of a lot out of him."

After each break, the movement would continue. Tom Schultz vividly recalled the drills: "One platoon would go out on a flanking search while the other platoons rested. Then, [that platoon] would come back and [the whole group] started moving again. Normally a big day of moving would take up maybe at the very most fifteen klicks [kilometers]. That was a big day because you were moving through a lot of garbage—undercover, triple canopy—a lot of places for enemy to be. You didn't just go walking down the trail, you did a lot of sensory stuff."

Gerry Barker, who served in the same division two years before Schultz, continued the story, drawing on similar memories:

> And then . . . oops "Looks like a good ambush sit."
> We flank some guys around the back side of the ambush site, breaking through brush with ninety pounds on their backs. They are on incredibly steep hillsides. That is II Corps area. That is exactly the way it was

every place we went. Pass [up] the machine guns, pass that damn [90]-mm recoilless rifle] up the hill, pass it down the hill.

Come to a stream . . . "Damn! Stream!"

"How deep is it?"

"I don't know, throw someone up front. If he thinks it's too deep we'll throw a rope across."

When we crossed a stream we fanned out on both sides and filled all the canteens. The medic would tell us it was contaminated.

"Don't drink the shit."

"You got a solution for it? Someplace else we're going to get some water from, kid?"

"Oh, well, Halazone tablets—iodine tablets."

"Put two in it. Medic says it doesn't look good." Then we were off and running again.

The first hump for each soldier was a sobering experience. Soldiers came to realize how terrific the physical exertion really was. Like most new people, Jerry Johnson was convinced that he would never be able to endure a year of what he had undergone that first day in the bush. But misery was a relative thing, and the first hump was usually the worst. John Merrell found that little sympathy was expended on new people. He also discovered that the column didn't wait for them.

"I was going up the side of a mountain that I had to climb hand over hand, and they were leaving me behind," recalled Merrell. "I was about three-quarters of the way up and I said, 'Bullshit, wait a minute.' I thought I was in good shape but I found out how out of shape I really was. And I never fell behind again because they weren't stopping."

Even the hardiest veterans found humping synonymous with agony. The region of the country a soldier operated in— the rugged terrain of the Central Highlands, the swamps of the Delta, the jungle, rice paddies, coastal strip, or near the DMZ—didn't seem to matter. Each possessed some quality that made patrolling there a tedious experience. Vernon Janick saw several areas of Vietnam, but he hated the rice paddies the most. "You were wet all the time and walking through them you'd sink in with all your gear," said Janick with more than a trace of exasperation. "Sometimes you would get in them up to your waist and the mud below was so thick you would just sink in and try to waddle through it. There was no place to fall. Some [rice paddies] were shallower than others. The only place you had for cover was right along the dikes. They were like little walkways. And the way we were trained, you never walked on trails or anywhere anybody else walked. . . . If you ever got hit, well, you just had to run for the closest dike. If you could get there fast enough, fine—otherwise, you just had to get down where you were."

Jon Neely operated in jungle and rice paddies throughout the south, but for him the swamps in the Delta were probably the worst.

> Some of our toughest going was when they would put us on boats and take us down the Saigon River to the Plain of Reeds. It was all marsh and swamp and the Viet Cong would set up. They were so lightweight, and they didn't carry very much equipment, so they could maneuver themselves around in that swamp pretty easily, whereas the average GI, after he got done packing all his food and ammunition and guns and helmet and everything else, he was pushing two hundred to two hundred and twenty-five pounds. He was not going to move around too quick. We did a lot of sinking in the mud.

Patrolling in the six- to twelve-foot-high elephant grass that covered the open areas in the jungle was also miserable. Elephant grass was unimaginably dense, and its sharp edges left a man's arms and hands crisscrossed with cuts. Jerry Johnson likened breaking trail in elephant grass to "walking up a mattress on a wall." It took everything out of a soldier. And elephant grass was excellent cover for an ambush. Johnson remembered that "You didn't know what was on the other side. You couldn't see over it. Couldn't see around it. You just pushed through the stuff." Men often took turns breaking trail in elephant grass. It was stifling hot exertion, for no air moved deep in the elephant grass. Pushing against the grass opened a passage and the hot air trapped near the ground would escape upward, striking at the men like the open door of a blast furnace. Ed Hoban recalled going on operations where he simply fell backward into the elephant grass time and time again to break trail through it.

The grassy swamps, paddies, and bamboo thickets also played host to leeches. Soldiers hated the repugnant creatures. Normally associated with streams and stagnant water, leeches were also prevalent in the tall grasses and stands of bamboo existing in many areas of the country. The creatures were totally unavoidable, and usually attached themselves as the men brushed against the foliage. Soldiers retained vivid memories of leeches crawling toward them in the mud or stretching out from a leaf. They had bodies the size of a piece of straw from a broom, or a pencil lead. At every opportunity soldiers operating in leech-infested areas would strip down to search themselves and each other.

Dwight Reiland's attitude toward leeches is indicative of the feelings most soldiers harbored for the parasites:

I think if you would ask what is the most hated thing about Vietnam it would have to be leeches. You'd get up and they would maybe be on your chest or your armpit or in your crotch or whatever. [They were] an insidious, evil, dirty kind of trespass on you. You didn't have to get in water to get into these things, particularly in the boggy, swampy, elephant grass type stuff. That was where you got them the worst, really. We had to push across the low land between a couple of ridges the first time I ever got a leech on me. It was open and we couldn't stop. We just hauled ass for half a mile or so to get across and make the cover of the jungle on the other side. As we were going across all the weeds and everything, our boots came untucked from our pants. Leeches were forever getting in your pants leg, but at least they couldn't proceed up beyond that. Everybody wore leech straps below the knee—a band around the calf. I saw leeches on the weeds and stuff and I knew that I was getting them on me. When we got to the other side and got into the jungle where we took a break, I pulled up my pants legs and I had like fifteen or seventeen leeches on my calves from the knee down. It's a hideous sight to pull your pants up and see them hanging on there like cocoons or something. It was sickening. Once they were engorged with blood, Jeez—they got like a half of a big fat cigar or something. I just hated them.

Willie Williams never saw leeches before his first operation in a swamp. He came out "almost covered with them." Steve Fredrick recalled waking up once with five leeches on his neck and head. To make matters worse, a soldier seldom felt a leech until it was almost filled with its victim's blood and ready to drop off.

Fortunately, a soldier's natural squeamishness prompted numerous "leech checks," and there was a wide assortment of proven methods for removing leeches. Michael Jackson burned them off with a match or a cigaret, a procedure done so frequently that it prompted machine-gunner Robert Sanders to remark, "I was sharing more cigarets with the leeches than I was smoking myself."[17] Burning was not the only method of leech removal. Army-issue insect repellent had a solvent that would dissolve the leeches' soft bodies. After a liberal dose of the bug juice, leeches would fall off and begin to decompose into soft blobs. If a soldier was particularly vindictive or desperate for amusement, he might, as Stephen Fredrick sometimes did, catch the detached leech, put it in an empty C-ration can, throw in a match and "just have a good time watching him burn." What soldiers did *not* want to do was simply grab the leech and pull it off. Doing so left a nasty round hole that bled profusely. Purists used the burning technique. They argued that using repellent to remove the creatures left angry-looking sores. Some soldiers removed leeches by applying salt from their C-rations, whereas others pushed a stick or match into the end of the leeches, turning them inside out. Ingenuity has always been a byword of soldiering.

Leeches had a particular affinity for the more personal areas of the body. Charles Gadd remembered a soldier in his unit who had one removed from the end of his penis. Medic Paul Gerrits had a leech attach itself to his testicles through a tear in the crotch of his pants while he was squatting down to treat another soldier for a snake bite. Historian Bernard Fall spoke with a young marine artillery officer who had a man evacuated while on patrol after a leech crawled through the man's penis into his bladder. Richard MacLeod, a rifleman with the 1st Squadron, 9th Cavalry, also mentioned a medevac for a man with a leech inside his penis. MacLeod claimed that although it might sound "highly unusual, it really wasn't." His unit became rather paranoid about leeches after a second man was denied a medevac for the same reason. The man began bleeding internally after several days and was finally flown out. After that, wrote MacLeod, some of the men began to put tape over the end of their penises.[18]

Like most things in Vietnam, leeches required some mental adaptation and once again demonstrated that it often was the "little things" that made life more miserable than it needed to be.

By midday, heat became the enemy, sapping the strength from each soldier as quickly and completely as it did the energy from the batteries in a field radio. Phil Yaeger noted that near the DMZ the heat was unbearable in the summer dry season:

> The rainy season started in late September and ran through Christmastime. Then it stayed dry for a while. Then you got another brief monsoon from February up until May. Then another dry stretch from May until sometime in September. That was the worst hot stretch. Out in the bush, loaded down with a flak jacket and seventy or eighty pounds of gear, hacking your way through triple canopy, the heat was just all around you. Under that canopy the air didn't move. It was just like being in a bake oven only humid. And even when you got acclimated to it there were times when you felt you just couldn't take another step.

Tom Magedanz captured the essence of patrolling during those blistering hot humps in the recollections he jotted down shortly after he returned home:

It was so hot we could wring out our T-shirts every five minutes or so. The sweat just ran and heat enveloped every part of our bodies. There were usually some small clouds in the sky and once in a while one would cover the sun for a few seconds and we could immediately feel the difference; it felt great. Any kind of breeze felt really good, too. We used to see clouds that might be moving toward the sun and we used to cheer them on. Using all the body English we could muster, we'd say, "Come on cloud. Get your dog ass under the sun. What do you think you're up there for anyway?" Or we'd say, "Buddha, no balls to rain. Buddha, not a hair on your gook ass, or else you'd make it rain and cool us off."[19]

New guys seemed to suffer most. They were usually the ones who dropped out with heat exhaustion. With the foresight gained from experience, old-timers such as Gerry Barker told squad leaders and assistant squad leaders and fire team leaders " 'to keep an eye on your kids. If you see a heat exhaustion case warn us. Get him down, get him cooled off, get water in him.' That was all it took—salt and water to make it go away. So that was the reaction. You tried to see it happening. You watched the complexion in your guys. But they were so damn dirty. And half of them were black. You couldn't always tell. We didn't evacuate guys for heat exhaustion. We'd stop and revive them, take some of the load off them, and get them back on their feet."

Procedures in Phil Yaeger's marine company were similar. "New people especially had to watch it," recalled Yaeger. "We'd usually medevac a guy if it was bad enough. You sat them down and pulled their helmets off and soaked them down good. If they were perspiring, generally you didn't worry too much about it. When they stopped sweating, a good squad leader would get on the hook [radio] or get the corpsman and let his platoon commander know."

In the north, where the marines operated, casualties from heat exhaustion or heat stroke took a heavy toll. Jeff Yushta remembered an operation on Go Noi Island in which his unit had a 20 percent medevac rate for heat stroke and heat prostration.

"Almost always it was new guys," said Yushta. "They hadn't pared down to a weight that would allow them to operate effectively. They hadn't learned how to ration water. I weighed about a hundred and forty-five pounds my whole life. I came back from there at a hundred twenty-eight. Seventeen pounds for me was a lot of weight to lose. There just wasn't a whole lot left. And losing that weight changed my whole body system. There was very little need to defecate because there was nothing getting through to my bowels. I didn't have to urinate often either because I was losing body fluid so fast."

When journalist Charles Anderson accompanied a group from the 3d Marine Regiment on patrol in 1969, out of the rifle company's 140 members, the group experienced 65 heat casualties, 23 of which were medevac'd in a period of three days.

One way to cope was to lighten the load each man carried. "The act of discarding part of what they had to carry," wrote Anderson, "sustained and lifted their now-initiated and hardened spirits. Getting rid of something made them feel better, made tomorrow more bearable." During the operation, Anderson saw soldiers tear apart their gear looking for things to throw away. He even saw them take razor blades to their flak jackets so they could remove some of the plate. This practice was not unique to that particular operation or to that unit. Jack Estes's squad leader in the 9th Marines cut the plates out of his flak jacket also, preferring the improved mobility and lighter weight to the questionable protection the armor offered. He suggested that Estes do the same thing.[20]

If the practice of cannibalizing flak jackets seemed endemic in the marines, it was because in many marine outfits the men were ordered to wear them. A marine's only choice in the matter was often whether he zipped up the jacket or not. Few did. Flak jackets weighed 6.7 pounds and were very hot to wear. Few army personnel wore them because they were not required to. William Harken's squad in the 2d Battalion, 27th Infantry of the 25th Infantry Division, carried only one flak jacket—for whoever walked point.

John Merrell was issued a flak jacket in the 4th Infantry Division, but he said that after he left the division headquarters and went to his battalion, he dropped it off because he didn't need it. "I wore a flak jacket many times over there but it was never mine. A lot of times we would come in out of the field on a three-day stand-down and the engineers would have them there. They would leave them in the bunkers."

Whether indicative of the random and infrequent nature of contact or the lack of faith that troops placed in the jackets, a 1969 analysis indicated that only 5 percent of army personnel wore them.[21]

After one o'clock, the day entered its hottest phase. Most units stopped for a siesta if possible, or at least slowed their movements. But the situation often required units to move during the heat of the afternoon, and the pace and duration of this continued movement depended completely on the availability of water. By afternoon, personal water supplies began to be exhausted. Charles Anderson observed marines wiping their foreheads and licking the sweat from their fingers. "The urea, dirty salt, and carbon dioxide they took in produced dizziness and nausea in empty stomachs." As Anderson observed, there was "little logic left by day's end."[22]

When water supplies were scant, a man's first drink in the morning had to be meted out in relation to the anticipated needs of the day. It was difficult to do because the first swallow every morning was the best drink of the day, according to Tom Magedanz. "In the morning the canteens would be covered with dew and the water inside would be really cool," said Magedanz. "We'd guzzle that fantastic water in the morning and then be pissed off at ourselves later in the day for being out of water, but it was worth it."[23]

In the Central Highlands and along the DMZ, Americans tended to patrol the mountaintops, where there was seldom a supply of water. The streams were always farther down slope in the valleys. Troops carried as many canteens as they reasonably could. However, in many units only two canteens were issued to each man. Paul Boehm's battalion commander believed that two quarts of water per man was adequate for a day. In Boehm's mind, two quarts didn't go very far. Phil Yaeger's standard issue was also two canteens. Individuals in his unit monitored their water consumption very closely, almost by the capful, because resupply could not be counted on. Tom Magedanz was issued three canteens and told that the water they held was supposed to last for two days or more. It obviously didn't. Magedanz remembered soldiers near the DMZ licking the dew from leaves and grass in the morning to supplement their water.[24]

Uncontaminated drinking water was scarce everywhere in Vietnam. When the men found streams or wells, they filled up their canteens, dropped in some iodine tablets to purify the water, shook it up a bit, and took their chances with whatever bugs or bacteria might migrate from their canteens into their stomachs. Phil Yaeger doubted that the iodine killed all the bacteria. He was convinced that it certainly didn't do anything to protect soldiers or marines from dioxin, which might be in the water. The dioxin he referred to came from defoliants such as Agent Orange, which leached out of the soil during the rain and collected in the streams and bomb craters from which the soldiers drank. Bomb craters, Randy Hoelzen later realized, "filled up with water in the rainy season and then evaporated. There had to be all kinds of residue in them," he reasoned, "because most of the trees were defoliated."

Tainted water wasn't a big concern when thirst was acute. Like everyone else, Jeff Yushta recognized the risk but took his chances. "We drank any water we could get our hands on," he said. "We were told not to, but we took our chances. I don't know if the iodine tablets helped or whatever, but you couldn't carry enough water. There was no way you could carry enough water to keep your body supplied in conditions like that. You couldn't have walked. Who wanted to carry a ten-gallon jug on their back?"

Getting sick was one way to secure a respite from humping the bush. Sergeant Fredrick never got sick, although he purposely drank water straight from the village wells. He tried other methods to escape the field as well. "I shouldn't admit this to anybody," he confided, "but I never took a malaria pill the whole time I was there. I wanted to get malaria so I could get the hell out of there. I never took one. That was probably a mistake, but I don't think so because I could have gotten killed there and malaria very seldom kills you if you have medical attention. So it was a pretty good bet."

Untreated water did claim its share of victims, however. Medic Jerry Severson, for instance, got worms. "I was down to a hundred twenty-eight pounds," he recalled. "Sicker than a dog. It was worms, and [drinking contaminated water was] just exactly how I got them. We ran out of water on one of our operations and we finally came on a stream. I filled a canteen and gulped water right out of it. Then I filled it back up, put my pills in there and away we went. But I think my system had been run down, because [I got worms] within a month after I got out of the hospital after I was wounded. So, I . . . went back in the hospital again."

As the day wore on, the sweating and suffering continued. Sweat dripped off noses, flies buzzed, and eyes burned. Towels became saturated. Canteen water got hot. Eyeglasses fogged up from perspiration. And when it seemed that nothing could possibly make matters any worse, humping had a way of producing that extra little misery.

Sweating, tired soldiers were often plagued by flies and other insects. Tom Magedanz detested the swarming flies that feasted on the soldiers' infected scabs and open sores. "If you had something in both hands it would drive you nuts because the flies would be on your arms," Magedanz recalled. "Everybody had jungle rot on their arms. You might have five or six sores on each arm and the flies would land on them. If you were carrying your rifle in one hand and machine-gun ammo or something else in the other, you couldn't brush the stupid flies off. Even when you did have a free hand, you'd brush the flies away and they'd fly up about six inches and land back down on a sore and start chowing down on your jungle rot. You'd move along sweating and your arms were numb; it was physically hard."

Vernon Janick remembered being plagued by "all kinds of weird things crawling around, especially during the monsoon season." But Janick's personal purgatory seemed to be populated by ants:

> Fire ants! Oh Jesus! They were big red ones. They
> usually made a big ball in a tree. I got a real good dose

of those once. I was the third man back. The point man
stirred them up. They'd hang in bushes and we always
had to chop new trails. We could rarely ever go on an
old trail. . . . Well, the first two guys really stirred 'em
up good, and I happened to be the third or fourth
through there. Naturally, they were just wild by then.
And Boy! I tell you. They just get down in you and they
just bite! Jeez. Just like somebody took a hundred cigarets and put them on you—just burn and sting. We had
a lot of that.

Then we had these other ones that were on the
ground. They were kind of weird ones, too. Big black
trails of them like a thick black tape. They made a
funny little noise when they crawled. They would burn
you when you touched them. Sometimes we would
walk till dark and then we would have to set up at night
and you would go to sit down and put your hand or skin
on them and boy, it just burnt!

Jerry Johnson was also intimately acquainted with red
ants. He acknowledged spending "many a time in the buff
stripping them off since I was usually the point man. . . .
When you went under a nest and brushed it, they would come
down and just eat you alive. They would stand right up on end
and you would have to strip completely down and the guys
would come up and spray you with bug dope and try to kill
them."

As each succeeding day and each succeeding patrol
passed, the fatigue and misery etched more deeply into the
faces and attitudes of the soldiers. If those days were devoid
of enemy contact, another problem began to surface that was
every bit as debilitating as physical exhaustion or the lack of
water. Soldiers, for myriad reasons, would relax their powers
of concentration. For many, fatigue was so great that they
moved beyond the point of caring about anything. It was a
problem that became a real challenge for NCOs such as Don
Putnam to rectify.

It got boring, especially when there was no contact. As a platoon sergeant I guess the hardest thing for me was to try and keep everybody alert. When there is no contact for a couple days or a week at a time you get real lax. Instead of people staying spread out they start to "cluster fuck"—grouping up. You tell them to spread out and you try to keep them aware. It becomes a hard job at times. All of a sudden you are shooting the breeze with your buddy and he should be fifteen— twenty feet in front of you. You kind of edge closer because you want to shoot the breeze a little bit, pass the time. If you are alert, you can walk for five or six or seven klicks and hardly say anything to anybody. You can do hand signals and all this other crap and you don't say anything. After a while, a person wants to talk to someone a little bit. They got things they want to say, to pass the time of day. And they become lax. That was the biggest problem I had when there was no enemy activity.

Soldiers were generally tense, sometimes afraid, and usually weary. It just happened that periods of inactivity or fatigue made it easier for the mind to lapse and vigilance dropped. It was sometimes called half-stepping. Others referred to carelessness as "diddy bopping." Soldiers were well aware of the truth in the saying, "A half-step may be your last step." When nearing the point of exhaustion, the men seemed to enter a state of semi-hypnosis and fixed their eyes on the man ahead.

Gerry Barker found that condition difficult to prevent and equally hard to remedy. "You had to keep your eye on the guy ahead of you and the guy behind you," said Barker. "You had to watch the guys watching their sector. You'd scoot up four people and wop a guy up side the head and say, 'You got something you are supposed to be watching, young man? It isn't his heels is it?' You were constantly watching your kids and you couldn't rest."

Marine Johnnie Clark said that men's minds sometimes wandered after they had humped a few kilometers:

We called it "World dreaming." Sometimes it was on air-conditioning or driving a car again. Sometimes it was strawberry shortcake and ice cream. My fantasies usually had long legs; chocolate ice cream was always optional. Fantasies had to be tempered with caution. It was wise to always be aware of where your foot was about to land or of the dark spot in the tree fifty meters ahead.[25]

Minds wandering in search of relief often focused on revenge. The enemy was responsible, and the enemy became the personification of all pain and fatigue. The enemy was something tangible. Enemy soldiers were visualized, given a face, a name, and an AK-47. Some soldiers even created their villains and imagined making them suffer. They shifted their mental fantasies of revenge to include the enemy's wives and friends—even their homes.

Soldiers tried to guess their day's final objective. Humping was easier when a soldier knew where he would end up. Knowing allowed soldiers to gauge distance against their endurance, and it provided a tired man with something to focus on and stagger toward. Columns got deathly silent in these periods of exhaustion. Minds began to conjure ways of getting out of the field: self-inflicted wounds, stumbling down a bank, inducing heat stroke. But seeing other men carrying on usually drove away such thoughts. Pride could carry men long after their muscles and limbs no longer could. "Half of it was you didn't want to let the others down," explained medic Paul Gerrits. "Nobody wanted to be known as a quitter. So you would go maybe five or six hundred meters and they would set you down to rest. You would just literally drop in place. Sometimes once you sat down it was a bitch getting back up again. But you would get up and go for another five or six hundred meters."

One of the worst things a soldier could do in the eyes of his fellow infantrymen was quit on a hump. Quitting separated soldiers from the undependables, and in the field there was nothing more loathsome than a GI who couldn't hack it.

Most days there was nothing to show for the effort; no enemy to count nor geography to claim. And most days there were no losses either. But with varying frequency, little vignettes would play themselves out in the heat of the day, without purpose, meaning nothing, occurring randomly. Fate would stretch out its fingers amidst the trancelike exhaustion, and someone would be touched. Paul Meringolo saw it happen:

> We'd been going all morning and all afternoon and probably covered seven or eight miles. Then, all of a sudden, one of the men in the company stepped on a mine. He was carrying a LAW. A LAW is a modern version of a bazooka. This particular fellow had been carrying this LAW sort of strapped over his shoulder. When he stepped on the mine, the mine engaged the LAW and the rocket fired and blew off part of his head. He was killed, obviously.
>
> There you are all day sort of going along. You are getting tired, exhausted from the heat, exhausted from moving along checking, wondering if you are going to run into something. By the middle of the afternoon this tiredness has taken over your body and all of a sudden something dramatic like that happens and it just sort of unnerves you. We called a medevac chopper and they took away the guy's body. And then we just started off walking again. It was like a surreal existence.

It was maddening, and there was no one against whom they could retaliate. Even as the man's body was being taken away and the retreating sound of the helicopter's blades faded in the distance, the space in the column filled in, and only a visual and audible impression of the event remained in the minds of those who were close enough to have experienced it. The incident became part of the unit's collective lore. Men not close to the deceased discussed the sympathetic detonation of the LAW with a polished and casual professional interest. Friends began the process of mentally suppressing the trauma and moving on. Each man knew that it could have been him; each man was glad beyond measure that it wasn't.

One black soldier lamented:

There was a lot of depression going with the constant strain of humping and firefights. I was really down lots of times. Most of the cats were. "Depressed" is an understatement. We were so down half the time we didn't know what we were going to do next, and we didn't care. We lost spirit 'cause we were just out there humping. Our [unit's] motto was "Drive On." No matter what happened, no matter what came down, we just drove on.[26]

All in all, Larry Gates believed, "Everything in Vietnam was a fight—the conditions, the elements, everything."

And there were times when there would be enemy dead in exchange for the effort. At such times, although there was no sense of being one step closer to winning, the feeling of revenge was satisfying.

"I can remember times when we got in a firefight and ended up with a body count of one or two and everybody else got away," said Donald Putnam. "One body! Everybody was elated! They felt like they had done their job, that things had happened like they were supposed to. It was great, something to show for all the effort. And they were just as high as the time we ended up with a [body count of] forty-seven. Something to show for the effort—that was the big thing. And every day was like that."

Perhaps Tom Magedanz expressed it best when he wrote, "Humping was like beating your head against the wall, because it feels so good to stop. . . . You can take off your pack, helmet, flak jacket, and ammunition, and you feel seventy-five pounds lighter. Your T-shirt is soaked with sweat and the breeze blowing on it feels beautiful. I don't think anything in the world feels better."[27]

There were other things, according to Charles Anderson, that made a man's months in Vietnam bearable: "A stream and a drink just ahead, the objective within sight and maybe a klick away, a letter on the way from the girl, R & R, the [other benefits] strung out along the way." Such things helped break up a tour of duty into chunks of weeks and days. If there was resupply it was cause for celebration. Sometimes there were treats on board the choppers: cigarets, pickles, fruit. No matter how trivial those treats might be, they were of infinite importance to the men in the field. A warm soda or candy was a big thing—a luxury—and it gave morale a boost. Such things soothed over the aches and thirst and helped in the final uphill push to the day's final objective. The climb was difficult, but men could sense the end of the trail like a horse smelling hay in the barn. It was also dangerous. Men were tired and less vigilant and the enemy knew the type of location that Americans liked to use for night bivouac. Those places were often booby-trapped. But once the site was checked over and cleared, once packs were shed and rations broken out, suddenly the day wasn't so bad.[28]

Time erodes the highs and lows of any experience, but most soldiers would agree unanimously with Vernon Janick that humping was "mostly being miserable." That people endured it as well as they seemed to was because they were able to maintain a sense of humor, according to Larry Gates. He remembered that during the monsoon, when the rice paddies were flooded, so were the bomb craters and shell holes that were in the paddies to begin with. Walking through them, a soldier might be in knee-deep or waist-deep water and then someone would walk into an old bomb crater and disappear completely. To avoid this happening, said Gates, "the point man would kind of feel for a hole with his leading foot when he set it down, and if he'd find one he'd say, 'Hole, keep right.' My lieutenant got the message wrong one time and the last thing I saw of him was his hand sticking out with his M16 in the air." The lieutenant didn't drown, but the image of that moment no doubt sustained Gates and the rest of the men in his platoon during many a hot and difficult hump.

Paul Gerrits was also quick to acknowledge that there were good times in the bush. "Don't get me wrong," he said. "Even while you were humping, someone was cracking a joke. Someone was telling a story. You would sit down and, say one platoon had to run cloverleafs [patrols], you sat almost all day some days and didn't hump. You would sit down and play cards. There were good times there. I'm not going to say the whole year was bad because if it was I would be in a looney bin somewhere."

By nightfall, the human spirit had rebounded a bit more.

Soldiers completed digging foxholes if the conditions indicated a need for them. The unit had radioed its position to headquarters and given supporting artillery units the grid coordinates for likely enemy avenues of approach in case the unit was attacked. Then men thought of home and the "freedom bird" that would fly them there when their tours ended. They fantasized about how perfect their return home would be. They thought about how many stars there were in the sky, and how beautiful a sunset was in Vietnam. They thought about women. Layne Anderson thought about McDonald's hamburgers and a chocolate shake and fries. Leonard Dutcher thought about a Pontiac G.T.O. The soldiers talked about their counterparts in the North Vietnamese Army, and about Viet Cong marksmanship. They admired the enemy's patience and his ability to make do. They talked shop in the language that accompanies the profession of killing. They spoke in a detached way about how the LAW had detonated and killed their comrade in the same way they might have spoken about a dead water buffalo. They discussed protests at home and how they would readjust to life back in "The World." And, like soldiers everywhere, they complained about "lifers" and "REMFs"—careerists and soldiers serving safely in the rear. They complained about the food, and the pay, and so-and-so's rotten feet.

Before dark they each cleaned their rifle and bullets, and broke down magazines and wiped the plate and the metal parts and oiled the spring. They carefully looked at the little 5.56mm cartridges and placed eighteen of them back into each twenty-round magazine so as not to put too much tension on the spring and risk a jam. They used toothbrushes and pipe cleaners and LSA oil and fussed over their rifles like jewelers repairing a Cartier watch. And they set trip flares and put out their Claymore mines, making sure the side labeled "FRONT TOWARD ENEMY" was in that position. They put a fragmentation grenade or two in a handy spot, and splashed on several handfuls of insect repellent. Then the men who had drawn first watch settled in as the others lay their heads on makeshift pillows, curled up in a fetal position, and drew their ponchos or poncho liners around themselves like a mummy. Some of them would sleep for two hours or four or six—until they were awakened by their biological alarm clocks or the men they would replace on watch. But their defense mechanisms, their instincts, never slept.

Each soldier spent a varied number of days in the bush. They would forget most of those days. The days of tragic consequence would be etched forever in their minds, but the overwhelming majority of their days were made up of monotony and fatigue, and the details concerning those days somehow melted away under the tropical sun and shrank in their memories.

CHAPTER 9

Hazards of the Field

January 9, 1968

Dear Mom and Dad,

Boy! It sure [is] getting hard to find time to get any letters written. I have been in the field since the 26th of last month so I am getting pretty grubby now. I will be going on R&R in a few days so I hope to get a break.

My best friend was killed by a booby trap two days ago along with another guy from my platoon. I sure miss him a lot and [I] know his wife will also. I don't know why it is, but it seems like the best guys always get killed first.

Have been getting a lot of mail lately, so much I hardly find time to read it all but I am sure glad to get it. It has been doing a lot of raining here. Hope it lets up soon. Will close for now.

Your Son,
Leonard[1]

For many combat soldiers, Vietnam seemed to be a continuing series of obstacles: natural, cultural, physical, and enemy in origin. The last of these, although hardly the most common, posed the greatest threat to soldiers in the field. There was more to Vietnam than enduring the fetid breath of the jungle and the clutching wait-a-minute vines; more than carnivorous ants and dysentery. Vietnam was an enemy seldom seen but always watchful. And so American soldiers, to varying degrees, found themselves plagued by booby traps, harassed by snipers, pummeled by rocket and mortar fire, and surprised by ambushes. Danger became part of the terrain, and most soldiers saw their personal mission as nothing more than surviving those hazards. In war, hazards are to be expected, and experienced soldiers anticipated them as best they could. There was no front line, no single direction in which one could point toward the enemy. One army did not thrust at the other across a main line of resistance. Rather, the soldiers waded into the countryside and struggled against currents of anticipation and fear, never knowing where danger might lie or even in what direction to face in order to meet it head-on.

Vernon Janick's experiences with the 4th Infantry Division in the Central Highlands during 1966 and 1967 were typical of what combat entailed for many U.S. Infantry soldiers throughout the war:

> We never got hit by anything really big. It was usually just a lot of Viet Cong. And they operated on their own as one or two here or there. We had constant booby traps and snipers. There were times they would pin us down for half a day, all day. You never could find them or see them or nothing. You would get up and move a little ways and *bam-bam-bam*.
>
> And the booby traps—everything was pretty well booby-trapped, so it wasn't real heavy action; it was an irritating action. One sniper would get you so mad. You would just get tired of being pinned down by that one guy and you would go bananas. You would get to the point where you just wanted to take that guy out.

During 1968–69 with the 198th Light Infantry Brigade, Layne Anderson was involved in only a handful of "real bad firefights." But the Chu Lai area harbored plenty of other dangers. "We got sniped at regularly," recalled Anderson. "I hated mortars worse than anything. We got mortared. Not real frequent, but frequent enough. Whether you were getting sniped at or were in a real firefight, there was always that chance that you might step on a mine or a booby trap, so you were always tense."

If a soldier participated in a dozen sharp firefights, one or two of which were against a large enemy force of battalion size or greater, his was an extraordinary tour of duty. Relatively few soldiers, particularly after mid-1969, were involved in such large battles.[2] Actions such as those that took place at Hamburger Hill or in the Hiep Duc Valley were unusual in their levels of combat intensity.[3]

Even in the period of heightened enemy activity between 1965 and 1969, there were long dry spells devoid of enemy contact. For Gerry Barker, "The reality of war was being bored for three months, getting in a fifteen-second firefight, and then being bored again." Dwight Reiland remembered contact being equally brief during his tour with the 101st Airborne Division in 1971. Combat for Reiland was measured in minutes, unlike the movies he had grown up watching, "where they fight all day and half the night and into the next day."

But throughout the days or weeks of inactivity separating periods of contact, soldiers were never able to lower their guard completely. Bryan Good quickly realized that although most of his days in the field were uneventful, something could happen at any moment. "Even when taking a break sitting on a mountaintop waiting for supplies—playing cards, cleaning your weapon, writing a letter—you still kept looking around," he said. "If you were cleaning your weapon your buddy next to you wasn't. He kept his all together. You were constantly wired. You just couldn't slack off."

The key to defeating the elusive, easily dispersed enemy forces lay in finding them. Reconnaissance units were assigned to that task both from the air and on the ground. Bob Emery's aerorifle platoon, which scouted for the 1st Cavalry Division, would typically "come down to check out a village or a trail or anything out there if someone made contact or if the scouts [observation helicopters] were fired on." Emery's unit would land under the protective cover of helicopter gunships and look for the enemy. "We'd go in and check out the area for bodies and make contact with the enemy if the enemy was still there. We would go out more or less as a full platoon and we'd search the area by squads."

Other cavalry units used vehicles to patrol the roadways and dry terrain when searching for enemy activity. Jerry

Severson served with E Troop, 17th Cavalry in the 173d Airborne Brigade. Their job, as he described it, was to "get out there ahead of everybody else and scout around and see where the enemy was, what he was up to, and how heavy his forces were. A lot of times it was done strictly on vehicles. . . . They'd throw us all on top of the APCs and down through the jungle we'd go, looking for whatever trouble we could get into. Usually we found some somewhere."

Both army and marine units also employed teams of personnel that were airlifted into enemy areas for anywhere from five days to two weeks to monitor enemy activity. These long-range reconnaissance patrol (LRRP) units, marine recon teams, and army Special Forces teams provided valuable information at considerable risk.

Unlike the small, silent reconnaissance teams or swiftly deployed aerorifle platoons, however, line infantry companies seldom enjoyed the advantage of speed or surprise. Heavily laden and a hundred or more strong, the line units moved laboriously through the jungle with what S. L. A. Marshall described as "the stealth of a brass band on a leopard hunt."[4] Marine Jeff Yushta was quick to point out that there was very little searching that was done successfully in the "search and destroy" operations in which he participated during 1969.

"You weren't seeking anybody out; they were there," explained Yushta. "If they came to you, you had a chance, but there was very little seeking out of Charlie. Charlie knew where you were before you knew where he was and he was laying the ground rules . . . But typically, if they flew you out on an operation and you were supposed to sweep those villes—if Charlie wanted to meet you, he would. If not, he melted into the bush and he was gone."

Michael Jackson was quite clear in his belief that the Vietnamese knew where the Americans were patrolling because of a general lack of discipline: noise, light, smell, even throwing away garbage. The pervasive attitude among the men in his unit in the 101st Airborne Division in 1970 was that if you were in an area near the enemy, they would know you were there.

That was certainly the case on Bryan Good's first trek into the mountains west of Phu Bai just before Christmas 1969.

His company's Kit Carson scout "shot a gook that had been following us. He knew who we were, how many of us were there, where we had come from—he knew everything about us. We had searched him and, hell, he had all that stuff inside his coat. . . . And we had only been there for that afternoon."

The sound of approaching helicopters gave the enemy ample notice of an American unit's size and location. Such audible warnings were often sufficient to allow the NVA or Viet Cong time to pack up their belongings and move out of harm's way, especially when the American operation was large and included the establishment of new artillery bases in an area. Special Forces sergeant Ray Leanna despaired of catching the enemy unawares when the arrival of large American units was heralded by such conspicuous fanfare. He recalled his impressions of an instance when his team had been shadowing an enemy force for several days, only to see their efforts wasted when "the infantry came in there with their helicopters and those 105s [howitzers] and set them up on top of the hills. Hell," he remarked with forgivable exaggeration, "I suppose you could hear them coming for an hour and a half before they got there. By the time they did get there, Charlie was gone."[5]

It was equally frustrating to the line companies that, despite helicopter mobility, they were seldom able to keep pace with the enemy if they chose not to be found. Gerry Barker recalled his experiences in the 1st Cavalry Division:

> The theory seemed to be that the VC would not be able to move out of their base areas, but very frequently we would move into bunkered areas and find that they had cleared out just before us—I mean, completely moving their supplies and everything. I remember once back in 1966 . . . we hit an abandoned, destroyed prisoner-of-war camp. No U.S., just Vietnamese prisoners. We found bunkers . . . twelve by twenty feet or so underground, two entrances to each one completely cleaned out. They had enough time with us arriving in the area the day before to clean out and move it. That is an awful lot of manpower. We never did find the stuff that was in there.

* * *

The VC and NVA, often well acquainted with the surrounding countryside, could use the terrain to tactical advantage, or as a sanctuary whenever possible. Local people often gave them sustenance and support, willingly or under duress, and were able to conceal supplies and ambushes.

Deciding where and under what conditions they were willing to fight was a prerogative the enemy seemed to enjoy throughout much of the war, and few American soldiers doubted the enemy's ability to control that aspect of the fighting. A 1967 Department of Defense study revealed that the VC and NVA shot first in more than 90 percent of company-sized firefights, whereas 80 percent of their larger contacts began with a well-organized attack. American offensive actions, however, seemed unable to destroy enemy forces in the field. Despite increases in battalion days in the field and a doubling of helicopter sorties in 1968, enemy losses remained consistent with previous levels.[6] After the enemy's 1968 offensives, MACV statistics indicated that the NVA and VC were effectively controlling the level of casualties on both sides.[7] Assistant Secretary of Defense Alain Enthoven attempted to explain these facts of life to his new superior, Defense Secretary Clark Clifford, in a memorandum dated 20 March 1968:

> . . . the enemy can control his casualty rate at least to a great extent by controlling the number, size, and intensity of combat engagements. If he so chooses, he can limit his casualties to a rate that he is able to bear indefinitely. Therefore, the notion that we can "win" this war by driving the VC/NVA from the country or by inflicting an unacceptable rate of casualties on him is false. Moreover, a 40 percent increase in friendly forces cannot be counted upon to produce a 40 percent increase in enemy casualties if the enemy doesn't want that to happen.[8]

Men in the field, like rifleman Dale Bertsch, already knew who held the initiative, at least in 1968 in the Mekong Delta region. "I think we were looking for Charlie, but he wasn't

looking for us," Bertsch admitted, "and that made all the difference in the world."[9]

The American soldier endured the miseries of humping
the bush and, in most cases, found nothing, saw nothing, and
came to suspect that he was achieving nothing. Like many of
his peers, Tom Schultz and his company would be flown into
desolate terrain to search with negligible results for four or
five days. Then the company would be flown somewhere else.
Schultz was unable to see any rhyme or reason to the process.
Twenty years later, however, he could still feel the futility and
frustration.

> We went out and literally busted our ass to get some-
> place. We're talking half a klick across a rice paddy,
> waist deep in the mud to get to a village only to find out
> that there was nobody there even though it was sup-
> posed to have been a Viet Cong supply depot or some-
> thing. . . . We were constantly on the move. We were
> always going someplace but never knew why! . . .
>
> "Well, what are we looking for? Are we out here to
> get shot at? Are we gonna shoot at somebody? Are we
> gonna find rice? Weapons?" There was no immediate
> return for all that effort except the sweat and the mos-
> quito bites and the leeches and the jungle rot.

Tom Birhanzel's experiences with the 199th Light Infantry
Brigade were similar. He likened the unit's operational planning to someone in the rear tossing them into the countryside
like a handful of darts. Paul Meringolo simply felt like a
pawn in a big chess game, "not really accomplishing anything, just acting on the latest whim of the battalion commander."

During the middle years of the Vietnam War one saw the
cryptic abbreviation IHTFP scrawled throughout I Corps.
The letters were not the 1960s' equivalent of "Kilroy was
here"; they stood for "I Hate This Fucking Place," and were
found chalked across the countryside wherever soldiers felt
that they truly had much to hate.[10]

Infantry soldiers in any war have often felt their efforts

were being wasted. Marine Jeff Yushta illustrated the unique frustrations of war in Vietnam:

> We were told to secure a ridge and this thing was al-
> most straight up. It was rugged climbing. We were
> loaded down. The temperature was absolutely—ah, I
> can't even think of a word bad enough! It was probably
> eight hundred feet high. If Charlie had the position,
> who cared? We weren't staying in the area. If he was
> dumb enough to climb up there, leave it to him. We lost
> about twelve guys to heat stroke and heat prostration
> trying to climb that ridge. When we got to the top there
> was nothing there, just a hill going down the other side.
> Somebody could have looked at a map and seen that.
> I'm sure somebody did. But somebody had it in their
> mind the ridge had to be taken in order to secure the
> area below. That is the Marine Corps. Take the high
> ground. Well, they could have flown us up there in
> choppers, too. They could have taken the hill with
> Phantoms [jet fighter-bombers]. But no! The book says
> a platoon of marines is going to go up that hill and they
> did!

This was not Mount Suribachi and there was no flag-raising—just a pause, a long pull from a hot canteen, and a very tired walk down the other side of the mountain. The Vietnam War differed from many of America's previous wars in that such ridges, whether fought for or not, were immediately abandoned to the enemy. That was a policy that gave rise to additional bitterness among the soldiers, especially when the lives of friends or comrades had been spent purchasing the real estate they were asked to walk away from. Yushta tried to understand the concept, but found it difficult:

> This was the modus operandi. I mean, Happy Valley
> must have been taken at least six or seven times and
> then just given back. And it seemed silly that with the
> manpower we were capable of mustering, the obviously
> far superior firepower that we had, why couldn't we just
> take something and hold it and not have to take it

again? The shortsightedness of the goals! But it seemed there was no plan in mind that I could discern at the level I was operating. I'm making a judgment. So I was sitting there arguing with myself: "Well, you don't have the whole picture here, but this is really stupid."

Giving up land for which they had fought was equally perplexing to professionals such as Gerry Barker, who, in spite of four tours in Vietnam, never came to see the sense of the policy. "We'd fight like hell for something and then leave it behind," said Barker. "That frustrated the troops because they didn't understand it and the army was lousy at explaining why things were happening that way. Now I realize it was because they had no answer to the problem. But at the time I didn't understand that. I felt they should have an answer."

The day-to-day existence of an infantryman in Vietnam was drudgery; having to engage an enemy on top of it made it easy for those soldiers to see their tour of duty as a series of variegated miseries—each to be conquered in turn, and always accompanied by the anxiety of never knowing where the enemy was or when he would strike. Usually, when it was least desirable, the enemy made his presence known.

Mines and Booby Traps

In November 1966 marine Ed Austin recorded a brief vignette in his journal that revealed one of the hazards of his occupation. "Today," he wrote, "a guy stepped on a mine that blew his leg off up to his knee. I had just passed over the same spot where he stepped on the mine."[11]

For the soldier who encountered them, Guenter Lewy noted, mines were "especially deadly depredations."[12] Casualty statistics from the war indicate just how deadly. The death toll from mines and booby traps in 1966 numbered more than a thousand Americans. In the first six months of 1967, another six thousand Americans became victims of such devices, more than five hundred of whom were killed. During the height of America's participation in the Vietnam

War, nearly one-fourth of American combat deaths were caused by mines and booby traps.[13]

Although a large number of American soldiers completed their tours of duty in the field without seeing a single mine or booby trap, there were many others decidedly less fortunate. Because of their randomness, no other weapon or tactic at the enemy's disposal was more economically effective in inflicting casualties while creating mental and emotional stress in the process. For commanders in the field, casualties resulting from booby traps were exasperating. To the men who put their lives on the line, the statistics meant much more.

If Americans remained in an area for any length of time, mines seemed to spring up with persistent frequency. The experience of the men in Company D, 1st Battalion, 9th Marines, during operations from Hill 55 south of Da Nang in 1966 provides an indication of how effective booby traps could be. Captain Francis J. West, who accompanied the unit in the field, noted that in five weeks the company lost ten men killed and fifty-eight wounded, all but three to mines. Only four of the wounded marines returned to active duty. The platoon's medic, who had been in the unit just nine days, had treated nine marines, all injured by mines.[14]

Enemy mines and booby traps came in assorted types and sizes, ranging from simple sharpened bamboo *punji* sticks to pressure-detonated or command-detonated explosives. *Punji* sticks were placed in pits or concealed in the tall grass along the trails. It was the latter type that Gerry Barker said he saw most frequently.

> I . . . remember looking at it and realizing all the ones that we had seen in pictures and in training were brown and this one was green bamboo right in the green grass. I thought it was a stiff blade of grass and I looked down and realized there was a second one pointed at me and then I pushed some of the grass apart and said "Shit!"
>
> I called to the rest of the guys around me and said, "Do you see what we are in?"
>
> These were stuck in the grass right alongside the road so that you could not get off of it comfortably.

They would have been great for an ambush. In fact that is what we assumed. . . . We used to find them around potential LZs or on LZs because they wouldn't hurt a guy walking but they would sure nail you if you were running.

Punji pits were equally as effective and difficult to find. Dwight Reiland's encounter with a *punji* pit illustrates both their design and the degree that luck sometimes played in detecting them:

> It was maybe eighteen inches deep with inverted sharpened bamboo stakes in it. What they would do is have a few at the bottom pointing up to hopefully get you when you stepped into it. If that didn't work, your first instinct was to yank back. And when you yanked back they got you with the inverted ones.
>
> We had sat down and I lit up a cigaret and was sitting there with a canteen of water and happened to stick my legs out to stretch or whatever and I pushed some of the cover off that thing. I thought, Oh my God! I didn't see it. Hell, if we had gone another ten feet. . . . Maybe my footsteps weren't lined up to catch it, but somebody would have stepped in that damn thing.

Explosive booby traps were more common than *punji* pits, especially in the later stages of the war, and they came in a variety of shapes and sizes. "Toe popper" was the generic term for small explosive charges or bullets set in a bamboo tube with a nail beneath the primer. The device required only the pressure of a weary foot on the nose of the cartridge to force the nail into the primer. Hand grenades, either homemade or of American or Chinese Communist manufacture, were more deadly. The most common means of employing them was to insert a grenade with its safety pin removed inside an empty can. This held the arming spoon securely in place until a trip wire pulled the grenade free and ignited its fuse. Grenades were also encased in clay mud balls with their pins removed. If a soldier stepped on or kicked the mud ball, the dried clay would cake off and the grenade would explode.

Tom Magedanz's friend Ruben Vela lost his legs and three other marines were wounded by one such device. The incident occurred in a place marines had grown to hate called, ironically enough, "Happy Valley." But what Magedanz and the others remembered most about the incident was that one of the wounded men's boots was accidentally left on the trail by the corpsman. "It served as a grisly reminder," he wrote later, "for in the days that followed, we passed by it several times."[15]

Kicking things was a habit common to Americans that the enemy used to his advantage. Jon Neely remembered walking into an area where there were a lot of palm trees and coconuts. "Of course the first thing the first guy did when he walked up there was kick coconuts on the ground to see which ones were okay and which ones weren't," said Neely. "One of them was booby trapped. The guy ended up losing his foot."

More powerful antipersonnel mines of Chinese manufacture were also sometimes encountered. These were directional fragmentation mines that looked like a small dishpan. Inside was a shaped charge made of TNT and up to eight hundred steel fragments that, at close range, could strip apart a human body as effectively as a large-bore shotgun. Jerry Severson encountered these, as well as more primitive varieties, with some frequency during 1967 in War Zone D.

"They would take a reinforcing rod and cut it up and put that in the front part of it," explained Severson. "Then they'd take plastic explosive, if they could get it, or, I suppose, gunpowder if they couldn't, and screw a blasting cap in the back and point it down a trail or whatever and you'd trip that and it would waste you!"

Larger mines were often command-detonated electrically in order to pinpoint specific targets. A member of Layne Anderson's platoon narrowly escaped his own annihilation by deactivating one such device. According to Anderson the man was walking along when he spotted a U.S.-made Claymore mine. "He unscrewed the cap and the cap and the cord went trickling through the woods. He was just white as a sheet. There was somebody on the other end of that detonator cord and he wasn't one of ours."

Claymores could be brutally devastating when linked together and detonated simultaneously. A chance series of events spared radioman Dan Krehbiel from just such a daisy chain that blew his platoon "to hell and gone" in the fall of 1969:

> My platoon got to go down to Trung Lap Village, a place that is always fun to go to. You could get stuff there: booze, dope, boom-boom girls [prostitutes]. I wanted to go with them, but this guy with more time in country wanted to go that way, so he took the radio. . . . I didn't hear them get hit, I just heard a guy get on the radio and heard the squelch break and I heard this guy in a real high-pitched voice saying, "Dustoff!"
>
> I stopped in my tracks and started listening. I listened and battalion said, "How many do you have wounded?" The only thing I remember catching out of his reply was, "Send a Chinook (large cargo helicopter)." That really freaked me out. The sergeant . . . got his legs blown out from underneath him. He crawled across the road to the radio and called in the dustoff. He was the one talking, legs gone, in shock, and he did it successfully and got help real fast. One of the guys killed outright was the RTO because the person who popped the booby trap, the Cong, waited for the guy with the aerial on his pack to get in the center of the ambush before he sprang it.

Of all the types of mines encountered, "bouncing bettys" were probably feared the most because of the nature and locality of the wounds they caused. The enemy scavenged the American M2 bounding mine whenever possible, or they fabricated their own using abandoned American M48 trip-flare canisters. When detonated, a small charge or spring would toss the small explosive charge, which had been sized to fit the tube, upward to waist height, where it exploded.[16]

Booby traps were almost nonexistent in the more remote areas of the Central Highlands, along the western border regions, and near the DMZ; but in the inhabited valleys and in the rural villages that had remained Viet Cong strongholds

since the days of the French occupation, booby traps seemed
an almost natural part of the terrain. In those areas, mines frequently appeared in patches along the trails and near open areas where the Americans were prone to hike and camp. Like
native flora and fauna, certain varieties of booby traps were
indigenous to particular locations. Marine Corps literature
admonished marines to remember that the enemy positioned
mines in areas where men relaxed or were most confident,
such as in the tracks left by armored vehicles. On the patrol
observed by Captain West, the marines were accompanied by
amphibious armored tractors (LVTs). The men had been told
to follow the fresh tracks left by the heavy vehicles. But fatigue, and perhaps a false sense of security, ultimately acted
against the men:

> . . . nine Marines had walked safely past, the tenth Ma-
> rine had wandered off the path of the treads. For twenty
> feet he had been following the dry trail of old tank
> treads. The VC had placed a mine on the old trail rest-
> ing against the torn fence. The Marine tripped a Bounc-
> ing Betty mine which flew knee high before it
> exploded, felling him and two Marines behind him.[17]

An army pamphlet warned soldiers that particular caution
was required near gates and entrances to villages. Soldiers
were also to be wary of the entrances to tunnels and around
cached enemy supplies, places where booby traps seemed especially prevalent. Souvenir items such as enemy flags were
particularly good indicators of the presence of the devices.[18]
It was also prudent to be suspicious of narrow or confined
spaces or routes offering easy access, as William Harken discovered when he was wounded by a booby trap on a well-
traveled footpath between two hamlets.

Other likely danger areas included clearings for helicopter
landing zones, rice paddy dikes, river shorelines, shady areas,
and, as Glen Olstad witnessed, water holes. "We were on road
security," said Olstad. "There was this little pond, and one day
we were out there playing in it—swimming, playing, guys on
guard watching. Next day we pulled into that same area and
one of the guys jumped off the track and ran across the field

Ed Hoban watches for enemy soldiers through the smoke and haze of battle during an operation in I Corps with F Troop, 8th Cavalry in the fall of 1971. *Courtesy Ed Hoban.*

Robert Bonesteel, a 9th Marine Regiment sniper, picks his way through elephant grass near Con Thien in the fall of 1967. *Courtesy Robert Bonesteel.*

Jack Freitag as a scout observer with Company F, 2d Battalion, 1st Marines, 1st Marine Division, in July 1966. *Courtesy Jack Freitag.*

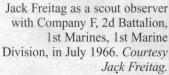

Doug Kurtz poses in front of a 9th Infantry Division aircushion vehicle at Dong Tam in the fall of 1969. *Courtesy Doug Kurtz.*

James Stanton of the 1st Marine Regiment, 1st Marine Division, on Hill 55 in the summer of 1969. *Courtesy James Stanton.*

Randall Hoelzen at LZ Jamie in August 1969. *Courtesy Randall Hoelzen.*

Basic trainees pose before graduation at Fort Lewis, Washington. William Harken is holding the guidon at top left; Stephen Fredrick is at far left in the second row from the top, wearing glasses. *Courtesy Stephen Fredrick.*

Sergeant Stephen Fredrick chows down on a C-ration while in the field with the 101st Airborne Division (Airmobile) in the Central Highlands. *U.S. Army Photo.*

Jerry Johnson and "Kim," one of the ubiquitous youths who sold Cokes to GIs, on Highway 13 north of Saigon in June 1969. *Courtesy Jerry Johnson.*

Leonard Dutcher catches a little sun west of Chu Lai in the spring of 1968. *Courtesy Paul Meringolo.*

Dwight Reiland flashed the two-finger peace sign as the helicopter he's riding in lifts out of a pickup zone near Firebase Bastogne in 1971. *Courtesy Dwight Reiland.*

John Merrell and "Ramona" pose for a friend in the Central Highlands in March 1969. *Courtesy John Merrell.*

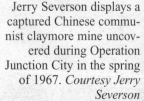

Jerry Severson displays a captured Chinese communist claymore mine uncovered during Operation Junction City in the spring of 1967. *Courtesy Jerry Severson*

Glen Olstad shows off a captured AK-47 assault rifle while standing in front of his M113 Armored Personnel Carrier near Nui Ba Den in 1968. GIs called the armor slabs protecting the vehicle commander (top right behind the .50-caliber machine gun) "chicken plates." *Courtesy Glen Olstad.*

Marine Jeff Yushta (right) poses with two of his buddies while operating in I Corps in 1969. *Courtesy Jeff Yushta.*

Tom Schultz lugs a mortar plotting board atop his rucksack during operations in the Central Highlands in August 1968. *Courtesy Tom Schultz.*

Tom Schultz (standing at left) poses with the rest of his mortar squad at a temporary firebase set up by the 1st Cavalry Division in Tay Ninh Province in the winter of 1968. The gunners from Company C, 2d Battalion, 7th Cavalry, have decked out their 81mm mortar tube with Christmas decorations provided by friends and families back in "The World." *Courtesy Tom Schultz.*

Marine Tom Magedanz poses during a break in "Happy Valley" near the DMZ on 2 July 1970. Two hours later, four men from his platoon hit a boobytrap about 150 meters away. *Courtesy Tom Magedanz.*

Mike Roberts, a 4th Infantry Division machine gunner, prepares to head out to the boonies from An Khe in July 1971. *Courtesy Mike Roberts.*

Machine gunner Layne Anderson poses with his M60 at LZ Gator, not far from the American Division's main base camp at Chu Lai, in September 1968. *Courtesy Layne Anderson.*

and dove in. The first sergeant or lieutenant, I don't know who it was, hollered at him to stop. He dove in and ran a *punji* stick right through his chest."

Soldiers were constantly warned not to establish patterns or to habitually frequent the same locations for night defensive positions or ambushes. Booby traps had a tendency to materialize in such areas.[19] Tom Magedanz told of a close call he had while serving with the 2d Battalion, 7th Marines:

> We were making our night pos, digging our foxholes. That hill had been used before as a night defense position, and there were some foxholes already dug. There was some trash, like C-ration boxes and stuff like that, lying around. Where the company CP was gonna stay, kind of at the center of the hill, there was an old sock lying there. The company radioman looked at it and just brushed it away—took a swipe at it with his entrenching tool to knock that sock away for some reason.
>
> Underneath the sock were two small bamboo pieces in a cross with two bare wires; the wires were not touching. The radioman said, "Hey, Captain, look at this." The captain came over and looked at it and they carefully dug down and found a booby-trapped 105 artillery round, a dud. Those wires led to a buried field radio battery, which led by wire to a blasting cap that was stuck in the 105 round. Luckily it didn't go off because he found it in time. Had he stepped on top of that sock instead of brushing it away, it would have blown and would have killed a bunch of guys.

Ninety-five percent of the mines and booby traps detected in Vietnam were antipersonnel devices, but vehicles were also at risk.[20] A study of the effectiveness of enemy mines on mechanized units between November 1968 and May 1969 found that, "throughout Vietnam, 73 percent of all tank losses and 77 percent of all armored personnel carrier losses were caused by mines."[21] Jerry Johnson's unit often operated with the 11th Armored Cavalry Regiment west of Saigon, where it sometimes encountered what he called "slapstick" mines along the roads and trails:

> They would take two flat pieces of wood and put a stick on either end of it to hold them apart from each other. Then they would wrap gum foil around it on each side and run two wires to that from a battery. When you tramped on that it would complete the circuit and the booby trap would explode. We had a tank commander killed, a TC we were working with, two days before he left for R&R. [He] was walking over a piece of corrugated steel that grounded out his tank, and his tank ran over the slapstick and he was standing on an eighty-pound charge. We were pulling security when we heard the boom. Barney Crawford and I—no one else would touch the guy—rolled him onto a poncho and put him on a dustoff chopper. You couldn't find [anything] from the waist down. Half his face was gone. That explosion was so violent that when he came back down there was pieces of him all over everything. He was a nice guy— he really was.

Although it was relatively easy to recognize the magnitude of the threat and quantify its negative effects, countering that threat remained difficult. Halting the Viet Cong's supply of explosives was nearly impossible. The enemy, relying heavily on unexploded American air and artillery ordnance to supplement its limited explosives reserves, scavenged everything from mortar rounds to aircraft bombs.[22] There was virtually no way to determine how many American casualties resulted from unexploded American bombs and artillery shells recovered by the enemy, but about eight hundred tons of unexploded ordnance was available to the North Vietnamese and Viet Cong forces each month.[23]

To restrict enemy access to unexploded ordnance, the marines began the "Voluntary Informant Program," paying rewards to Vietnamese who brought in or pointed out unexploded munitions such as grenades, dud artillery rounds, and aircraft rockets or bombs.[24] It was inherently risky for any civilian to carry explosives, however. A soldier encountering such a person would likely assume the scavenged device to be in VC hands even if, as Paul Gerrits witnessed, those hands were very small:

> We were walking through a village near Phouc Vinh and I had the funny feeling there was somebody walking in back of us. I turned around to say something and I saw three people following us a couple hundred yards back, so we got off the road. The rest of the company kept walking. There was a curve in the road and Knapp jumped out and confronted what turned out to be three kids and one of them had a grenade in his hand. He shot all three of them. Turns out the pin was still in the grenade.
>
> I guess they were noncombatants. What had happened, I suppose, was someone dropped a grenade and they were bringing it back, doing us a good turn. It wasn't intentional. But who wants to risk checking to see if the pin is in?

The significance of the American soldier's material affluence and his slovenly habits is evidenced by the fact that 90 percent of the material used by the enemy in the construction of mines and booby traps was of American origin.[25] The enemy was quite adept at modifying that material so that the most innocent pieces of garbage were frequently altered with lethal effect. While walking point near Lai Khe, Jerry Johnson recalled finding several LAWs that hadn't been properly disposed of. He said that the enemy

> took them and put in plastic explosive and filled them up with nails and glass and anything they could find and packed both ends shut. Boy, that would have been a dandy Claymore.
>
> I can't remember the guy's name, [but a guy] from one of the platoons was killed with one of those P-38 can openers you got in your C-rations. It went right through his throat: shrapnel in a booby trap. They even had a five-hundred-pound bomb we found. They had enough nerve to fool around with a five-hundred-pounder.... The

mortar [rounds] had those fins on them. They would break them off and use them as shrapnel. They even had some of the crude booby traps like the bouncing bettys and stuff like that. They used old commo wire or old Claymore wire. Anything we threw away they used.

Farther north, Paul Meringolo encountered unique booby traps made out of empty ammo cans. "It was just sort of frightening to think what they could do with makeshift pieces of equipment," he explained. "We were always being told to be careful not to throw away cans, not to throw away batteries, to make sure we destroyed things before we discarded them because if we didn't, the enemy would use them against us. Unfortunately, like most Americans, we got lazy and you threw away things—cans, half-used [radio] batteries—even though we knew we shouldn't. And they would usually be used against us somewhere along the line later on."

Normally, the presence of a trip wire or some other triggering device was the only clue that a hidden explosive device was nearby. At times, however, the enemy left warning signs. While patrolling the Ho Bo Woods with the 25th Infantry Division, Dan Krehbiel learned that there were signs that the Viet Cong used to warn one another that they should watch out for booby traps in that area.

They just planted 'em in likely spots where GIs walked: on the road instead of off the road, on the rice paddy dike instead of in the swampy, messy paddy. The GI typically will take the easy route every time. Why bust your way through a hedgerow when there is a little opening? So they'd plant one there. And that is how it went.

We learned to look for something that shouldn't be there: a cigaret pack in the middle of nothing, for instance. How did that cigaret pack get there? It was put there for a reason, and that was for one Viet Cong to tell another one, "Don't come through here." You learned how to spot odd things; anything that looked out of place would catch your attention.

Some units defused booby traps, but most simply blew them in place. As Jerry Johnson observed, "If the booby trap was set, they knew we were there anyhow, so we weren't giving away anything." In the minds of many soldiers it became prudent as well to clear the locations where mines were likely to be found—whether or not one was actually uncovered. Ron Flesch explained:

> If a marine opened a gate that had been booby-trapped, five or six grunts were usually wounded in the ensuing explosion. Though it was routine to check the gate for tampering, sometimes you could not detect the booby trap, as the VC were very clever. My approach was simple: I would just throw a frag grenade and blow the whole damned thing up. Let the villagers build a new gate. Five or six marines was simply too high a price to pay.[26]

Terry Tople's squad carried a grappling hook for searching enemy bodies just in case they had a grenade concealed beneath them. Tom Magedanz said he heard of units that simply shot an M79 grenade round at a corpse.

Keeping soldiers dispersed in booby-trapped areas was imperative, and platoon and squad leaders such as William Harken were always fearful of momentary lapses that could become fatal. One incident on an operation in "Booby Trap Alley" near Firebase Crockett cost Sergeant Harken four members of his squad. The unit sat down for a break and, despite the sergeant's warnings, four men clustered together. One of the foursome, the unit's medic, leaned over and picked up a discarded mortar round lying on the ground. "Of course it was booby-trapped," Harken sighed in resignation. "It killed him and another guy. A third man wound up with a plate in his head and the other man suffered two broken arms, a broken leg, and shrapnel all over his body."

The constant attrition due to booby traps made everyone particularly conscious of foot placement. Marine Vince Olson said that the men in his platoon were often "afraid of where to step, afraid we might make the next step and get blown up. Even more than getting shot at, it was just the suspense. You might take the next step and get your leg blown off."

Tim O'Brien captured the mood of desperation and uncertainty that accompanied each soldier as he picked his way methodically across a field full of lethal possibilities:

> You do some thinking. You hallucinate. You look ahead a few paces and wonder what your legs will resemble if there is more to the earth in that spot than silicates and nitrogen. Will the pain be unbearable? Will you scream and fall silent? Will you be afraid to look at your own body, afraid of the sight of your own red flesh and white bone? You wonder if the medic remembered his morphine. . . .
>
> It is not easy to fight this sort of self-defeating fear, but you try. You decide to be ultra-careful—the hardnosed realistic approach. You try to second-guess the mine. Should you put your foot to that flat rock or the clump of weeds to its rear? Paddy dike or water? You wish you were Tarzan, able to swing on the vines. You trace the footprints of the men to your front. You give up when he curses you for following too closely; better one man dead than two.[27]

It is not surprising that the men feared these devices, for the effects of a powerful enemy antipersonnel mine were devastating. O'Brien recalled the effects of a dud 105mm shell that his black friend Chip detonated. "He died in such a way," the rifleman lamented, "that for once you could never know his color."[28] Journalist Charles Anderson graphically described the human debris of a marine sergeant and his radioman left by a large booby trap:

> The mine accomplished just about what the Russians who made it and the North Vietnamese who planted it had in mind. The only things left inviolate on those two human bodies and their clothing was the propriety of boots on feet, although the feet were ripped from their legs. The mine mixed trousers with calf muscles and tendons with genitals with intestines with

bladders with shit with livers and spleen and kidneys and stomachs, and jammed the oozy mass upward into lungs and throats. Then it burned hands and arms and chests and faces to the texture and appearance of dried prunes. Just like it was supposed to do. What happens to human beings in mechanized warfare has absolutely no poetic or theatrical possibilities.[29]

When flesh was reduced to detritus for Graves Registration personnel to dispose of, anger often became rage and men's thoughts focused on revenge. But in most cases, as Dan Krehbiel noted, there was nobody to shoot back at when somebody got hurt.

Men dreamed of paying back the enemy, and sometimes the recipients of this pent-up rage were simply those closest to the scene of the disaster. Tim O'Brien recalled how, "After a booby-trapped artillery round blew two popular soldiers into a hedgerow, men put their fists into the faces of the nearest Vietnamese, two frightened women living in the guilty hamlet, and when the troops were through with them, they hacked off chunks of thick black hair. The men were crying doing this."[30]

On rare occasions the guilty party did fall into American hands. Jon Neely's squad exacted some payback on one such enemy soldier following a booby-trap incident on Highway 1 north of Saigon. There was no mercy from men who suddenly found in their hands the personification of all they hated, and there was no remorse in the aftermath:

About three to four minutes after we heard over the radio that a track from 1st Platoon was going in for a hot meal, we heard a large explosion. It was right back where the road was, so we jumped on our APC as fast as we could and headed back there. The Vietnamese had set a land mine in the middle of the road and when our 1st Platoon track came through there the enemy ignited it and blew the track up. There were six guys on the track and four of them were killed instantly. Two of them were really messed up pretty bad, but they

eventually would make it and they would go back to
The World.

We were lucky that we saw the gook . . . we saw a
guy running out in a rice paddy and we figured it was
the guy who had set up the land mine. So a couple of
us took off after him. We got out there and we grabbed
him and we found a detonator in his clothing. Now normal procedure would be to take him back to whatever
base camp happened to be around there and let them in-
terrogate him. Well, tempers didn't last that long and I
would say we probably put around two hundred—two
hundred and fifty bullets in the guy.

As the war progressed, American soldiers used their Claymore mines for more than perimeter defense or ambush. Men
frequently planted booby traps of their own beneath enemy
bodies or chose a likely location to lay trip wires made with
two metal clips from an M16 ammo bandolier, nylon fishing
line or commo wire, a plastic spoon from a C ration, and batteries from a radio for an electrical supply.

"Anything tripping the wire pulled the plastic spoon out,
closing the metal clips and completing the circuit to the electrical cap on the Claymore," Dwight Reiland explained.
"And—*Boom!* Anything that tripped that got a Claymore in
the face, and a Claymore was a devastating mine." Reiland
noted with satisfaction how "insidiously effective" those
booby traps could be. "Nobody had to lay there and hide or
be quiet or remain hidden or anything," he said. "The thing
was there, ready all the time. It never fell asleep."

Snipers

Throughout the Vietnam conflict the enemy sought to
avoid exposing his forces to the overwhelming firepower that
Americans could bring to bear. Consequently, a soldier's contact with the enemy frequently consisted of nothing but
sniper fire. Grenadier Bryan Good of the 101st Airborne Division said that the enemy would usually "just let go with a
half a dozen AK rounds and you would hit the dirt and won-

der where it came from." Like most soldiers, Good found such attacks irritating because there was seldom a chance to react with any hope of success. "You would call in artillery and go through the whole rigamarole. Heck, they would be long gone."

Tom Schultz was equally familiar with the frustrating routine. "It was, 'Get down, there's somebody out there.' We would find some cover and start shooting. We never knew whether we hit anybody or did any damage, and normally we'd go and sweep the area after the contact and all we would find were empty cartridges."

Brevity and the near certainty of negative results almost universally characterized such attacks. After a three- or four-minute exchange the enemy would disappear and, as Jeff Yushta recalled, "We never had any success in running them down. Usually, after the initial contact, we hoped we got our licks in, and they took off and we figured we would run into them a little later."

Fortunately the haste and often extreme range of the enemy's fire made such attacks irritating but seldom costly in terms of American casualties. Close calls, however, seemed to occur in abundance. Ed Austin wrote in his diary of seeing a fellow marine bend over to get some water from a well. "There was a pop and his helmet almost fell into the well. He took it off and looked at it. There was a hole completely through both sides. It missed his head by less than an inch."[31]

Not all sniper fire was ineffective, however. When Robert Bonesteel joined the 1st Battalion, 4th Marine Regiment, in October 1967, he discovered that the squad to which he was assigned had lost nine men killed by a single NVA sniper. Understandably, fear of snipers was rampant. "It was a big thing at that time to let your cloth helmet cover hang down rather than tuck it in between the steel helmet and the inner liner," Bonesteel recalled, "because when you had a helmet on there was a real nice spot to aim at right in front of the ear."

Like booby traps, a sniper's bullet increased the sense of frustration and futility that soldiers felt. Frustration was certainly evident in September 1966 when persistent sniper fire pinned down Vernon Janick's company for more than a day on the outskirts of a small village:

> They had a real good scope on us. Anytime anybody got out of the hole to make a move, *crack-crack, crack-crack!* I was a grenadier and I just plugged in everything I could in there and we stayed there all day. Just couldn't make a move.
>
> Well, that night we knew we must have got a few of them because you could hear people crying and carrying on. That was getting to piss me off, too, because of all the aggravation. We just couldn't seem to get them. The next day we made a sweep and found a couple of bodies in a rice paddy, but we never found the weapons. We figured there had to be more, so we just about tore the place apart. We looked it over real good. Never did find anything, though, so we moved out after that.

The enemy's harassing fire also included large-caliber weapons. While in War Zone D in 1967, Jerry Severson remembered encountering a lone Viet Cong with a 57mm recoilless rifle. "He had everybody scared," said Severson. "He'd fire one round into the side of a jeep or an APC or a three-quarter-ton truck that was hauling some guys, something where he could do some damage. One round! Then away he'd go. We don't know whether he went in a tunnel. We never found any tunnel complex. But there was lots of bullets fired out there trying to get that guy. We never got him as far as I know."

Snipers were often selective in choosing targets; NCOs, officers, and radiomen were high on the priority list. The first man whom Steve Fredrick saw killed in the field was a young RTO hit by sniper fire while crossing a rice paddy. This apparent selectivity in choosing targets made everyone a bit conscious of being near an antenna, giving obvious commands, or saluting while in the field.

Sergeant Gerry Barker recalled that during Operation Masher-White Wing in 1966, a squad leader was pointing and yelling orders to his men and he was shot. "They were looking for the leader," Barker recalled. "It was the kind of thing that made us feel we were being constantly observed—that we were constantly in somebody's gunsight. That really eats on you."

The loss of men to enemy action hurt units deeply, not only in terms of experience and manpower lost, but in terms of friendships severed and lives prematurely extinguished as well. Tom Magedanz's account of the death of a fellow marine killed by sniper fire in April 1970 in the Que Son Valley brings a measure of understanding to one of the hazards of the field—and perhaps explains something about the greater human element of war:

> We were kind of lax. We had taken a break; we had been humping all morning. It was really hot and a couple guys got together and started talking. There got to be too big a group, and the sniper took advantage. I had just finished talking to Jim and I sat down and leaned against this stone wall. He was leaning against the other side of it talking, so I was maybe ten feet away. There was an automatic burst from an AK, and he was shot in the neck and killed. Chuck Streiff was hit in the arm.
>
> Chuck said Jim's throat was hit from the side and was more or less shot away. He could hear Jim gurgling until he died. They were both taken away by the same medevac chopper. . . .
>
> I remember Chuck shouting, "Corpsman up! He shot me right in the arm!" And I remember Ledbetter yelling, "Oh my God—Jim!" when he saw Jim laying there hit bad. I yelled, "Put out some rounds." Bradley was already shooting in the air just to make the gooks get down. Then we tried to set up a better defensive perimeter and wait for the chopper. I went back once to check and Sergeant Reed told me Jim had died.[32]

Ambushes

Enemy small-arms fire produced only 16 percent of America's wounded in Vietnam, but it accounted for 51 percent of the U.S. servicemen killed in combat.[33] Many of these casualties were the result of ambushes, a tactic to which the enemy and the terrain in Vietnam were particularly well suited. The frequency and severity of the enemy's ambush threat was widely recognized and the services warned their personnel accordingly. The army, for example, noted the enemy's ability to detect operational patterns in a unit's movement or methods.[34] The enemy took advantage of such laxity or repetition with frequent success.

Bryan Good's unit, Company D, 1st Battalion, 327th Infantry, was the victim of an ambush born of repetition. Two previous trips up a muddy mountainside in late April 1970 had been uneventful. On 1 May, the company was ordered up the hill a third time. Everything that day had gone badly and Good vividly remembered that no one wanted to repeat the maneuver a third time.

We were getting low on C's and instead of bringing us C's and water they dropped us off some beer and cigarets. We were all thirsty and hungry, so everybody had a couple of beers. That was all we had. Then up this shitting hill we go again. We got to the top and there was a trail watcher there and Brock, the pointman, got twelve rounds right through the gut. That's when Rick, the slack man, got two or three rounds off at him and his '16 jammed. All I heard was the twelve rounds of the AK and the two from the '16. Rick was up there cussing and banging his M16 against a tree.

The rest of us finally got up on top of the hill and then all hell broke loose. About thirty of them at least were up there around a little horseshoe formation. . . . The lieutenant had his hand blown off that day. There must have been at least a dozen got medevac'd out.

The mountains and jungles offered the enemy excellent concealment. The foliage was so thick that it was not uncommon for the enemy to spring an ambush when an American unit was only five to fifteen meters away.[35] In less densely foliated areas, the enemy's preparations and creativity served him well. The Viet Cong, for example, often wore freshly cut foliage on their fiber helmets, along with a cape of camouflage material. Moving through a rice paddy and into an open area while on patrol one day, Dennis Foell saw "what we thought were trees start moving. That was the closest I can say that we actually saw the enemy—after all the trees started moving. They definitely were very good in their camouflage."

Excellent fire discipline, noise discipline, and immobility at point-blank range guaranteed that the enemy would inflict maximum casualties, while proximity reduced or negated American air and artillery support.[36] Prudence naturally dictated that the enemy would not ambush large American forces unless they were in considerable strength. Sergeant Don Putnam was reminded of that uncomfortable thought when his mechanized infantry unit went into Cambodia during the 1970 invasion:

> We had always believed that the only time the gooks would ambush us was when they had us outnumbered. If they had you outnumbered they would take you on. So we were moving into Cambodia with a company of tanks and our full battalion. While moving down a road, we got ambushed. I was on the lead track of our platoon and they RPG'd three tracks in front of us.
>
> When you are moving in a mechanized column and you get ambushed, the tracks alternate all the way back, creating a herringbone effect, and the guys bail off and start laying down fire on both sides. I came off the top of the track and the first thing that entered my mind was that our shit was weak. They wouldn't mess with us unless they had us outnumbered big time. It probably only lasted for a half an hour to forty-five minutes. They didn't have us outnumbered that time, but that was the first thought. If they were willing to mess with this big column of APCs and tanks and everything that is going with it, they must be pretty strong.

The enemy often baited their ambushes with small-arms fire or even human lures to tempt overeager Americans. Once a platoon found itself inside such a trap, casualties could be fearsome. S. L. A. Marshall described the ambush of an ill-fated patrol from the 1st Infantry Division on 11 December

1966. A platoon was moving through the jungle north of Soui Da, following in the footsteps of a patrol that had covered the same area the day before. As the column advanced into a clearing, the pointman saw three uniformed figures standing with their backs turned and their rifles shouldered. When they darted toward the woods, the lead Americans gave chase, spreading their unit out across the clearing. It didn't occur to anyone that the enemy soldiers might be human bait. Seconds later, the platoon was flanked by concentrated automatic weapons fire from the dense forest twenty-five meters away. Over the course of the next half hour, the thirty-man platoon was nearly wiped out, suffering twenty-four dead and emerging with only two able-bodied soldiers.[37]

It was also dangerous to move rapidly to the aid of a platoon being ambushed. Secondary ambushes were often placed along the routes that a relief element was expected to travel when coming to the aid of a stricken unit. In other instances, the enemy would remain in the ambush site using one destroyed American unit to lure in another. Vernon Janick remembered the fate of two platoons from his company in the Central Highlands in 1967: "We had one whole platoon walk into an ambush and all but one man died. That guy played dead. The other platoon that went in to rescue them . . . hell, they lost two-thirds of them. So that was about half; two platoons, or half the company, got wasted. We were all spread out into four platoons. By the time the rest of us got there they were pretty well all cleaned out."

Enemy tactics also took into account the American soldier's dogged determination never to abandon a dead or wounded comrade. This facet of unit solidarity produced numerous additional casualties and set the stage for one of the most difficult aspects of combat in Vietnam. In July 1969, the 3d Platoon of Company H, 2d Battalion, 1st Marines, fell victim to an ambush dug in on the side of a trail. The enemy left heavy vegetation in place, but cleared a narrow field of fire. Their opening burst hit the point man in the legs. As men rushed to his assistance, they were felled in succession with shots to the legs, and then, if possible, killed with shots to the head or back. Within a few minutes the NVA killed six and wounded sixteen more without losing a single man.[38]

Marine Phil Yaeger saw similar things happen while with the 3d Marine Division, and he hated the enemy for it. "Marines have a long history of not leaving their dead on the battlefield and the North Vietnamese were well aware of that," he explained. "So, they would try to drop somebody right in front of a bunker knowing full well that we would try to get to them. And we would! We took a lot of casualties retrieving casualties."

Sergeant Willie Williams lost a number of friends while with the 25th Infantry Division in 1966, but his most bitter memory was of struggling to retrieve a man he knew he was helpless to save.

"I got hit trying to get to a friend of mine who had been hit," said Williams. "He wasn't dead yet, but he was hit real bad by machine-gun fire and everybody that had gone out to get him had gotten hit. So I had my M79 man fire at this bunker while I tried to go get him and I got hit with grenade fragments. The guy I was going after [eventually] died. I couldn't get him out. But he wouldn't let me come to him anyway. He told me if I tried to get him I would get killed and he would shoot me before he would see Charlie get me."

Indirect Fire

The majority of casualties in both world wars and Korea were caused by artillery and mortar fire. In Vietnam, however, the enemy's limited access to artillery and the absence of a stable front line behind which to establish artillery concentrations (except across the demilitarized zone in I Corps) denied him the use of large-caliber indirect-fire weapons in most campaigns. Nevertheless, mortars, rockets, and light to medium artillery produced nearly two-thirds of America's casualties there.[39]

The most frequent type of indirect fire experienced by Americans was the standoff rocket or mortar attack during which no other military action, such as a ground assault or sapper infiltration, took place. These standoff attacks came in two degrees of intensity: harassment, which involved the firing of a half-dozen or so mortar rounds at a position, and

so-called attacks by fire, which were more intense applica-
tions of up to thirty or more rounds of rocket or mortar fire.[40]
Standoff attacks exacted a heavy toll of American and South
Vietnamese military and civilian casualties while posing very
limited risk to the enemy. As analyst Thomas Thayer noted:

> Although an attack required advanced planning, lo-
> gistical support and was military in style, the target was
> not assaulted. A standoff attack was generally a means
> of exerting military pressure on a target which the com-
> munists could not hope to or did not desire to defeat.
> The communists inflicted an allied combat death for
> every fifty to sixty rounds they fired and while they
> sometimes suffered casualties from allied counterbat-
> tery fire, they usually escaped unharmed.[41]

Enemy forces relied on 61mm and 82mm mortars, which
were slightly larger than their American counterparts and
thus capable of firing either American- or Soviet-made mortar rounds. The enemy, of course, appreciated the ability of
their mortars to fire American projectiles, since they were often more readily available than their own rounds. That puzzling fact led Tom Schultz to wonder just how U.S. material
made its way into enemy hands. "The Russians make an
82mm mortar; we make an 81mm," he observed. "Obviously
82mm projectiles won't fit an 81mm, but an 81mm will work
in an 82mm. So we encountered Russian-made 82mm mortars that we captured in bunkers and we would find cases of
81mm ammo lying beside them. I don't think they bought
that stuff through a defense contractor. It had to come off the
docks for bucks."

Although the suspicions of the young soldier were typical
of many Americans who were skeptical of the South Vietnamese government's integrity and could imagine the scope
of black market activities in Vietnam, other sources of
American-made munitions were also available to the enemy.
The most obvious source was material captured by the enemy
from ARVN bases or units destroyed in the field. Munitions
were also captured from American bases, and U.S. mortar

rounds could be purchased on the international arms market. In truth, there were numerous sources of supply.

Locating a clandestine mortar tube used by the enemy for harassing fire was, of course, difficult under any circumstances, but in John Meyer's Combined Action Platoon, every once in a while there was some luck:

> The local VC had a mortar which they would bring out every so often when they felt they had the opportunity, and [they would] crank off a few rounds in this direction or that direction. We kept running sweeps trying to find where this mortar was stashed. They figured it wasn't too far from the general area where the rounds would come from—but the enemy would fire a couple of rounds and go hide it again. There was no reacting to it. Then one day while looking for it, one of the PFs [Popular Forces] walked into the river to cool off and he stepped on it. They had buried it in the mud on the river bottom. They would just get it out when they needed it. It was just a fluke to go looking for something like that and come up with it the way they did.

Mortars could be quite accurate, especially when the enemy knew the exact location of a target. On occasion, this vital information was provided by civilians, or at least the presence of a civilian preceding a mortar attack was blamed for the accuracy of the enemy rounds. Paul Boehm survived his first mortar attack, but recalled that a somewhat strange event had preceded it.

> A mamasan walked up to the perimeter, and a derelict—I don't remember his name, he was in Layne's platoon—took her to the Old Man's CP [command post]. He got upset because they didn't blindfold her or anything—just walked her up. The Old Man told the guy to get rid of her, so he took her out to the perimeter. It was morning and our ambushes had come in and we were just hanging around waiting to move out. There weren't a lot of foxholes dug because most of the company had been out on ambush.

So she walked out, took off, and it couldn't have been twenty minutes later we got mortared and the first round landed right next to the Old Man's command post. She paced it off and it was perfect. I mean, they lobbed the first round right dead on. And then they worked them all around.

Because the enemy often observed American units as they set up their night defensive positions, it was customary for many units to set up before dark and then move to a new position a few hundred yards away in the last minutes of twilight. No one complained of the extra movement, however, because on occasion mortar rounds would fall into the vacated locations.

The enemy's mortar fire was usually rapid and sometimes very accurate, and his mortar tubes were normally close enough for GIs to hear the hollow *ploomp* as the projectiles left the weapons. Experienced troops could tell about how long it would be before the shells landed—but no one could predict where. On more than a few occasions, the rounds found their mark.

It is often said that one never forgets a first command. When Tom Schultz became a squad leader his men were more than simply soldiers, they were his friends. Shortly thereafter, on an evening that never seems to stray far enough from memory, his squad was nearly wiped out. Thinking back on the incident, Schultz recalled:

[There was] a guy, I can't remember his name, he was just one man. First name, last name, I can't even remember it. I can still see him, dark hair, mustache— quite a handsome man. When he'd left California to come to 'Nam he'd just got word from the Red Cross that his wife was in the delivery room but they wouldn't let him go back to see his baby. He was a schoolteacher from Louisiana. He'd been in country for three months. There was also a Hawaiian boy from Seattle. We called him Pineapple. He stood about five foot one. Always jolly. Finally there was Rick—from back East some-where—Philadelphia or somewhere. Nice guy. Those three guys were all in my squad and they all died on the same night.

I had been moved into the squad leader position after six or seven months because I was the ranking man. There were eight of us in the squad. We dug our night defensive positions and the lieutenant called the squad leaders from the platoon back to talk. We had a little pow-wow for ten or fifteen minutes talking about what we would be doing the next day. My squad had two holes in the perimeter. It was just dark. I had just left the meeting and they were all back in the two holes and . . . *pop* . . . *pop* . . . *pop*.

"Mortar!"

We had about twenty seconds before the rounds would hit. They got both my holes. It wasn't very pretty! There were a lot of people after that and before that, but they are the ones I remember most. You live and work with people who get shot to hell—it's hard to understand. And there is no reason—never was, never will be. Three dead, two wounded. And I happened to be in the right place for ten minutes.

Ground Attacks

Sometimes American units were the targets of enemy ground assaults. Large-scale assaults were the nightmare of any soldier. Attacks launched against larger installations, such as battalion firebases or brigade or division base camps, were seldom successful because of the firepower of those well-established defenses. But in the field, and at smaller outposts, American positions were often manned by no more than a hundred men, dug in and alone in the jungle where fire support was more limited and the enemy's chances of success were much improved.

Marine Jeff Yushta's small perimeter was overrun by Viet Cong on Go Noi Island. It was the unit's second time on the island within a few months, and the marines had hit the enemy hard. According to Yushta:

We set up that night in a pretty bad spot. They were wise enough to know that we were not operating at full company strength and they hit us that night. It was about two o'clock in the morning and they knew we were exhausted.

They penetrated our position real early. A company can't set up in that big a position anyway. I doubt that our positions were more than a circle with a diameter of a hundred and ten meters or something like that. You tried to set up in somewhat of a circle with the command post in the center, but the terrain would often have an irregular shape to it. And I am sure they saw us set up and they hit us where we weren't ready to take them. They came through and we really didn't take that many casualties. We didn't get too many kills either. I think it was more or less their way of saying, "Look, you are pissing us off here in our backyard and we can do whatever we want to you."

That was the first time I'd been in a position that was overrun and it was a little disconcerting. You always felt a sense of security when you set up for the night even though you were in an unfamiliar place. There were Claymores and trip flares, and a couple of marines nearby that will help you out. You were dug in. Somebody would almost have to crawl right up on you before they could kill you. That belief got shattered.

One other aspect of that evening left the young marine with a lasting sense of sadness; a split-second decision, made in the confusion of battle, which could never be undone:

I felt we were getting more pressure from a certain area of the perimeter that night. . . . I saw they were going to penetrate us. Nobody said, "Go over there." There was no way to contact anybody. I thought that area needed to be shored up and I took two guys, one from each hole next to me, and headed for that area. One of the men got cut down on the way there. When we got there the enemy attacked from a totally different direction.

Now I say to myself, if he had stayed in his hole he probably would have survived. But I was processing the information that I had at the time, and I don't think I could have made any other decision.

In another instance, Sgt. Willie Williams led one of two ambush patrols outside of his company's perimeter and found himself on the fringe of a larger attack against his company in the Ho Bo Woods. Unknown to Sergeant Williams, while he deployed his men to the east of the company's hastily dug perimeter, a battalion of NVA regulars and Viet Cong prepared for an early morning attack. Williams remembered the night of 5 April 1966 vividly:

We were about a half a kilometer from the perimeter and we fired on the advance party that was coming up to our lines. At the time that this happened, I didn't know that the force was that large, or we wouldn't have fired on it. We only saw about fifteen or twenty Viet Cong and we opened up on them. Then, in the distance, we could see the hardcore troops [advancing] by columns. I called back in and tried to get permission to return to friendly lines and I was told we had to stay out. They were getting overrun.

So we divided the patrol into two groups and there were two bomb craters, so part of us stayed in one bomb crater and the other half went to the other one. We never fired another shot but we threw grenades and tried to get the artillery to fire on the main column. But we couldn't get artillery to come because they were walking it through the perimeter because they were being overrun. It was fearful [in the shell hole] because at any minute if we had been spotted, we would all have been dead. We just sat and prayed for daylight.

In the morning I went out to check for any enemy we had killed, and again we couldn't find one complete body. I know we killed quite a few, but we couldn't find a single body. Then, that morning, I called back in to the base camp and they sent an APC out to get our dead and wounded. When we got back in, it was rough because most of the people that I had known were either killed or wounded back in the perimeter. They got completely overrun.[42]

Williams's strong suspicion was that his company had been left exposed as bait, a sentiment shared by many field soldiers. American firepower could be brought to bear effectively only on concentrations of enemy soldiers in known locations. It followed that the best way to locate and destroy enemy forces was to have a unit in the field stumble into them, pull back, and then let the air power and artillery do the killing. Afterward, the infantry, as Randall Hoelzen put it, would "walk back into it and see if there was anything left." But the process definitely left Hoelzen and many others feeling as though "we were bait . . . a walking target for an ambush."

Jack Freitag referred to the platoon he operated with as a "SLIP unit," a "Sacrificial Lamb Infantry Platoon." He was the artillery forward observer with a small force of marines setting ambushes in an area near the village of An Trac southwest of Da Nang. The unit was located in the middle of a pro–Viet Cong area; in retrospect, Freitag said that he thought his unit was used "as bait to draw the enemy down on us. Then they would call in the big guns and kick ass." He wasn't very happy about it. His unit, with an average of eighteen men, took—by his reckoning—more than forty casualties during the two months they were at An Trac.

In the years following the war in Vietnam, the enemy and his abilities have been given over to some exaggeration by American soldiers who undoubtedly believed that they were facing a foe who appeared to have every advantage. There is always some need to overrate an enemy's ability in order to place one's own efforts in a better light. However, the accounts given by some former American servicemen seem to assign to the Viet Cong and the North Vietnamese Army a level of sophistication they did not deserve.

Gerry Barker was one of the few who challenged such descriptions of the enemy:

I've heard more bullshit about how good the VC and the NVA were than they were in reality. What I saw in

Special Forces made me realize there were lots of terrible errors on the NVA and VC side. They were lousy in the jungle to begin with. NVA and VC were not quiet in the jungle. I watched them make every bit as much noise as Americans did. They didn't have as many contraptions, which helped them, but the VC could not sneak through the woods. If there was any possible way to get to a trail, they would. They definitely got sick. . . . They got terrible infections. They had leprosy going around in Laos beyond belief.

What they were good at was outworking us. I will hand them that. They outworked us. If anybody deserved to win based on effort it was them. I think that the error we made was never defeating the ideology. . . . I don't think that the guys around me either in the infantry companies or in SF underestimated them—not on racial grounds or any other. Usually, we had very limited contact with them. But I did hear a lot of BS about "Sir Charles"—how good he was and that sort of thing.

Soldiers encountered obstacles every day. There were both natural impediments and, with random frequency, obstacles of enemy origin. Wherever one went in Vietnam there were the rocks as well as the flowers, the bamboo vipers and malaria-infested swamps as well as the vibrant greens and silvers of a landscape seemingly cut from an Oriental silk screen. There were glorious sunsets and rainfall beyond belief. Occasionally, too, there were the hazards of the field—man-made traps awaiting a single misstep, a clear field of fire, careless repetition, or bad luck. Each night as the men dug their defensive positions there was always a chance, albeit slim, that more than darkness was gathering around the perimeter. And with each new dawn came the gnawing question, if not today, when? If not me, who?

CHAPTER 10

Change and Coping

December 12, 1967

Dear Mom and Dad,

Well, I've been in Viet Nam for two months now almost so I am getting to be a hard-core trooper now. I've changed a lot over here. You'll probably hardly know me when I get home. I guess this place would change anyone.

I enjoyed the pictures that you sent me, especially the one of you and Dad. Well, it won't be long now and it will be Christmas. I hope you all have a merry one. I've been getting a lot of mail the last few weeks and I have been glad to get them. Please tell everyone thanks a lot because it makes today a little bit better to get some mail. It's still been raining a lot over here and will probably rain a lot until April or so. Will close for now. Write more later.

Your Son,
Leonard[1]

With every day spent in Vietnam and each minute exposed to combat, soldiers such as Leonard Dutcher evolved from inexperienced, wide-eyed recruits to "hard-core troopers." Like soldiers in all wars, they became by degrees pragmatic, efficient, hardened, and cynical. Coming of age in the bush was a significant personal achievement, one in which most soldiers took genuine pride. Even soldiers who harbored misgivings about the war and America's role in it tended to derive some satisfaction from having endured the rite of passage that combat symbolized. Steve Fredrick's sentiments were probably consistent with those of most infantrymen who survived their baptism of fire and felt deserving of the recognition that survival had accorded them. He tried to describe his feelings to his parents after a month in the bush: "I was awarded the Combat Infantryman's Badge last week. It means that I have been in battle and under enemy fire. It probably doesn't mean much to you at home, but I am proud of it as now I am a real soldier."[2]

Combat initiated a metamorphosis within the new men, the result being most often a soldier who could do his job under fire, endure the daily conditions of life in the field, and divest himself of the philosophical and emotional baggage that might otherwise impair his ability to cope and survive. Plotting this change over time demonstrated, as journalist Ward Just discovered in 1966, that an infantryman's tour of duty in the field was marked by three distinct stages:

> The first three months were new and strange and efficiency therefore low, the middle six months filled with activity and bustle and efficiency therefore high, and the final three months preoccupied with home and family, and staying alive ... and efficiency therefore low.

The pattern was so universal that Just claimed, "MACV mathematicians and psychologists could describe a soldier's efficiency curve as precisely as a missile's parabola."[3]

Sergeant Michael Jackson didn't need mathematicians or psychologists to explain a pattern that was obvious to many infantry soldiers:

> From the first month to the third month or maybe even the second month you were a cherry and you were not respected. People saw you as a liability and stayed away from you. ... From the third month to the tenth month you couldn't find a finer soldier because by then you had learned the ropes; you knew what to expect. There was some sense of camaraderie and you basically knew what to do and who you could count on. So, from the third month to the tenth month you were a

pretty good soldier. From the tenth month till the twelfth month you weren't shit because you were short.

Sergeant Gerry Barker, however, believed that men decreased in efficiency much earlier in their tour than the tenth month. He agreed that men reached peak efficiency by their third month in country, but he expressed a strong opinion that they began a long slide by the time they hit the midpoint of their tour. "I think it got to their morale when they realized how long that tour was going to be," he said.

Soldiers rather quickly came to appreciate just how long their year in combat would be; for many of them, it bordered on eternity. An anecdote recorded in the diary of air force Capt. Richard Sexton revealed something of the way in which a combat soldier saw the length of his year-long tour: "Eighty days have September, April, June, and November. All the rest have ninety-three except the last month which has one hundred and forty."[4] The probability of being killed or sustaining injury in that time period made the actual length of a one-year combat tour strictly relative. Those who experienced the most contact and casualties had little reason for optimism as they counted off their days. Such men developed a sense of myopia toward their DEROS date. Often one of a soldier's first priorities was to get past his initial fears and alter his thought processes in order to cope with the mental stresses of soldiering and the fight for survival.

Once this was accomplished, the path toward one's DEROS date entered a long, dark tunnel that extended well beyond the range of most soldiers' vision. Although the standard tour for enlisted personnel was twelve months in the army and thirteen months for marines, the prospect of a year in combat seemed like a lifetime to most men, and they were unable to contemplate completing their tours unscathed.

It made little difference how long a tour of duty in Vietnam might be when each day in the field exposed men to death or injury, and brought with it the accompanying frayed nerves and brooding anticipation. Terry Musser remembered "looking in anticipation for the same damn things to happen. Instead of it being a guy two guys down on your right that got it, it could be you the next time. Fear of the unknown! Expectation is probably worse than getting shot, although I was never shot. . . . But I think having to look forward to it time after time takes its toll."

At the first hint of action, however, nervousness gave way to a visceral rush of adrenaline that sent soldiers into an intense and sometimes strangely euphoric stage of alertness and reaction. Even when Vernon Janick was "dog dead tired," he remembered how all of a sudden "you came alive." And while under adrenaline's enigmatic spell, rifleman Jeff Yushta found that combat reminded him of a Fuji commercial for color film. "Everything became very brilliant in color and all the sensory organs seemed to max out—sight, hearing—and time seemed to slow down," he said. "And then afterwards, what a huge rush! I think that is why I don't get excited about anything anymore. It is something you can't explain. Terrifyingly exciting would be the two words."

Medic Paul Gerrits's experiences under fire were similar. Sight, sound, everything became intensified, leaving him with a strange sense of invincibility. Phil Yaeger probed his reactions and said that he never felt more alive or more on top of what he was doing than when he was in combat. "It wasn't exhilarating in the sense that riding a roller coaster is," he explained, "but the chemicals in your body take over to such a degree that you are just rushing beyond anything that anyone else would ever experience otherwise."

This adrenaline rush had a rejuvenating quality as well, which, for a number of soldiers, became somewhat addictive. Jeff Yushta tried to explain its impact:

> Most combat experience for soldiers is 90 percent boredom and 10 percent sheer terror. And here you are on these "search and destroys." You have had enough of this place to begin with. Everything is a pain in the ass. It's unbelievably hot. You are carrying sixty pounds of gear. You are pulling leeches off. And nothing is happening. And then . . . *pop!* Charlie opens up. And there is a five-minute firefight and you are refreshed! You are ready to go again. And then you go three or four klicks—same conditions. You just go down. And your

mind tells you, "You remember how we fixed that last time? We can do it again."

Tom Schultz expanded on that theme. "Maybe that is what we are all addicted to," he mused. "You don't get that kind of adrenaline rush in anything you do in this life. Adrenaline is a high-powered drug, however it is triggered. We are just creatures of response, right?"

But, the sober side of combat was never farther away than a medevac helicopter or a poncho-covered corpse, as Tom Magedanz discovered while patrolling in Happy Valley during February 1970. "Most of the time we would kill one or two NVA," said Magedanz. "For a while it was almost a game because we weren't losing anybody. Guys were sort of giddy or sort of happy if they killed NVA because it was like you were doing your job. But after Zoodsma was killed . . . that kind of cooled everybody's jets. That was a shock to everybody."

Americans were wounded or died—often in agony—with varying frequency, leaving soldiers to ponder each day, as Tom Schultz did, "Who's turn is it? It's somebody's turn. They didn't come to play."

As infantry soldiers became intimately acquainted with their own mortality, they acquired a determination to survive—to outlast, as Charles Anderson put it, those little "rice-powered bastards" no matter what. So the men faced their dilemmas, assessed their chances, and took whatever steps were available or appropriate in order to cope with the reality of their daily existence.[5]

Some soldiers took their lives a day at a time, choosing not to look beyond the immediate present. Others thought of themselves as being dead already and hoped that, with some luck and a bit of combat skill, they could slowly pull themselves through the tunnel toward the light that represented life and a trip home at the end of their tours. They became cynical and hard and distant because such qualities would help them to survive. They would change in other ways as well, depending on what they experienced during their personal wars in Vietnam.

Surviving the first months of combat propelled each man

closer to veteran status and gave him a leg up onto the plateau of effectiveness. Survival also helped alleviate some of the initial fears that soldiers brought with them on their first trips into the bush. Medic Francis Whitebird remembered that experience translated directly into self-confidence. "As time went on I realized I could make it out there as a medic," he explained. "After a while I became very confident in myself."

Optimism could, however, be heavily influenced by the degree and type of contact that a soldier experienced. At a time and in a place where firefights were few and enemy activity was limited mostly to booby traps, optimism might be quite high. Dan Krehbiel was confident that skill and precaution could make a difference. He also understood that, for others, it might not.

"Some guys in the other areas were in heavy combat . . . and guys got hurt every day, and it was a whole different flavor of war," said Krehbiel. "I was so happy I wasn't in I Corps or the Highlands, from what I've heard, because I knew what I was doing in III Corps. If you walked carefully and paid attention and didn't slough off, you could make it."

John Meyer was equally optimistic. After several months with his Combined Action Platoon south of Da Nang, he admitted: "I never believed for a moment that I would get hurt. It never occurred to me. The only thought I gave to it was, 'If I'm killed I'm not going to have to worry about it, so there is no sense worrying about it.' I always did what I had to do and I never really gave any regard to that matter."

Meyer's convictions helped him through six months of operations, but they were incapable of stopping shell fragments. A booby trap brought an end to his optimism. In the moments following the blast, Meyer recalled, "I kind of melted like the air went out of me. I know things changed at that time permanently. I never had quite the same outlook."

Confidence and savvy, without a touch of luck, were seldom sufficient to guarantee a soldier's survival for an entire tour of duty. The most cautious and prudent soldiers could, and did, die in battle. This fact forced soldiers to view their own futures with a certain degree of fatalism. The insane and inexplicable randomness of battle generated a sense of helplessness toward those exigencies against which no amount of skill or precaution could insulate a soldier. The idea of chance and luck grew to singular importance. Marine Ron Flesch, drawing from his experiences in 1965, wrote of this chilling aspect of combat. "Eyes aim rifles and fingers squeeze triggers, but fate decides who's in the wrong place at the wrong time, who's on the receiving end of the bullets. Being on the good side had no bearing on the situation."[6]

The relative forces of skill and luck were more specifically described by army lieutenant James McDonough:

> We would learn how little our decisions determined our futures. Rational decision-making or technical and physical skills may save you once or twice. But a man in combat is exposed a thousand times. A gust of wind blows at the right moment to take a mortar round ten yards farther to explode. A tree grows fifty years only to absorb a grenade fragment that would have otherwise entered your heart. A blade of grass or bent branch deflects a speeding bullet enough to send it harmlessly through your flopping shirt—or savagely through your brain or liver.[7]

In a short story written immediately after his return from Vietnam, Steve Fredrick equated his tour there to a carnival game: "Step right up, only one thin lifetime; and if you beat the game, you get time back plus a chance to spend it somewhere else. A game of chance, a game of skill. Step right up!"[8]

The death of others always gave pause to the living and caused them to wonder when their turn might come. Logically, there was no reassurance in asking the question, Why not me? Some soldiers became despondent and accepted the fact that sooner or later it *could* be them. They lost an appreciable fear of death and resigned themselves to that possibility. Rifleman Paul Meringolo was one who came to accept that there could likely be a fatal end to his tour in Vietnam:

> As I experienced various things further on through my tour of duty, I felt I wouldn't survive. It just seemed that as the days and months progressed I really felt I

wasn't going to get past this experience. Getting infused into the infantry and the everyday aggravations that you had to deal with: physical and mental exhaustion, somebody might trip an antipersonnel mine, or you might experience small-arms fire—the uncertainty. Every day your psyche and your physical being made you think how in the heck am I ever going to get past this? This was interspersed with the death of a close friend at an unexpected time and these became cumulative feelings. It is not like you could pass it by and have maybe one or two good days and go on to something else. If there was a period of relaxing or noncombat between these experiences, you fed on thoughts of what had happened and you knew it was going to happen again. So it kept adding on and on to the point where, for me . . . [I knew], something was going to happen that would affect me personally.

Glen Olstad entertained a similar sense of fatalism while serving with the 25th Infantry Division in 1968. "There were times that you didn't know why you were still alive or hadn't been seriously wounded," Olstad recalled. "I would say most of my tour I did not actually expect to come home. Someplace, sometime I expected I'd make the wrong move. We never talked about it, but I think everybody I was with felt the same way. We talked about home in the past tense. I can only remember one man that I was with that planned on what he was going to do when he got home. We all wanted to go home, but that was too far into the future."

Often the sensation of doom was more pervasive than specific. Gerry Barker suffered feelings of foreboding in each of his four tours in Vietnam. "I had premonitions that this was it," said Barker. "Now I suppose it was teenage melodrama or something else, but yeah, each time I was pretty certain I would not come back. I was surprised when I did."

There was very little a soldier could actually do to alter the conditions of his employment. Living to fight another day meant having to endure the same stresses and fears over and over again. But as long as a soldier lived, he also learned. Mike Meil did. An older NCO hollered at him not to jump as he leapt off the top of his APC one morning. Meil narrowly missed landing on an antipersonnel mine hidden by the roadside.

"I didn't have any idea it was there," Meil recalled. "I guess I wasn't looking for it to begin with. How *he* knew it was there I don't know. It was too far away for him to see it. He told me, 'You knew when we came in that the enemy had been here and probably set booby traps because we ran across tunnels in a creek bank. You saw the locations. You should have expected personnel mines.' "

There were no simple rules, no pat, easily remembered phrases that guaranteed survival. A soldier had to be careful and watch veterans to learn the tricks of the infantryman's trade. Every encounter with a booby trap or incoming mortar round improved combat skills and taught lessons. An ambush survived was a lesson learned and each fragment of knowledge improved one's odds. The will to survive drove men to become better soldiers. They developed an ability to truly see their surroundings and not just passively look around. They began to sense and feel, relying on past experiences to interpret the present. They walked in each others' footsteps not only because of the mines and booby traps, but because it became second nature to do so. They developed a strong camaraderie. They shared a collective mood and acquired a collective wisdom, a wisdom that was uncomplicated and could either protect a man's life or at least make it a bit easier to endure.

The cardinal rule was condensed to three letters: CYA (cover your ass). It was a new man's first lesson and the last admonishment to friends when an old-timer headed back to The World. More than mindless repetition, the phrase embodied the idea that each man was ultimately on his own. In the soldiers' minds, the military hierarchy itself seemed to scheme against their survival, and soldiers came to see themselves as expendable commodities. So each man took responsibility for his survival and learned the tricks of the trade. Soldiers learned to trust their instincts as well as their newly attuned senses. They also hedged their bets with lucky coins, extra boonie knives, pocket Bibles, and superior firepower.

The soldiers' apprehensions changed as their awareness of the dangers increased. Continued enemy contact demonstrated clearly the simple fact that the longer a soldier was exposed to battle, the more likely it was that he would eventually come to harm. It was a realization that quieted the enthusiasm of the new man and heralded his coming of age. After his first operations in the fall of 1968, a member of the 101st Airborne Division wrote, "There aren't very many of the enemy around here. They are mostly hard-core Viet Cong and they are hard to find. Nobody really wants to find them that bad anyway."[9]

Sergeant Michael Jackson observed similar feelings within his company of that same division in 1970. "I would say that people who [went] over there at seventeen, eighteen, nineteen years old—teenagers, white, Mom, apple pie, Chevrolet, 'Let's get the VC'—after three or four months had a different outlook. If they believed in search and destroy when they first got there, they were soon believing in search and avoid."

Soldiers never got used to battle, but they did become more adept at coping with its stresses and avoiding its pitfalls. Richard Holmes noted that continued actions

> do not strengthen a soldier's courage and willingness to fight; rather, they are debilitating. Whereas their first few battles had helped such men grow in confidence and improve in tactical ability, subsequent actions tended to have the reverse effect. The loss of their friends affected them deeply, and they began to feel that their chances of survival were diminished with each action.[10]

What Tom Magedanz remembered most was "just progressively getting more and more tired, emotionally tired, too, and under more and more strain as time went on." The stress was worse for men who experienced close calls or wounds. Such soldiers were left with no illusions as to the reality of war and the personal stakes for which each man played.

Jerry Severson's ten-man squad was hit by a command-detonated mine while providing road security during Operation

Junction City in Tay Ninh Province in early 1967. The mine killed two men and wounded five others, including Severson. "I felt the thing hit me and I heard the blast, saw the smoke, whatever," Severson recalled. "I pulled my shirt out and blood was running out of my chest right over my heart. I thought, Well, it's curtains for you. When the blood runs out you're done for. Then I heard the other guys screaming and, me being medic, I took off and my legs went out from under me. I didn't even realize that I had been hit in both legs. I got up finally and started patching guys up and seeing how bad off they were. You do what you can. I started working on the guys I figured would come out of it."

When Severson returned to his unit after his release from the hospital, he discovered that he had won a new degree of respect from the men. He also had a new attitude that made him see things differently.

"It was real to me then, and when they shot, boy, I'd duck! I started looking for something to hide behind because there was none of this jumping right up and running out in the face of the enemy and all that good garbage anymore, no sir!" said Severson. "I found myself a hole I could get into and stuck my head out very carefully when looking around corners and things like that. I managed to function and do the job all right, but I had a whole different attitude toward it. I was scared! I was scared to death most of the time after that."

Men came to realize the futility of dwelling on their fears. The necessity of coping with fear and channeling it into some benign form was a key part of the process of maturing into a veteran combat soldier; it was a process that could hardly be overstated. According to Paul Meringolo:

> You just wouldn't be able to go on and make it through a year tour if you were always worried about it. It seemed through some metamorphosis, that after you were in country a month or so you learned to live with this fear. It doesn't go away, it just wasn't as overpowering as it was in your first days. You got accustomed to it. You adjusted to the reality of seeing dead bodies and the possibility of being ambushed or the possibility of hitting booby traps and mines.

After you were there that short while, you realized that you couldn't function in any capacity if you let that feeling [of fear] overpower or control you. So you somehow slowly evolved into just doing what you had to do and realized that you had a long time to go. Most of the time during the war you weren't thinking about death on a day-to-day basis, you just got on with what was happening. Believe it or not, the killing or the experiences became commonplace and you learned to adjust and adapt. If you sat back some nights and thought about it, you realized how frightening it was.

Accompanying his loss of innocence, Steve Fredrick also realized an increased sense of cynicism toward his government and the people who ran it. But most of all, the young sergeant was quick to point out, "I came to realize right then and there how goddamned short my life might end up being."

Soldiers began to react automatically to the spontaneity and violence of combat with a single-minded intensity that often surprised them. Tom Schultz remembered that in the first moment of battle a split-second debate took place in his mind between his fears, his sense of obligation, and his desire to live. "There is a side of you that tells you not to do anything, there is a side of you that tells you [that] you have to do something, and there is a side of you that does something," explained Schultz. "Whether it is right or wrong you do something. You don't just lay there and whimper until it's over. It's really strange."

Jerry Severson said he experienced an initial flash of panic, after which, "If you did see something move, then you shot at it—I think in most cases probably without even aiming at it. But you would quick point over in that direction and pull the trigger and hope to hell you hit something. It was just total reaction rather than a lot of thought going into it in my case. I imagine my heart had to be going two hundred and twenty miles per hour."

During the first moments of combat Jerry Johnson recalled wishing he could have crawled up inside his steel pot with just his feet sticking out. But, as he began to focus on doing his job, he discovered that the anxiety subsided.

Likewise, marine scout observer Jack Freitag found that when the shooting started, "I wasn't concerned about anything else as much as just getting my gun's placement right. So really I had my mind so occupied that I wasn't thinking about anything else."

Reaction could be so automatic that a man under fire might feel detached from his actions, separated from the control of his own response. As Layne Anderson put it, "You don't really think, you just act on instinct." It was a sensation that Paul Meringolo described as "almost like being on automatic pilot. Your feelings and your actions are sort of taken over by this internal machine," he recalled. "Everything is moving at an accelerated pace and you are swept along with it. And even though you are a part of it, you have this excited detachment about it. You make no value judgments, no conscious decisions, you just flow with the experience."

Phil Yaeger believed that such detachment was psychologically defensive:

> You go on automatic or you don't survive. I won't say I didn't think, I just didn't react to the horror around me. My emotions shut down. I think it is typical of marines. I mean, the training will only take you so far and then you suck it up, you just do it. I wasn't even especially scared when it got that bad. Not like I was when I first got there and not like I was a month before my DEROS. Everything between those two extremes was pretty much one foot in front of the other—automatic pilot. And that was reinforced by losing people I was close to.

Many soldiers experienced the progressive erosion of morale as their tours continued. Much of this was the result of the cumulative effect of stress over a long period of time. The thought process leading to such changes in attitude was described by Paul Fussell, who delineated the evolution of fear as he observed it during World War II. Fussell noted that fear manifested itself in three stages. At first, soldiers rationalized that nothing would happen to them for whatever reason they chose. This self-persuasion was eventually replaced by the belief that something *could* happen, and it was important to ensure as far as humanly possible that it didn't. Soldiers in Vietnam rationalized that by being more vigilant, digging their foxholes a bit deeper, carrying more ammunition, avoiding tunnels, wearing a flak jacket, or myriad other precautions, they might ensure their survival. But as time passed, men who saw considerable combat often came to the decision that, "death and injury are matters more of luck than of skill," making inevitable Fussell's third stage: "It is *going* to happen to me and only my not being there is going to prevent it."[11]

Whereas most men conditioned themselves to function under fire and a few men came to enjoy it, there were a few for whom the stress of exposure to battle was simply too much. But fleeing the battlefield was not common in Vietnam if for no other reason than that, in a war without fronts, soldiers had no way of knowing which way to run. Operating in isolated platoons and companies, most troops were too far from a rear area for men to entertain any hope of seeking safety there. Survival depended on staying with the group rather than running away from it. Only men in total panic took flight, and such instances were rare. Vernon Janick, for example, recalled only one such instance occurring in his two tours with the 4th Infantry Division.

Sergeant William Harken said that he was compelled to physically subdue one of his men:

> I had a short-timer with just two weeks left. He was the most scared individual I've ever seen in my life, bar none! He made it three hundred and fifty-one days. He thought he was going to die. I had to literally keep a hold of him. He was going bonkers.
>
> "I don't want to die! I don't want to die! Get me out of here." So I just grabbed a hold of him. He was just a little guy. Physically I held him down. Then, fortunately, the last thing I remember he went on sick call back to Cu Chi and I never saw him again.

The only way to escape field duty was to hide out in the base camps or forward firebases, either by feigning illness or injury, by refusing outright to return to the field, or by getting transferred to a noncombat job. Outright refusal could result in jail time in Long Binh in a facility known derisively as LBJ (Long Binh Jail). Steve Fredrick knew men who refused to go to the field, but his personal code of honor made the act an alternative he never considered. By December 1968, however, Sergeant Fredrick's attitude had softened. "I'm . . . waiting to take a prisoner to Long Binh Jail down south," he wrote in a letter to his father. "He is an American and the reason he is going to jail is because he refuses to go to the field and be a line doggie. He has been with us for longer than I have and I guess he just lost his nerve. I can't really blame him."[12]

David Sartori had a similar experience two days before Christmas that same year. While driving a truck, Sartori saw a black GI, being taken against his will back to the field, jump from a jeep and collapse. The two soldiers escorting the man claimed that he was faking unconsciousness on the roadway. Sartori later recalled in a letter:

> Suddenly the heretofore "unconscious GI" sprang to his feet and withdrew a fragmentation grenade from his pocket and pulled the ignition pin: however, he still held securely onto the trigger handle. As the MP approached he extended his hand holding the grenade under my chin. The MP got his attention and I ran onto the road. . . . Additional MPs with the Criminal Investigators arrived. The GI finally surrendered the grenade to my MP buddy.
>
> The man was not ill. He just wanted out and that's what he got. He was a typical case of what I refer to as "probation justice." Like thousands of men in the Army, he had been given the choice of either go[ing] Army or go[ing to] prison by a civilian probation officer. These people had disciplinary problems as civilians and they certainly aren't rehabilitated because they don the uniform of "Whitey's army." Our stockade on Long Binh Post is filled with these types of veterans from civilian courts.[13]

Although there were few ways by which a soldier could avoid the hazards of field duty, there always seemed to be a few who sought by whatever means possible to remove themselves from danger. Very few men chose the extreme of desertion, but there were those who were prone to hide during combat and not take part. A few others chose to wound themselves so that they would be evacuated safely out of the field. Vernon Janick recalled two such instances. In the first incident, "a man had his buddy shoot him in the calf. The other guy I remember started jabbing himself with a *punji* stick. He pissed and shit in a little thing and stirred the stick in there so it would get him infected enough to get out." Janick was quick to admit, however, that "there was a lot of talk, too. A lot of wishing it would happen. Sometimes it was so miserable that it went through your mind anyway—wishing for that million dollar wound to get you out."

The number of self-inflicted wounds will probably never be known, since such wounds were probably recorded as accidents or passed off as having occurred in combat. On patrol with a company from the 5th Mechanized Infantry Division in 1971, *Stars and Stripes* correspondent Dan Evans recorded one such occurrence. The men had been in the field for two weeks and had suffered several casualties killed and wounded. They were tired, and resupply had been poor. On a Sunday morning a GI shot himself in the foot with his M16. The shooting was officially recorded as an accident, but Evans was told by the men in the unit that the man just wanted to get out of the field.[14]

Soldiers generally treated self-inflicted wounds as none of their business. In Jerry Johnson's unit the men knew of one particular soldier whose wound was self-inflicted, but no one disputed the man's claim to having been shot by accident. "One guy saw him do it," said Johnson. "But he wasn't going to rat on him because the guy had a loaded weapon and he didn't. I would say he was afraid he would nail him some night back in the company area. Everybody's got enemies at least every once in a while, and you just didn't know [if] the guy was nuts! He might get you in your bunk or something. They didn't have to medevac him, he was already in the rear. They just took him down to the aid station."

A few men developed the habit of hiding during contact. Such behavior did nothing to assist group survival, and the practice was heartily discouraged by the others in the unit, particularly if the shirkers were new NCOs or officers. Jon Neely recalled serving with one NCO school graduate who was fantastic at barking out orders but was of little value in combat. According to Neely:

> The first firefight we got into after he joined our unit, everybody was doing their job. At that time I had been moved up to squad leader, so I was going around making sure everything was alright and that everybody was doing what they were supposed to be doing. I just happened to look around and I couldn't find the guy. He was nowhere around. I thought maybe he'd been hit or something.
>
> Well, about two minutes after the firefight was over, one of the guys found him crawling out from underneath an APC. He got so scared, that was where he went. So we had a talk with him, if you want to call it that. [We] drummed it into his head that everybody had a job to do including him, do the job or we'd find something else to do with him. Well, he never did straighten out. Fortunately for him, we got him transferred out before he got shot by somebody other than the enemy.

Tom Schultz's company had similar problems with a captain, and Schultz's disgust for the man remained long after the officer was relieved of his command. Schultz remembered little about him other than that he was short in height. Time had erased the name, but not Schultz's memory of the man leading the unit into two ambushes and then lying on the ground vomiting when the shooting started.

Some men, as Larry Gates came to understand, simply could not withstand the strain of combat and those men did not return to the field. Gates personally felt no animosity for them. He had been in combat and understood the shallow meaning of words such as coward.

"The fact that you . . . may get killed at any minute plays on a person's mind," Gates explained. "We did have one casualty because of that. He made it through a thirty-day operation, but he didn't come back out with us three days later. So we lost one man to the strain of it all. It's not a matter of being a coward, it's just a matter of what you can put up with and for how long."

David Sartori witnessed a dramatic example of combat fatigue in the 199th Light Infantry Brigade's chapel. A man in the front pew arose and preached incessantly to an almost empty church for fifteen minutes prior to the start of the service.

> Since he had no odor of alcohol, eyes normal, I assumed he was neither intoxicated nor drugged, but rather psychotic. I phoned our emergency ambulance and we took the poor devil to the hospital on Long Binh. . . . The man said he was against killing and believed in love and not hate. He wanted to go to heaven and leave the wicked world behind.
> . . . It was the worst psychotic case I've ever seen. He was in that condition for a week and hanging around the Chapel. Two days later the GI was medevac'd to San Francisco. He had been on an APC with the 17th Cav and saw too much shit too soon.[15]

A few found their existence impossible to endure, for whatever reasons, and brought an end to their lives at a moment of their choosing. Suicide is always an enigma. To die by one's own hand in time of war is doubly puzzling. John Merrell witnessed one incident involving an ARVN soldier:

> Our company was told to create an LZ in the middle of the jungle on top of this hill for the ARVN. They were having a big assault in this area and the choppers would come in so far, drop them off, and another set would come in and take them the rest of the way. . . . All these ARVNs would come in and we'd go try and see if we could talk to them. It was something to do. We were standing there just like I'm talking to you, and they had the same stuff we had: packs on and grenades and stuff. One guy pulled the pin on his grenade. Suicide, see. That sort of blew me away. I found out how fast I was. He killed himself. Blew his head right

off. . . . What his friends said afterward was that he
didn't want to be in the army. He was afraid or something. He just didn't want to be in the army, so he ended
it. That was weird.

The records show that 382 Americans, including just 23
marines, committed suicide in Vietnam.[16] If the numbers are
correct, marine John Meyer's Combined Action Company
was an unfortunate statistical rarity. "In the six months I was
with this company, our company strength was never over a
hundred men," said Meyer. "And out of those hundred men,
two committed suicide on the eve of their return to the States.
It is—well—I can't explain it. I don't understand it. You'd
think they'd be in anything but a suicidal mood. To me that is
a pretty high rate of suicide."

Jon Neely saw a man in his platoon commit suicide aboard
a barge while guarding the Ben Luc bridge. Neely remembered the man as very quiet and withdrawn.

> He would get off by himself and just sit there and
> clean his weapon or stare off into the countryside. This
> one particular night it was his time for guard duty and
> the rest of us were supposed to be sleeping. For some
> reason I couldn't sleep and my squad leader . . .
> couldn't sleep, so we were sitting up at the one end of
> the barge just quietly talking about back home and dif-
> ferent things.
>   He said, "I think it's about time for him to throw a
> charge in there [the water]. He hasn't thrown one in a
> while." So we got up and started walking down towards
> the guy and he was clear at the other end of the barge.
> We saw him light a fuse. He had a stick of C-4 and he
> lit the fuse and instead of throwing it he held it up
> against his chest. We hollered at him, but he wouldn't
> move it. Of course the C-4 went off and just instantly
> killed the guy.

The strain endured by soldiers in war is cumulative. Soldiers in Vietnam realized that they had few alternatives but to
face the danger and press onward. For some, there was sim-

ply no ability to cope any longer. For others, it was not merely the fear of death that fueled their apprehensions, but the acknowledgment that there might well be things that could happen to them that were worse than dying. As John Dollard noted in his study of fear in battle, the anxiety that new men experienced of being labeled a coward rapidly gave way to a fear of being crippled or disfigured. The greatest fear was of wounds to the abdomen, eyes, brain, and genitals.[17] Similar attitudes certainly existed among soldiers in Vietnam.

Looking back, Michael Jackson said that although "I was afraid all the time I was over there . . . I really didn't fear dying—being killed. What I did fear was being handicapped—really messed up. I didn't want any pain and I didn't want to come back without everything I went over there with. My sense was, having seen what I saw, if I was going to be killed I wasn't going to be in much pain. It would be [snap of the fingers] just like that. I certainly didn't want to die, but I had my doubts [about living incapacitated]."

Resignation to one's fate was simply one of many methods by which soldiers attempted to reach a workable compromise between their unavoidable exposure to the dangers of combat and the almost overpowering desire to avoid that danger. So infantrymen assembled a vast array of mechanisms and attitudes that enabled them to cope with their dilemma.

Coping often took the form of adopting precautionary behaviors—positive actions in the field that helped soldiers stay alert and alive. Machine gunner Dennis Foell's precautions in the Hiep Duc Valley probably saved several lives. His squad had just finished digging in when "they started hitting us with mortars. The first one that came in was a dud round and hit the CP. It went right through the poncho liners they had strung up there to make shade. . . . Then they came in pretty good and our foxhole was dug big enough for approximately four or five men. If I remember correctly I think there were like fourteen guys altogether from other squads who had piled in. I fortunately happened to be on the bottom."

Jerry Severson believed in the value of foxholes too, and dug them even when he was at a firebase. "I'd wake up in the hole a lot of times and not even remember getting into it," he said. "A lot of times, we weren't even taking incoming rounds. It was our own artillery shooting out. As soon as you heard something go off, you were in a hole."

Some soldiers carried extra weapons or ammunition, whereas others faithfully wore helmets or flak jackets. In lieu of genuine ways to reduce their exposure to danger, soldiers often tried to allay their fears by treating the symptoms of their distress rather than the cause, which was beyond their ability to control. One such method was the observance of superstitions and the adoption of good-luck pieces.

Don Putnam carried a silver dollar given to him by the proprietress of a local tavern near Green Bay, Wisconsin. She gave silver dollars to six boys headed to Vietnam. All six came back. Putnam still carries it. Other soldiers might carry a bullet or shell fragment that they believed had positive qualities simply because it came close to them and missed. Some men carried pictures of loved ones or articles of women's clothing, or went through whatever rituals they believed would afford them some degree of safety. There were soldiers who might squirrel away a personal possession owned by a man who had survived his tour. Others tried to stay near someone they thought was lucky, hoping that the luck was contagious or at least radiated an aura from which they too might benefit. Other men were considered jinxes and so were avoided. Places could also be considered cursed or simply bad luck to be near. Some GIs felt especially uneasy in Vietnamese cemeteries. Such sites were often selected for night ambushes or defensive positions because they were on high ground and the raised burial mounds offered good cover. Similarly, locations in which a unit had previously suffered casualties could be eerie. Such areas often contained skeletal remains of enemy soldiers as well as the debris of battle. Soldiers have always been superstitious about such places.

Religious beliefs provided comfort for many soldiers. Jerry Severson carried items representing both the religious and the secular realms. "I carried Roy Froy, one of those fuzzball things that had eyes and feet," explained Severson. "When I went over there my sister gave me that thing and, boy, that was important! Another thing, not that I was ever a religious person, but I had a little Bible with me and the only time I ever read it was in the hospital after I was wounded."

"With the Man upstairs looking down at us, who do we fear?" Jeff Beatty wrote to his mother from the Central Highlands. It was a line from a prayer book she had sent him. The devotional and Bible returned home, along with other miscellaneous personal effects, but not the son who had been comforted by their words.[18]

Many infantrymen chose to help ease the pain of their existence through self-medication. This generally took the form of communal drinking bouts when a unit stood down or entered a base area and could relax. The practice helped make sleep easier by numbing the body and clouding the memory. Other drugs of preference, such as marijuana and hashish, were cheap, potent, and readily available, especially later in the war, for those who chose to use them.

According to Jon Neely, "Everything was right at your disposal. If you wanted marijuana, any gook kid could run and get you a big bag for a five dollar bill." A country that seemed to have little else had easy access to drugs and liquor. By 1968, even in the more remote villages, corpsman John Meyer recalled, "All you had to do was wave some money at the Vietnamese and say *tuc fin* and they would be back with the marijuana in no time."

"Anytime you got back to a big firebase like Tay Ninh or Long Binh," claimed Paul Gerrits, "you could give a mamasan a carton of Salem cigarets in the wrapper and the next morning she would sell you back the same carton of cigarets filled with marijuana and rewrapped in cellophane. The price," he recalled, "was about ten dollars a carton and the mamasan kept the Salems."

Marijuana cigarets were also frequently purchased in what the soldiers called "party packs," ten prerolled joints sealed in a plastic bag. They typically cost about a hundred piasters, or fifty cents.

One soldier said of his first encounter with smoking marijuana in 1970, "It was a wonderful experience for me. It really worked as an anesthetic and helped me escape. There were none of the terrible side effects that came from alcohol: no throwing up, no dizziness, no stomach pains, which I had been getting. And I got the same escape that I had from alcohol. It was really a valuable tranquilizer to us guys."

Those who grew tired of marijuana could purchase OJs—joints soaked in opium—or they could buy marijuana cigarets sprinkled with skag (heroin). Skag and opium were also available in various forms, although their use was far less widespread. Dwight Reiland, for example, recalled that in 1971 there was only one man in his unit who snorted skag.

Apart from marijuana, the only other drug that enjoyed anything approximating widespread use was speed, typically sold in liquid form and used by soldiers to help them either stay awake in the field or celebrate in the rear. Corpsman John Meyer remembered that the most readily obtainable source for speed was to purchase one of several French pharmaceuticals available on the black market. Along with a barbiturate or downer appropriately nicknamed Number Ten, there was, according to Meyer, "a popular form of speed the marines called moon juice." Meyer thought that the product's brand name was Obeseatrol, and noted, "it was some kind of amphetamine-laced weight-control product." Meyer found the idea of the dietary liquid absurd. "I don't know how the hell this ended up in Vietnam," he said, shaking his head, "because there weren't too many obese Vietnamese. It had to be meant for the black market to sell to the troops."

Marine Terry Shepardson also remembered the liquid in the little bottle. "One teaspoon every eight hours for weight control," he said with a smile. "But a half a bottle would do wonders for you." According to Jon Neely just half an ounce from the four-ounce bottle and "you were guaranteed you were going to be up all night flying high."

Soldiers did not use alcohol or narcotics to any great extent while in the field; the danger inherent in such a practice was obvious. Once safely back in a rear area, however, the binges became truly epic. According to Michael Jackson, soldiers were either "boozers or heads." And as John Merrell suggested, "What's the difference if you sat down and smoked two joints or drank a six-pack of beer except that the army gave you the beer. Either you got your warm Black Label beer and liked it or you didn't." Whatever one's preference, Michael Jackson claimed, "everybody would get messed up when they were in the rear, and nobody really had a problem with it because everybody felt pretty secure in hootches close to bunkers."

Coping might also involve nothing more than keeping focused on the mundane aspects of everyday life and avoiding thoughts about the perils of operating in the bush. A soldier might clean his rifle with fanatical diligence or develop a compulsion for rearranging the equipment in his pack. The responsibilities of NCOs and officers kept their minds occupied with practical matters ranging from foot care to resupply to oral hygiene.

For most soldiers, the stresses of combat also made it necessary to disconnect or redirect their emotions. In the process, anger often came to be the only feeling some soldiers could recognize. Sergeant Willie Williams saw a lot of friendly casualties in 1966 during his first five months in Vietnam. It made him realize what war actually meant, and that realization prompted a lot of hate. Probing his own reactions, Williams said simply, "After that, killing didn't bother me."

Marine Phil Yaeger underwent a similar process after he experienced the carnage of his early battles along the DMZ. "I don't think I was 'right' from Mutter Ridge on in the sense that I am now," he explained. "I was reprogrammed to fight a war. I was good at it. But I just shut down all my emotions, or attempted to. I could feel anger, but I couldn't feel anything but anger. And in that sense I wasn't right, and it took me a long time to get even close to being right."

Rifleman Tom Schultz strove to maintain control of his emotions as well. "It's no longer a game, and you try to divorce yourself from your feelings because emotions will kill you in combat," Schultz said. "I guess you become somewhat hardened to the fact of death. Sure you feel remorse for what you do, and you feel sympathy for the families and all that, but you cannot get tied into it or you'll lose perspective and make mistakes. Then you don't make it. That's the way it was. I changed in that way."

Emotions could never be totally suppressed, however; as a compromise, soldiers tried to remain aloof. Some saw their actions as nothing more than being part of the job. Ed Hoban tried to maintain the attitude that he was doing "what I *had* to do, and at that time that was my job. To this day a job is a job. I think anybody who is in that situation would feel that way, too." Still others were able to cloak their fears in the rationalization that there was nothing to be helped by worrying, so it was best not to think about anything.

Paul Gerrits relied on both methods to help deal with his stress. He described his attitude as "pretty good while I was over there. I was doing my duty. I was going to do it the best I possibly could without any bitching. If something came up that was beyond my control, why should I worry about it? Why worry about something you can't possibly control?"

Like many of his peers in the field, Dan Krehbiel chose to adopt the attitude that nothing he experienced really mattered. His rationale was perfectly logical to anyone serving in the field with no way out.

"I never really understood what I was doing there," Krehbiel admitted. "I numbed myself to that question and all other questions and I subjugated them to the one thought that it doesn't mean anything. That was an expression we used, 'Fuck it, it don't mean nothing!' We used that expression for everything. Coarse though it may sound, it was the catchphrase. Your best buddy, your card partner, could get killed. You'd say that and keep on moving. 'It doesn't matter. Get home. It's okay.' You just numbed out."

The only problem with such detachment was that few soldiers could really convince themselves of it. Jeff Yushta saw through the veneer. "When you lost a good friend it hurt. And when guys went home—rotated out—that hurt. You put on a good front and said to yourself that nothing meant anything; but deep down it did."

Genuine humor also made coping with daily life more bearable and was a treasured commodity in the bush. But a grim, gallows humor permeated the war as well, serving as a facade for toughness and levity. Like a callus on the soul, dark humor and sardonic laughter revealed pain and hurt beneath the surface. Perversely, making a joke about death helped men overcome its horror and made the killing easier to inflict or to accept afterward by demoting of the enemy to a comedic parody of humanity. Enemy skulls bedecked with unit patches, sunglasses, cigarets, or a boonie hat cheapened

death and made it easier to deal with. A few soldiers mutilated the dead or took parts from enemy corpses as trophies.
Such souvenirs occasionally found their way into the men's
billets or were even mailed home. Events in the bush frequently revealed the dark humor of men hardened to normal
emotions. Mike Meil remembered one incident he thought to
be quite humorous in 1967, yet it seemed strangely perverse
twenty years later:

> We ran into an NVA regiment. This time we were
> riding personnel carriers back in and we ran into some
> shit. We got in a hell of a battle. There were so many
> bodies around there that they were just lying all over all
> shot up and crawling or dead. . . . There was a dead
> body laying out and his legs were extended and the
> driver turned to me because I was riding up alongside
> the cupola behind the driver's hatch. He said, "Watch
> this." He ran over the dead soldier's knees and the force
> of the weight of the tracked vehicle on his legs sat him
> right up into the side of the vehicle. His face came right
> up flat into the side of the personnel carrier, which was
> really morbid. But Jesus—we just had a hell of a
> chuckle out of that. As morbid as it was, we thought it
> was funnier than hell. And [the driver] turned around as
> he looked at me and said, "That's neat." You laugh
> about this shit and then you think sometimes, How can
> you?

Genuine humor, on the other hand, served to take some of
the sting out of life in the field. Every unit had its clowns who
somehow made the worst bearable and helped everyone endure beyond their limits. Such men were worth their weight
in gold in helping to maintain a unit's morale.

Oddly enough, fatigue could also sometimes make it easier to function in the bush and cope with the stress of combat.
Fatigue often made the troops feel invincible, or just too tired
to care. Vernon Janick knew the feeling well. "Some days you
were more gung ho than others," he said. "There were times
over there when you just didn't give a shit. You would just go
ahead and say, 'Fuck it!' You know? Do it anyway. Not care.

We had a lot of those times. You got so fed up with everything you didn't check for booby traps, or you checked a bunker by just jumping down in there. You just wanted to get them so bad that you didn't care. But at other times you were really super cautious. It varied, you had mixed feelings."

After heavy contact and numerous long operations, Willie Williams had seen too much to care any longer about much of anything. The stress and fatigue he endured each day had altered his outlook completely.

"I don't know if I wasn't afraid—that's a toughy to answer," Williams admitted. "But I didn't care. Life didn't mean nothing to me and I wasn't afraid of dying. If it happened, it happened. That was the attitude I had. Then I got to a point of where I felt that I was immortal—that I couldn't be killed."

As infantrymen learned to cope with the dangers of their occupation, they also began to develop a cynicism that changed their commitment to the war itself. Although their combat efficiency increased during the first three months, their commitment to the stated aims and goals of the war began to slide in the opposite direction.

Disenchantment had always existed, even in the first years of America's involvement in Vietnam, but it became more obvious and widespread by mid-1968, when the undeclared war grew ever more unpopular in the wake of the Tet offensive and the presidential election campaigns. The actual experience of fighting laid the groundwork for changes in the attitudes of American combat soldiers toward their government's stated objectives in Vietnam and toward the government of South Vietnam. These attitudes were passed on from veterans to new guys, resulting in a slowly maturing pessimism that was inherited and inculcated in the squads and fire teams—where it really mattered. At what was literally the grass roots level, soldiers knew exactly what they were fighting for; being shot at made that obvious. What became obscure in the daily attrition was the purpose: what they were hoping to achieve for all the effort. Unfortunately, most soldiers were unable to find any apparent purpose for the sacrifices they had witnessed or made. The cause in Vietnam that had seemed so necessary and immediate in 1965 was remarkably devoid of genuine meaning after only a few lives or enemy contacts or rotations. Commitment to the war and its ideals was replaced by practical considerations that were, of necessity, self-centered.[19]

Although most soldiers in Vietnam wanted to "win" in some ultimate sense, the goal of the man in the field was to simply survive to make it home again. That thought came to dominate the actions of nearly every soldier. The realization that they were fighting to get home again put an end to many of the predilections they entertained when they went overseas. Some veterans say that they fought for God and country and to stop the spread of communism. Far more fought because their pride, self-respect, and sense of self-preservation demanded it. For most, there did not seem to be any loftier concerns than those.

Many soldiers, such as Steve Fredrick, believed that in principle America was justified in being in Vietnam. It was not until Fredrick got home that he detached himself enough from the war to question that aspect of it. He was quick to admit that once the shooting started he immediately put aside any notions he may have entertained about philosophy and politics. His motivation for fighting became extremely simplistic:

There are people out there trying to kill you. That does something to you. And then, when you actually start to see it happen, I mean, you're right up close and there is blood and guts and gore and you get your own hands bloody, you have to change. I realized what had happened to me. I'm a poor little sodbuster from Iowa who got stuck over there and was told to kill people. . . . It doesn't matter what you think or what you do. What matters is to survive and stay alive for a year. That was just the most important thing that there was. If something would have got in the way of me staying alive, I'd of had to kill it. That's what made me fight. It wasn't that I thought I was fighting for my country or saving Vietnam or anything. It was me, Steve Fredrick! And if I didn't kill it, it would kill me. That's what it boiled down to.

What made Sergeant Fredrick's sentiments the norm among combat troops in Vietnam was the fact that, as the years went by, the situation seemed to stagnate. Throughout the war success was measured by the effort rather than the achievement. There was no denying the effort, and using such a yardstick left room for glowing optimism. But as soldiers kept returning to fight for the same terrain, as casualties mounted during operations that mirrored previous ones, the disparity between effort and result weakened their resolve.

American soldiers also viewed the Vietnamese government and its armed forces with contempt. It was a government that most soldiers believed to be corrupt and hardly worth defending, which prompted GIs throughout the war to wonder why they were enduring all that they were. Sergeant Gerry Barker remembered that, back in 1966, his men were making jokes about the Vietnamese government. While in the hospital with malaria, Barker met then Vice President Nguyen Cao Ky's wife as she came through his hospital ward giving cigaret lighters to the wounded Americans. The feelings of the man in the bed next to Barker seemed to express with absolute clarity an attitude common to many. "Boy," he sighed, "I almost feel contaminated taking this."

In April 1967, the Reverend Dr. Martin Luther King, in his "Declaration of Independence from the War in Vietnam" given at Manhattan's Riverside Church, noted that during the conflict, apart from the usual brutalizing process to which soldiers are exposed in any war, "We are adding cynicism to the process of death, for our troops must know after a short period there that none of the things we claim to be fighting for are really involved."[20]

As new men began to witness the deaths of their comrades, they found it increasingly difficult to explain why their lives were being spent inflicting more death. It didn't take long for marine Jack Freitag to discover that:

> We weren't fighting for democracy or the country. I realized that the majority of the people in that country did not want us there. . . . I bet I went through hundreds of hamlets and little villages over there, and I never had

a Vietnamese come up to me and say, "There's VC over there."

We'd go ask them, "Where are the VC?" But they were all VC. They fed them and clothed them, sheltered them. . . . And I thought it would be just the opposite when I got there. I thought the people in the South that weren't carrying weapons would be on our side. It was apparent that they weren't.

We fought for survival and each other's survival. I don't think we fought for democracy or freedom for the country because we knew that wasn't the case.

In coping with the fear and hardships, GIs struck back at what they believed to be the source of danger or frustration. In the process, they developed hatred. Mike Meil remembered that he built up a hatred simply because he was scared.

There was a possibility that they would kill you and the more opportunity they had, I think, your feelings grew stronger and stronger. You didn't feel wanted, supposedly, by the South Vietnamese. When I first went over there, I was under the impression that I was there to help them. As time went by, I felt the majority of them didn't want us there. . . . It was much easier for them to accept the communist regime rather than get their ass kicked from two different sides. And I guess you built up a hatred because you were so confused. That was the only way that you could protect yourself.

Most soldiers came to equate their enemy or any obstacle to their survival as merely that—an obstacle. Such feelings reduced the enemy, as Paul Fussell noted, to being simply an impediment to each infantryman's safe return home.[21] Lieutenant Michael Lanning saw the enemy in exactly that way. He defined his duty as an officer in terms of overcoming that obstacle, not for the furthering of his nation's aims or for some greater goal, but to secure the survival of each of his men.[22] A sentiment expressed by one of Lieutenant Lanning's men seemed to encapsulate a simple truth about how Americans saw the war they were fighting: "It's not who's right, but who's LEFT!"[23]

If the guilt felt by soldiers after eradicating those impediments to their safe return was not exactly overpowering, neither was there any real sense of accomplishment. Men matured in the field without gaining any insight into why they were fighting; they were merely able to strip away the reasons that were false. As time passed, it got easier to pull the trigger, easier to look at the corpses. As Willie Williams noted so succinctly, "The first time I actually saw a person and fired, it was difficult. After I saw the way our people were dying, the trigger pulled easier. Everything I did was for survival."

Marine Vince Olson felt much the same way after seeing "a lot of killing and fighting in the short period of time (1967–1968) I was there. It didn't bother me a bit to shoot an NVA or a Viet Cong. Even today I don't think it would bother me, because I was in combat. If I'd shot somebody right at first before I saw any of our men get killed, it might have bothered me more. But I think after you see somebody get killed by the enemy it takes some pressure off your conscience somehow."

The transition to soldiering was a regressive one. Men sensed that whatever they had become as soldiers was less than what they had once been. They had been provided with the means to act violently, and they saw enough violence directed against them to make them want to retaliate in kind. The possibility of death convinced them that they could no longer maintain humanistic sentiments in combat that might come between physical survival and the niceties of a distant and civilized world. Most men conditioned themselves to kill, but, like William Harken, they got no pleasure from doing so. In battle, response was usually instantaneous, and such programmed behavior overrode many of a soldier's internal controls. As Steve Fredrick put it, "What a man can do when he has to—that or die—is pretty incredible."

Gerry Barker was a bit more philosophical:

> Nobody comes out of war with respect for themselves. That is the biggest thing you lose. . . . A person who goes through something like Vietnam realizes how

terribly afraid he was. You would sell your mother to get off that damn helicopter before that infil[tration]. I don't think any of us came back feeling like we were successful. I think that is the thing the experience robs you of. You were vulnerable. You weren't very good at what you set out to do, and you lost that feeling of immortality. You realized that a seventeen year old who is a whole lot more on the ball than you can get killed. I think that really cuts your legs out from under you. . . . You weren't the same person anymore.

Even in wars with clear-cut causes, the actions of the man on the battlefield are survival centered. Paul Fussell quoted a private on the Anzio beachhead during World War II as saying, "If we killed we could go on living. Whatever we were fighting for seemed irrelevant."[24]

Journalist Ward Just noted a similar attitude in 1966. According to Just, "All of the arguments and the doubts became irrelevant when men fought to survive. The idea was that men were not fighting for any reason, or any ideology, but because they were there; they fought for their friends."[25]

Private Tom Schultz couldn't have agreed more. "The primary concern of every soldier excluding none that I knew, with the exception of maybe the higher-ranking officers captain and above," he said, "was getting home alive."

Dan Krehbiel gradually came to harbor serious misgivings about his reasons for fighting after President Nixon promised to withdraw American troops from Vietnam.

As I was going over there I felt that there was at least a reason for being there. When I got there, I found out there really wasn't; and as it went on, it got worse and my feelings got worse and I developed antiwar attitudes and I went home completely cynical; completely the reverse of patriotic.

The enemy was willing to die, really willing to die for what they believed in—a lot of them anyway—and we weren't. We just weren't. All we wanted to do was go home. In my war that's how it was.

Dwight Reiland decided that he was there simply because he had no choice. "There was nothing you could do about it," he said in despair. "You knew you were there for the time. You questioned the why. It didn't seem like you ever accomplished anything. You couldn't say, 'Today we gained a couple of square miles out near the A Shau,' because as soon as you walked out of it you hadn't gained anything. . . . It all seemed like such a waste of time. What purpose did it serve? You just pretty much resigned yourself to the fact that it was just kind of a black spot in your life. You had to get through it, get out of there, and forget about it."

The reason it was so difficult for soldiers to focus on a motive for fighting in Vietnam, other than in terms of their personal survival, was because they "were fighting for a mythical Vietnam which had been celebrated by American leaders but which did not in fact exist."[26]

Enlisted men were not the only ones who had trouble clarifying what they were being asked to die for. In 1974 Brig. Gen. Douglas Kinnard surveyed 110 American generals who had served in Vietnam and learned that 70 percent of them had never been clear in their own minds about America's military objectives.[27]

In a war where much was uncertain, change remained constant. The process of maturing and coping continued throughout each soldier's tour of duty. As combat experience broadened, the protective covering of the psyche was continually stretched and pulled to provide the insulation necessary to continue coping. If the cover was pulled too far in any single direction, or in too many directions at once, it began to tear. Most soldiers managed, but they often found, as Ed Austin did, that they had to give up something in return. Austin confided to his diary five months after his arrival, "I first came to Viet Nam to convert men to Christianity. Now, most of my thoughts center around killing V.C."[28] As Richard Ogden put it, "The fight to remain alive was one problem; the fight to remain human was quite another."[29]

CHAPTER 11

Offensive Operations

March 29, 1968

Dear Mom and Dad,

Received your latest letter yesterday and was glad to hear from you again. We are still in the field and it sure is hot out here, [it] is really hard to keep enough drinking water on hand to keep from drying out. The way it sounds now we will be out for quite some time this time. I'll write whenever I find the time but don't think I'll be able to write as often as usual. . . .

Well, I have less than six months left in this rotten Army and then I can kiss this place goodbye and say "Hello, Wisconsin!" I sure miss you all much and will be glad to get back and start living a decent life again where I don't have to kill someone just to stay alive like over here.

I sure hope Harold don't have to come into the Army 'cause they will send him over here before he knows what's going on. . . . I better close for now as there will be a chopper coming any time now.

> Your Littlest,
> Len[1]

The Olympian powers that planned the insertions of infantry soldiers into the remote locales of Vietnam did so in the hope that the enemy would be present. But what intelligence personnel and staff officers looked forward to as a stroke of luck or a golden opportunity was often greeted with apprehension and skepticism by the soldiers who would carry out their plans. For the grunts, being transported into the bush—

whether by helicopters, tracked vehicles, small boats, or simply on their own feet—marked the beginning of yet another experience that would likely prove to be unpleasant.

For infantry soldiers in Vietnam, helicopters were the most frequent harbingers of violence and death, and the tattoo of their rotor blades conditioned a response that still evokes powerful feelings and vivid memories. "Helicopters always scare me," said Sgt. Steve Fredrick. "Even when I hear them today they make my heart beat faster because I rode in helicopters for hours and hours, and almost every time I did we had combat. Those were incredibly exciting times. Boy, you talk about a rush! But you also knew something was going to happen or something was happening someplace, and you were going to be in it pretty quick."

The start of each new operation began with the familiar presence of anticipation and terror. It was the prelude to a routine that Paul Meringolo described vividly:

> We geared up before the helicopters arrived. We were carrying extra C-rations and ammunition besides normal packs and gear. Everyone was stooped over from the weight we each had to carry. Our platoon was to be the lead element. That meant we would be on the first helicopter out. We broke up into groups of about six on opposite sides of the runway to wait for the helicopters to come. There wasn't much talking at these times; everyone was pretty much into their own thoughts of what might be awaiting us and dealing with the internal fear those thoughts created. I can remember hearing and seeing the helicopters as they came into view. There were eight to ten of them and the sound of the helicopter blades is one that I think haunts every infantryman that served in Vietnam. They circled to pick us up. I also have to tell you that situations like this come about as close as it is to a John Wayne war movie because even though we were scared, that adrenaline was certainly firing through our bloodstreams.
>
> It took all our effort to climb into the helicopters under the weight of our gear. All the helicopters lifted off

and turned toward the mountains and the uncertainty of what we were heading into.[2]

Infantrymen took their positions on the floors of the helicopters out of convenience or habit. Some dangled their legs out the side openings; others chose interior positions leaning against the transmission housing in the rear of the cargo area. Still others rested against the pilots' seat backs and faced rearward. Some sat on top of their helmets—for comfort as much as protection. As they waited, the welcome surge of adrenaline began to replace their hungry, hollow feelings with a surprising giddiness. Then heartbeats accelerated with the staccato pulse of the forty-foot blades as the pilots added power and pitch and coaxed their birds upward into the humid air.

Once aloft above the lush greens and browns of the jungle and rice paddies, the war became suddenly distant—almost sanitary—and a pleasant transformation began. Although helicopter flights into the bush were relatively short, the experience itself could be intensely pleasant. Journalist Charles Anderson noted: "One's outlook on the world and the war underwent a dramatic improvement . . . near[ing] ecstasy."[3] Steve Fredrick recalled that it seemed "forty degrees cooler up there." During the wet season, Matthew Brennan appreciated the way the rotor blades kept out the rain and dried the men's clothing.[4] Robert Emery enjoyed the flights because, once aloft, he felt removed from the disgusting realities of the war. "You'd see beautiful scenery up there," he recalled. "You didn't see the death and destruction—or smell it." But for infantry soldiers, such pleasures always seemed to be short-lived. The war waited patiently below, its presence betrayed in part by the bomb craters that shimmered in the sunlight and marched away to the horizon.

Although men enjoyed the reprieve from the heat and the hostile environment, they also felt the strain and tension. "You would get a pretty hollow feeling in the pit of your stomach," Sergeant Fredrick recalled. "Fear is what you would call it." But the fear, according to Fredrick, was partially controlled by keeping one's attention focused on the business at hand. There was equipment to check, and men glanced at each other for reassurance, their hands assuming a death grip on their weapons. All the while, crew members and infantrymen alike anxiously scanned the terrain ahead for red signal smoke or green tracers, either of which indicated that the landing zone was "hot," meaning under enemy fire.

A helicopter was most vulnerable while descending to land, and soldiers were, for the most part, convinced that their choppers were large, slow, thin-skinned targets. Rifleman Paul Boehm tried to imagine helicopters as the enemy would see them—through their rifle sights. It was not a vision that inspired confidence. Like many soldiers, Boehm stepped out onto the landing skid as his helicopter flared to land, reasoning that the quicker he got out of that "giant beer can," the safer he would be.

Jeff Yushta felt the same way about exiting the cumbersome CH-46 Sea Knight helicopters that his marine unit used in 1969–70. The vulnerability of helicopters, however, was at least partially deceptive, and experience tempered Yushta's initial distrust of the machines. "You would think putting one bullet in a helicopter should bring the thing down," he said. "But there is so much empty space that they had to hit a critical fuel line or something to do a lot of damage."

Being in the lead helicopter, or "first lift," could be particularly worrisome. The lead ships were truly descending into the unknown and there would be few friendly troops available to lend support if they ran into difficulty. Fear and excitement were oddly juxtaposed at such times.

Sergeant Donald Putnam found it exhilarating but also very scary: "You go in and you don't really know what's there," he explained. "It could be three or four guys that decided they wanted to mix it up a little bit. It could be three or four dozen guys. It could be a thousand guys. . . . So there is that little fear of the unknown."

Under such conditions, according to Sgt. Michael Jackson, "the odds weren't good. If the landing zone was boobytrapped, or if it was going to be a real hot LZ, . . . you would probably get it."

Later lifts often proved to be just as dangerous. The limited size of many landing zones sometimes necessitated bringing in only one or two ships at a time. Experience taught

Terry Musser that "Charlie would know [that] any other choppers coming in would probably land in the same place." If the enemy was present, the soldiers arriving with the second or third lifts were likely to take as much fire as those who landed in the first wave of the assault.

The inevitable attrition of helicopters by enemy fire was not lost on those awaiting their turn to be flown into battle. Dennis Foell had to wait to be picked up in the summer of 1969 while his battalion, operating in I Corps, engaged elements of the 1st VC Regiment in the Hiep Duc Valley. He recalled seeing seventeen or eighteen choppers show up for the battalion's first lift, but he said that there were only three or four choppers left by the time it was his platoon's turn. That final run into the LZ on that combat assault was memorable for Foell because, "Flying at treetop level and being a machine gunner myself, I was trying to assist the door gunner a little bit by shooting out of the helicopter. The pilots were doing an excellent job, but as we flew over, the trees would brush against the chopper every once in a while. It was kind of a nerve-racking situation there."

Fortunately, hot LZs were relatively rare. Jerry Johnson estimated that of his fifty-some assaults with the 1st Infantry Division, only four or five were hot. His experience seemed typical. Statistically at least, the threat of being killed in a helicopter as a result of enemy fire was exaggerated. During the war, some 5,260 Americans died in helicopters, but 43 percent of those losses resulted from accidents. Only 8 percent of army personnel and 4 percent of the marines who were killed in action in Vietnam died in helicopters. Rare as such occurrences were, enough infantrymen saw burned wreckage, charred human remains, or damaged helicopters limping away over the trees trailing smoke to convince themselves of the potential risks involved in a helicopter assault.[5]

During Randy Hoelzen's tour with the 1st Cavalry Division in 1969, he saw medevacs and gunships go down, but never a "Huey" troopship during a combat assault. Even so, he admitted that the fear of being shot down was always on his mind.

Robert Emery, a grenadier with a scout unit in the 1st Cavalry Division, was the sole survivor of a helicopter shot down while leaving an LZ near the Ia Drang Valley in 1966. The Huey in which he was riding had reached treetop level when bullets began passing through the ship. What followed became the start of a nightmare for Emery.

> I could hear the rounds go *thunk, thunk, thunk* coming through the ship. There was one that came through behind the pilot in front of me. I was sitting in the "Hell Hole," which is just behind the pilot. There was one round that came through a water can, and rounds ricocheted and flew into my leg. At almost the same time, the medic screamed. He was sitting in the compartment between the pilot and copilot, right behind me. He screamed, and as I looked at him there was a big silver flash and the chopper fell. I landed on my back outside the chopper. I probably passed out for some time there; I'm not sure how long.

Emery lay still while enemy troops inspected the wreckage. A short time later he was struck in the head with a rifle butt by an enemy soldier and left for dead. After spending the night alone in the jungle, he was rescued.[6]

Landing zones, hot or cold, were almost always given a thorough artillery or aerial rocket preparation before the landing took place.[7] As the artillery or rocket prep ended, helicopter gunships raked the landing zones with machine-gun fire, and the door gunners on each troopship assisted by hosing down the surrounding terrain as the helicopters plunged into the landing zone and disgorged their human cargoes. Paul Boehm was caught off guard by all of the preparatory fire during his first helicopter assault. Said Boehm, "All of a sudden the door gunner opened up and I about shit my pants. I thought, Christ, I'm dead." But the outgoing fire was not in answer to enemy rounds, it was simply standard operating procedure.

It was also often standard operating procedure, although seldom publicized, for the infantry, in the haste and excitement of a landing, to have to jump from their helicopters while they were still five or more feet above the ground. The resulting injuries were unfortunate but not uncommon: the price paid when—out of diffidence to enemy fire or fear of hidden obstructions—a pilot would go no lower. Terry Musser elaborated on those jumps with a bitterness that came from experience:

> When you watch movies about Vietnam, and you see an assault into a hot LZ, every chopper lands. They put their skids down on the ground. I don't think I ever once while I was over there was in a chopper that landed before we got out. In other words, we were jumping from four to ten feet or better. That was when you were over elephant grass. Of course nobody knew how tall it was, so the chopper would stay above it and you would jump off. All of a sudden you had a ten-foot jump. That is a rude awakening.
>
> At that time I weighed about a hundred and forty-five pounds, so I had almost a third of extra body weight just in equipment. At Fort Benning when we went in [training] they always landed those choppers. . . . I found out that when you get hot LZs, they don't land those choppers. They get as close as they think they dare and you jump out. But when you have all that weight it wants to keep going after your body has stopped. I think we probably had more injuries just getting off the choppers than we did from enemy fire in that first LZ.

Machine gunner Layne Anderson recalled sharing a hospital ward with half a dozen men from the 198th Light Infantry Brigade, all of whom suffered broken legs or back injuries as a result of a helicopter insertion. A crippled lieutenant prompted Leonard Dutcher to write, "Having to jump is not a nice thing to have to do, but it's done every day over here."[8]

On rare occasions, a soldier might be helped out of a helicopter door by an overanxious door gunner. Jerry Johnson once received such a "boot-assisted takeoff." He didn't appreciate the help.

> I guess they were afraid that if they landed on something it might tip a tree up into the tail rotor or some-

thing like that. It wasn't a nice exit. I was kicked in the back by a door gunner. I was waiting for a *Chieu Hoi* to get out in front of me. I almost killed the *Chieu Hoi*. I fell on him. I happened to see that door gunner about two flights later and I said, "You ever do that again— you're dead."

He knocked me right on a log. I could have killed myself. It wasn't that I was holding back, I just couldn't get out. There were too many guys ahead of me.

Once on the ground, visibility for both soldiers and helicopter crewmen was often obstructed by flying dust and debris as the emptying choppers hovered with rotors at full pitch, straining against the hot air. It was difficult to see and harder to hear as the men crouched, oriented themselves, and followed their comrades through the elephant grass and natural debris that seemed to litter most LZs. The cacophony of gunfire, low-frequency rotor noise, and screaming jet turbine engines rendered the ears momentarily useless. The men moved quickly to secure their portion of the LZ's perimeter or simply to get away from the clearing as rapidly as possible. Either way, it was never like training. According to Jeff Yushta, the Marine Corps

prepared you for frontal assault World War II tactical maneuvers, and here you were fighting in thick jungle. . . . You came off a chopper in Vietnam and everybody was supposed to run and fan out. There were fourteen combat-loaded troops coming out of the CH-46s and they were supposed to be in two lines of seven. The first guy out was supposed to run about a hundred yards before he dropped down. The rest were supposed to drop at twenty-yard intervals, or something like that. Well, half the time you couldn't run thirty feet. You'd hit something you couldn't pass. It didn't take long to discover that, if you were the first guy out of the chopper, you hit the deck because there would soon be seven guys on top of you, and the bottom of the pile was about the safest spot to be.

The jitters they felt, which had peaked just before touch down, were dissipating and the men reacted out of habit. Once on the ground, soldiers felt a little more at ease. They were back in their element and landing zones usually afforded some cover in the tall grass. Terry Musser, however, found that keeping contact with the others deploying out of an LZ could be difficult.

> Being an RTO, at least I didn't have to figure out which way to go. Whoever I was with, platoon leader or squad leader, I just followed him. You didn't have much choice. That was probably the hardest part, trying to keep up with him when a lot of times there was so much mass confusion. If you zigged or zagged wrong in that elephant grass you could just lose sight of everybody. . . . If he came under fire, about the time he stopped, you were still running. So there was a lot of OJT [on-the-job training] on what to do or not to do when you got there the first few times. . . . The biggest thing was to get off the LZ, especially if it was hot.

Even if the LZ was uncontested, soldiers had little doubt that the enemy knew of their presence. But hostile forces could be surrounded or cut off and overwhelmed by firepower if they chose to fight. With that goal in mind, the pointmen struck off on an azimuth and the rest of the unit trailed after. The hunt was on. Sometimes they would operate in small groups, using the enemy's hit-and-run tactics. At other times they would hunt like the rajahs of India, with hundreds of men beating the bush to drive the "game" toward waiting rifles, artillery, and air power. Sometimes they were very successful.

Night Ambushes

Although it was often conceded by the men in the field that the night belonged to the enemy, nearly every evening throughout the length and breadth of Vietnam, American troops prepared to contest the enemy's claim to those hours of

darkness with the deployment of scores of small ambushes.
Some were defensive, to provide security for a small firebase
or company night defensive position (NDP). Others helped
keep enemy mortar teams at bay and provided early warning
of an attack against main positions.

Phil Yaeger, a 3d Marine Division grunt, participated in
some forty or fifty ambushes during 1966 and 1967, none of
which was ever sprung. He was quick to explain, however,
that near the DMZ the general consensus was that "divisions
weren't going to move around at night, and that is what was
out there."

More enemy movement was usually to be found farther
south among the villages and in the western border areas,
where the enemy was prone to move after dark. Mike Meil
said that his cavalry troop often went on ambush patrols in
the Central Highlands.

> Sometimes we would leave from our perimeter and
> go in on foot. A majority of the time we would go in by
> chopper. We'd always go in just as it was starting to get
> dark. They would drop us off so Charlie couldn't see us
> coming into the area. On a few occasions they dropped
> us off too early. That is what you had to watch out
> for. . . . The object of it was for you to ambush them,
> not for them to ambush you. And we, on occasion, had
> it reversed. But we would go out if we'd get information
> from within the unit or . . . even intelligence reports of
> VC or NVA working out of a certain village or what
> have you. We would go out and set up a night ambush
> patrol and the whole object of it was to make contact.

Ambushes were also set along the trails leading into Vietnam from Cambodia and Laos. These were intended to harass
and disrupt enemy forces as they brought in supplies and infiltrated troops from their border sanctuaries and staged them
farther into Vietnam. Jerry Johnson's company ambushed the
infiltration routes west of Saigon and frequently encountered
enemy pedestrian traffic and the heavily laden bicycles used
to transport materiel over the jungle trails. Similarly, Doug
Kurtz spent many a night on the Plain of Reeds hoping to

catch the enemy as he moved out of hiding. On some nights their vigilance was rewarded.

> One night on ambush we probably had been set down for two hours and we were right on a little stream. . . . We liked to work the streams. They would walk in there looking for their rockets and stuff. You could hear them coming. Everybody started waking everybody up. We were just waiting for them—you could hear them talking just as plain as day. It was like they were just down the street. Somebody yelled, "Open fire! Get 'em!" Everybody started shooting. We got every one of them. . . . Then, because we blew our cover, we went back to the base. The next day we went out and checked them over . . . and took the bodies to Firebase Gettysburg.

Civilian populations could be given some small measure of protection against Viet Cong recruitment and tax collection by laying ambushes in and around the villages. Donald Trimble was a member of a marine Combined Action Platoon (CAP) in which American marines and Vietnamese village militia worked jointly to provide security at the local level. On Trimble's second day in the bush, the beginning of Tet 1971, he was part of a four-man ambush team. Shortly after dark he watched enemy soldiers putting up posters and Viet Cong flags within thirty feet of his place of concealment. He was, understandably, "scared to death."

> I had an ARVN at my back, so I reached around and grabbed him to pull him around because I was gonna get his M16. He grabbed my hand and we held hands there for a little bit. I didn't know it at the time, but the Vietnamese men hold hands customarily. . . .
> I saw them throw a great big flag up right in front of me, and there was no question about who they were. So I pulled the ARVN who was behind me around, and I showed him. He got real excited. Of course so was I; my heart was beating a thousand miles a minute. I told the ARVN to open up on him and I'd shoot some flares

at the same time. Well, I pinged off my flares . . . and he opened up with his M16 about four feet in front of us. The dust just flew. And the VC opened up on us, so I quick grabbed the M16 away from the ARVN. They were running down the path, shooting backwards at us and I heard bullets go by me so close that it hurt my ears. . . . I emptied two clips and I threw him back his gun and I grabbed the M79. I shot up a few more canisters of light and then I started reconning the area with high explosive.

During the firefight, a second CAP team moved to aid the men on ambush and were themselves ambushed by a rear guard of Viet Cong. No one was hurt, but the events gave Trimble pause.

"There were drag marks in the two hootches," he recalled. "It looked like someone had just slaughtered a pig. We didn't go in, and we didn't throw grenades. We just went back up the path and took down the flag, took down the posters, and returned to our patrol base, where I reflected on what had just taken place."

The majority of ambush patrols were uneventful. Still, just as Americans were often victims of well-placed enemy ambushes, so too was the enemy frequently made to suffer at the hands of small bands of soldiers waiting silently for an enemy to enter their "kill zone." Consequently, many soldiers preferred ambush tactics to the company-sized search-and-destroy operations.

"We had some of our best body counts outside of an overrun situation when we'd set up ambushes on old firebases," said Paul Gerrits. "We'd abandon a firebase and set an ambush in the tree line for five or six nights after we left. Anybody that walked in—we'd grease them. Or we would ambush a trail. That's when we got our best body counts and the most kills. We were most effective and lost the least amount of people when we traveled in small groups and waited for them."

Sergeant Willie Williams enjoyed some success on ambush patrols as well, but he preferred them simply because he felt more in control with a smaller group of people. But not everyone liked ambushes or saw the sense in them. Jeff Yushta, for example, questioned the concept of sending out four-man "killer teams," as his unit's ambush patrols were called, because they occasionally backfired. "What the hell were they sending four guys out there in the middle of the dark for?" he wondered aloud. "Charlie knew the area. He knew you were going out. If he was moving in front of you, he would just set up and wait for you. We had that happen. And they just kept doing it."

Ambushes were nerve-racking contests played for the highest stakes possible, but Randy Hoelzen still found them to be strangely satisfying. "There *was* a risk element," he agreed, "but at the same time there was a feeling like—we're taking it to them for once. It was our turn."

Specific techniques used on ambush patrols varied among different units, but a look into the numerous defensive perimeters scattered across South Vietnam on any given night would have revealed parties of men engaged in similar preparations. Typically, a company sent out several ambush patrols of from four to six men, although some units might use squads or even platoons of twenty-five men or more.

The location of an ambush depended on intelligence reports and the savvy of the men in the field. According to Sgt. Steve Fredrick, most of his unit's ambushes were set up along trails or intersections, just as a hunter would stake out game trails. Often, several ambush teams would be positioned to provide mutual support.

Every unit had volunteers who liked ambushes. Mostly, however, men took their turn as the duty rotated between the squads. As darkness drew near, the men going out were pulled into the middle of the perimeter and given a chance to eat. Then they blackened their faces, inspected their ammunition, grenades, Claymore mines, and trip flares, and gathered for a briefing by their patrol leaders. When it was dark enough to conceal their departure, the teams slipped out, hoping to melt into the darkness as they moved toward their assigned locations.

It took consummate skill and confidence to navigate in the darkness of the jungle and, by a circuitous route, reach a predetermined ambush point. Simply orienting with a compass in the darkness was difficult. At its worst, it resulted in tragedy.

"You are trying to go through jungle six hundred meters to someplace," Jeff Yushta explained. "It is dark before you get there. I never met anybody that could walk a straight line with his eyes closed. And we had a team that went out, made a loop, and came back in on part of the perimeter where no team had gone out. The people on the perimeter there opened up on them and they took casualties."

Soldiers were often afraid that they might become victims of an enemy ambush while trying to set up their own. In the darkness, eyes were useless, and the men became acutely aware of each vibration and sound, no matter how insignificant. To their heightened senses, even the sloshing of the water in their canteens seemed deafening. The metallic click of a rifle against the underbrush or their own elephantine footsteps seemed to shout a warning to the enemy. The sense of isolation and vulnerability haunted their minds. Being suddenly four hundred to a thousand meters away from the rest of the company with only a handful of other men left many a soldier talking to himself and silently whistling in the dark.

At the ambush site, the men took positions along the enemy's most likely avenue of approach. Phil Yaeger's ambush patrols would normally move past their planned location while it was still daylight and then "double back after dark to set up. If not more than fifty yards, you could double back and get into your site with as little movement as possible. I had things set up in the column so that when we doubled back we could form the radius and stop and we would be in the ambush position. All we would have to do is sit down."

The men often sat within arm's reach of each other, and no digging was allowed. In the darkness, the usual weapons of choice were Claymore antipersonnel mines and fragmentation grenades, which would not betray a soldier's location. The M16s were generally reserved for emergencies. Other weapons taken on ambush were matters of preference, which varied within each unit. Sergeant Barker's platoon never took M79 grenade launchers on ambush because they wanted them with the company if they had to get an ambush team back in. Other units left their M60 machine guns behind because of their greater bulk and the difficulty in moving quietly with them.[9] It was common in Phil Yaeger's battalion, however, to take one or two machine guns on an ambush, especially when they were near the DMZ. The real killing power was provided by the Claymore mines placed at the ends and along the center of the ambush.

One never knew what he might encounter on an ambush patrol. Phil Yaeger had a man gored by a wild boar one night, and Donald Putnam was attacked by a rat while setting up an ambush near a rice paddy dike. Said Putnam:

> I went up to supply and had gotten a pair of baggy fatigue pants. There were no strings in the bottom, so they were hanging open like balloons. I was walking out by this grave and I had all this stuff on my back and a rifle in my hand and I'm whispering to these guys . . . and this thing runs up my leg. I dropped my rifle. It shocked the hell out of me. An M16 hitting the ground doesn't sound pretty—it clatters. . . . I was hopping around with a pack on my back and all that shit was making noise. The '16 was on the ground. The two guys with me had already hit the ground. They figured if there was anything out there it was going to fire and kill me. Finally I got the rat out and picked my '16 up. I was a bundle of nerves. I was shaking like a leaf. It scared the hell out of me.

Fatigue was also an enemy that Steve Fredrick remembered wasn't always easy to overcome. "You didn't have anything to sleep in—no poncho, no poncho liner, nothing," recalled Fredrick. "You were not supposed to sleep at all when you are on an ambush. But Christ, you can't stay awake all day *and* all night, so we would work it out among ourselves who was going to stay awake for this period and who was going to stay awake for that period."

In many units, half the team slept while the other half kept watch, but nerves and two-hour-watch rotations meant that men got very little sleep on a night ambush. Medic Jerry Severson said that he was given Deximil to distribute as needed when he was on ambushes with E Troop, 17th Cavalry.

Anything that could go wrong on an ambush usually did. Snoring could erupt without warning, or a man might cry out in his sleep. Men prone to such things were tended to closely. It was also easy to lose things—from a hand grenade to a starlight scope—in the darkness. Navy corpsman John Meyer once lost his glasses.

> I picked up the starlight scope and started scanning the horizon. Something was wrong. I couldn't get it to focus. I couldn't see anything. I realized I had lost my glasses somewhere. I didn't have a chance of finding them. I found a pair of prescription sunglasses in my fatigues, which was better than nothing, but it wasn't real good for finding things in the dark. I managed to get through my watch okay. Then I had to find my relief and wake him up. It was *really* dark out there and I couldn't find him. All I could see was a lump here or there where somebody was maybe sleeping. But I didn't want to wake everybody up to find the guy I needed. I was crawling around on my hands and knees whispering "Ski? . . . Ski? . . . Where are you?" No response. Finally I stopped for a moment. "Ski? . . . Ski?" I heard somebody groaning. I looked down and saw I was kneeling on his chest.

On rare occasions, the faint rattle of equipment or the squeaking of pack harnesses suddenly transformed darkness and shadow into substance as enemy soldiers appeared out of the night. At such a moment, adrenaline exploded into the bloodstream. James Stanton explained the sensation:

> It is two o'clock in the morning and you are half asleep. Nothing is happening. All of a sudden you hear twelve guns start all at once. That is adrenaline! Your heart starts beating so fast you think it's going to pop out of your shirt. . . . Even if you were here and all of a sudden an ambush is popped somewhere nearby, you hear all hell break loose and you can be doing nothing, but your heart is going ninety miles an hour. You are just waiting and waiting and waiting—hoping they

come your way because you got to let it out somehow. . . . It gets you goofy.

At times enemy soldiers were uncomfortably close before
they were detected. Said William Harken, "I was always
scared at night, so I was always awake and alert. I relaxed in
the daytime." He discovered how mistaken he had been in his
belief when "one evening two enemy soldiers got to within
maybe fifteen or twenty yards before I knew they were there.
I know I put three rounds in the chest of one of them. One
was a tracer round. But we could not find a body. We found
two weapons, a pair of Ho Chi Minh sandals, and things like
that, but we could not find a body."

Sergeant Willie Williams's military career nearly ended
under similar circumstances in 1966 near the Ho Bo Woods
northwest of Saigon. Williams's men had set up at the edge of
a rice paddy on a bright

moonlit night and there was nothing going on, so we
were more or less relaxed. I had taken my web gear off
and laid it behind the dike and everybody just got comfortable.

Then all at once we saw about fifteen people. I don't
know where they came from, but they stepped out of
the hedgerow and they were only a few meters away
from us. When I saw them, I jumped up and yelled. I
didn't have my weapon or nothing and some [of] our
guys started shooting. I saw one enemy soldier take aim
on me and he fired. I didn't feel nothing, I just
screamed. I don't know if it shocked him when I
screamed, but he pulled off and it was a bad shot. I remember him firing; I saw the flash. I fell back behind
the dike to the rice paddy and I started pitching
grenades.

That morning, when we got back, I went to get some
water in my helmet and when I got back to the APC I
didn't have any water. My steel pot had been hit. . . .

Ambushes were usually backed by artillery support. Map
coordinates were given to the artillery in advance and the

ambush team could, if necessary, call for and adjust the artillery fire for protection or to exact heavier casualties on the enemy force. Artillery gave an ambush team tremendous power. Marine scout observer Jack Freitag described one such ambush that worked to perfection:

> We were lined up along a riverbank and all the dope [artillery coordinates] was set up. . . . We didn't know how many were coming. We didn't know if it was a company or a platoon or a battalion. We counted so many . . . sixty-seven I believe, and I had all the dope set so it was fire at my command. We had no M60s. No M79s. They were carrying mortars and rockets and all kinds of crap.
>
> They had a woman out in front of them about twenty yards. When they got to about the middle of us, artillery fire landed about fifty yards on the far side of them. And then [the enemy] kind of walked leisurely toward us. We didn't open up yet. And then we opened up and they panicked. They started dropping everything and they were running, screaming. I kept walking up the artillery and they left blood trails going all over.

Firepower in the form of artillery and air strikes could also be the saving grace for an ambush team that would have otherwise been overwhelmed by the force it attacked. Under normal circumstances, an enemy unit too large for the ambush team to handle was allowed to pass unhindered. Sometimes, however, the ambush team was unaware of just how perilous its position was. Sergeant Donald Putnam experienced such a night when the sniper accompanying his team sighted four Viet Cong moving down a rice paddy dike. The sniper killed one Viet Cong and the other three sought cover and returned fire. Within minutes, however, Putnam's team began taking fire from hootches on three sides and the situation began to deteriorate.

> I called [the captain] and I said, "Hey, I need ammo. I'm hurting." About twenty minutes later I was back on

the radio saying, "I need ammo and I need it now. It is getting real sparse."

He said, "I can't get you a chopper. There ain't nothing available. Can you pull out?"

I said, "No. We got open paddies behind me. . . . If I pull back they're just going to cut us apart. We'll never make it from here to the next dike. They'll nail every damn one of us."

Fifteen minutes later the situation was desperate. At the last minute, however, the help arrived, and once again fortunes shifted.

[Captain Muehlstead] come up there with just minutes to spare because we were down to nothing. . . . He brought up the tracks and we proceeded to kick ass and take names at that point. And this went on from eleven-thirty at night until two-thirty in the morning. We called and had illumination hanging the whole time. We called for arty to work the wood lines around behind them. Finally, we had gunships on station and then we also had jets on station that bombed along the river that ran behind us and took care of the wood lines back there. We were up all night and wrapped it up at daylight.

All that was left was the tally, and that had to wait for daylight.

"There was an ARVN compound down the river and we got in contact with them and had them work up towards us," said Putnam. "Just before we met up, the ARVNs found forty-seven bodies stacked up like cordwood along the river. It was all the ones they had dragged out the night before. They were all fresh trails. So we had forty-seven bodies there and a couple lying back where we were."

On most nights, nothing disturbed the men on ambush except the mosquitoes, the dampness, and their own stiff joints and muscles. The dawn would begin to tint the eastern horizon and the teams would collect their Claymores and move cautiously back toward the company perimeter or to a pickup point. Some outfits brought their ambush teams in while it was still dark, but most waited until just before dawn. As the company conducted its stand-to, the ambush teams hailed the troops on guard and passed back inside to a breakfast of C-rations and the start of a new day. Usually there was nothing to report—no contact and no friendly casualties. Sergeant Vernon Janick, however, survived one unforgettable night in the Central Highlands near the end of his second tour that was like no other night he had ever experienced.

Janick and three others were sent out to establish a listening post (LP) about a thousand meters from the company's night position. The unusually great distance of the LP from the perimeter bothered the sergeant, but the four men followed orders and completed digging two holes just before dark. After registering defensive artillery on the tree line and clearing in front of their position, there was nothing left for the foursome to do but wait, and listen, and worry. Things progressed normally until about midnight. Then, said Janick,

> the first watch woke me up and there was a rattling in the high elephant grass and I could hear something crawling, so I called for flares. Just as they popped, about five of them jumped out of the elephant grass and opened up on us, so we opened up on them. Then, out of the tree line, all kinds of crazy shit started. We got hit bad.
>
> Well, Willie, this black guy I had in the hole with me, said, "I'm getting the fuck out of here, man!" I said, "Where the hell you gonna go?" Anyway, he crouched and moved up out of the hole and just as he rose up he took one in the neck. He just dropped right there, half over the foxhole. I pulled him in and called for artillery and opened up with everything I had until I ran out of ammo.
>
> I didn't know what happened to the other two guys at the time, but I knew I wasn't getting any fire from them. I picked up Willie's M16 and emptied it out. I had nothing left but a couple of grenades, so I just called in more artillery and told them to open up and just move it back and forth so many meters out and

keep it coming. It was nearly on top of us. It was the only thing to do. I don't know how many there were of them out there, but by the sound and the muzzle flashes it was pretty heavy.

After about ten minutes, the artillery stopped. I was pretty scared. All I had was two grenades. It got really quiet. My ears were ringing, but I was listening hard. I turned off the radio because I didn't want to have them hear the squelch. Hell, I just sat there, grenade in hand, alone with Willie's body. I had this horrible feeling because I was down in the hole and I didn't know what was up there. I was afraid they would come crawling in and I would get a bayonet in the head. My eyeballs were popping and my ears heard more than what was probably out there. It was a long night. Time just seemed to drag.

I must have finally dozed off 'cause it started to get light and I remember kind of waking up. I got up real slow and crawled out of the hole and looked around . . . [long exhale] *whew!* I was the only one left there. The other two guys were dead, too. That was rough. I was drained—nothing left. It was close enough to the end of my second tour that I didn't go back to the field. I would have probably never been the same.

Large-Scale Operations

The efforts of a single infantry company were often just one tiny part of a much larger coordinated effort involving battalions, brigades, or even whole divisions of men participating in very complex large-scale operations. Such colossal orchestrations of men and materiel were usually conducted with one of three missions in mind.

Most frequently, large-scale operations in Vietnam were of the search-and-destroy variety. These operations usually employed maneuvering and blocking forces that were assigned to search a given area and destroy what was found there rather than seize ground in the traditional manner. Clear-and-secure operations were initiated when allied forces sought to drive the enemy from populated areas in order to provide security for a given period of time. These operations involved securing towns and villages as part of the pacification program in order to weaken the guerrillas' hold on the civilian population. Typically, units might protect a rice crop to keep it from falling into Viet Cong hands, or they might guard a village being harassed by local Viet Cong forces. Finally, operations were conducted to protect highways or other transportation arteries, as well as to provide security for base areas and important military and civilian installations.[10]

The typical infantry company engaged in all three types of operations, sometimes simultaneously. Throughout the Vietnam War, U.S. forces, either in conjunction with ARVN forces or alone, conducted hundreds of large offensive operations beginning with the marines' four-day-long Operation Starlite in August 1965, and ending with Operation Jefferson Glenn, involving the 101st Airborne Division and the ARVN 1st Infantry Division, which was terminated on 12 October 1971 by President Richard Nixon's announcement that American troops would henceforth operate only in a defensive posture.[11]

The soldiers humping the bush seldom knew the name of the operations in which they were participating, and, if they did, it was of no importance. The men were typically concerned only with the rumors of where they were going and how long they would be out in the field. For them, one operation was the same as the next: a progression of hot, tiring days, fitful nights, and occasional violence and terror. Gerry Barker remembered his second tour with the 1st Cavalry Division in late 1966–1967 as one of utter fatigue. His unit was put through one operation after another. "We went on Crazy Horse with the Koreans first," recalled Barker. "After that we went down to where the 101st was on the coast and worked inland from there. Then we came back up and worked with the marines in Masher-White Wing, Eagle Claw—that series. That was when we went through the An Lao Valley."

Similarly, marine Phil Yaeger went into the field in July 1966 during Operation Hastings and remained there through Operations Prairie and Prairie II, which ended in March 1967. "We'd pull out for a while," Yaeger recalled, "and we might spend a few days in a perimeter and get a hot meal. But then we would be right back into it again."

The tactics of most search-and-destroy operations were simple: Seal the enemy in a given area and then drive him toward the waiting guns of a blocking force. Layne Anderson remembered trying to clear the Viet Cong–infested part of the Batangan Peninsula known as Pinkville in 1969.

"We weren't very friendly going through there," Anderson claimed. "Everyone was taken prisoner when we went through on line with eighty-five hundred people, the battle-ship USS *New Jersey,* constant air support, constant illumination. . . ."

In similar operations on Go Noi Island south of Da Nang, Jeff Yushta recalled "sweeping their area trying to catch them. I suppose somebody would call it a classic pincer maneuver where you are supposedly sweeping him towards another force and there is no way out."

The analogy often used was that of a hammer and anvil coming together. On occasion the system worked, but often the anvil or the hammer was porous enough for the enemy to squeeze through, or, having been tipped off, escape the trap before it closed. Operation Double Eagle began in January 1966 against the 325th NVA Division, which intelligence had confirmed was on the border of Binh Dinh Province. It ended in February after the units involved encountered only snipers. Prisoners taken during the operation credited the absence of the enemy's main force to prior knowledge of the operation down to the actual time and place of attack.

Operation Cedar Falls also sought to exterminate a large enemy force, this time in the Iron Triangle northwest of Saigon. It also failed to corner the main enemy forces, although the enemy still lost more than 700 killed and an additional 280 were taken prisoner.[12]

Even the lowly private in the field suspected that his missions were sometimes being compromised. Looking back to 1965 and 1966 in the Central Highlands, Terry Musser wondered if "maybe we were working *too* close with the Vietnamese. . . ."

There were certainly some unintentional leaks on the American side. In December 1969, American forces overran a Viet Cong communications monitoring station on the outskirts of Saigon that had been listening in on U.S. voice and Morse code transmissions. Handwritten copies of American messages found in the monitoring station indicated that each evening the enemy listened to 11th Aviation Group radio messages to learn where American units would be airlifted the following morning. The Viet Cong had even broken the frequency designation codes so that they had access to the command frequencies used during operations.[13]

But whether the enemy was destroyed or simply had vacated the area ahead of the approaching Americans, when the operation ended, the allied units left the area to the enemy, allowing him to filter back in again. This made it necessary to return repeatedly.

Jeff Yushta's company attacked Go Noi Island three times during his one-year tour. "You got to know some of these areas," said Yushta, "and they knew you. It was like visiting an old neighborhood."

Operations might be measured by the intensity of the logistics effort necessary to sustain them, but they boiled down to intensive patrolling by rifle companies and the exertion of each individual soldier engaged in searching for the enemy. Jon Neely's participation in large-scale operations generally meant getting "sent out to set up ambushes or go on sweeps. And they said, 'Just go out and make contact and pull back,' and then they would send in gunships or something like that to clean up."

Air and Artillery Support

Success in Vietnam was often derived from a simple three-part recipe that was enthusiastically supported by most soldiers in the field. The ingredients were to make contact, pull back, and let artillery and air power do the work. Jon Neely, in recalling his impressions of the 9th Infantry Division's artillery support, used one word: fantastic.

"If we got into a big firefight and we were totally outnumbered or whatever the case might have been, we called for artillery and those guys were right on target," explained Neely.

"They would hit the area that we needed and keep bringing it until we told them to stop."

Most men described their artillery support with the same superlatives. Jerry Johnson was quick to acknowledge the artillery and air power he found so comforting while serving with the 1st Infantry Division. "We always worked under our fire support, whether it was artillery or our own mortars," said Johnson. "If we were out of their range, there was an air strike available on call at all times." Because of such ample firepower, Vernon Janick discovered that firefights usually didn't last very long. "We took advantage of a lot of air strikes and artillery," he said, "so as soon as we got hit, well, we called in air strikes. . . ."

Though a few critics claimed that the practice interfered with the infantry's traditional job of closing with and destroying the enemy, and thus reduced the soldier's sense of purpose and accomplishment, most men in the field seemed to relish any application of firepower, prudent or not, that reduced the element of risk to themselves.

"You had all this firepower at your disposal and you learned to use it," said Jeff Yushta. "There is nothing chicken about sitting down and calling in a Phantom strike on a bunker. It was smart business. Our lieutenants learned to operate in those parameters. They didn't say, 'Gee, wouldn't the captain be impressed if I led a charge up to this thing and we overwhelmed it?' First of all, they were going to get very little support from their men in this overwhelming attack. Once they learned that, then you got to a functional point."

The use of air and artillery made good sense to GIs in the bush because the enemy could be tenacious when backed into a corner and nearly impossible to extricate without firepower. Tom Schultz's unit always hoped to encounter the enemy on the move. Otherwise, he explained, "if they were dug in in an area, we'd back off and throw air in on them, because you were not going to break them loose."

The enemy's resilience became obvious to Gerry Barker during Operation Crazy Horse. In order to dislodge the entrenched enemy, the GIs were forced to resort to "corkscrew and blowtorch" tactics similar to those used against the Japanese during World War II.

Said Barker, "They divided a hill up into segments and artillery batteries had less than a kilometer, less than a grid square to shell. The artillery fired nonstop except when tac-air was going in. They pounded that damn hill, and when we went up the hill it was like burnt cork. I mean, it made the kind of crunching sound that burnt cork does. There wasn't a tree left intact on the damn hill. They shelled it for a week. We still ran into fire. Caves! We had to clear the damn hill with hand grenades and flamethrowers."

Oddly enough, considering the vast amount of artillery support available in Vietnam, only 30 percent of the artillery ammunition expended was actually fired in direct support of allied ground troops. The remainder was fired in conditions of light or inactive combat, a practice known as harassment and interdiction (H & I). H & I fire was targeted on likely enemy locations. Whether the H & I was designed to use up old allotments of ammunition, or whether artillery commanders were rated on the amount of ammunition they expended, as soldiers often jokingly surmised, a lot of ordnance was fired into the countryside seemingly in hopes of randomly locating the world's most unlucky Viet Cong soldier.[14]

Major General Rathvon McC. Tompkins, who took command of the 3d Marine Division in November 1967, was an outspoken critic of the practice. He maintained that most H & I fire was "utterly worthless" and "a great waste of ammunition."[15]

Although H & I fire admittedly killed a few enemy soldiers, it occasionally killed friendly forces as well. Phil Yaeger lost two men to H & I fire while on an ambush patrol outside Cua Viet a month before he left country. Yaeger had set up in a cluster of pine trees on top of a sand dune with a rear guard on the other side.

They were firing H & Is and one of them came in short and missed. It came over . . . and clipped the top of the dune. Then it went down and detonated behind us so the squad radius wasn't hit with any shrapnel. It totally wasted the two guys in the rear.

That was total frustration. . . . I did everything right. There was nothing wrong except one round of ammunition. That happened to be the round that passed right over our site.

Perhaps because of the effectiveness of artillery support, Jon Neely noted, "There were very few times that we had to call in for jet fighters to drop napalm or heavy bombs. Most of our air support was [helicopter] gunships and, again, anytime that we called in they were right there."

Particularly lucrative targets were given lavish attention by the air force at astronomical cost: They were targeted for B-52 heavy bomber strikes known as Arc Light missions.

In a remote border valley in the Central Highlands, John Merrell's company reported hearing tanks or motorized vehicles one day. Merrell remembered that it was around 10 o'clock in the morning when they radioed their report. Soon after, the company was ordered out of the valley to a nearby hill. What followed was, in Merrell's words,

probably the most beautiful sight that I've ever seen. They walked the bombs right up to the base of the hill we were sitting on. That was the first wave. Then it started way across the valley and we were getting nervous because they weren't stopping and they walked the bombs right up to the base of the hill again. Then they walked them across the valley the other way.

I can't understand why, but we went down into the valley after the raid was over and we walked down the lanes created by the bombs, and there were massive lanes. A B-52 drops big bombs and they just clear out the jungle. It was like a four-lane highway—it was just that big. You could walk down into a bomb crater and not see out the top standing down in the bottom. That's how deep they were. That was probably one of the neatest things I saw when I was there. You don't get to see that too often.

Another thing Merrell never saw with any frequency were enemy casualties resulting from a B-52 raid. On this occasion there was no "debris from tanks or anything. We didn't find any dead bodies either." But, Merrell was quick to point out,

"That's the way we operated over there. Firepower was wasted in my opinion. Of course," he added with a laugh, "I have a lot of opinions now."

The firepower advantage was appreciated, but there was sometimes a brief tinge of sympathy for the enemy who withstood the onslaught of fire. Jon Neely remembered how "even in the heat of a battle, drenched with sweat, nerves on edge, when the gunships came in, it was nice to just sit back and watch those guys work. But," he admitted, "you just had to wonder how the enemy ever stood those air strikes being called in on them. The firepower that they brought to bear was awesome."

Just how awesome the air effort was in Vietnam can be seen in the statistics. During the Vietnam War, the United States engaged in what was, according to Thomas Thayer, "the largest and costliest air effort in history."[16] American and South Vietnamese aircraft flew 3.4 million combat sorties (90 percent American) in South Vietnam, North Vietnam, Laos, and Cambodia between 1965 and 1972, and dropped the equivalent of seventy tons of bombs for every square mile of Vietnam and five hundred pounds of bombs for every man, woman, and child in the country. This amounted to three times as many bombs as were dropped during World War II. In 1968–69 alone, the United States dropped on *South* Vietnam more than one-and-a-half times the tonnage dropped by all allies on Germany throughout World War II. There were 21 million bomb craters in South Vietnam alone.[17]

Yet despite this tremendous effort, two-thirds of the total air strikes were preplanned raids attempting to interdict enemy supply and personnel movements by striking against roads and trails, supply caches, and troop movements. Only about 10 percent of the tactical air strikes in South Vietnam were flown in support of allied ground forces in contact with the enemy.[18]

Having witnessed such overwhelming firepower, many soldiers and marines expressed a profound thanks that they had not been subjected to the same aerial pounding as their opponents. But some also confessed to harboring a certain respect or sympathy for those who fought on beneath the bombs. "When the Phantoms would come in, or the gunships, or artillery," Phil Yaeger said, "I sometimes felt it wasn't quite fair. That doesn't make any sense, but I felt that way a lot of times."

Tunnel and Bunker Complexes

Fortified enemy defensive positions meant bunkers—dugout positions reinforced with timber or bamboo and covered with earth. They were difficult to locate and hard to destroy. Bunkers were often connected by trenches or tunnels, and they were located to provide interlocking fields of defensive fire. Assaulting such positions was difficult and dangerous. Moving on line into such a complex required discipline. Without that virtue, as Tom Schultz learned, tragic consequences could and did occur.

"One time we swept some bunkers and this guy who had been there only a month or so got ahead of the sweep and came out of a bunker holding something up and somebody just blew him up," recalled Schultz. "It wasn't anybody's fault; he moved out of sequence. The bunkers were all camouflaged and it was triple canopy [jungle] and he moved ahead a couple of bunkers, and when you got guys covering the sweep and someone jumps up holding something—well, he got blown up."

Soldiers searching for the enemy frequently encountered his dens—subterranean habitats that were legendary. Often the diggings were modest temporary affairs. Ed Hoban repeatedly found the entrances to holes and tunnels in I Corps, but saw nothing large or intricate:

"Some of them turned out to be little spider holes going nowhere," he explained. "Others would basically go in and you could get three or four people into them. I didn't see anything that was ever connected to anything else. Hiding spaces like a small cave were pretty much all we found."

The first step in clearing a tunnel complex was to toss smoke grenades into the entrance. The smoke, Jerry Johnson explained, was used to find other exits or entrances. "Usually, the smoke would flow through. That way, everybody is not standing watching the hole and a good comes out another one and shoots you. That way you could cover all the entrances."

Tear gas or CS gas grenades were also frequently used to clear tunnels and caves. Actually a fine powder and not a true gas, the CS compound when inhaled quickly irritated the eyes, nose, and throat, and caused chest pains, vomiting, and choking. The gas was especially useful as a nonlethal means of expelling enemy soldiers or civilians from a tunnel or cave without endangering American lives.[19]

Just how effective CS gas could be was revealed in an incident that could easily have had tragic consequences. According to Mike Meil, "This moron lieutenant takes a gas grenade, and I'm down inside that son of a bitch [bunker] about fifty or seventy-five feet in the dark going through different tunnels and I'm feeling for booby traps to make sure that I'm all right—don't get into a bunch of soup. He throws that gas grenade down and there I am! I'm sucking this gas—coughing, gagging, looking for air—and I got to feel my way back out of the hole without hitting any booby traps and do it fast because I'm running out of oxygen! I got out of the hole, but I was one mad sonofabitch. And I think I chased that lieutenant . . . screaming at the top of my lungs at him that I was going to kill him."

It was just as common to throw deadly missiles in a hole before sticking one's head inside. Ed Hoban, for one, never crawled into a tunnel that he hadn't fragged first. Mike Meil couldn't have agreed more. On more than one occasion Meil followed a grenade down a hole and found dead enemy soldiers.

Most soldiers had no desire to be the first to enter a tunnel of any size, so the job of investigating the enemy's subterranean lairs, like most unpleasant tasks, devolved to men who, for reasons known only to themselves, liked probing around in the close confines and oppressive darkness of the tunnels. After a few tunnels, however, most men had had enough. The duty would then be passed along to someone else who was interested in souvenirs or spelunking. In the absence of volunteers, the task would fall on the heads of those soldiers of lowest status or smallest stature. Jerry Johnson remembered the selection process well. It consisted, he said, of someone asking, " 'How about one of you guys going down in?' I was the new guy," sighed Johnson, "the FNG. I had to go down."

Being alone below ground generated enormous anxiety for Johnson, who found no joy in exploring tunnels.

> Tunnels were maybe thirty inches in diameter. You would go down head first. You never went down feet first because you didn't know how deep it was. Guys would help lower you down. Usually you would hit the bottom right away with your hands. But you didn't know if you were going to hit booby traps or *punji* stakes or what. Going down hands first you could slide on down and crawl through as best you could, a .45 [pistol] in one hand and a flashlight in the other.

Soldiers carried a pistol for weaponry but flashlights were optional, some preferring instead to move by instinct and feel, believing that the flashlight simply made the exploring soldiers easier targets.

"Close your eyes for a minute," said Ed Hoban, trying to describe the feeling, "and imagine yourself crawling into a small, dark tunnel. Give yourself a penlight and a pistol. Now tie a rope around yourself so they can drag you out if you get shot in the head. Throw in a few snakes and rats and then pray there aren't any gooks between you and wherever you are crawling to."

Jerry Johnson concurred. Inside, soldiers usually found the accommodations quite spartan. Said Johnson:

> After going through a narrow passage you would break into a room so small you could barely sit in it. There might be a table there, maybe an oil lamp, and little spaces to store stuff. They were multi-level too. You could look up and see trapdoors. You would have to be careful that they weren't booby-trapped, or that somebody wasn't up there. One time I went to move a trapdoor and I could faintly see something move. I shot up through the trapdoor and popped it open, but there was nothing there. But firing a .45 in a confined area

like that was just deafening. I came out and I just couldn't hear for a couple of hours.

Large tunnel complexes were marvels of engineering and utility. Mike Meil encountered one group of tunnels in the Central Highlands that "had a hospital and an armory in it. . . . It was a big son of a bitch," he said, shaking his head at the memory. "Must have been probably somewhere from a hundred to two hundred adjoining holes to it. It was . . . set up real nice. They had a surgical-type deal in it, lights that operated from a generator. . . . It was somewhere around fifty or sixty feet deep into the hills."

Paul Boehm toured a similar tunnel complex farther north and discovered, along with barracks and hospital facilities, a classroom with a stage, and a fully ventilated mess hall complete with bamboo plumbing.

No matter what the size of the tunnel complex, investigating them always involved risk, which some units simply felt no compulsion to accept. By 1971, Dwight Reiland claimed that his unit really didn't "give a damn whether anybody was down there or not. We would throw a few white phosphorus grenades or frags or whatever down there," said Reiland, "and if [the enemy was] in there their asses were grass. If they weren't in there, what's a couple of grenades? Who cares? I wasn't going to crawl in that damn hole. If they wanted a body count, they could say there was one in there."

Rumors of bamboo vipers and other reptilian booby traps were also often associated with tunnels. Although explosive booby traps and *punji* stakes were frequently found below ground, snakes, despite tales to the contrary, were rarely encountered. Jerry Johnson saw snakes on only one occasion, hanging from the entrance to a low cave. The only creatures Ed Hoban encountered in tunnels were rats, which sometimes crawled over him, giving him one more good reason to frag tunnel entrances. The only creatures that contested Mike Meil's underground explorations were birds. Meil explained that the enemy would "use birds as a warning device." According to Meil, the Viet Cong would sometimes "tie strings to the [birds'] feet and anchor them down. When you got close to the area the birds would raise holy hell and alert the enemy, who would race out the other end."

Sometimes, however, the Viet Cong were unable to escape. Tom Magedanz heard rumors in the spring of 1970 that some of the men from a neighboring company were ambushing enemy soldiers underground near Hill 953. The North Vietnamese and Viet Cong were in caves. "Some of [the men had] malaria," Magedanz recalled, "and Golf [Company] would go inside the caves and shoot them. Then they'd drag the bodies away, hide in the caves, and shoot other gooks who would try to go back in."[20]

Most divisions created special units employing men called "tunnel rats" who were assigned the task of exploring the enemy's larger underground haunts. But more and more frequently as the war progressed, the smaller holes were sealed with explosives, for safety's sake if nothing else, and the search for Charles continued elsewhere.

Targets of Opportunity

In most operations, infantry soldiers occupied themselves with patrolling by day, ambushing by night, and sometimes getting lucky and finding the enemy in the open. Tom Schultz recalled one incident involving just such an unexpected opportunity:

> We were set up in dense jungle and it was like an oasis, a sand oasis in the middle of this jungle. . . . We were set up there in a night defense position. It was early morning and the sun was just coming up and here came—there must have been fifty coming across the sand from one wood line to the other, perhaps a hundred fifty yards from us. We got everybody positioned and we got the mortar tube set up and approximated the distance. On the count of three, everybody pulled the trigger. We knocked down, I don't know—fifteen? Twenty? The rest of them got away.

Small ambush and reconnaissance teams frequently operated during daylight hours, typically camouflaging themselves on high ground and observing enemy movement. When targets of opportunity were sighted, artillery fire was called in and adjusted by the team's observer.

Layne Anderson and Paul Boehm both took part in what the 198th Light Infantry Brigade referred to as "killer teams." Composed of about a dozen men, the teams operated in the bush for periods of up to two weeks. They were flown out to the field by helicopter just as darkness fell. According to Layne Anderson they would "run like hell to get up on a prearranged location and you would dig in and camouflage yourself as well as you could and spend the night there. Next day you would just sit there and observe, never fire a shot. Call in artillery. On the next night you would get the hell out of there and go to another prearranged location."

Infantry companies usually spent the daylight hours maneuvering into blocking positions and waiting, or patrolling assigned areas of operation constantly searching for the enemy. Occasionally, opposing forces blundered into each other.

A hastily prepared ambush early in John Merrell's tour provided him with an appreciation for several truths about the accuracy and effect of small-arms fire. Merrell's company walked into an abandoned VC base camp one afternoon in the Central Highlands. "There were campfires still burning," he remembered. "The huts were there. They had the trees pulled down over the top and so forth, so we immediately put out security, and they saw four guys coming down the trail."

Merrell's unit set up a hasty ambush, and when the enemy "walked around the bushes, the first guy saw us and we opened fire. We probably spent fifteen hundred rounds, somewhere in there. We put all that firepower out probably fifty or sixty feet. We put that firepower out in such a condensed area. You know how many bodies we found? One! You know how far away he was? A hundred yards! I counted twenty-three bullet holes in him. And he still went a hundred yards. None of us could believe it."

The first of many lessons Merrell learned about war was that it was "harder to kill a human being than a person thinks.

You see on TV a person gets shot and falls down dead. Most of the time it isn't that way. . . ." Another truth revealed was that in the aftermath of a battle, there was often very little to see.

Private Merrell's experience demonstrated, however, that success in battle was almost always the result of a one-sided advantage of opportunity resulting from seeing the enemy first and initiating the contact. One-sided firefights produced easy kills without sacrifice, and soldiers relished them. Without having been in combat, it is difficult to imagine the sense of relief and momentary euphoria that triumph on the field of battle evokes. Men killed so they could live, and at the time, many of them reveled silently in their moments of revenge or their joy at surviving. Such men were neither psychopaths nor warmongers—simply realists who wagered their lives and enjoyed winning intensely. Their viciousness was not premeditated; it was simply a by-product resulting from the dynamics of two groups of men wishing to remain alive—each at the expense of the other.

In war there is little room for sentiment, and in lieu of romantic trappings, the dispassionate student is left with a strangely macabre sense of reality about killing in wartime—a sense of the spontaneity and genuine, though momentary, blood lust. This was a facet of combat poignantly revealed in the following account by Vernon Janick.

Right after Christmas [1966] we stopped for one day to get all our mail and resupply, and the stuff came for the whole company all at once. It took a couple of choppers just to drop all that stuff off. So we thought we would maybe get a couple, three days to set up and kind of enjoy that stuff. The next day they told us we had to mount up and move out. They'd spotted an NVA outfit somewhere out there, so we were pissed because it was the first time in a long time we'd had something good to eat, sweets and stuff, and we would have liked to have stayed there. There was no way that we could eat it or carry it all with us. We divided up what we could. Ate what we could there. We had to bury the rest. . . .

Well, the NVA weren't where they thought they were. They were somewhere else and were watching all this. We moved out and all of a sudden I didn't know what was going on. Our platoon was told to get on line. We must have circled. While we were doing that, the NVA came down from the hills and started digging all this stuff up. They thought we went the other way. So I presume the old man [company commander] knew where they were. . . . And we got on line and I didn't quite know what was going on but as soon as we came out of the clearing, there them suckers were, just digging up all our stuff. We were told not to open fire. We got closer and closer and closer and they were so busy digging they didn't see us. All of a sudden, when they did, they all just kind of scattered and we opened up. We had a solid line of iron, you could say. There was no way anyone was going to get by there. We just wiped them all out. I think there was eighteen.

I had the M79. You can shoot one [round], then you got to quick get another one, open it up, and put another one in. One [NVA] I know I got for sure because all his guts spilled out. Just about a direct hit right in front of him tore him all apart. Anyway, we were glad for that. It was a good kill—easy. We didn't take one casualty because they were so surprised.

Friendly Casualties

Soldiers operating in the field lived with constant reminders that every day might be their last. They also understood that if they were wounded and made it back to a hospital, they would likely survive all but the most critical injuries. Accordingly, in the hierarchy of priorities in a combat unit, the immediate care and evacuation of the wounded ranked high on the list, and the collective efforts of a unit were seldom more intense than when trying to save a wounded comrade.

In order to save the wounded, according to Tom Schultz, everybody did their best. "We were schooled in emergency first aid," he said, "but no more than getting the bleeding stopped and treating for shock." It was the job of the navy corpsmen and army combat medics to stabilize the wounded and treat them to prevent the onset of shock. "Sometimes," medic Jerry Severson admitted, "you were bandaging a dead man. But you didn't tell him that. You gave him every hope in the world. At times you knew damn well he didn't stand much of a chance, but you patched him up. Sometimes the chopper would get there before he died, and sometimes it didn't. Either way you did all that you could."

Shock, according to medic Francis Whitebird, could be as lethal as a wound itself. "We'd ramble on about nothing and keep talking trying to reassure the guy that he was going to be all right and that he'd be going back to The World," said Whitebird, "but he would know there was something wrong with him. He wouldn't look down. He would look straight up in your eyes. You had to have enough guts to look right back into his eyes and say, 'There's nothing wrong with you, just a little gunshot wound here. I'll call the medevac. That's a million-dollar wound man. I wish I had one just like it.' You had to pep the guy up."

Less serious wounds could wait until the fighting ended, but for the critically wounded, minutes meant the difference between life and death. And in combat, circumstances often dictated drastic measures. Tom Schultz recalled how on one occasion he helped a medic perform a tracheotomy in the field. "A guy got hit by a mortar round," recalled Schultz. "The round took part of his face and knocked his teeth down his throat so he couldn't breathe. It took four of us to hold him, but the medic cut his throat and put a tube in, and the guy lived."

For the wounded, the initial surprise and subsequent pain often came to dominate their impressions of events that would alter their lives forever. Kenneth Korkow, wounded at Khe Sanh, recalled two thoughts going through his mind:

> Number one, I'd been knocked on my butt three times before by incoming rounds and never had a scratch. This time I knew they had greased me good, but I was still on my feet. It blew off my flak jacket, it

ripped a boot off, it blew my helmet off. I was a mass of blood, but I was still on my feet. The other thing that was ironic was that they got me with a mortar, which was the same thing I'd been getting them with. There was some perverse humor in that. Through the grace of God I did not feel intense pain. My nervous system just went numb. I didn't scream.

Sergeant William Harken's initial reaction to being wounded by a boobytrap was disbelief and fear. "The first thing I grabbed for was my privates," he explained. "They were there, so that was cause for a little bit of relief. Then I got mad. I turned around and took a few steps back up the trail because I was angry and I wanted to shoot the first Vietnamese I saw." Pain, however, stopped him short. "All of a sudden it started to hurt, so I decided I better lie down. The medic come over and said, 'How you feel?' God I hurt. I told Doc to take care of the pain. They gave me a shot, threw smoke, and next thing I knew I was on a helicopter."

Jack Freitag's last act in the field was to put down his map and reach out to pick up a wounded fellow marine. Then, according to Freitag:

A bullet picked me up and threw me right back where I started from. The medevac helicopter was already there and they got us and put us on the chopper. I never felt panic. I knew I was hit bad when I tried to push myself up and couldn't move my legs. I was paralyzed from the waist down. I didn't think much of it at that time, I just tried to bandage myself. There was just a little peephole of a wound in front, but when I reached around in back, my hand just kind of disappeared into my body. I could feel bones and flesh and shit. I thought, Oh Christ, this is bad.

I never lost consciousness. I was aware of everything that was going on. I wasn't in shock. When I got on the chopper, the crew chief told me to put a pressure bandage on the wound in front. Then he lifted me up and somebody said, "How is he doing?" and I could see him shaking his head while he tried to put on a bandage.

I was right by the door and the crew chief got everybody strapped in and then went over to his M60 and started pumping away. The shell casings were falling by me and I was lying there and the helicopter made a turn and I could see the gooks coming out of their spider holes and shooting up at us and the crew chief was shooting down, and that was the last picture I remember of Vietnam.

Tragically, there were those whom no amount of effort could save. They were the thousands of soldiers whose trip home began in a poncho gripped at the corners by men who were unashamed of their tears. War is laden with intense emotion, but whether it was a close friend or a complete stranger, Phil Yaeger, like many soldiers and marines, was humbled each time by the intensity he felt when witnessing death. "There is nothing more personal that you can do," he explained, "than share in someone's death. If somebody close to you died, there was a real emotional bond, broken—snapped! And that hurt. If it was a total stranger, it was eerie. I felt like I was sharing their entire life if I shared their death."

Yaeger recalled one occasion during which he had been powerless to prevent the life of a fellow marine from slowly evaporating before his eyes. It left a profound sense. "I wasn't up front at the time he was wounded," said Yaeger, "but a corpsman and I got up to him and a couple of other marines helped us drag him back. We looked and looked and couldn't find any wound. While we looked, the life drained out of him. I didn't have the vaguest idea who he was, but that memory of him will always be with me."

Having served as an infantry soldier, Randall Hoelzen's greatest wish was that the people back home would come to understand that the death of a soldier is equally as important and significant as the death of a civilian. Bonds of friendship that had been cemented beneath the light of a flare or the canopy of the jungle were not severed easily, and the lives of comrades were not surrendered without a fight.

Understandably, the memories of the deaths of friends and

comrades are often jealously guarded. In the late summer of 1971, Dwight Reiland's squad began a patrol outside the perimeter of a new firebase west of Phu Bai. As the men picked their way through the debris left from the clearing of the small patrol base, there was a sudden explosion. Wounded in the blast was Reiland's closest friend and mentor, Robert Pulaski. With great difficulty, Reiland recalled:

Pulaski tripped a boobytrap and it blew [the] hell out of him. Evidently, the enemy stole some of our explosives or something. There was some power in that thing, and it blew off his legs. I was just in back of him and I saw where the explosion took place, but I didn't see Bob at the time. Anyhow, I got up to where I thought he should be, and there he was on the other side of a log probably fifteen or twenty feet away. The explosion blew one leg off about midway between the knee and the groin, and the other leg was blown off at the calf. He didn't have a shirt on. All he was wearing were pants and boots and his equipment. The explosion left his body naked. His testicles were gone and his penis was just barely attached. It just split him open.

God! I looked over that log and I saw him there and he was just kind of quivering and he was taking very shallow, rapid breaths. He was unconscious but he was trying to breathe.

The enemy used that boobytrap as the trigger for a little ambush. We took a few rounds, so I jumped over that log by Bob, and I started hollering for Doc. Just then Lawton come diving over the log beside me.

By the time Doc got over there, Lawton and I both had our belts off and had twisted a couple of tourniquets around Pulaski's legs. When Doc got over there he said, "You know, I think he is dead." And then he said, "But that's not for us to decide."

The others on the firebase heard the explosion and the enemy rifle fire and began to lay down covering fire for the patrol. At the same time, efforts were begun to get the wounded man extracted. A resupply helicopter happened to be unloading at the time of the ambush and, while the supply helicopter was being readied, a stretcher was hurried down from the hill. Meanwhile, Reiland continued:

> Doc gave Bob a shot of morphine, maybe a couple of them—I don't remember. Anyhow, we tightened the tourniquets and started loading him on the stretcher they had brought down. Then we took a couple more rounds of enemy fire so we had to lie there a little bit until we knew that we could carry him up the hill.
>
> When we got him up there, the helicopter pilot and the door gunners had literally kicked out the tubular aluminum frames for the seats to make room for the stretcher. The leg that had been blown off at the thigh was there and so we put that on the stretcher, but we never did find the other one. We went down to see if we could, but we never found it. Then they took off with him.

Looking for the leg was a last act of compassion by men who had done everything they possibly could for their friend. They knew in their hearts what was confirmed an hour later: Bob Pulaski was dead on arrival at the hospital. "We had some other guys killed," Reiland said, shaking away the memory, "but that was the one that hurt."

It was hard to let go, harder than words could express, yet they were gone and life in the field continued. The dead and the wounded rotated home, part of the strange migration of souls that marked the beginnings and endings of lives and tours and friendships. But the planes that carried the aluminum caskets back to America had not come to Vietnam empty. The one-year cycle of lives continued uninterrupted on the grand scale. It was tragically finite only where families and friends were concerned. In a matter of hours the news would travel westward, followed in a few days' time by the remains. But for those soldiers there would be no DEROS, and no joy in their homecoming.

The Numbers Game

At a personal level, survival was synonymous with winning. The measure of success for GIs in the field was the arrival of the helicopters, which, after two weeks or a month or more, took the men back to a more secure area for a few days of rest. Units were usually rotated to a small firebase to pull guard for a week and dry their feet, drink some beer, write some letters, and get a little sleep. There was always a chance of enemy activity during an extraction, but usually the helicopters lifted from the jungles with a collective sigh of relief from their human cargo.

The sound of the rotor blades was suddenly one of the sweetest on the earth, signaling a temporary reprieve from the war—or at least the more dangerous aspects of it. As the choppers rose into the cooler air, men relaxed and smiles broke out. Feet dangled over the skids and the war passed by harmlessly below. It was good.

At such times men reflected on many things. They relied on themselves, trusted each other, and were proud of themselves. They understood what it meant to be alive, and they sensed their increasing maturity and self-reliance. They were indispensable to others as they had never been before and, having come through another operation, they were genuinely imbued with the attitude that there was probably nothing they couldn't do. Such moments were worth remembering; they were what most soldiers would choose to remember. The soldiers were suddenly young men again, alive, joking in the company of true comrades. "It was a real hot day and I was sweaty and dirty," said Ed Hoban, recalling one such moment years later. "The sweat was just dripping off my face, and someone handed me a Marlboro cigaret. The sweat dripped down that cigaret and I had my feet hanging out the side of the chopper and we were flying along. It was over. We knew we were heading in for the day. That tasted so sweet!"

But to the Olympian powers that planned the insertions, the success of the American war effort in Vietnam was subject to quantitative measurements: shells fired, bombing missions flown, weapons captured, defectors returned, hamlets secured, and, most importantly, the number of reported enemy kills. The most commonly used yardstick for measuring success was the "body count." Such grisly arithmetic produced the kind of data that analysts needed to plot success in the absence of ground gained or other traditional indicators. Although one would expect no misunderstanding of the definition of bodies physically counted in the field, there was considerable room left for interpretation.[21]

Military Assistance Command Vietnam (MACV) regulations required that body count be substantiated by counting bodies of "males of fighting age and others, male or female, known to have carried arms." In addition, "Body count made from the air will be based upon debriefings of pilots or observers which substantiate beyond a reasonable doubt the count was in fact KIA." As Guenter Lewy suggested, "It was a figure conducive to estimates," and both inflationary and deflationary effects made accuracy difficult.[22]

The rugged terrain and frequent night attacks made it very hard to search for and locate enemy bodies after a contact. The enemy also placed a high priority on recovering casualties, which helped prevent accurate counts. Because of such difficulties, field commanders were inclined to estimate the enemy's losses without hard evidence. Although most tried to be accurate, for others, body count became a work of creative fiction.

There were many ways a unit's body count could be inflated. Some units made claims based on circumstantial evidence. Blood trails might be substituted for enemy corpses. A captured weapon or pieces of a body would likely be treated as if it were a body.[23]

No matter how it was done, inflating the count was a common practice in the memories of many soldiers. In Jeff Yushta's company, cheating was "definitely part of the game. . . . We fudged our body counts. If somebody had been blown in half and you didn't know which piece went where, [you] made it two instead of one. And if somebody would say, 'I know I got him, but they must have dragged him away.' Okay, we'd count that. If there was any feasible way to raise the count without getting to be absurd, it was done."

John Merrell, on the other hand, could not recall "any of

the time I was there that the body count was ever misrepresented—by us anyway!" He maintained that his company's body count was "honest coming in from the field." If there was cheating, Merrell believed that it was done by those in command "farther up the line."

That was precisely where Gerry Barker felt that his unit's body counts were being exaggerated. "During my second tour," he explained, "we had a firefight . . . and I called two [bodies] into the company. I heard the company relay it as two bodies. But when we heard it farther up the line, it was already five. We just laughed."

Jerry Severson recalled occasions where the tallies were thrown off by accidentally or intentionally counting the same bodies more than once. On one occasion he remembered seeing six bodies, "but, when they totalled them it was, 'How many did you get?' 'Well . . . I got six!' They would ask someone else, 'How many did you get?' 'I got six.' 'Well, that's twelve. How many did you get?'. . ."

MACV issued guidelines for factoring additional dead based on standard percentages by type of encounter and terrain. Nowhere were the counts larger, or the truth probably more liberally interpreted, than in the evaluation of enemy casualties from high-level bombing missions.

Paul Meringolo's company was conducting a routine sweep of some villages when orders came to vacate the area for a B-52 raid. Meringolo was deeply impressed with the destructive power he witnessed, but he was totally bemused by what happened afterward:

> When the operation was over, we discovered that we got credit for a hundred and forty-one NVA being killed! We hadn't the slightest idea how that was determined, but we were told it was because our intelligence felt that there had been an NVA unit operating in the area. Because of the kill ratio of such a bomb drop from a B-52, they gave us credit for those kills even though on that operation we didn't see one single VC nor NVA soldier.
>
> . . . We very well may have destroyed or killed some of the enemy, but we also may very well have not killed

anybody. But that was what Vietnam was all about—
numbers! Numbers that had to show that we were accomplishing something whether in fact we were or not.

Exaggerated counts never seemed to be questioned higher
up. Officers who tried to render accurate body counts had to
fight against a current of pressure to produce results—on paper if not in truth. Guenter Lewy asserted that this manipulation of reality affected not only battle news, which was edited
and revised until it was acceptable to those higher up, but also
friendly casualty reports, pacification reports, food distribu-
tion status—anything that lent itself to statistical measure-
ment as a demonstration of progress. Lewy quoted Maj.
William I. Lowry as saying, "Duplicity was so automatic that
lower headquarters began to believe the things they were for-
warding to higher headquarters . . . the paper graphs and
charts became the ultimate reality."[24] This situation was reinforced, as Shelby Stanton points out, by the fact that the
unquestioned tallies "were readily rewarded by medals, promotions, and time off from field duty."[25]

Incentives offered to the enlisted personnel were usually
the result of increasing pressure from above to produce more
kills. Charles Gadd, for example, claimed that his unit was
"constantly under pressure to turn in a body count, and the
word was out that companies with the greatest number would
get to spend more time at Cocoa Beach. It was an accepted
thing to cheat on a body count report—all of us had been
guilty of this."[26]

Bryan Good remembered that in early 1970, something
resembling a bounty existed in his battalion. "Anybody who
got a confirmed kill," he recalled, "got a three-day pass to
China Beach in Da Nang." Good was quick to point out, however, that there was very little desire to collect. Few men were
willing to risk their lives for a three-day vacation. Besides, he
added, "The kills were a joint venture. If they did offer a pass
to someone . . . whoever was there longest got it."

Just how many such rewards were actually handed out is
certainly subject to debate, but conversations with enlisted
veterans strongly indicate that if anyone benefited from high
body counts, it was the officers far more than the soldiers.

Gerry Barker knew that enlisted men were not rewarded for body count in his unit, but he suspected strongly that officers were. Certainly a platoon leader or company commander's efficiency reports were based upon body count, he said.

Correspondent Ward Just offered further amplification. War, he noted, was a rare opportunity for career officers because combat command is considered essential. Add to that the pressure on officers to produce results in order to get the exemplary individual efficiency ratings needed for advancement. "It is not for nothing that the reports are called progress reports," Just quipped.[27]

The grim accounting of casualties required a double-entry ledger, however. Not surprisingly, GIs having seen the official tallies of enemy casualties, were naturally suspicious of friendly casualty reports. Gerry Barker summed up his unit's view with the observation that "reports of casualties were always fiction. We would read in *Stars and Stripes* that some fight that had taken place had produced light casualties, and we would say that meant everybody that was wounded weighed less than a hundred and ten pounds. We didn't believe anything anybody said. The things that we *could* see [made the casualty reports sound] ridiculous."

What the soldiers saw gave them excellent reason to doubt press releases concerning American casualty statistics. Willie Williams said that he learned through correspondence with his wife that the information his division was giving family members living in Hawaii was a little misleading:

> They used to have one day that they would take the dependents of the soldiers that were still at Schofield Barracks—a lot of the wives were still there—and they would meet and they would show film clips and they also had a little bulletin that they would give them as to what was happening. And our casualties were always "light." When we lost the whole company, it was listed as "moderate." We never had "heavy" casualties, even though the time we got overrun we didn't have forty people that walked away from that. And that's talking about two hundred and forty-three men in a company. We didn't have forty that walked away.

In data processing, the adage is "garbage in—garbage out." When changes in policy and tactics are based on reported data, accuracy becomes even more imperative. Yet few seem to have believed the data upon which progress was measured, and the sense of disillusionment grew as the war continued. In a survey conducted at the Army War College in 1968, of the 65 officers questioned, many of whom had been battalion or brigade commanders in Vietnam, 60 percent indicated a belief that the estimates were based on actual count. A second study of 173 general officers by retired Brig. Gen. Douglas Kinnard in 1974 showed that 61 percent believed the count was "often inflated." Only 28 percent thought that the count reflected any degree of accuracy.[28]

There were at least four attempts to corroborate body count statistics by extrapolating enemy casualties from captured documents. The results varied, but the most complete analysis put enemy losses at about half of what had been reported. In 1968, however, North Vietnam's Gen. Vo Nguyen Giap, in an interview with Oriana Fallaci, acknowledged the loss of about a half million men in the war up to that point, which was more than the official tally of 435,000.[29]

Whatever the truth, the enemy was able throughout the war to make good his losses. In December 1964 total enemy strength was estimated at 180,700. Three years later, the enemy had increased his total force to 261,500. About 45 percent of North Vietnamese males between the ages of fifteen and thirty-four years were serving in the People's Army of Vietnam. This meant that in early 1968, when U.S. forces were achieving their greatest successes the North Vietnamese had sufficient manpower to replace their losses and maintain the same size force in the field for another thirteen years— even at that rate of attrition.[30]

The numbers often seemed so ridiculous that more than one veteran commented sarcastically that American soldiers apparently killed the whole country. In any event, the official tally listed 850,000 enemy war dead, the equivalent of killing about 40 percent of the enemy's total force each year. Allied forces lost 222,000 soldiers killed in South Vietnam. America's share was 21 percent, and of those 46,620 Americans who died in combat, the U.S. Army and Marine Corps accounted for 95 percent by the war's end in 1973.[31]

Tremendous effort was expended on the collection of data, and certainly there was much to learn from it, but the one statistic that mattered for the United States in Vietnam was also the single statistic that was most accurately kept. As one intelligence officer summarized so eloquently, "His is not an army that sends coffins north, it is by the traffic of homebound American coffins that Giap measures his success."[32]

CHAPTER 12

The Bitter Angles of Our Nature

April 3, 1968

Dear Mom and Dad,

I'm hoping this letter finds you well and are getting nice weather. We are waiting for the choppers to pick us up this morning and take us to a new location to do some hunting. I guess we'll only be out about three more days and then we are supposed to go to the rear and get a few days rest. I sure hope I'm back in on my birthday so I can drink some beer.

I've been hearing that [President] Johnson is trying to get the war stopped this summer. What he'll probably do is get it messed up more and we'll be doing more fighting than ever. I suppose if they declare war over here I'll be here until the end. I sure hope they get it settled cause I want to come home soon. The day I hit the States again will be the happiest day of my life.

Your Son,
Len[1]

In combat, it is often the narrowest of lines that separates laudable behavior under fire from excessive or atrocious behavior. Writing about the violent nature of the war with the Japanese in the Pacific during World War II, John Dower pointed out that "atrocities follow war as the jackal follows a wounded beast."[2] A generation later, Stephen Banko, in a Veterans Day address to students in Buffalo, New York, admonished his youthful audience: "If I told you the full details of some of the incidents that resulted in military medals, you'd be more convinced that such deportment merited seven-and-a-half to fifteen years at Attica."[3]

Atrocities occurred in Vietnam as they have in all previous wars. But, as former marine lieutenant Philip Caputo points out, what has often been ignored are the causes that triggered them.[4]

In Vietnam, as so often happens in modern war, the momentum generated by battle and the destructiveness of the weapons used not only increased the loss of civilian life, but also helped foster brutality. The soldier's aggression was further exacerbated by the frustration, exhaustion, and physical discomfort generated by the climate, terrain, and assorted impediments of the bush—not to mention the incredible complexity of distinguishing friendly villagers from the enemy. The Vietnam War combined the very worst elements of guerrilla tactics, terrorism, and ruthless conventional military action. There was ample opportunity for excesses of fatigue or absence of character to manifest themselves in isolated acts of brutality and violence. Additionally, inexperienced platoon leaders and young NCOs operating in small, autonomous units were often put under tremendous strain as they sought to carry out their missions and maintain discipline. On occasion, leadership was sadly lacking.

Of the tens of thousands of men who served in infantry units in the field in Vietnam, the majority, such as Larry Gates, never participated in any act of physical violence that could be construed as an atrocity. Gates said that he never witnessed such an act by any of the men with whom he served, and he took pride in the fact that, "Our company was pretty humane. We captured prisoners. We didn't cut any parts off the dead. We didn't inflict any more pain than what our weapons would allow us to do. We weren't imaginative about it at all."

Premeditated acts of violent behavior were rare in the field, but they did happen, and many soldiers, though not condoning such behavior, could understand the emotions that precipitated it. Jeff Yushta reasoned that, "Everybody lost a little bit of themselves there and I know some good guys that went over the edge a little bit. . . . And I say to myself, 'Well, they were just subjected to more than I was, and if they went over and came back, what they did while they were on the other side is kind of something they didn't have control over.' I know them now to be good people."

Even when provoked, most soldiers resisted the temptation to seek personal vengeance. Displays of restraint received little notice precisely because there was nothing sensational about them. Jerry Johnson recalled policing up after one of his first battles:

> It was the first time I saw a dead dink. He had a fifty-caliber round right through the head. I mean he was dead! And I picked him up [by the shoulders] and looked and [then threw the body back down]. I wasn't really mad, it was just handling the body rough. And some guy said, "Hey buddy—shoot him." I looked around and said, "What do you mean shoot him?" There was a news team—two guys. They had watched me and wondered what I was going to do to the body. I wasn't going to do anything to it. I just picked it up like that and threw it down and the guy said, "Shoot it."

Johnson was angry and a bit surprised, but he did not take the bait. "After all," he reasoned, "the guy was dead. What could I do to him?"

Those who have not experienced combat often expect restraint and civility to come easily for soldiers during wartime. It is hard for them to appreciate how difficult it is to live up to that expectation. Soldiers whose lives are in jeopardy during battle are often angry, and the emotions unleashed by aggression and the instinct for survival are a powerful force. Combat soldiers are witnesses to intensely traumatic scenes of carnage; they are agents empowered to inflict similar physical destruction upon their enemies and they understand that they could easily suffer the same fate. The violence and brutality to which they are occasionally subjected sometimes engenders responses of a similar nature, creating a spiraling escalation of violence and revenge, resulting in atrocities being committed by both sides.

Part of the blame for excessive brutality on the battlefield results from men becoming desensitized to violence. Rifleman

Mike Meil, for one, was somewhat taken aback by what he witnessed when he first arrived in Vietnam. "I always thought to myself, Jesus! These guys are goddamned crazy!" Meil recalled. But as the months in the field passed, he discovered he became just like them. "I guess you feel that in order to survive you have to be crazy. You do things that people would never expect to hear or see about back here in the United States."

Over the course of their tours, men became hardened in direct proportion to the amount of combat and carnage to which they were exposed. Callousness was often a by-product of that exposure, and too much exposure caused emotional debilitation. As John Ellis notes, there is no getting used to combat: "Each moment of combat imposes a strain so great that men will break down in direct relation to the intensity and duration of their experience. Psychiatric casualties are as inevitable as gunshot and shrapnel wounds in combat."[5]

Resulting acts of brutality are usually episodic, a result of emotional trauma, inexplicable displays of senseless violence that are clear indicators that the fabric of one's humanity is becoming frayed.

Tom Magedanz recalled one such display during a patrol in the Que Son mountains. Magedanz's squad fired into a clump of bushes, killing two NVA who had fled from the approaching marines.

"One of them was a woman," Magedanz remembered, "but she was NVA; there's no question in my mind. They both had, not complete uniforms, but they had green shirts and trousers. And she was kind of a pretty woman. Not like the old women in the village who work so hard and were all wrinkled and everything. This was a pretty girl and pretty well fed also. One of our guys—I don't know why or what he was thinking of—he just kind of lost it. But he shot her in the face a bunch of times and blew away half her face."

The transformation Jon Neely underwent in 1969 seemed almost incomprehensible to him in retrospect.

After I had been in country six or seven months, I really started to get into going out into the field and getting into contact. I was getting to the point where I enjoyed what I was doing so much that after one particular firefight, we went over to check on our body count, and one of the first things that I did when I approached one of the dead Vietnamese or Viet Cong—I had seen evidence of this before, and for some reason it just struck me as something to do at this time—I reached down and cut one of the guy's ears off and poked a hole in it and hung it on a chain. It seemed maybe cruel and inhumane, but the longer you were there, [and] the more you saw what they did to your guys, the more you turned around and did it to theirs. . . .

I had become, I don't know, part animal I guess you could call it. And from that point, it just seemed like I had regressed or something. I kept turning more and more animalistic. I was enjoying the contact. I was enjoying the firefights and enjoying killing, and at one time I displayed as many as thirteen ears on this chain that I had hanging off my gear. I look back on it now and I wonder to myself, Jeeze, what the heck happened to me? I have a totally different set of beliefs now than what I had when I was over there, and I wonder how I let myself get that way.[6]

Although some men realized that they had allowed themselves to change, most soldiers chose to blame their aberrant behavior on external elements, the most common being that their actions reflected the enemy's behavior. Although he did not attempt to justify brutality on such grounds, Philip Caputo noted perceptively that, "Men who do not expect to receive mercy eventually lose their inclination to grant it."[7]

Prisoners of War

When a soldier raises his hands in surrender, he takes a perilous step, for in most cases, he is hoping to be spared by the very people he was trying to kill only moments before. In nearly all wars soldiers have been reluctant to take prisoners, and all too often enemy soldiers have been "dispatched" while still in the gray area between combatant and formal prisoner.

Several factors undoubtedly contributed to such actions. The intensity of combat might have made it impossible for some soldiers to restrain the raw emotions unleashed during battle. Certainly, there is a reluctance to assume any degree of risk beyond what is absolutely necessary. Additionally, troops at the point of attack were often engaged in numerous activities that commanded their attention. A potential prisoner might have been seen as a dangerous distraction, if not a genuine hazard. And soldiers, friend as well as foe, fought in fragmented groups; while one individual or small group was no longer returning fire, a neighboring group might well have continued the fight, confusing the issue of who was truly a combatant. But American soldiers generally assumed, either as a product of their training or as part of the acquired wisdom and lore of the veterans in their combat units, that the enemy would not surrender anyway.

Terry Musser noted that, during his combat tour in 1965–66, there was a genuine paucity of enemy POWs. According to Musser, "We never had the opportunity to get that many of them. Once we got involved, there wasn't much quarter given. If they were wounded, they literally—whether they were VC or NVA—believed that we would kill them anyway. They would crawl off or die in the brush. I saw an awful lot of blood trails. But we never did take that many prisoners."

Like their elders in the Pacific during World War II, infantrymen in Vietnam accepted as fact the notion that a wounded Viet Cong or NVA soldier would feign surrender in an attempt to kill any Americans foolish enough to approach. According to Michael Lanning, when his men approached a wounded enemy soldier, they usually continued to "shoot and throw grenades at the body" rather than risk possible Viet Cong perfidy.[8]

In a war without fronts, there were also logistical problems concerning prisoners. This caused Tom Magedanz to observe pragmatically:

> If it was a wounded NVA, he wasn't taken prisoner. They were killed. Usually, if there was a little firefight

or some shooting, if you heard another squad off in the distance shooting, a few minutes later you'd hear some more shooting. They would be finishing off the wounded ones. I guess it's not a good thing to do, but I just can't see calling in a medevac helicopter in the mountains to pick up a man you just got done trying to kill and risk having a helicopter shot down. That's one thing. But to kill a prisoner who is healthy is something else. I didn't see that happen.

Wounded soldiers were sometimes dispatched with little regard on the battlefield by men from both sides. But the practice was hardly endemic to the Vietnam War.

During World War II, correspondent Eric Sevareid described the shooting of German prisoners and Italian civilians during the Italian campaign. Edgar L. Jones, a correspondent in the Pacific, provided some additional disquieting perspective:

> What kind of war do civilians suppose we fought anyway? We shot prisoners in cold blood, wiped out hospitals, strafed lifeboats, killed or mistreated enemy civilians, finished off the enemy wounded, tossed the dying into a hole with the dead, and, in the Pacific, boiled the flesh off enemy skulls to make table ornaments for sweethearts, or carved their bones into letter openers.[9]

Some Americans treated Japanese corpses with practically no regard, and collecting human body parts became so flagrant that the commander in chief of the Pacific Fleet found it necessary to order in 1942 that, "No part of the enemy's body may be used as a souvenir. Unit commanders will take stern disciplinary action."[10]

American soldiers were convinced that it was the enemy who set the pace and tone with respect to the treatment of prisoners. Terry Musser looked back at the remains of 1st Cavalry Division units he came upon after they had been overwhelmed by the enemy, and wondered aloud, "Maybe they all went out fighting, but they all went out. That happened all the time.

Well, there has to be one wounded person someplace that doesn't get killed immediately! But there never seemed to be any survivors unless they were buried in a shell hole with a bunch of bodies on top."

Perhaps because of the difficulty of moving POWs into Cambodia or Laos and then north, the enemy usually killed Americans, whether wounded or not, rather than take them prisoner. That fact became evident with the first battles between Communist and U.S. forces in the fall of 1965. Army Specialist Jack P. Smith's unit, Company C, 2d Battalion, 7th Cavalry, was ambushed while moving in support of other units in the Ia Drang Valley. Wounded and virtually helpless, Smith recalled how, "All night long the Cong [actually the 66th NVA Regiment] had been moving around killing the wounded. Every few minutes I heard some guy start screaming, 'No, no, no, please,' and then a burst of bullets. When they found a guy that was wounded, they'd make an awful racket. They'd [enemy soldiers] yell for their buddies and babble awhile, then turn the poor devil over and listen to him while they stuck a barrel in his face and squeezed. . . ."[11] Later, the rifleman learned that two of his close friends had been found executed together, both shot in the back of the head. Understandably, such experiences cultivated a strong desire for revenge.

Sergeant Gerry Barker discovered in late 1966 that if he wanted prisoners, he had to act quickly.

If you couldn't get to the troops fast enough they would kill them. It was always that way. I was telling this to my father one time in Vietnam there in Saigon and . . . in fact I was expressing exactly the frustration of, "Damnit, I just had a couple of good soldiers kill a prisoner!" He was telling me how in the Philippines, when he was there in World War II, that it was so bad they were giving three-day passes and a hundred dollars for bringing in a prisoner. It wasn't that the Japanese wouldn't surrender, it was that our rosy-cheeked American boys were killing the damn prisoners. That, unfortunately, was a fact of life in combat. It was hard to get them to do it [take prisoners]. I had the same trouble with the 'Yards [Montagnards] later on. They did not bring in prisoners.

That was the dark side of soldiering, and Barker suspected it had been the same in every war. But he understood the soldiers' motives. Prisoners died, he reasoned, because "the kids were damn angry."

> You just lost your buddy a month ago and you aren't over it yet. You are scared to death and you are hostile! Scared! You suddenly have the object of your terror there at your mercy. . . . And you know he is going to go back to a prison camp and be warm and safe and dry and you are going to stay out there. It takes a lot of self-control not to shoot him. I always stressed with my kids the intelligence value of prisoners. Sometimes that worked if I watched them close enough.

Leadership can do only so much, however. Ultimately, it was up to each soldier in the frenzy of battle or the frustration of its aftermath to decide in his own mind whether or not the man before him would receive mercy. The abuse or murder of an enemy soldier *after* he was formally taken into custody and disarmed appears to have been extremely rare, though. If a prisoner *was* killed after his surrender was accepted, it was seldom in cold blood. According to Jim Raysor, on one occasion his recon team took a POW

> down to this creek and waited for a chopper. We were sitting there and we had him in a half circle. There were eight of us. We were all smoking and drinking coffee, just having a good time, taking a lunch break waiting for this chopper to come in. When we heard the *wacka-wacka-wacka* from the chopper this guy flipped out and started yelling some Ho Chi Minh stuff and started going across the creek. As soon as he started yelling and hit the water everybody just spun on him and lit him up. I mean, Jesus, I don't think anybody missed him. I don't think anybody shot less than ten rounds on

automatic. It was tough to explain when the chopper landed.

If an enemy soldier became a prisoner, treatment seemed to be no worse than what was de rigueur in Vince Olson's unit. Olson never saw men in his unit physically abuse prisoners. There were, however, times when "we would make prisoners carry our packs and stuff like that so we wouldn't have to carry them," he explained. "And sometimes, we had them out walking point . . . looking for booby traps or snipers. If they were getting down, or ducking, or looking a little bit funny, we knew something was going to happen. We used them as decoys—something to give us a little advantage. But as far as beating them or anything, we never did that."

Vernon Janick recalled, however, that the treatment of prisoners in his company was a bit more brusque. "Sometimes we got a little carried away," he admitted.

> We roughed them up a little bit sometimes and then sent them in on a chopper to wherever they took 'em. . . . Just slapped 'em up and stuff—kicked them. Especially the ones we captured on the run with weapons and stuff. You had no mercy on them for sure. Just all the irritation and stuff that you were getting before that. You would get so mad that when you did get one. . . . It was just like a dog that bit you. Boy! When you get a hold of that sucker. . . .
>
> Like I say, at first we went through them a little bit and then sent them in. Took out our frustrations a little bit. They had this ugly, mean look to them that just made you automatically butt-stroke them and stuff like that. You built up a real hatred for the NVA or any enemy.

The mistreatment of prisoners or refusing to accept surrender was more common if Americans had been killed or wounded. Ed Austin succumbed to his baser instincts after helping load on a medevac helicopter the man for whom he had carried a radio during most of his tour. But Austin's rage, and the behavior it inspired, left him subsequently very confused. Austin later wrote in his journal:

> Freitag was shot today. It is his spine so he should be going home. Davis was also hit. Both by the same sniper. And we captured the sniper (three others too). I got hold of the VC that shot Jack. I went out of my head and almost beat him to death. I felt mixed up afterwards. I was glad I did it, but felt I had no right to. He was blindfolded and his hands were tied behind him, and I beat him with a rifle butt.[12]

In a few cases, previous experience was cited as justification for not taking prisoners. A POW taken by Willie Williams killed the platoon's medic, Carlos Sanchez, later that same night. Sergeant Williams could not recall how the prisoner got loose, "But he physically killed Sanchez, and I made an oath then that I wouldn't take any more [prisoners]."

Stories of prisoners being thrown from helicopters or placed before makeshift firing squads were standard fare. But, like most rumors, what soldiers heard differed a great deal from what they actually saw. Sergeant Steve Fredrick pointed out that:

> Stories build and grow and get embellished, and Vietnam vets, like all vets, like to impress civilians with war stories and have them look at you like you are different, strange, and even a little scary. . . . Generally, these are men who have gained little other notice for worthiness or respect in their life, so they are trying to parlay one year in Vietnam into a lifetime of wonder, respect, fear and noteworthiness. . . . [13]

The value of prisoners sometimes seemed overrated to the men in the field, especially because of the language barrier. The inability of most Americans to communicate with the Vietnamese became a constant source of frustration, and sometimes, as Tom Schultz relates, led to brutality:

There was one situation where we had been in a ville and interrogated everyone, and everybody was cordial and had their identity cards in order and had the right amount of rice. We walked out with some feeling of security. Well, you were never really secure, but these people were cooperative.

We walked out of this ville about four hundred yards and set up an NDP. We were just taking our packs off and starting to get laid back for the night when we caught fire from two sides. On paper, according to battalion—according to brigade, we were fired upon, so we could go in there and fire. We did not go in and kill anyone, but we destroyed the village and destroyed the rice. And we found a tunnel and we found a man in the tunnel with a rifle. We took him back to where we were setting up night defenses. We didn't have an interrogator and by some, oh, unreasonable quirk, the company commander thought he was going to make this Vietnamese speak English. He slapped the shit out of him and bloodied him until he couldn't talk. We tied him up and sent him back on the chopper the next day.

Prisoners sent to the rear for questioning were eventually handed over to the South Vietnamese for processing. What happened after that remained a mystery to most soldiers, but they were well aware of the barbaric interrogations conducted by the South Vietnamese, which they sometimes witnessed in the field. Charles Gadd recalled seeing National Police troopers beat several POWs on the soles of their feet with bamboo poles until they bled. "It didn't take long before they had every one of the POWs answering their questions," Gadd later wrote.[14]

Rifleman Paul Boehm was similarly taken aback by the Vietnamese Rangers who occasionally handled interrogations for his unit:

They would beat them upside the head a little bit and then shoot them. Or they would take and . . . I've seen them put prisoners in a push-up position with a bayonet on the ground: stick a bayonet in the ground under them and drop a sandbag on their shoulders—see how long he can stand it . . . before he ends up on top of that bayonet. Weird sight.

. . . Sticking the head in the water always worked good. Basically, they just beat the living piss out of them. They would butt-stroke them all the time if they got the wrong answer. But then, after so many times, is a guy going to say it just so he doesn't get his face smashed again? So whether they were getting the truth out of them—who knows.

Such behavior was not practiced solely by the Vietnamese. Gerry Barker remembered seeing the marines take a couple of prisoners near Khe Sanh with exactly the same results: brutality that achieved nothing. It was, Barker decided, "more for their own satisfaction than anything."

Americans in the field commonly believed that many prisoners and suspects who were sent to the rear ended up being released. As Don Putnam explained, "That hurt, because you knew you were going to face the guy that night or the next night." He dutifully continued sending back prisoners, although he acknowledged that, "I would be a liar if I sat here and said there weren't times that I would just as soon shoot the guy knowing that was what was going to happen. But no matter how strong my animal instincts got, I still wouldn't do it. I'd take them back and go through the same silly process again. . . . I don't know what the answer to that is. I guess I can sit here now and say I'm glad I didn't change, although at times that frustration was so great I would have liked to."

Rudyard Kipling once observed, "There is an accumulative cruelty in a number of men, though none in particular is ill-natured."[15] On occasion, soldiers became a law unto themselves. This is a facet of all wars, played out time and again, as it was one sultry day in the Que Son Valley. A marine recalled hearing of an incident in a sister platoon where a prisoner was taken who had "tight cords around his thighs to cut off the circulation." It was generally believed that the cords prevented the man from feeling much pain and reduced bleeding while he was crawling through barbed wire around the base camp. "Anyway," noted the chronicler, "the rumor was that 1st Platoon decided that this prisoner must be a sapper—an especially feared type of NVA soldier, and they beat him to death."[16]

Mutilation

Mutilating corpses was another practice that had its adherents in Vietnam. In its least objectionable form, some individuals left "calling cards"—unit shoulder patches, printed business cards, or regimental crests—laid on or affixed to a corpse after a battle in order to identify the outfit responsible. Most units discouraged the practice, but in a few organizations it was widespread. Gerry Barker remembered B Company, 1st Battalion, 8th Cavalry's "Death from Above" cards, and Michael Lanning's unit ordered yellow three-by-five cards in English and Vietnamese that read, "Compliments of the Old Guard, 2d Battalion, 3d Infantry." Some men left an ace of spades or a division or separate brigade shoulder patch. Donald Putnam's platoon sometimes deposited cloth patches with an enemy corpse; William Harken's platoon left a metal pin embossed with the battalion's "Wolfhound" insignia.[17]

More excessive were calling cards that were carved into the forehead or chest of an enemy soldier. When Robert Keeling first joined his mechanized unit in late 1969, he remembered being told about two men in his company who were "butchers, I guess you might say, because every time they would kill an NVA or a VC, they would disfigure the body. What they would do is carve AKA on their foreheads—Ass Kicking Alpha." Keeling wasn't sure why, although he said that some men in the unit claimed the enemy seemed to be scared of the company and very seldom attacked it.

Irrational as it may seem, some GIs accepted the notion that such brutality discouraged the enemy from messing with them. Such rationalization had no real basis. Most units operated in the same area for weeks at a time, and the enemy was well acquainted with those whom they were fighting. But, as Robert Keeling indicated, one of the reasons for the identification left on corpses was the belief that a marked corpse somehow offered added protection. It is doubtful that the enemy was frightened by mutilations any more than Americans were. Such acts probably prompted anger and an increased probability of responses in kind, but more than one GI justified violating enemy corpses because it put fear into their adversaries and, as a consequence, reduced the likelihood of contact.

Sergeant William Harken believed that "because of what we did—the Wolfhound crest, sometimes the ace of spades, the removing of an ear—we were never in an ambush. We would ambush people, but we were never ambushed. [It] made sense to me. And I believe the enemy knew who we were, too. I firmly believe it."

Most of the mutilation, however, probably resulted from frustration, a desire for revenge, or outright callousness. Johnnie Clark remembered that after the death of a machine gunner in his unit, a man who was both popular and just thirty days shy of going home, a member of his squad carved their unit designation across the chest of a nearby corpse and tacked an ace of spades to his forehead.[18]

Occasionally, whole bodies were used as warnings, and the exhibition of corpses, although very rare, represented the sometimes twisted logic of war. Jon Neely claims that he saw such displays from time to time at Dong Tam, but said he doubted their worth. Sometimes, according to Neely, "They would string the dead VC up on the barbed wire out in front of the base camp and hang signs on them stating this is what's happening to VC and trying to persuade the local villagers not to side with the VC, but to swing over to the South Vietnam government."

Sergeant Willie Williams witnessed a similar act shortly after his unit began setting up its base camp at Cu Chi in 1966. "The colonel had the first Viet Cong we killed strung up on a post and put out in the wire in front of our perimeter," said Williams. "The body stayed there and just deteriorated. Supposedly this put fear in the Cong and also it was because they mutilated a lot of our men."

Perhaps the most publicized form of mutilation in Vietnam was the removal of ears from enemy corpses. Ears were collected as trophies, a means of "counting coup"—of keeping an individual record of kills, to "gross out" new guys or, in a

demented way, achieve some degree of status.[19] Military life
has sometimes held an attraction for those with violent ten-
dencies, and although such men are a small minority in the
military, the relative freedom of action they were accorded on
the battlefield in Vietnam sometimes left the door open to
atrocious behavior:

> Every army has its quota. They show up in any
> prison camp, habituals or amoral characters ready at
> the drop of a hat to betray their fellows. Education and
> social background seem to have had little bearing on
> how men will respond under pressure. . . . In any mili-
> tary company there will be four to seven percent mal-
> contents, troublemakers and oddballs. They stay
> estranged to the outfit.[20]

Men sometimes attempted to justify the practice of taking
ears with the rumor that a Buddhist could not go to heaven if
his body was not intact or properly buried. It was entirely untrue, but it provided a hollow excuse. The bodies of people
killed with automatic weapons or artillery were rarely intact.
Still, Jon Neely explained, "One of the reasons that guys did
things like . . . taking ears or taking fingers was the Vietnamese belief that if any part of their body was missing, they
wouldn't bury them—they would just let them lay there and
rot. And a lot of times that was what you wanted, evidence of
a kill. You wanted the population to see this. You wanted other
Viet Cong or NVA to see that one of theirs was dead."

Vernon Janick recalled men in his company in 1966 who
kept "ears, teeth, fingers, and [stuff] like that." On occasion,
in Sgt. Gerry Barker's platoon, enemy KIAs would lose an
ear or the gold fillings from their teeth. But Barker was quick
to point out that it was usually the same one or two men who
engaged in the practice. Jack Freitag mailed an ear to his
brother. He never forgot that ear, or the tall Viet Cong with
the perfect teeth to whom it had belonged and who continued
to haunt his dreams long after he returned home.

The fuss over collecting ears confused more than a few
soldiers. Cutting an ear off a corpse did far less damage to the
integrity of the corpse than a single round from a .50-caliber

machine gun. As Tom Magedanz observed, it certainly wasn't the worst that could happen:

> A few guys in our unit cut ears off dead gooks. I'm not sure why, but it didn't seem particularly wrong, at least compared to killing him in the first place. I think it was a way to suppress our own fear because seeing the body was jarring, horrifying evidence really of what could happen to us. Back home people were always appalled by stories of taking ears, but not about killing, and I couldn't figure out why.[21]

Later in the war, the practice was more visibly discouraged. In 1968, Jerry Johnson recalled that when he arrived in country, "They sort of read us the riot act, talking about the Geneva Convention and all that. 'You will not take ears, scalps, or any of that stuff. That is a no-no.' " Johnson could recall only one or two people out of the hundred men in his company who ever took an ear. Sergeant William Harken saw it happen only twice during his four months in the field in late 1968. In 1970, Donald Putnam remembered seeing men walk "up to a body after a firefight and empty a clip into them . . . as a way of venting steam. But as far as cutting body parts off, no. I never had anybody do that—never!"

Jeff Yushta recalled seeing some marines mutilate bodies in late 1969 and early 1970, but he was adamant that such acts were not condoned at any level in his unit. Nor were such acts a part of Phil Yaeger's war experience in 1966. Yaeger was quick to cite the leadership in his unit as the reason.

"I've heard a lot of other vets who have taken ears or disfigured NVA bodies," said Yaeger. "I never did that. I never saw that. I guess my battalion commander wouldn't have tolerated that. I don't think my platoon sergeant would have tolerated that. *I* sure as hell wouldn't have tolerated it. But it happened. Both sides did it."

In rare cases, despite quality leadership—or more frequently in its absence—men in the field were as ethical as their situation and state of mind allowed them to be. Jack Freitag saw the remains of men in a platoon from I Company, 3d Battalion, 1st Marines, that were discovered in the village of

An Trac south of Da Nang in late 1966. The unit had been "wiped out" and the dead mutilated. According to Freitag, "All the bodies were in a little bitty . . . Catholic Church. And all the . . . marines were mutilated. The lieutenant was tied up with concertina wire and his balls were cut off and stuck in his mouth. His ears were cut off. His skin was stripped across his chest and they pulled . . . you know, they cut it so deep and they actually pulled muscle tissue and stuff down. So we all wanted revenge."

Whether such stories were true or not mattered little. It was not what was true, but what men believed to be true that motivated them. Stories of enemy acts of mutilation were standard fare in Vietnam, and for some, like Jon Neely, that knowledge came firsthand.

> It wasn't good enough just to be in a firefight and kill an American. It seemed they just wanted to see how far they could go with dismemberment, humiliation, [anything] to make the American look bad. They would kill a guy first, or even torture him . . . they would cut different parts of his body off and sew them onto other parts of his body. It is difficult to explain this.
>
> Same way with the Vietnamese civilians that the Viet Cong thought were siding with us. They would torture them in many different ways. They didn't like to just kill Vietnamese civilians. They liked to torture them and leave them as a symbol of what could happen if they didn't support the Viet Cong.

Emergency room nurse Pamela Davis saw two Americans who had been brought into her evacuation hospital suffering from wounds received when the Viet Cong had gouged their eyes out with bamboo sticks. Davis was haunted by the memory:

> The screams of these young men as they lay in the emergency room seemed to penetrate the whole base. Anger then came through. Not just the frustration and helplessness, but real anger, and it was frightening. I found myself having to watch the troops, the doctors,

and myself when the Vietnamese came in so that we wouldn't do things we would be sorry for later.[22]

Phil Yaeger fought against the same feelings of rage during Operation Hickory in May 1967 when "four people out of another platoon in my company were wounded and finally killed in front of NVA bunkers. We tried for four days and when we finally got to them they had been mutilated pretty badly. We blew the bunkers, retrieved our dead, and left," said Yaeger. After a moment's reflection he added, "but that wasn't satisfactory. I wanted revenge."

War, according to the most oft-repeated cliché, is hell. Most people, even without the benefit of experience, would certainly agree. But the cliché loses its impact if one has no more understanding of the meaning of hell than the meaning of war. Gerry Barker defined war as "using whatever means available to beat somebody else whatever the reason, right or wrong." Michael Jackson was more direct. "War," he decided, "is fucking people up. That is pretty crude and blunt, but that is the raw truth of the matter." And Kenneth Korkow, a marine veteran of Khe Sanh, saw war as "dirty back-alley street fighting—killing the other guy before he kills you." Under such circumstances, he admitted, "I became very hard." So did many others.

Those engaged in combat in Vietnam certainly understood the meaning of war. Tragically, so did the civilians caught in the middle. But even without atrocities, war has always been profane, ugly, and disgusting—all of the things that prompted one World War II veteran to exclaim, "There are so many stories I could tell you, so many horrors, but I shall try to push them all behind me, for I do not wish to remember them . . . that is true of us all."[23]

CHAPTER 13

Civilians?

April 9, 1968

Dear Mom and Dad,

Hope this letter finds you in good health and [you] are making out alright. Everything here is going along fairly well. It still is hot here, but I'm getting used to it now.

Well, only a few months more and I'll be home again. It seems like it has been about three years since I've seen the farm and you folks. You probably won't hardly know me the first time you see me. I feel like I've aged about ten years over here.

Well, have to close for now. [I'll] try and write some more tomorrow.

Your Son,
Len[1]

Occasionally, the essence of an experience over a period of months or even years can be encapsulated in a single event. Such salient moments flavor the memories forever, even as the vagaries of climate or soil can produce a wine of exquisite vintage or render it sour and unpalatable.

For Larry Iwasko, what began as an evening like many others in the Republic of Vietnam ended in a lingering sadness. With a brevity common to soldiers in time of war, Larry described his experience in a letter to his mother in words that clearly revealed his personal pain and disillusionment.

Last night I killed a nineteen-year-old girl and a baby about eleven months old with a hand grenade. We received fire from a bunker and I had to blow it with a hand grenade. The girl and baby were in it and she fired upon us with an AK, which is a gook rifle. I was sick when I saw what I did, and still am, but I had no other choice. All I want to do is serve my tour and get the hell out of here.[2]

It would be difficult to find a more poignant declaration of what the war in Vietnam could mean. Yet Iwasko's experience was not unique. His was simply one of many individual tragedies played out against the backdrop of a war that, for too many Americans, suddenly took on the trappings of a Gothic novel.

Chance imposed upon rifleman Mike Meil a similar tragedy. While traveling in a convoy en route to his cavalry unit in the field, a jeep passing Meil's armored personnel carrier hit an antitank mine, blowing the vehicle and its occupants into the air. Meil and the others in the convoy reacted as they had been trained and as they had been told:

Everybody was reconning by fire. I wasn't. I had seen movement, and I was firing in the general area that I saw the movement. [Afterward] I went out to the area where I had seen the movement and I found a woman and a little girl lying there dead. I was in shock. I didn't know exactly what to do. I never reported the incident to any officers or anything, but I told another guy that was coming out to the unit at the same time I was. We figured it was best just to keep quiet about it, so I just left them lay. For around fifteen years I never told anybody other than that one guy. . . . That was an everlasting impression in my mind. I was eighteen years old, never realizing what it would be like to kill somebody—least of all a woman and child. It was . . . unexpected . . . quite a shock.

The killing of civilians, whether intentionally or by accident, graphically demonstrates war's insanity and waste. Civilian casualties are a sadly unavoidable part of modern war; but those destined by chance or circumstance to participate in an action that results in such deaths are left with a searing emotional trauma in which guilt and self-doubt render all other rationalizations meaningless.

Because the Viet Cong chose to fight amidst the civilian population, and because they wore no identifying uniform, distinguishing them from the local peasantry was often impossible. Identifying the competent combatants was made even more difficult, not only because large numbers of women served in the enemy's ranks, but many Vietnamese of all ages sympathized with or were coerced by the Viet Cong into participating in the war in ways that endangered American lives.

During training, soldiers and marines were told that old men planted mines in the roadways and little children hid grenades in their shoeshine boxes. Regrettably for both sides, later experiences sometimes demonstrated the truth of such stories. Glen Olstad's squad on one occasion brought in a very old man after he was seen planting a mine; Sgt. William Harken was horrified to see a young boy explode when the grenade he was holding behind his back detonated. Such shocking incidents did much to harden the attitudes of GIs, while at the same time reminding them that anyone could pose a threat to their survival.

Marine Jeff Yushta described one such incident involving his platoon:

> We were supposed to be on an operation where nobody knew where you were, which was a joke now that you look back on it. But these kids would come out of the bushes with Styrofoam coolers, like they sell at local grocery stores, with ice and Cokes. . . . There was this little kid and he'd been following and he knew right where we were going to be and he was waiting for us. He knew when we got there we were going to be thirsty. He would sell out. . . .
>
> You got [warned], "Don't ever drink anything a Vietnamese tries to give you; it could be poison!" Here were cans of Coke. Mr. American product. You sucked them up pretty quick. And he had a Styrofoam cooler that was booby-trapped.

Now, I have no idea if he was going to put it some-place and wait for somebody to come and take some. It appears to me that whoever set it up knew the kid was going [to die], too. I can't understand that. As a parent I can't understand involving one of my children in something of that magnitude.

The Viet Cong often demonstrated little or no concern for the Vietnamese people caught in the middle, no matter what their age, and the Americans' sense of alienation from the Vietnamese intensified whenever they observed such brutal-ity toward each other. Corpsman John Meyer remembered watching a group of American combat engineers repairing a bridge on the road from An Hoa to Da Nang in 1970. "They had paused for a break and the corpsman with them began playing with some kids trying to score a few points," said Meyer. "Two Viet Cong came down the road riding a motor-cycle and threw a satchel charge right in his lap. Killed him and a couple of the Vietnamese kids, and wounded some other kids and maybe some marines. The corpsman," Meyer recalled with a rueful smile, "got the bridge named after him."

Sergeant Gerry Barker, however, looked back on two tours during which he admitted having "relatively little contact with civilians," and maintained that civilians "didn't do any-thing to us. We always heard about it. We heard about the grenade in the gas tank at An Khe. We heard this, that, and the other thing. But we never, in either of the two companies I belonged to, saw firsthand a case of that. It never happened in our company. I would bet it was more rumor than reality."

Sergeant Steve Fredrick agreed, remembering that he had been warned against trusting Vietnamese civilians as far back as basic training. "Maybe that was true and always in the back of my mind," he reflected, "but it was easy to be friendly with them, too."

Civilian duplicity was undoubtedly exaggerated, but the tales were taken to heart by American soldiers, and often pro-vided the basis for soldiers' attitudes and, more tragically, their actions.

The Viet Cong often used local populations as sanctuary

or shield, depending on their needs. The ease with which the Viet Cong could alter their identity from farmer to fighter by simply picking up a rifle or by hiding it again was well known to the Americans who tried to sort them out.

Captain Francis West observed the process while accompanying a platoon of marines northwest of Chu Lai. As a second group of marines swept the area looking for Viet Cong, the platoon that West accompanied looked out over the pastoral landscape below. Just ahead they saw "a group of armed VC run across a rice paddy and enter a large house. Moments later they reappeared wearing black pajamas, straw conical hats, and carrying hoes. They split up and waded into the rice paddies."[3]

The difficulty in identifying the Viet Cong infuriated Jeff Yushta. "I could respect the NVA," he said. "They put on the uniform and they came at you head on. It's funny. I never believed that there was honor between warriors on opposite sides of a battle, but I see that there is. But dealing with the Viet Cong was real hard because they didn't stand up and fight like men." After a moment the former marine added, "It was real easy for me to dehumanize the Viet Cong."

Civilians in wartime are always at the mercy of trespassing armies and are necessarily compelled to rely on the discipline and decency of each soldier to keep them from harm. Sometimes that harm was nothing but undisguised barbarity. Dennis Foell recalled:

We came through [a hamlet] early one morning and asked if there had been any movement. We could see that there had been. But they kept telling us, no, there was nothing there. Most of them were little kids or older mamasans, but there was a girl; I would've guessed her to be somewhere between fifteen to eighteen years old, and she was a nice-looking girl. Of course there were many jokes made by GIs, you know, how fine [she was] and everything.

The next day when we came through again, right away the mamasans came out and wanted a medic to come and check their daughter, so we went over there. She was lying there in definite pain. Apparently, the [previous] night some NVA troops had come through and raped this girl. I don't know how many there were, but she was bruised and pretty badly swollen. One of the medics decided to call in a medevac, and she was flown back to Chu Lai.

Villagers were certainly intimidated, teased, and, at times, roughly handled by GIs, but few were brutalized or mistreated without provocation. Far from abusing the people, American infantry units often provided medical care where it was needed. Many individuals, such as rifleman John Merrell, handed out C-rations and played with the children. Tom Magedanz discovered amidst the drudgery and occasional chaos of the war that

> people are the same everywhere. If you go in their hootch they give you a stool to sit on and some tea or water to drink and everyone sits around and smiles, although conversation is limited. The thirteen-year-old girls go to the corner to giggle, and the little kids start to show off and get silly; and of course, Mamasan is embarrassed at the way the kids are behaving. It's the same everywhere. Nothing made me more homesick than visiting a Vietnamese family like that (even if I wasn't exactly invited).[4]

Dan Krehbiel agreed, in part because his company commander made them take a look at the people. "They were just raising their families and going out to the fields, and that is all they really wanted to do," he said. "They didn't care who ran the government. After we got to know certain people and saw them fairly regularly, the fear lessened. I had some good memories of some of those people."

But Krehbiel also felt the undercurrents of fear and intimidation among the villagers. "Although they were openly friendly at times," Krehbiel admitted sensing that "secretly they despised us. I felt that all the time. This artificial smile would come on them. They were scared to death of us. They were scared of the Viet Cong who came in the middle of the night if they didn't resist us. They lived in fear all the time."

Villagers were caught in a situation in which noticeable assistance to either side could bring retaliation from the other. One of the first times John Meyer heard a burst from an AK-47 rifle, it came from two Viet Cong dressed as ARVNs who walked into the home of a village security chief. They assassinated the man along with one of his children and an old man unfortunate enough to be visiting. Meyer learned quickly that such acts told the people who was really in charge. "The people in the village could smile at the marines all day long," he said, "but when the Viet Cong asked for something, they were going to get it. If the hamlet security chief could be assassinated in broad daylight, anybody could be had. That pretty well set the tone for things."

Meyer's Combined Action Platoon had daily contact with villagers, and the marines strove to keep relations amicable and to protect the village from the Viet Cong. Yet it seemed that every success was "pretty well countered." One such success story involved

> a young boy maybe ten years old [who] had gotten thrown off his water [buffalo]. Somehow in the fall, his eyelid was pretty well torn off. . . . I managed to get him medevac'd, which was not easy to do because you have to find somebody that will take in a Vietnamese civilian. . . . But the CO we had at that time spoke the language fluently. He prided himself on his rapport with the Vietnamese and he made an effort to get this boy medevac'd. We got him to a doctor and got the eyelid sewed back on. And we were quite popular in that village for a certain period of time. . . .
>
> One day we returned and they just told us, "Go away!" They didn't want us around anymore. It was obvious to us the local Viet Cong cadre had gotten to this family and warned them off of associating too closely with the Americans.

Marine Don Trimble was equally aware of Viet Cong terror tactics. He recalled a Catholic couple who lived in one of the villages where his CAP unit frequently rested during the day. "The husband was a physician," said Trimble. "They lived in a very nice brick home, or it used to be once upon a time. The VC came in and shot him in the back one night and left him totally paralyzed from the neck down, so she took care of him."

Though not precise, statistics detailing Viet Cong terrorist acts from 1957 to 1972 reveal that 36,725 persons were assassinated in South Vietnam and 58,000 more were abducted. In many instances torture was used, and in numerous cases, such as the disembowelment that Austrian journalist Kuno Knoebl witnessed, the rest of the villagers were forced to watch.[5]

Richard Ogden's platoon came upon the appalling aftermath of what their unit's Vietnamese interpreter learned had been a Viet Cong execution:

> In the center of a tiny courtyard, we discovered the body of a man about forty years old, clad only in a pair of shorts. The body lay chest down in an enormous pool of blood. . . . The head had been severed cleanly above the collarbone, leaving the entire neck with the head.
> To see your first dead was shocking, but to see a human head totally separated was horrifying.[6]

As the villagers returned from the jungle, Ogden saw them carrying a little boy whose skin over his chest had been peeled away in long strips. Through the interpreter they discovered that

> The villagers had been forced to watch the torture of the child and the anguish of the father, who was held and made to observe closely and listen to the screams of the boy. Then they cut off the father's head in the presence of the mother and forced her to hold it.[7]

Some NVA and Viet Cong terrorist attacks, rather than being selective, were directed against entire populations in hamlets and refugee camps in order to demonstrate the government's inability to provide security. In December 1967, VC and NVA forces systematically murdered Montagnard refugees with flamethrowers in the hamlet of Dak Son northeast of Saigon. The massacre left 252 dead and 50 more wounded.[8]

The Viet Cong repeated such massacres periodically. In June 1968 seventy-eight civilians were killed and many more wounded in the hamlet of Son Tra in Quang Ngai Province. Two years later, on 14 June 1970, an NVA sapper battalion led by Viet Cong invaded the village of Phuthan eighteen miles south of Da Nang, where, according to Lawrence Stern of the *Washington Post,* the enemy "methodically dropped grenades and satchel charges into the mouths of bunkers, killing an estimated one hundred civilians."[9] Tom Magedanz was in the area at the time of the Phuthan massacre and later wrote:

> Two NVA companies killed 102 civilians by LZ Baldy in June of 1970. They mortared the ville and then went through throwing grenades and shooting anyone that moved. A marine platoon from Baldy was sent to help, but they got pinned down and couldn't move. There wasn't much they could have done anyway.[10]

In light of such atrocities, Americans at times saw civilians as victims, but they also patronized them or remained deeply suspicious and distrustful.

James Amodt's candor from the Central Highlands in 1968 is revealing:

> Despite army propaganda pamphlets that exhort the soldier to mingle with the indigenous peoples and adapt and respect their customs ("We are their guests"), . . . some of the inhabitants are trying to kill us. . . . We are told to trust no one; we trust no one. And so the people we do come in contact with are bastardized by us. It is similar to Mexican-American border towns. The natives only sell—their services, their goods, and their bodies. They are generally curt (perhaps because of the language barrier), greedy, and unstinting in their hatred for us.
>
> For our part we either feel they are insufferably ig-

norant and immoral, fit only to wash our dishes and clothes, or we are patronizing. They are collectively known as "Gooks" (pronounced Goddamn Gooks).

In this area there is also a large percentage of mountain people, the Montagnards (pronounced Gooks). . . . Those I have encountered are as lovable as the Vietnamese. Some of our soldiers live with them and act as advisors or black-market agents. At various times we others are sent out to stay in the village for a night to entertain the ladies and augment the supply of beer and other black-market items. In turn, the Montagnards turn us on with pot, locally known as "number one cigarette."[11]

Many African-American soldiers, however, tended to see the Vietnamese civilians as people of color like themselves and empathized with them in terms of oppression and discrimination. Michael Jackson recalled that the Vietnamese employed at Camp Evans would point to African-American soldiers and say, "Soul: same-same."

Said Jackson, "I saw racism against the Vietnamese by white soldiers, which to me suggested the same kind of arrogance and treatment that I had seen in my country. So I generally saw the Vietnamese civilians more as victims than as terrible folks who were out there trying to spread communism."

Yet, as a combat soldier, Sergeant Jackson discovered that the regard he held for the Vietnamese civilians and their ancient culture often evaporated under fire. On those occasions, he explained:

When there were people in my company who were killed or hurt, or when we had to move at night, which was completely stupid, or when we were humping eighteen hours a day and it was hot as hell, and everybody was sweating and everybody [was] wondering why the heck are we doing this—no resupply of food or water—my psychological state was, Where are the damn gooks? I want to shoot their damn heads off. So that was the dichotomy. On the one hand, as civilians, I saw the people as victims. On the other hand, as a soldier, when I'm tired and just beat to hell and don't give a shit—or when I've seen Americans fall—give me some gooks, because I want to mess them up! That was the sort of dual perspective that I had to live with.

Unfortunately, the treatment of the Vietnamese people by American soldiers who were tired, scared, and frustrated by the people's lack of cooperation often degenerated into crudeness, vulgarity, and excess, although such actions were neither systematic nor, in most cases, intended.

Nonetheless, as soldiers progressed in their tours of duty and became more and more desensitized by the war, their attitude and self-control often eroded. The change was often evident in the men's writing. Ed Austin, for example, noted in his diary at the end of his first week in Vietnam in September 1966 that he was troubled by two marines who were "cursing every Vietnamese they saw" from the back of the truck in which he was riding. According to Austin, "They shouted 'fool' at men and 'bitch' at the women. They are worse than animals; sick with self-glory and self-praise."[12]

Barely six months later, however, Austin noted that his unit had moved to Viem Tay 1. "About 1500 this afternoon five of us were throwing rocks at some kids when a sniper round came in and hit 2nd Lt. Deter in the pants leg."[13] The change from casting a disapproving eye at the insults of others to the casting of stones, while trivial in comparison with the death and despair painted on some of the pages in between, is insightful.

The occasional boredom of American soldiers, when coupled with their imagination, aggravation, and general lack of respect for the Vietnamese, was, as Charles Anderson described it, "at least counterproductive and often just plain disastrous."[14]

John Meyer noted an incident in which the handler of a mine-sniffing dog who had been temporarily attached to his CAP unit fed C-4 (plastique explosive) to some ducks and a dog in one of the villages. "They started foaming at the mouth and went into convulsions," he said. "It ate them up something fierce." The incident was particularly disastrous because, as Meyer explained, "he did this to a family that we had real good relations with in an area where we had been fairly popular."

While resting on a hilltop, Tom Magedanz watched several men in his platoon entertain themselves by killing a water buffalo, "shooting it to see what an M79 would do, and what an M14 would do, and so on."

Other men's activities, however, were not restricted to animals. Soldiers recalled those who tossed smoke grenades or CS gas into crowds just for kicks as they passed through villages. Layne Anderson recalled seeing some men in the back of a deuce-and-a-half truck "swinging ax handles at Vietnamese on motor scooters and bicycles as they rode down the highway from Chu Lai."

Gerry Barker nearly came to blows with members of another platoon under similar circumstances. The men were "throwing C-ration cans at civilians as we rode through villages," said Barker. "They would hurl C's at the civilians just as hard as they could, not like they were giving C's to these poor civilians; they were trying to hurt them. I stopped it, but I damn near had to fight them."

However, on the way to the rifle range at An Khe, Sergeant Barker admitted to a slightly different attitude:

> The Coke sellers and the beer sellers were always there and there was an altercation over paying one of them. Apparently, all the girls that sold Coke and beer worked for one Vietnamese guy and two of my guys kicked the shit out of him. Not only did I not report it, I made sure that all of us had alibis. I felt that my guys had to keep in mind that we were there trying to win hearts and minds, but if it became a dispute between the Vietnamese and one of my guys, there was no question—my guy right or wrong! But that was where my bread was buttered.

Locality and mission also influenced the degree of respect shown to the people and their property. Sergeant William Harken maintained that on his company's operations, gardens were trampled and furnishings were sometimes knocked about, but that was the extent of what he saw as mistreatment of civilians.

Josh Cruze was far more critical of the search-and-destroy tactics used by his marine unit, and the conduct of some of the men in his platoon left him ashamed:

> We used to go into hamlets—go into their personal belongings and tear pictures of relatives down, turn over furniture, break dishes, set fire to hootches. I thought, this is so un-American. This is not what we are supposed to do. These are all people. Little kids were crying. My friend shot some woman that was innocent. You think, this guy's going to get paid back, and he did. We were on patrol and we got sniper fire from a tree line. . . . Who do you think got hit?[15]

When soldiers encountered booby traps or received enemy fire, maintaining discipline and self-control were infinitely more difficult. Vince Olson understood the plight of the civilians, although their reluctance to help Americans was always a source of bitter frustration. He remembered how, after receiving incoming fire from the NVA,

> we'd go down to the village and ask where the enemy were. And they'd always point to the mountains, or they'd say they couldn't understand. But you knew they could understand what you were trying to say, and I tell you, it really got on your nerves. I think they knew, but they were too scared to tell you. It is hard to tell what happened to them at night.
>
> They were probably more scared of the Vietnamese hurting them, because it might have been one standing right beside us. If he didn't have a uniform on, it could have been an enemy standing right beside them and they didn't want to tell you. I suppose they reacted the best they could to kind of protect themselves.

Jeff Yushta also struggled against the tendency to view all villagers as the enemy. Looking back, he compared the situation in Vietnam to contemporary America. "Everybody wanted you to believe that the Viet Cong could not operate in an area unless the people supported them. But," explained Yushta, "look at the gangs in a neighborhood: just because there is a gang there doesn't mean everybody in the neighborhood is against you. The Viet Cong were like a gang. We have people in our cities here in the United States who are terrorized by people."

Try as they might to convince themselves that villagers meant them no harm, GIs learned from experience that most Vietnamese cared very little for them. Like many soldiers, Dan Krehbiel asked himself, "Where does culpability begin? Those people knew what was going on in their country. Did that mean they were all enemies by definition? They didn't tell us about booby traps. By God they knew they were there! Did that make them Viet Cong by their inaction? I never thought of them that way, but I never trusted them."

In 1967, north of Qui Nhon in the Bong Son Plain, Gerry Barker was convinced that some villagers were VC, and that many more were sympathetic to the Viet Cong. But, he added, "I don't blame them for that. If the Saigon government were my government, I'd have been a communist!"

Jack Freitag's company swept a village in November 1966 in which there was no question as to the loyalty of the inhabitants. The village was supposed to be encircled during the night, but as the men approached across open paddies in a driving rain, they heard an eerie *bong . . . bong . . . bong*. As they shivered in the paddies, waiting for dawn, they could hear "babies crying, chickens, all kinds of commotion." At daylight, they moved in across a bamboo bridge, above which was displayed a large Viet Cong star. As they moved into the village, Freitag recalled, the marines

blew up everything that we could see that was booby-trapped. And every step of the way we had to. Lieutenant Gains was a "mustang." Everybody respected him. He and Sergeant Cox were disarming or blowing up everything. At the end of the village, where they got out through a tunnel system, there were *punji* sticks lined up back and forth. There were no women, no children, no chickens, no nothing in the ville. Everything was gone except for the pigs and the water buffalo. They took the dogs; they took everything.

We were trying to disarm everything and we were in this hootch and all of a sudden we heard a loud, deafening explosion. The biggest chunk that you could find of Lieutenant Gains was the chest cavity and his pelvic area, nothing else. Cox was mangled up also, but not quite as bad.[16]

As the marines loaded the remains of their lieutenant in a poncho, they must have contemplated the strangeness of a war in which there was so seldom an enemy to shoot back at. In World War II the enemy's homes and factories were bombed into rubble—along with their unfortunate inhabitants—because the industry and people supported the war effort. In Vietnam, a plant in which booby traps were fabricated did not have two smokestacks and a railroad siding, only a thatched roof.

When the situation allowed, or when the presence of allied troops could truly guarantee civilians a measure of security and freedom from enemy intimidation, relations between Americans and the South Vietnamese could be amicable. In only one instance during Dan Krehbiel's tour of duty did this occur. Still, that one interaction left a lasting impression on the young radioman, and possibly on the people of a village as well. Said Krehbiel:

There was a whole village of people that we helped out . . . because our company commander . . . knew how to speak Vietnamese. Right on the border, just before the invasion of Cambodia in 1970, was this village that was being threatened with extinction because the chieftain refused to play along with the NVA and Viet Cong. They threatened the whole village; said they were going to destroy it. We were in the air to begin a five- or six-day patrol and all of a sudden we took a right turn and landed outside of this village. We walked into it and the village came out to greet us. . . . The company commander came back and said, "We are gonna stay here for a while. These folks have been threatened, so we are gonna secure it for them." And . . . it was the easiest time we had. They were fun people. They were happy to see us for a change, and it was just remarkable—altogether different view. And we went on patrol every three days and that was it. We eventually got to know the bartender and the little village tavern and got on just fine with them. We were there for nineteen days. It was like R&R almost.

Patrolling less friendly villages, on the other hand, nearly always generated apprehension and suspicion. Marine Vince Olson later realized that:

After you were in Vietnam awhile in a combat situation you could just about do anything. You'd see your buddies get killed and you had to take your frustrations out on something. Sometimes, when we'd be on operations, they'd burn down villages. They were made out of grass and all it would take was a match and the whole village would be in flames. I don't know, everything gets tied up in you and you gotta take your revenge out somehow. You tried to ask the people where the enemy was and they wouldn't cooperate with you. You really didn't want to just turn around and shoot them because you knew that wasn't right. You sometimes didn't know what they were, so you would torch a village or something. But normally you got the word from higher up; somebody would tell you to do it.

Not surprisingly, the more hostile an area was, the more frustrated and hostile was the Americans' attitude toward the people living there. Paul Boehm's unit operated in the vicinity of My Lai, in the region known as Pinkville. It was, he remembered, "the most heavily mined and booby-trapped area in Vietnam that I was in."

You would take fire from a village and you would burn it out. In most cases you would just completely level [it]. And the women and kids weren't even there in those cases. They were off in a hole somewhere. We would find whole villages in tunnels. The VC would be in the village shooting at you. You'd go in there and find it completely empty. So you'd just burn it. You'd burn it, kill the animals, take your frustrations out on a pigpen with a machete or something—that type of thing. If a guy got wounded or someone got hit, then you'd . . . totally destroy [the village].

Author Tim O'Brien operated in the same area and described the mood of the men in his company as "boiling with hate" as they "triggered one mine after another." O'Brien's unit walked through the village of My Khe 3 into ambushes and had taken casualties without any warning from the villagers. There was also constant sniper fire. O'Brien later admitted, "It took little provocation [after that] for us to flick the flint on our Zippo lighters. Thatched roofs take flame quickly, and on bad days the hamlets of Pinkville burned, taking our revenge in fire. It was good to walk from Pinkville and see fire behind Alpha Company. It was good just as pure hate is good."[17]

On one operation in the area, Paul Boehm remembered hearing a rumor about a sniper who sighted in his rifle by shooting a civilian off a bicycle. The man's captain, the story went, only verbally reprimanded him. Apparently, anything could happen in Pinkville.

To an American soldier, the villages were labyrinths filled with nooks and crannies and hiding places, peopled by women of all ages and men who were either very old or very young. Stepping through the hedges into a hamlet, the soldiers encountered a world of bewildering wooden implements and alien bamboo and palm-leaf structures. There were cooking pots and stone jars, dirt floors, and root cellars that seemed as ancient and enduring as the frozen smiles of the people. And, like the roots of a tree, spreading out beneath many of the villages were tunnels and bunkers and storage pits.

Gerry Barker was particularly frustrated by the storage pits found in every village.

Every grunt I ever talked to had been shot at out of a storage pit. So we'd get cagey. The second time we ran into a storage pit we grenaded it. Now, Vietnamese villages are built out of mud and the floor is about six inches above the ground. . . . If you got people laying on the ground in a firefight, how high are the bullets? About a foot up, right? So, there is no place for a Vietnamese to hide. So where does he go? In the storage pit. And we were grenading storage pits.

The couple of fights I saw in villages we always nailed civilians that way. I watched more damn grunts yank civilians out of storage pits: "Look at this! I got a VC!"

And yeah, take my position as a platoon sergeant. What do you do [if] he's hiding [but] I don't really believe he's VC. So I tried as much as I could to keep the guys in control and keep things in perspective. But I am here to tell you that we killed civilians in storage pits. And I couldn't tell you now, with all the wisdom of forty-six years, how to avoid it.

Additional civilian casualties occurred when people fled during a search. As Sergeant Barker explained:

They would dart off into the jungle and we would find them hiding. I don't know about you, but if I was five feet high, and a bunch of these six-foot bastards dressed in green came into my village, guns a roaring. . . . So again, we tried as much as possible . . . to handle them gently. But that was *after* we shot at them first, because, if you go out there traipsing through the jungle and you see somebody in black, the first inclination is for somebody to squeeze off a couple of shots, and then you find out.

"Oh, it's three women."

They may not have been hit because, thank God, our guys were generally lousy shots. But that is really what happened all too often. In fact, it happened a lot.

Most squad and platoon leaders tried to give suspicious people the benefit of the doubt, though they were more prone to do so at the beginning of their tours than toward the end.

Sergeant Donald Putnam, on the other hand, maintained that people tended to run away from Americans for a reason. He claimed that he was inclined to shoot first and ask questions later. "If they were still able to answer, fine! If not, that was okay, too. I don't think we ever made a mistake and shot an innocent civilian. At this point I don't really care. . . . Nobody [in my platoon] got killed. And that, to me, mattered a whole lot more. . . . Somebody else can sit and judge, but I felt I did what was right."

Frequent attempts were made throughout the war to alter military policy and tactics in order to minimize civilian casualties—often at the cost of additional Americans killed and wounded. In May 1966, Ward Just accompanied a 1st Infantry Division unit operating on the fringes of the Michelin plantation in Binh Duong Province. The battalion's commander entered the village of Than An under machine-gun and mortar fire and saw five VC fleeing from the village. He chose to attack without artillery or air strikes in an effort to spare the lives of civilians in the area. His men found weapons, uniforms, and tunnels beneath houses in the scattered hamlets. The soldiers worked their way forward. There were no civilian casualties. There were no Viet Cong casualties either. However, fifteen GIs were shot. The battalion commander later told the commanding general who flew in after the operation, "Maybe if I had it to do over again, I'd do it differently."[18]

Some units did do it differently—and the civilian casualties resulting from air strikes and artillery occasionally exceeded those suffered by the enemy. In most cases, however, commanders were hesitant to spare firepower and risk heavier American casualties. On the other hand, sometimes the degree of response seemed extravagant.

On 15 April 1970, Company B, 1st Battalion, 5th Marines, engaged enemy troops near the hamlet of Le Bac 2 on Go Noi Island. Air strikes called in during the attack killed a dozen enemy soldiers, but Marine Corps records indicated an additional thirty people died in the nearby hamlet as a result of the bombing.[19] Jeff Yushta was there:

> We ran into a ville and we took heavy fire and we
> called in F-4s [Phantom jet fighter-bombers]. They laid

down some pretty heavy napalm. And then we swept the village. One of my vivid memories was a stack of thirty-some bodies that other marines and other people after us had just thrown in a pile. It was just a jumble of arms and legs. I can still see it. There was a kid in the pile and there was no way for me to tell whether he was killed by small-arms fire or the air strike or whatever. I was battling some real conflicting thoughts there. I knew it was a free-fire zone. We were doing a job that I still felt had to be done. But I can't make any sense out of why these people were involved in this. It was one of the things that made you hate the Viet Cong. They involved what we would call innocent people. Nobody was innocent there, I guess.

You just can't be that selective in a firefight, not with the type of weapons that we were using. We are talking about automatic weapons, not single shot. You see an enemy, you pull a bead on him and take him. Somebody opens up on you, basically, everybody opens up. If it is out there, chances are it is going to take something, because there is a wall of lead. And I can't make any sense today out of how all these women and kids would get in the middle. That just doesn't come together. And there is no way to selectively napalm an area.

The lopsided asymmetry of firepower in the war often saw enemy small-arms fire countered with air strikes and artillery. Frequently the enemy was able to goad the Americans into such overreaction. When, as a result, civilians were killed by indirect fire, soldiers and marines often felt intense guilt and sadness. On one such occasion, Jack Freitag's platoon sat down to eat C-rations and took sniper fire from a large hootch. The unit's response included several volleys of 105mm artillery rounds from a nearby battery. Afterward, they found casualties, but the snipers were not among them. Said Freitag:

We went in there and found this old man lying dead underneath a bamboo bed. An old lady was on top of him with her hands folded. She was split wide open across her chest. She was going, "Marines Number One!" This was one of the first times I called artillery with my radioman Ed Austin, and I saw that he was giving her his C-ration cookies. He felt so sorry for her. He turned around and he said, "Get a corpsman over here!" Then he walked out and I could see tears in his eyes. . . . He said, "Those people weren't shooting at us. . . ." He felt like he was responsible.

I tried to make excuses because I gave him the coordinates for the grid and everything. I said, "Ed, they feed them, they clothe them, they shelter them. Their children are VC. Don't feel bad for them. You can't. You'll never make it." He got over that but he prayed a lot.

As the war progressed, attempts were made to limit the use of artillery and air strikes in populated areas. Such policies were not popular with the soldiers who relied on the support of the big guns. Willie Williams recalled the frustration caused by that policy one evening in October 1966 while he listened over the radio to the fate of a sister 25th Infantry Division platoon in Tay Ninh Province:

On this night, [Sergeant Wolmack] and Sergeant Garland took a reinforced patrol out. They had been out there about a half hour and I heard them calling back over the radio and asking for artillery fire because they were being followed by a large number of Cong. They were refused because there were friendly houses in the area. So, about a half an hour later we heard the firefight, and then it ceased and we lost all radio contact. After a period of time, when we couldn't get radio contact, I went out on patrol and there were two other patrols searching for them. We couldn't find them that night.

The next morning we found them. They had been annihilated—mutilated! And we found everyone except Sergeant Wolmack. The company searched for about a week as far up as the Oriental River, and every village we went to, the local people would say, "Yes they got him, he's a prisoner." But we never found him.[20]

Civilians were sometimes warned by the allies of impending attacks. Naturally, in such cases the enemy was alerted also. But despite the warnings, civilians often refused to leave an area. During Operation Junction City, Jerry Severson's unit was told that South Vietnamese government forces had cleared the civilians from the area of operations. Unfortunately, the unit encountered civilians, and Severson noted sadly, "If they came out from behind a tree or something like that, a lot of them got killed."

Donald Putnam encountered the same problem during the Cambodia invasion in May 1970. "Supposedly," he recalled, "everybody in front of us was going to be enemy."

> The first village we came to, we had the artillery lay down a pretty heavy barrage. We went in and started clearing the village. It was full of friendlies. We started clearing bunkers and we had no Cambodian interpreters—not a one. I remember the first bunker I cleared. I cleared it using standard procedure: Being as I didn't speak Cambodian, I couldn't say anything. And I probably wouldn't anyway. . . . I pulled the pin on the grenade, popped the spoon, waited three seconds, tossed it, and followed it in. There were five people lying there—none of them dead, all wounded. No weapons, no nothing! I grabbed my RTO and got on the horn and called the Old Man and said, "There's something wrong! I just cleared a bunker and these people don't have weapons. They look like peasants to me."
>
> Well, I no more than said that and they started getting calls from everybody else that was clearing bunkers. It turned out this village had never been evacuated. They took to their bunkers when the first shells started coming in. We spent the better part of a day having choppers come in . . . and evacuate those people.

Curfews were initiated in populated areas to help restrict the movement of civilians in and out of their villages after

dark. People caught out after curfew were usually taken in as
suspects. Those who ran often became Viet Cong by default.
Steve Fredrick remembered how one evening, while enforcing the curfew, his squad shot a woman fleeing across the
paddies:

> We yelled the Vietnamese word for stop. She took
> off running. We didn't know then whether it was a man
> or a woman or what. It was too far away, so we opened
> up. We hit her, and I had to go out with about five other
> guys and find out what we hit. And Jesus, here was this
> old lady lying there sobbing and moaning and a big
> part of her hand was blown off. That was terrible . . . It
> was after the curfew, a couple of hours after. For all we
> knew she was out there laying booby traps on the rice
> paddy dikes. . . . You just didn't know. But it is still a
> pretty disgusting feeling when you are supposed to be
> a soldier—shooting old women.

Although often criticized, curfew policies in Vietnam were
often far more humane than the enforcement procedures imposed by the Americans in earlier conflicts. Corporal Sam
Gillis of the 1st California Volunteer Regiment serving in the
Philippines during the insurrection in 1899, for example, detailed in a letter how, "We make everyone get into his house
by 7 P.M. and we only tell a man once. If he refuses, we shoot
him. We killed over 300 natives the first night. . . . If they fire
a shot from a house, we burn the house and every house
near it."[21]

According to Peter Braestrup, former *Washington Post*
Saigon bureau chief, soldiers in Vietnam were probably "bet-
ter disciplined than their elders." He further noted that "less
damage and fewer civilian casualties were inflicted on the
South Vietnamese than on the Koreans during the Korean
War."[22]

Restrictive policies to protect civilian lives also sometimes
included guidelines that allowed shooting only if a unit was
fired upon, or prohibited the return of fire until permission
was obtained. Layne Anderson, like most soldiers who risked
their lives under such restraints, found these so-called rules

of engagement ridiculous. He remembered that during one operation

> We got pinned down in a rice paddy and called in artillery to help us out. They said, "Sorry, we can't shoot into that village with indirect fire because it is friendly." We went out into areas where they said you can't shoot at them unless they shoot at you first. Well, we adhered to that. But they had other goofy rules that didn't make a lot of sense. You had to holler halt before you fired in certain areas. But it was just a bunch of bullshit. I began to believe that the way we were going about it we could never really win with the restraints we had.

John Merrell could not have agreed more. During the latter part of 1969, "when things were really getting rocky back here in the States," Merrell went on patrol, where he remembered being told, "Don't shoot unless fired at." It was his view that "we weren't kickin' much ass because we weren't going after them."

Civilian lives were definitely saved by such policies, but the restrictions made the job of American soldiers all the more difficult and possibly more dangerous. Jerry Severson, like many soldiers, wondered: "What the hell are rules and regulations?" It appeared to Severson that the people in charge were playing at war as if it were a sport. He added in despair, "The thing is, they were playing their sport with lives, people's lives."

The actions of men in the field were dictated by survival first and policy second. Most men were as ethical as their present situation and past experiences allowed them to be. As Capt. Michael Lanning put it, "We in the jungle made our own rules and followed those made by others only to the extent that it was to our advantage."[23] Jerry Severson was equally pragmatic. "They taught us how to operate according to the Geneva Convention," he said, "but actually you did what you needed to do to survive and that was it. . . . A lot of people died over there that didn't need to, but you didn't know. Once they were shooting at you and it was for real, it was hard to decide who was a good Vietnamese and who was a bad Vietnamese. In the woods you just got by."

Disciplinary action was seldom taken against soldiers who violated the rules of engagement, so those rules were open to creative interpretation and application.

Because, to borrow from Mao Tse-tung, the guerrilla warrior swam freely in the sea of the peasantry, the designation of "free-fire zones" became the tactical equivalent of draining the lake to catch fish. Supposedly, such zones were devoid of civilians—innocent or otherwise; as the name implied, there were no restrictions imposed on shooting in such areas. Although anyone encountered in a free-fire zone could be considered enemy, most units used discretion and did not shoot people on sight.

Doug Kurtz, who operated in the south on the Plain of Reeds when it was a free-fire zone, explained that there were often times when they "would see a sampan and there would be three or four people in it who weren't supposed to be there. We didn't shoot them. We turned them over to the ARVN or detain[ed] them till the ARVNs came and picked them up. We didn't just shoot everybody we saw."

Ed Hoban's aerorifle platoon almost always operated in free-fire zones. Hoban said, "When we went down it was 'rock and roll' baby! We were never on safe." But he was quick to add that he never saw the men in his unit kill indiscriminantly. Neither did Jim Raysor, the leader of one of the 101st Airborne Division's long-range reconnaissance teams. Because his six-man team operated alone deep in enemy territory, being seen by a civilian could compromise the team's mission and result in its annihilation. Raysor discovered that he had to be flexible and creative in dealing with civilians in such remote places. On one occasion, for example, his unit

> stopped in this village to bathe and this old mamasan, I mean old, she looked one hundred . . . walked into the village. There was a discussion. "Well, what are we going to do with her? We can't let her just walk out of here." In other instances where we had done that . . . we got ourselves in trouble, especially when working in such small groups. There were these old concrete urns,

maybe three-foot urns, eighteen inches across, they
used to put water in, and they had a concrete deal that
slid over the top to keep the bugs out. Well, we put her
in that figuring if somebody comes along, they'll hear
her.

In order to clear a region of civilians and create a free-fire
zone, soldiers were required to round up villagers and sever
their ties to the land by moving them to refugee camps. Doing that was probably the most difficult of all operations in
which American soldiers took part. Gerry Barker described a
relocation operation on the Bong Son Plain in which his platoon took part:

We would go into these villages hitting booby traps,
largely *punji* stakes, but occasionally grenade traps,
which were extremely common in that area. We hit
them on the way into the village and then we would
have to be nice to the Vietnamese. It was hard to make
my men do it.

We would hit the village fast, almost at a dead run,
fan out to the outside of the village, pull everybody out
of their houses, push them to the middle—not give
them a chance to take cover or run off. Just herd them
toward the middle, keep pushing them down the street.
The Vietnamese interpreters were told to tell them,
"Don't go near a house or we'll shoot." And we would
go through the houses throwing them in the middle and
herding them all into the larger streets and still larger
streets until we had them all in the middle of town.
Then we gave them to the Vietnamese and they would
take them out. Then we would . . . burn the village to
the ground, destroy their animals, destroy caches of
crops, that sort of thing. We frequently would find
weapons doing this.

The effect of such actions on the Vietnamese people was
predictable, but what has nearly always been overlooked was
how difficult the job of relocating civilians was for the GIs

who were ordered to conduct the operations. Gerry Barker and his men hated the missions because they

> just ate at your troops. That was awfully tough on a guy. It was hard to keep control of the platoon after that. I think it really hurt their ego doing that job. They felt it was wrong and it made them more brutal. And there is no right answer. You can't shoot the damn villagers and you can't expect the villagers not to hate you. There were enough farm boys there amongst us to realize the farmer's attachment to the land. There we were taking him off it, burning his crops, killing his livestock. And then we said, "Love us. We are Americans fighting for your freedom." How does even the dumbest infantry-man live with that?
>
> I don't think there was a kid left in my platoon after one of those missions who thought that we were doing anybody any good. That was just impossible. Can you imagine the shrieking and crying and the pure ha-tred . . . from the Vietnamese when we did that to them?

The question of atrocities committed against civilians in Vietnam has been a troubling and complex one. Correspon-dent Charles Anderson claimed that "between one-third and one-half of all Americans who served in Vietnam committed one or more atrocities." Obviously, this is an exaggeration. Only 10 to 15 percent of all the soldiers who served in Viet-nam went into the bush, and a minority of those soldiers were guilty of any excesses. There is probably a little more valid-ity to Anderson's assertion that during the Vietnam War there were "literally tens of thousands of incidents of malicious in-tent and atrocious result." But again, his definition of "atro-cious" is not clearly stated, and certainly extends well beyond even the most liberal use of the term.[24]

On the other hand, James Martin Davis maintained with equal veracity:

> Anyone who thinks there were no atrocities com-mitted in Vietnam has no idea what this war was all

about. There were atrocities committed every day, but they were committed by the Viet Cong and the North Vietnamese soldiers.[25]

The massacre at My Lai was not the only atrocity committed by the Americans during the Vietnam War, and many former infantrymen allude to that fact. The official records show that 201 army personnel and 77 marines were convicted by courts-martial for serious offenses during the war. It is naive to assume that those figures represent the only Americans guilty of a capital crime against the Vietnamese. It is interesting to note, however, that in the case of 95 soldiers and 27 marines convicted of homicide, only 25 percent of those acts occurred in the field.[26] The figure is probably low, however. GIs in the field were not likely to report the excesses of their fellow soldiers and marines. Furthermore, courts-martial panels quite likely took into account the extraordinary emotional stress and frustration of fighting a counterinsurgency war, so that the low number of convictions for acts occurring in the field is understandable. At the same time, it is reasonable to suspect that the number of atrocities involving American troops will probably never be accurately determined.

Although atrocities such as the My Lai massacre were inexcusable, they generally occurred without forethought on a spur-of-the-moment basis, triggered by emotional reactions to enemy contact, frustration, large numbers of friendly casualties, or a desire for revenge. The Viet Cong and NVA, while guilty of the same human failings, also took civilian lives with calculated premeditation as part of a systematic campaign of terror designed to subjugate the civilian population.[27]

In any event, civilians became casualties in a war that refused to leave them alone. They fell victim to Viet Cong booby traps and American artillery fire, as well as to the frustrations of men on both sides carrying rifles. The men carrying rifles, however, were not without conscience.

In the spring of 1967, intelligence officers found evidence of a large buildup of NVA regulars in the Que Son Valley, a traditional Viet Cong stronghold.[28] During April, while his company patrolled that densely populated area in southern I Corps, forward observer Ed Austin wrote to his parents:

> There are more civilians killed here per day than VC either by accident or on purpose and that's just plain murder. I'm not surprised that there are more VC. We make more VC than we kill by the way these people are treated. I won't go into detail but some of the things that take place would make you ashamed of good old America.[29]

His shame stemmed from an operation a week earlier that Austin bitterly described in his diary: "We got one VC with weapon at 7:00. At 7:30 we went through a ville. The guys killed two men—murdered them—and two water buffalo calves, all just for kicks. They also made a girl undress and stood there laughing at her standing there nude. We got a lot of sniper fire."[30]

Also angry because civilians were being killed by artillery fire, the forward observer noted in frustration in his journal a few days later:

> I just went to a meeting. I leave at 0230 with two platoons to search a ville. We will probably kill a bunch more civilians. I'll tell you about it when I get back.[31]

The story would remain untold, for hidden among the innocent there was always the enemy. Eddie P. Austin was killed that morning by small-arms fire from elements of the 3d NVA Regiment, which had assembled in the valley to assault the marine outpost.

CHAPTER 14

"Short!"

June 1, 1968 (116 days to go)

Dear Mother and Dad,

Hoping this letter finds you in good health and having better weather than me. We are having our summer monsoon rains now and a lot of hot temperatures. It rains every day from about four in the afternoon until about midnight or later.

When we first got here, we knew there was a war going on, as the bullets were flying thick and fast. We are still in the same area, but it has quieted down a lot now. We have cleared most of the enemy out and what's left don't want to do much fighting anymore. I hope we will go back to Chu Lai where it is a little more safe and secure.

The time is going by a little faster now and I am getting anxious to get out of here and back home. Today my platoon is on an observation point on a mountain where we can see for miles around, so I have some free time to write a few letters. I wish I could write you all every day, but it seems like the only time we stop is at night and there is no moon to write by now.

I can't wait to get back and drive your tractors again, especially the new one. Maybe I can do some plowing with it this fall if I can still remember how to drive one. I haven't put my hands on a steering wheel for a long time. I should be on my way on the 26th of September so I will probably get to Los Angeles on

the 28th. Well, I'll sign off for now. [I'll] write again
soon.

Your Son Far Away,
Len[1]

The one piece of knowledge upon which Leonard Dutcher
and his fellow soldiers could anchor their hopes and gauge
their progress through the war in Vietnam was the date that
each man became eligible to return home. Every soldier was
assigned a personal DEROS date, every marine an RTD (rotation date), with the understanding that once he fulfilled the
obligatory number of days, he could, in the words of Paul
Fussell, "purchase his reprieve" and return home. Precisely
because American soldiers entered and left the war according
to a personal rotation schedule, it became nearly impossible,
as Charles Moskos noted, to "overstate the soldier's constant
concern with how much more time—down to the day—he
had remaining in Vietnam."[2] DEROS dates, Moskos asserted,
were the "paramount factor affecting a soldier's combat motivation." With the exception of general officers, every soldier's DEROS date was unequivocal; thus forewarned, nearly
all soldiers, both in the field and in the rear, began anticipating their day of deliverance well in advance. This resulted in
a soldier's final weeks in Vietnam evolving into an unabashed
struggle to keep his appointment with a homebound airplane—no matter what.

The policy of individual rotation in Vietnam differed dramatically from the world wars, in which American soldiers
served for the duration. Rotation in Vietnam had its prece-
dents in the policy established during the Korean War, in
which soldiers rotated home on the basis of accumulated
points. Soldiers serving in Korea needed thirty-six points to
get home. On line he earned four points a month; serving in
a combat zone, three; in country but beyond the reach of enemy action, two. Most infantrymen in Korea served approximately a year; support personnel served eighteen months.
The system favored soldiers serving in combat.[3] In Vietnam
there was no such distinction. Not only did every soldier
DEROS in one year (marines RTD'd in thirteen months), but

every soldier in Vietnam also received the same combat pay, regardless of his duties or the location of his posting.

Despite the differences, however, the similarity of defensive attitudes and behaviors of soldiers who can sense the end of their personal participation in any war is hardly surprising. British journalist Max Hastings noted that commanders in the Korean War disliked individual rotation schedules precisely because the men became "increasingly cautious and reluctant to accept risk as they grew 'short' and approached release date."[4] When peace negotiations in Korea began in earnest, men became all the more reluctant to take risks. Corporal Bill Patterson, who served in Korea with the 27th Infantry Regiment, noted that, "It made it awfully hard to get people to do things, to go out on patrol. A man would just say, 'Aw, I'm on short time.' "[5]

Soldiers felt exactly the same at the end of World War II. Marine Eugene Sledge, for example, exhibited what many Vietnam veterans would have recognized as "short-timer's fever" while assaulting Kunishi Ridge on Okinawa in June 1945. As Sledge explained:

> We all knew that this was probably the last big fight before the Japanese were wiped out and the campaign ended. While I plodded along through the darkness, my heart pounding, my throat dry and almost too tight to swallow, near panic seized me. Having made it that far in the war, I knew my luck would run out. I began to sweat and pray that when I got hit it wouldn't result in death or maiming. I wanted to turn and run away.[6]

Soldiers in Vietnam, already reluctant to expose themselves to danger as their individual tours came to an end, became increasingly aware after 1968 that the war would probably end sooner than later. This knowledge, noted Charles Moskos, gave rise to "the quite rational feeling of not wanting to be the last man killed in a closing war which characterized the low morale of the American ground forces after 1969." Such an attitude was like a case of "short-timer's fever" writ large.[7]

Randy Hoelzen was troubled by just such thoughts in 1970:

> A good part of this period was when Nixon was president and he promised the American people an honorable peace, and Kissinger and the North Vietnamese were negotiating in Paris. Every sign was that eventually there was going to be a peace agreement. That is a weird feeling. Am I going to die today and then tomorrow there is going to be a peace agreement? I remember being on the choppers going to a new site and all of a sudden they changed directions and I thought, Maybe this is it—peace has just broke out!

Counting the days and crossing off another number on their short-timer calendars intensified in importance as the men passed the midpoint in their tours. The aging process in the bush was measured not only by the passing of each day, but also by the transience of people who constantly appeared and departed against a backdrop of numbered hills and oddly named villages. Over time, what had formed the collective experience of an entire unit became little more than a vainglorious memory shared by a dwindling handful of familiar faces that inexorably vanished—rotating home or disappearing prematurely on a medevac helicopter. Their savvy, like much of the equipment they carried, had been bequeathed to them by those in whose footsteps they had followed. Added to the weight of their inheritance and their weapons was the still greater burden of responsibility thrust upon them as they advanced by seniority into the leadership roles of the squads.

After eight or nine months, soldiers had passed the zenith of their effectiveness. By the tenth month they had become "old soldiers" and nothing impressed them much anymore. They had hardened in the places where it mattered most, and they showed their age in the creases around their eyes and in the scuffed, cracked leather of their rotting jungle boots. The scars of their military service showed both outwardly and inwardly: Ringworm, bad feet, jungle rot, and the angry red welts of healing wounds and infected cuts all left their mark. The men were tired in body and spirit. Many were in ill health, having been weakened by malaria or dysentery, which—in concert with their poor diet, sleep deprivation, and nervousness—took a terrible toll.

Sergeant Gerry Barker remembered that at the end of his 1967 tour, "I was so damned tired my only question was how to keep thirty people alive, particularly since there was an officer for only two of the seven months I served as a platoon sergeant." In the end Barker contracted malaria and, upon returning to the field too soon, was stricken by hepatitis as well. As a result, the twenty-one-year-old NCO was medevac'd home looking like little more than a walking skeleton.

When Phil Yaeger's tour came to an end, the marine recalled simply, "I was fried! I physically wasn't well." Vernon Janick, after two tours in the Central Highlands, had "lost spirit and . . . just didn't feel right. I was drained; nothing left. I was just pretty well washed out."

Seeing the finish line kept them running, especially those who were running on empty and might otherwise have given up. In that respect, as psychologist James Goodwin explains, DEROS did its job:

> For those who had been struggling with a psychological breakdown due to the stresses of combat, the DEROS fantasy served as a major prophylactic to actual overt symptoms of acute combat reaction. For these veterans, it was a hard-fought struggle to hold on until their time came due.[8]

Although the tantalizing promise of home evoked an intense desire to survive—to "make it"—at the same time it fueled the long-suppressed fear that they would not. This sense of vulnerability awakened a paranoia that, in the last days of a GI's tour, something would come between him and his long-awaited flight home.

"You started feeling vulnerable again," Phil Yaeger explained. "You started worrying about it. That numbness started to wear off. Your focus was on that flight date and all the things that *could* happen."

Ironically, being short evoked feelings of fear similar to those experienced when a soldier was newly arrived. Paul

Meringolo recalled the fear he felt during the last few weeks of his tour:

> You got preoccupied with it. You tried to realize that you would probably be going home if nothing happened. And that fear that was there for the first couple weeks or so started to slowly take you over.... You found yourself fighting off thoughts of home which became more prevalent as you got closer. It seemed unreal that you would actually be going home, yet it was about to become a reality. So, the more real that became, the more you feared something happening.

"You'd been there a long time, but you could have only one day left and make a mistake," said Tom Schultz. That nervousness encouraged many infantrymen to consider additional ways of assuring their survival. "Is there enough time for me to get my teeth pulled, break a finger?" Schultz remembered wondering. "What do I have to do to get those last days eaten up?"

Sergeant Gerry Barker observed that at the tail end of a man's tour his performance fell off dramatically because he would get "short-timer's cramp and do dumb things." Barker remembered men would invariably try to "get out of things toward the end. They made stupid mistakes and they would sometimes get to be know-it-alls. They could be an insubordination problem, but usually with the squad leaders, not with me. It would occur at the lowest level. And they got real sheepish when you called them on it. Very frequently they got scared. They got real frightened as they got short."

Safe Havens

In order to compensate for decreasing combat efficiency and escalating paranoia, the demands on short-timers were often unofficially reduced, providing many combat soldiers with a period of disengagement and decompression before they went home. When possible, soldiers were sent to the relative security of a firebase or base camp to sit out the last weeks of their tour. If a rear job was unavailable, soldiers sought safety within the combat unit itself.

Dan Krehbiel got out of patrolling in 1970 by volunteering to join his company's mortar platoon. Krehbiel saw the move as his best chance to get off line.

A lot of guys got out after six or seven or eight months of combat and took jobs in supply, or as a company clerk, or a battalion clerk, or something—anything that got you out of combat so that you could live out your short-timer life in reasonable comfort and security. I kept looking for a job like that but never got one. I finally nailed down the mortar job because the mortar platoon was safer. They might be out in the field in little patrol bases, but at least it wasn't like being on ambush every night. It was the creature comforts. You didn't have to sleep in the rain. You could build makeshift shelters. You weren't on the move every night. . . . Anyway, I figured mortar platoon was a pretty good deal.

Krehbiel's plan, however, had one unforeseeable flaw.

Two weeks after my training was over and I was made a mortar squad leader, the new battalion commander ordered all the mortars to go back out to the field with the infantry, so all of that went out the window. I gave up my twenty-five-pound radio and picked up a twenty-five-pound base plate instead, and went out again.

When Gerry Barker led his 1st Cavalry Division platoon in 1966–67, he was seldom able to have men posted to the rear simply because they were short. Because of that, Barker did what he could to minimize their nervousness. "I tried to never let a guy know when his last mission was going to be, or when he was going in [to the rear]," Barker explained. "I tried to keep them off ambush patrol the last month or so, because everybody thought ambush patrol was the worst. . . . I

tried to send them in without warning so nobody knew
[when] he was going in. . . ."

Although some units, especially prior to 1969, kept their
personnel in the field almost until the day their planes departed for the United States, others pulled men from the field
well before their rotation date. The policy was well enough
established in Leonard Dutcher's company that he was able to
confidently write:

> I counted up my days again today and it comes to
> 166 left before I get on the bird going home. I guess
> that they pull the soldiers out of the field about ten to
> twenty days prior to leaving Viet Nam to check them
> out for anything that he might have caught over here.
> So I have only about five months left to do in the field,
> and then I can take it easy the rest of the time.[9]

Throughout the long middle of their tours, when home
was but a distant dream, soldiers longed for a reprieve from
the field. It was a possibility that became more likely as they
progressed into the long-awaited double digits. In time, many
soldiers made a chance acquaintance, collected on a debt
owed, pulled the right strings, or reaped a just reward for the
job they had done in combat. Those left behind watched as
the fortunate ones amongst them parceled out the canteens
and other gear they would no longer need, and caught the
supply chopper back to the rear to sit out the remainder of
their tours enjoying electric lights, soft cots, and real food.

Those who received choice postings almost always believed that it was a reward for their efforts in the bush. They
were probably right. Those who watched with more than a little jealousy as the lucky ones said good-bye were apt to believe that such jobs were ill-gotten.

There was no formal policy for assigning field soldiers to
the rear; rather, there was a surprising assortment of ways and
means for a fortunate few to avoid the bush in the twilight of
their tours. One such way, albeit a rocky one, was the de facto
policy in many units that allowed soldiers who had been
wounded three times to be relieved of combat duty. After being awarded his third Purple Heart for wounds, Charles Gadd

was given a job at Firebase Sandy. Similarly, marine Vince Olson was transferred to Okinawa after his third wound and Jon Neely was given the option of a rear-area posting, which he declined.[10]

There were other ways out besides collecting Purple Hearts—a dangerous hobby at best. After eight months as a point man, Jerry Johnson traded his flak jacket and web gear for the white jacket and towel carried by the waiters in the private mess of the 1st Infantry Division's commanding general. Like Johnson, every man in the mess was a decorated combat veteran. Dennis Foell received a similar posting, becoming an enlisted aide to Brig. Gen. John Donaldson, assistant commander of the Americal Division. Foell recalled his selection for the job:

> I came in and the general said that I had approximately nine months in the field and had been through Hiep Duc [Valley] and a few other little incidents that had happened around there that they considered quite significant. He asked me if I wanted the position, and I said, "Yes, I'd be quite interested." At that time I was still an E-4, but I was to be promoted to E-5 the next week. He said if I accepted this [rear job] I would go back to the bottom of the list for E-5s. I said, "Okay, no problem with that." One of the options they gave me was that if I was selected and wanted to go back to the field, they would waive E-5 and promote me to E-6. I suppose to some people that would have been important, but I guess at that point, getting out of the field sounded more important to me.

After nearly ten months in the field, Dwight Reiland landed a job in the rear with the 101st Airborne Division. His experience was typical of that of many other former infantrymen.

> Captain Quigley [the company commander] left in October or November, but there were four of us that must have endeared ourselves to him. Anyhow, he got

us jobs in the rear when he left so I was pulled out of the bush and my job happened to be company clerk.

Keith Oskings, a friend from Ohio, got the supply sergeant's job. And another guy got the chaplain's jeep driver job. That was the job everybody wanted because chaplains didn't act like they were in the army at all, . . . Jeez! There was no better duty than working for one of those guys.

Not everyone knew his guardian angel, but for most infantrymen it was a senior NCO or officer who made the arrangements. Though he was never able to confirm his suspicions, Randall Hoelzen speculated that his benefactor was the platoon leader for whom he had carried the radio when he initially joined the 1st Cavalry Division. Whoever his anonymous benefactor was, Hoelzen was thankful for the job as supply clerk.

Safety could also be acquired by reenlisting, an unpalatable prospect because it meant extending one's term of military service by several years. But once out of the field, the remaining obligation both in Vietnam and stateside would be served in the real military—the one with the haircuts and formations and pettiness that characterizes military life for so many soldiers. It seemed a high price to pay—unless a soldier's assessment of his future chances dictated otherwise. Those interested in re-upping had no difficulty in locating their nearest recruiter. Perhaps it was coincidence, but it seemed to Robert Keeling that, after any particularly bad firefight, "the first thing the army did was send out a reenlistment officer." Like overzealous lawyers at an accident scene, their presence was often viewed with contempt by the men in the field, who resented their playing on men's fears and tempting their frayed nerves with promises of leave back to the States and safe occupations in the rear.

Bryan Good was accosted by a reenlistment NCO while working out of Camp Eagle in 1970. Good turned down the man's offer and forgot about the incident, until subsequent events refreshed his memory. After a particularly bad scare, Good, who was recently married, decided that he'd had enough. Along with C-rations and new ammunition, the resupply helicopters deposited the recruiting NCO with whom Good had spoken earlier. When the sergeant asked if anybody wanted to reenlist, Good didn't hesitate.

"I told him my name and he looked it up and said, 'Hell, you can have anything you want.' I said, 'Let's . . . get the hell out of here.' That was it. I never said good-bye to nobody or nothing. I was gone that fast."

The deal the rifleman struck was straightforward—reenlistment for three years from that day. In return, he was pulled immediately from the bush, guaranteed a job in the rear, and given a $640 cash bonus and a thirty-day leave back home in the States. He took the leave immediately. Upon his return, Good was assigned duty as a turbine engine repair technician at Phu Bai. Although Good's unit lost an infantryman, it gained a conscientious man in the rear.

As the war progressed, a small but ever-increasing number of soldiers simply refused to serve in the field any longer. After about six months of combat, Randall Hoelzen was sent to the hospital at Cu Chi suffering from intestinal worms. When he returned to his brigade rear area, Hoelzen was surprised to discover a

whole contingent of people back there shamming. They were saying they weren't going to go back out. And so they just kind of used them for whatever duties they could make up for them, and then either sent them to LBJ [Long Binh Jail] for a while, or, I suppose, they got a dishonorable discharge after that. We had one guy that got wounded and said he wasn't coming back and he didn't. There were lots of guys that went that route. And it was my perception that there were a lot more blacks that did that than whites. And of those blacks that were in the rear at that time [1969], there was a strong feeling of, "This isn't my war." And they let you know it. They were telling their comrades—other black soldiers—"You are stupid to be fighting this war." Maybe they were right.

In many cases, however, pride limited the extremes to which one might go in order to secure a rear-echelon job, though nearly everyone had days when he dreamed of such good fortune and schemed about how to accomplish it. Steve Fredrick saw two possible avenues available to him when he wrote his father in February 1969.

> I have talked to the right people and it is possible for me to get out of the Army 90 days early to go to college. This would mean that I would get out of Vietnam 60 days early. Right now I have about 200 days left here, but if things go right I can have that cut to 140 days and this is important because 60 days can be at least 60 lifetimes.
>
> I would like to have you get me registered in a school (any school) which has a session beginning approximately June 22, 1969. I must be registered for at least 12 hours. . . . What college doesn't matter for the one semester. . . . Then, send me the registration papers and the acceptance with maybe a schedule of classes so I can get the paperwork done over here. Time is important because the paperwork will take a long time . . . but I think I know the people that it will take to get this thing pushed thru. . . .
>
> There are some jobs in the rear areas which I am trying to get. If I can, then I know I will make it back. There is only one trouble; my Company Commander . . . doesn't want to lose me because of the job I do. He has sent some men the same rank as me to the rear because they couldn't tote the load. That's good for them, but I couldn't do that because I have too much pride in myself. And besides, I feel I should stay with my men and do the best job I can in keeping them alive. Don't get me wrong, if I can get a rear job, I'll take it, but I could never have it said that I was in the rear because I was a dud or was scared.[11]

There was no mistaking Fredrick's elation when he was able to write a few days later:

> I have some of the best damn news I could have short of coming home. I now have a rear echelon job.

The sergeant major was impressed by my ability to do things, and he gave me a choice of two jobs. I could be platoon sergeant for a long-range reconnaissance platoon, or be the platoon sergeant back in the rear for supply and transportation. I took the rear job. I sleep in a nice, warm place at night. I'm about completely out of danger. I will almost certainly be coming back to "The World" in one piece. Music will be the one luxury I will afford myself besides a nice bed and showers each night and beaucoup beer. I guess you could say I'm overjoyed at my good luck. I still have a lot of work to do as we have about 1,000 men who depend on this platoon for everything from food to ammo.[12]

Unfortunately, the demand for rear jobs greatly outstripped their availability, and because politics was involved in securing those jobs, jealousies and frustration often surfaced. This was most keenly felt when a sense of injustice, real or imagined, was exacerbated by sentiments of racism. Tim O'Brien noted in his memoir:

The officer corps is dominated by white men; the corps of foot soldiers, common grunts, is disproportionately black. On top of that are all the old elements of racial tension—fears, hates, suspicions. And on top of that is the very pure fact that life is at stake. Not property or a decent job or social acceptance. It's a matter of staying alive.

With either the hunch or the reality that white officers favor white grunts in handing out the rear jobs, many blacks react as any sane man would. They sulk. They talk back. They get angry, loaf, play sick, smoke dope. They get together and laugh and say shit to the system.

And this feeds the problem. Pointing at malingering and insubordination by blacks, the officers are free to pass out the jobs to white men. Then the whole cycle goes for another round, getting worse.[13]

Both blacks and whites were unquestionably sensitive to their parochial interests, so accusations of racial prejudice after 1968 were possibly the results of both sides seeing only what they wished. Sergeant Michael Jackson asserted that in his battalion of the 101st Airborne Division in 1970, there seemed to be more blacks in the field than in the rear. His experience was that the blacks in his company weren't getting rotated to the rear "after six months, or seven, or ten months or twelve months."

Earlier in the war, Sergeant Willie Williams felt that there was definitely a "bias in being on the front line . . . there was a lot of racial difference there." And whereas black soldiers tended to remain in the field, Williams noted with some anger that "whites would go to brigade somewhere in the rear echelon."

As casualties and the disproportionality of blacks in combat became a matter of public debate, the military apparently became more sensitive to the issue and sought corrections.

Gerry Barker recalled: "In the beginning, in 1966 and early 1967, they weren't raising much hell about percentages and my platoon was about half black. Later in 1967 they started noticing things like that, and it was very obvious that we were getting more whites in. They got it back to about 25 percent being black. The army was very strict about that later in the war. But in the early days—yeah—there was a higher preponderance of blacks but the army did good work to visibly correct that!"

In an article for the *Naval War College Review,* Comdr. George L. Jackson noted that, in 1967, reports indicated that African-Americans made up 11 percent of the total enlisted strength in Vietnam but accounted for 14.5 percent of army combat forces and 22.5 percent of army personnel killed in action. He went on to note that, due to educational and other deferments, 30.2 percent of qualified African-Americans were drafted compared with only 18.8 percent of qualified whites. In response to these inequities, the Department of Defense readjusted force levels to achieve more equitable proportions.[14]

That the inequities seemed to have been corrected, as Sergeant Barker suggests, is indicated by statistical data.

Baskir and Strauss demonstrated that in 1965, 24 percent of KIAs were black. In 1966, the figure fell to 16 percent, and by 1968 blacks made up only 13 percent of combat fatalities, a figure that declined to only 9 percent by 1970.

Thomas Thayer, citing data from the Office of the Assistant Secretary of Defense, showed that blacks accounted for 12 percent of military deaths in Vietnam through March 1973. As Thayer explains, "About 14 percent of enlisted deaths and 2 percent of officer deaths were black." The percent of blacks in the armed forces in 1973 was 13.5 percent enlisted and 2.3 percent officer. Thus, "Blacks did not bear an unfair burden in the Vietnam War in terms of combat deaths despite allegations to the contrary."[15]

By 1970, however, many white soldiers believed that the military had overcorrected. Jeff Yushta observed that in the Marine Corps, in his estimation, "Blacks were getting a better deal than we were, and less questions were asked."

The growing sense of African-American pride surfacing in America during the late 1960s soon manifested itself in Vietnam. Marine Tom Magedanz recalled that blacks in Vietnam

banded together, wore slave bracelets [braided from boot laces], carried power sticks [swagger sticks], and referred to whites as "the beast." Whites reacted as you might expect. Blacks gave each other "the power" [or dap], a complicated series of handclasp-handshake movements, as a greeting. From a distance, or just walking by, two blacks always gave each other the raised fist salute. "Give me some power, Bro—been bleedin' for the beast." Whites would laugh and talk about it behind their backs and trouble was always seething beneath the surface.

But in the bush we needed each other so much that we got along pretty well. The rear was a different story. In Vietnam if you wanted to get out of the bush bad enough, you could; and there were groups of troublemakers—black and white—in the rear. The farther back in the rear you got, the worse it was. And blacks and whites who were friends in the bush felt intimidated or awkward together in the rear.

Throughout the war the races worked closely together in the field if for no other reason than that necessity required it. Tom Schultz believed that there was less opportunity for racial discord because, in a combat situation, one simply couldn't afford it. "You worked together, you lived together, and you died together," said Schultz. Marine Kenneth Korkow agreed.

In combat, superficialities of race were unimportant when your life is mutually dependent upon other lives. Any barriers come down real quickly. It becomes a performance-based acceptance at that point. The guy is either a coward and you don't want him with you, or he is a responsible marine and you want him with you. It is that simple. And it doesn't make any difference how tall he is, what color his eyes are, what color his skin is. It doesn't make a difference how smart he is. Those things are all moot points. It is what kind of marine he is, how he responds in combat!

Most soldiers' memories of life in the field remain largely unscarred by racial incidents or epithets. John Merrell, who grew up in a small, midwestern town where he had never met many blacks, served in a squad that was predominantly black and developed strong friendships with many of his squad members. He recalled with obvious sincerity that when his friend Larry Nigh rotated home, "He gave me his picture because he knew that I didn't have one. And when he got on the truck to leave he wouldn't let go of my hand. I never forgot that."

Despite the sudden increase in military discipline and nitpicking in the rear, most men were still enthusiastic about their new lease on life. While getting settled into his supply sergeant's job at Camp Evans, Stephen Fredrick wrote home:

I am really getting along great. I don't think I will ever have to go back to the line. I have a cooler in my room now with ice in it to keep my bottle of Jim Beam and my Miller High Life cold. I also rigged up a TV aerial out of a water pipe and charcoal grill and commo wire and we bought a TV from the Seabees. As you can see, I am really starting to enjoy life.[16]

Men in the rear found themselves enjoying a comparative safety and ease of living that their friends in the field could only dream about. But they also experienced a bittersweetness, stemming from the sense of guilt that came from leaving friends and comrades whom they had entrusted with their lives. Few men dwelled long on such unpleasantness, however; nearly everyone who secured a rear job was able to justify his actions: Things changed; the constant rotation weakened their unit loyalties. "Leaving my squad wasn't quite as hard as I imagined," acknowledged Charles Gadd, "since most of the old-time vets had been either killed or sent back to the States because of serious wounds."[17]

Randall Hoelzen's sense of abandonment was neutralized in part by his understanding that "people rotate like crazy out of there." Looking back, the former rifleman reflected, "If someone would have told me that there was going to be a helicopter in ten seconds, I would have been in it. There was no hesitation about leaving the field—no second thoughts. But I knew I was going to become a rear-echelon motherfucker as soon as I went back there. I was willing to make that sacrifice."

Having served time in the bush was a status symbol, something that a majority of those in the rear could not claim—at least at the time. But many soldiers sensed, as did Hoelzen, that "twenty years later at the American Legion club it would be the guys who served in the rear that would be telling the war stories and people back in this country would not recognize the difference."

Time spent away from the field did not, however, insulate the former grunts from news of firefights and casualties in their old units. Those who escaped the field were compelled to struggle with some degree of survivor's guilt whenever they were confronted with the news of losses among the men they left behind. But as Randall Hoelzen remembered, survivor's guilt was usually neutralized by survivor's instinct.

Steve Fredrick, however, was reminded of the obscene carnage of war when his unit, the 3d Battalion, 187th Infantry, pushed into the heavily defended A Shau Valley in early May 1969. While the battle raged, Fredrick loaded helicopters with materiel for his company in the field, and he watched as the helicopters climbed out of Firebase Helen and headed westward into the mouth of the A Shau. A horrifying number of those choppers returned with casualties. Fredrick helped off-load stretcher patients and corpses. It was intensely emotional for the former platoon sergeant, and it caused tremendous soul-searching. He wrote to his father as the assault into the A Shau began:

> It has really been a big hassle around here lately. The brigade is in the A Shau Valley and they are catching hell. We have been working day and night to keep them supplied. I am really glad I'm not on the line [be]cause my old platoon went in first and they got the first three choppers in the combat assault shot right out of the sky by small arms, automatic weapons, and rocket grenades. A lot of boys I used to have got hit. The goddamned war, and I mean just that, is a terrible thing.
>
> The people back there take for granted that it will soon be over because the damn government puts out these kinds of rumors. All the while our finest young men, the forgotten ones, are over here dying in the spring of their life.[18]

With each day that the battle raged, Fredrick's bitterness intensified. Then, on 11 May 1969, the 101st Airborne Division began to move up the slopes of Ap Bia Mountain. After four assaults and ten more days of continued battle, the mountain became known throughout Vietnam and America as "Hamburger Hill."[19] Fredrick had been a platoon sergeant in Company B, which led the initial assault against the bunkers and fortified trench works that the NVA had built there. His empathy for those in the battle intensified still more. As the assault on Hamburger Hill continued he wrote:

> I suppose you have been hearing the news of the 101st going into the A Shau Valley. Whatever they say, don't believe it because we have been getting our ass

kicked. We have lost over 300 men killed and wounded
in the last five days. . . . I have had to take the bodies of
a lot of my friends off the choppers in the last few days.
It is a hard thing to comprehend.[20]

Years later the memories of those helicopters and their cargoes were still disturbing. "Guys that I knew. . . ." He sighed,
his voice trailing off. After a minute he added simply, "It was
pretty heavy stuff." Fredrick contemplated volunteering to return to his unit, but his instincts for survival were too powerful. In the end, he conceded quietly, "I just couldn't do it."

Most soldiers reassigned to the rear had few regrets. In
many cases their lives were so improved that some men voluntarily extended their tours of duty in order to receive an
"early out" from the military when they returned to the
United States. Soldiers with two years' active duty would, if
all went according to plan, have served approximately eighteen months of their military obligation when they returned
home. After a thirty-day leave, these soldiers would still face
the onus of five or more months of active military service
based somewhere in the United States. It was not an attractive
proposition. By extending in Vietnam for an additional sixty
to ninety days, however, they became eligible for release from
the military when they returned from overseas. Extending for
six months brought the added benefit of home leave.

The enticement of a free trip home for Christmas encouraged marine Larry Iwasko to consider extending. In June,
Iwasko wrote with unbridled enthusiasm, "[I] will be home in
157 days . . . I'm coming home for Christmas—so be on the
lookout."[21] In the aftermath of several firefights, however, extending became less attractive. In September he advised his
mother:

I will not be home for Xmas after all. We have been
seeing too much action lately, and I can't see extending
and taking a chance with my own life. For the past four
days now we have gotten into firefights every night. . . .
Two nights ago I was point man on a patrol and we almost walked into a U-shaped ambush. We killed six
and wounded three. One of our men was lightly

wounded and that was the only casualty on our side. Well, I am sorry if I had all of your hopes up, but I am only trying to keep myself in one piece.[22]

Extending was more desirable, however, for those stationed in secure areas. While guarding the air base and facilities at Tuy Hoa in early 1971, machine gunner Mike Roberts not only experienced little enemy contact, he also enjoyed the enticing amenities offered on the base and at the nearby beach. He decided, "Hey! Wow! If it was going to be like this, instead of coming back to the States, I might just as well re-up for a couple of extra months and stick it out there."

Roberts's battalion was unexpectedly rotated out of Tuy Hoa shortly after his original DEROS date, however, and the unit was sent to An Khe in the Central Highlands, where Roberts found himself humping the bush again. Fortunately, there were no serious repercussions. It was a fact of life for any former grunt that, in time of need, he might lose his rear job and be returned to the bush. It didn't happen often, but the possibility added an element of chance to be considered when contemplating whether or not to extend.

That was precisely what happened to medic Jerry Severson in 1967. Severson had what he thought was an airtight deal worked out with the brigade surgeon to act as liaison between his company and the brigade's medical detachment at Pleiku.

The deal was I wouldn't have to go back to the field. I had been over there a year. I extended for two months so I could get a ninety-day early out. I'd already gone from "I'm gonna be a career soldier," to getting a ninety-day early out. I knew damn well if I came back to the United States I'd have thirty days leave coming and then four months active duty left, and I didn't want four months of spit and polish anyplace. So, I thought, if I can find a real cushy job the last two months over here I can make it. So fine!

I'd done my duty so they let me slide for a couple of months in country. The only problem was that B Company of the 504th Infantry got overrun and they lost eleven medics. I went back out in the woods again knowing that I didn't have to be there. I watched the plane leave that I should have been on. . . . I'd committed the fatal sin, I could have been home, but instead I was back out in the woods again.

For those still in the field, time continued to drag, edging inexorably toward the final day labeled DEROS or RTD on the short-timer's calendar. Soldiers and marines who were unable to land rear jobs cursed their bad luck and wondered if the military had forgotten them completely. While they waited and hoped, they took whatever additional precautions they could think of to insulate themselves from harm.

Tom Magedanz's anxiety intensified as his RTD date drew closer. "You always worry," it seemed to him, "but you're getting closer to where you might make it if you can just keep on." So, he did the only thing possible—he kept on going, pretending that "none of it was real." His final days in the field, however, took an abrupt turn for the worse when his unit was ordered back into Happy Valley:

I had about ten days left in the bush, and I did not want to go back to Happy Valley. July 2 is when Kirkendall and those guys hit the booby trap and everything, and I was pretty nervous. Kirkendall had only twenty days left when he got hit. I carried more ammunition, and, on one hand, tried to be a little bit more careful. But, on the other hand, on a couple of patrols, I remember I maybe took some more chances than I normally would have and I'm not quite sure why. We didn't run into anything. It was just kind of the last fling in the bush or something.

But then we got lucky and on July 6th we got choppered south of Da Nang—south of Marble Mountain. It was still in the field, but it was in this kind of sandy area close to the ocean and there was nothing going on. That was a good break for me.

With two weeks left to serve in his year, Paul Meringolo was finally granted deliverance from the bush, as well as a measure of solitude:

I was able to sit back in the security of the firebase, which made it a little bit better. That little bit of security was better than going out on patrols. But one day we had a patrol that got some fire and was pinned down. Even though I knew I didn't have to, I saddled up. I wanted to get out there and secure those positions and help the men out there on that patrol. The fact of going home, for me at that time, was overridden by my loyalties for the people I was with and my [sense of] responsibility.

Robert Keeling also found his loyalties as strong as ever despite having only two weeks left to serve. His mechanized unit was called upon to secure a pilot shot down outside An Khe and a medevac helicopter that had been downed attempting to rescue him. Keeling's APC was placed at the bottom of a hill to provide fire support as the men from Keeling's unit moved upward on foot. Almost immediately the advancing soldiers took fire and Keeling remembered thinking that they would need a stretcher to carry the men down.

"I started up the hill, which was stupid on my part, but I went up with a .45 [pistol] and a litter," recalled Keeling. "At the top I ran into a hell of a contact with two other guys [Americans]. . . . One guy got knocked down right off the bat. I grabbed his machine gun. . . . I mean I was scared! There was no saving him so I used his M60 as much as I could and helped this other guy back to a track. . . . [Then] I went back and got the other guy and hauled him over to the track. He was dead."

Keeling was awarded the Bronze Star for valor, but the medal and its citation lie buried in a drawer, out of sight. "Every time I see it," he explained, "it reminds me of old Skeeter . . . it reminds me of a dead man." It was Keeling's last contact. With two weeks left in country, he went into base camp resolved never to come out again. He didn't have to.

In the waning years of the Vietnam War, American units began to disband or redeploy to the United States. The standard practice was for several battalions to pool their old-timers, usually men with nine months or more in country, and send them home with the colors of a battalion scheduled for redeployment or deactivation. Personnel with less time in country were then reassigned to units remaining in Vietnam.

Dan Krehbiel humped his mortar right to the end. His battalion was scheduled to withdraw, and the short-timers were going home early. Sergeant Krehbiel was one of them. "There were," he recalled with genuine pride, "about ten of us who got early outs—early DEROS orders. But right up to that last day, I was in the field."

Others received early outs, known in the jargon of the infantry as "drops," for the same reason. Layne Anderson's was a seven-day drop. He spent 358 days in Vietnam, noting with a touch of sarcasm that the army gave him his seven days out of the goodness of its heart.

Not all early departures were joyous occasions, however. Phil Yaeger left Vietnam three weeks before his scheduled RTD because his father had suffered a heart attack.

Michael Jackson also left Vietnam under difficult circumstances. He had been in a firefight when word came over the radio for him to report to the rear. Jackson didn't know what was happening, but his first thought was of his parents.

> It took two days for me to get back to the rear and they said, "Sergeant Jackson, two days ago when we called you to get back, your sister was deathly ill and I want to tell you now that she died."
>
> I started crying. . . . The executive officer used to be in the field but rotated to the rear after six months. He was a real good soldier, a real good officer even when he was in the field. He took me in his arms. And that experience—in terms of the compassion that he showed and the support—I will never forget him.

FIGMO

With the end now clearly in sight, soldiers' shortness accelerated at an almost exponential rate. Mike Meil knew that he was short but wasn't sure of the exact day he would be freed from the field. When that day arrived, it caught him somewhat by surprise.

"I knew that I was short, that I should either be going home or getting the hell out of there pretty goddamned quick because of the time I had," Meil recalled. "They came out and called our names; 'Hey you guys, get your shit together, say your good-byes. You are heading home!' It was difficult. I think I gave away everything that I had. . . . I grabbed my shit and hugged a few guys and cried a little bit and headed back to Pleiku."

On 11 July 1970 it was Tom Magedanz's turn. Like others who had gone before him, Magedanz anxiously awaited the day, dreaming of the final honor accorded each marine in his company who was rotating home.

> You got to pop your own smoke so the helicopter coming to pick you up could see where to land. But since we were just south of Da Nang a few miles I was picked up by a tracked vehicle called a Husky. I remember I was sitting by the radio that day and it came down off the company radio that they wanted Echo 4 Mike 7885 sent to the rear and that was me. An E-4 is a corporal, Mike stands for M in Magedanz, and 7885 was what was called my "Zap Number," the last four digits of my service number. So they called out my zap number and said to get to the rear, and I went in on that Husky.[23]

Throughout the Vietnam War there were literally millions of men who, in one way or another, "popped their own smoke." For some it was a final thumbs-up as the helicopter taking them to the rear lifted out of the jungle. Others flashed the two-fingered peace sign as they began the first leg of their long journey home. They were the fortunate ones, the men with smiles that reached from the DMZ to the Delta, the ones who went out standing up. They were the vast majority.

They were sent to the brigade and division base camps to fill out reams of paperwork, a tradition that the military bureaucracy calls out-processing. It seldom took more than a day or two, but there was still apprehension, even that far in the rear, that a random rocket or sapper attack might send a man home in an aluminum casket in the belly of a "freedom bird."

Those recently arrived from the bush felt strangely naked and vulnerable without a weapon. Steve Fredrick wrote home from Camp Eagle in May 1969, "Every time I hear a loud noise I hit the ground, jump, or my heart skips about a yard. It's a real hassle."[24] Jerry Johnson spent his final week at Di An, and every night he went to a bunker to ensure that he would be going home. Dwight Reiland, however, found that his last days at Camp Eagle in January 1972 were more akin to "being away at college and the end of the school year is coming up and you knew in this case you probably weren't going to see them again."

In 1967, with one week to go, Jerry Severson was convinced that he would somehow die. He returned to Bien Hoa just in time to hear the rumor that "clairvoyant" Jeanne Dixon had prophesied that an American unit would be overrun. Naturally, every unit that heard the prediction fancied itself the target. Severson spent his final night in Vietnam at the 173d Airborne Brigade's rear area crouched in a bunker listening as enemy rockets roared overhead and landed on the air base beyond. The base wasn't overrun; Severson just spent a night without sleep. He knew then that he would make it home—if only the plane didn't crash on the way.

Doug Kurtz drank his last night away with friends he had made in the rear at Dong Tam. He couldn't sleep anyhow. There were a lot of maudlin promises to visit each other back in The World. Of course, Kurtz realized that he would probably never see his friends again, although he remembered making all sorts of plans to do so. Robert Keeling gave his short-timer's calendar and boonie hat to the next guy scheduled to DEROS and left his tape recorder on the APC for the others—tokens of farewell for the men with whom he had shared so much.

One of the happiest days in a GI's tour was the day he got his printed orders announcing his trip home. That day was inscribed on short-timers' calendars with the acronym FIGMO, which in the jargon of grunts stood for "Fuck it, I got my orders!" Dan Krehbiel thought he had. Ready to enjoy his early

rotation home, Krehbiel suddenly discovered himself hope-
lessly entangled in the web of army bureaucracy.

> I would have been ten days early but they lost my or-
> ders. Absolute truth. Eleven days later I finally got per-
> mission to go down and get new orders cut, and I was
> so pleased at that decision because I figured I could
> pick where I was gonna go—training cadre at Fort
> Leonard Wood, Missouri—and do something I liked to
> do and be close to home. Well, naturally, they found my
> old orders. Those dirty rotten bastards found my orders.
> "Son of a gun, our fault! You should have been home
> eleven days ago. You're going to Fort Hood, Texas."
> And I told them, "No! I don't want those. I want new
> ones. You made me wait, just cut me new orders."
> "No, I'm sorry, we can't just do that," the guy said.
> It was real strange. I threatened him. I had never
> threatened anyone before—and not since—but I threat-
> ened him. I said, "If you want to live, you grimy little
> son of a bitch . . ." He was a guy in the rear. He was
> never in the field. It was not his fault; that was how he
> fit into the army machine. But I held it against him and
> took it out on him and said, "How dare you control my
> life, you little weasel." And he said, "I'll go tell my of-
> ficer on you," or whatever. Eventually, they said,
> "Here's your orders, now get the hell out of here." They
> didn't update or change anything. I went to Fort Hood.

The road home now began to look familiar. It was, after
all, the same road they had come in on. From the brigade and
division rear areas soldiers caught flights to the replacement
centers through which they had entered Vietnam. Most men
spent their final few days in transient barracks checking bulletin boards for a flight manifest with their name on it. Few
men had to perform duties, so the majority spent a lot of time
at the various clubs drinking. Robert Keeling recalled that in
Cam Ranh Bay he entertained himself flushing toilets, playing with a light switch, and eating ice cream.

John Merrell said that he got out of the bush only twenty-
four hours before his scheduled flight, but the plane was de-

layed. He was stuck. Cam Ranh Bay, however, offered some amenities. "Nobody messed with you," he recalled. "You just slept." His favorite place at Cam Ranh Bay was the mess hall. "After eating C-rations for a year," Merrell said, "fresh-cooked food tasted good."

Tom Magedanz spent two days in Da Nang waiting for his freedom bird. What he remembered most about Da Nang was having to sleep on a cement floor in the transient facility while waiting for the airplane.

Captain Robert Steenlage found Cam Ranh Bay backed up with the December rush. Since it appeared that he would have a day or two to wait, he took advantage of the resources at his disposal. "Cam Ranh Bay was just like a resort area—a beautiful place right on the ocean," Steenlage recalled. "So I went down to the beach in a swimming suit. I hadn't been in one of those for a long time."

The resulting sunburn was severe, but Steenlage's fear that the medics would keep him in Vietnam because of it was even more discomforting, so he didn't seek treatment. His starched khakis were torture, but far worse, he was going home as a virtual "untouchable" to the bride he'd left behind.

Once on a flight manifest, the men exchanged their military scrip for greenbacks, and cleared customs. About twenty-four hours prior to departure, they were given a shakedown inspection. The men were formed up with their baggage at their feet and told to dump the contents of their duffel bags on the ground. Charles Gadd recalled that the search seemed degrading—until it turned up a "pile of confiscated illegal merchandise" that men had been trying to smuggle out of the country. A second shakedown twelve hours later turned up "another box of contraband."[25] Later in the war, soldiers were screened for drug use by undergoing a mandatory urinalysis.

Once the men had passed muster, they boarded the buses with wire screens over the windows—just like the ones they had ridden so long before in the opposite direction—and were transported to the air terminals. Names were called off the flight manifest and everyone answered in as nonmilitary a way as they dared. The men were then marched to the terminal waiting rooms while the planes were readied. Finally a voice over the loudspeaker began instructing the men to board the aircraft, beginning with the highest-ranking officers.

Dan Krehbiel got to board his flight first—his only consolation for being held over for so long. According to Krehbiel:

> I got to Long Binh and was immediately scolded for being eleven days late. "Where the hell have you been?" "You have been AWOL." All that good stuff. They were going to write me up for an Article Fifteen [nonjudicial punishment] because I was eleven days late leaving the country. And I said, "No! Why don't you read the rest of the report here?"
>
> "Well! Hell!" they said. "You should have been out of here eleven days ago." So they put me on the next manifest. In fact, they called my name first out of this entire two-hundred-man manifest. My name came first, then came a brigadier general. That was great.

The men had changed a great deal in their one-year life as combat soldiers, but just beneath the surface there were flashes of what they once had been. While sitting in the reception center at Da Nang awaiting his flight home, Ed Hoban ran into his former high school track coach. His reaction was instinctive. Upon seeing the former coach, the combat veteran reverted immediately to another place and time: "I had a cigarette, and I hid it from him," he said. "That was interesting now that I look back at it."

As they took their seats in the civilian airliners, they could smell the United States in the appointments about the cabin, but all eyes focused immediately on the "round-eyed" flight attendants. The air-conditioner came on and the seat-belt light drew their attention. If there were fears of a last Viet Cong rocket attack, the thoughts were suppressed. The plane taxied out, did a quick run-up, and began its takeoff roll. Reflecting on that moment, Tom Magedanz said, "I remember when the wheels left the ground, I looked out the window to get a last look. I just kind of stared at the countryside and tried to remember what it looked like at night and just tried to remember the whole experience. I don't remember any cheering or anything like that. It was just quiet in that airplane when we left."

Jerry Johnson's image of that moment of departure was similar in many respects, although like most soldiers he remembered cheering:

> As soon as those wheels were off the ground, man, the plane just erupted—everybody started yelling and screaming and hugging each other and we knew we were on our way home. . . .
>
> In a way it was relief and in another way you looked back and you said to yourself, That was something I'll probably never, ever experience again. It didn't make you want to reenlist or go back for another tour though [laughter]. It was amazing to me that I actually acted like that. You had to be part animal sometimes. Was that really me? You know—I'll never ever tell anybody what I went through. That's something I thought. When I was up in that plane it got real quiet and everybody just sat there thinking.

EPILOGUE

Eating the Toad

Elation was eventually replaced by monotony as the DC-8s and 707s settled in at altitude and fixed their noses onto the great-circle routes that would take the soldiers home. The cramped quarters and relative isolation afforded the men little to do but stare into space and ponder the mysteries of the life they had just lived. Flight attendants were kept busy emptying ashtrays, slapping stray hands, and providing tiny bottles of booze—or mixers for those who had purchased their own "Texas Fifths" at the PX prior to departure. Some returnees slept fitfully on the way home, but others struggled with a haunting sense of vulnerability that had not yet fully abated.

Dan Krehbiel's flight from Yokota Air Base, Japan, was rerouted because of a typhoon in the Aleutian Islands. In the worst of the turbulence, Krehbiel was sure that he was going to die. And Jerry Severson experienced a nightmare so vivid that a flight attendant had to come to his aid. In his dream, the plane

> was going to crash. I was just sweating and twitching. The stewardess finally woke me up. It was so real—so damned real—it was unbelievable. I dreamt we were about fifty miles out to sea and running out of fuel and the pilot didn't know whether he could make the airport or have to ditch in the sea. Christ! We were coming in right over the buildings and down in between some of them trying to make the airport. Whew!

As their planes winged westward, they crossed an invisible boundary far more real than the international date line;

they exited a world of fear into a land free of booby traps and ambushes, where thunder was only that, and where one could sleep securely. It would require time to adjust, a lifetime perhaps, but they would no longer be living with constant fear.

Pandemonium inevitably erupted in each aircraft when the landing gear made contact with American soil. The elation soon faded, however, as the soldiers began the tedious process of passing through customs and, especially later in the war, a gauntlet of protesters. Exchanging catcalls and obscenities with the antiwar demonstrators made little impression on them at the time, however. The soldiers were insulated by their numbers and too elated to let it bother them. In addition, many flights arrived at night, so that no one was there to diminish the impact of their arrival.

After clearing customs, the men were bused to processing centers to begin what would, for some, mark the end of their military service. The rest anxiously waited to begin the thirty-day leave authorized for them en route to their next duty stations. Overall, the mood was euphoric.

Perhaps because of the long flights and their cavalier attitudes, soldiers' memories of events at the processing centers are a bit vague. Donald Putnam remembered walking into the Oakland center.

> They had us all spread out by tables, two or three guys to a table, standing up, and this guy started giving instructions. We had been on the plane for hours. We were dead tired. We didn't care. A third of us were getting out of the army and that was it! We were done! History! He said, "We guarantee you will be out of here in twenty-four hours or less." I remember standing there thinking, this is the first guarantee I have had in two years. If this man lives up to this, he is a hero. He explained how the process would go and then they just started us moving.

Paul Gerrits said that he spent eighteen hours standing in line and waiting. Men filled out forms and answered questions. They reviewed their military records, verifying the length of their leave and orders for duty afterward, or examining their discharge papers and getting briefings on veteran's benefits. Most, such as Dwight Reiland, found the process almost enjoyable. Coming back through the Fort Lewis, Washington, center Reiland was fed a steak dinner and "treated as a human being instead of an animal."

There was one vision, however, that appealed to Randall Hoelzen's sense of irony as he moved through the Oakland processing center. After visiting each of the various desks, he went back to a gymnasium-like area where he and his comrades waited on benches for their turn at the next station. While sitting there, Hoelzen noticed that:

> Off to one side away from the seating in the gym sat this sergeant at a desk with a "Re-Up" sign. He was a *very* lonely guy. I can never forget that. All those guys sitting and talking and waiting and this guy just sitting at his desk. Nobody was coming to him. It was kind of humorous.

The men were given brief physicals as well as a cursory psychological examination. They were also measured by tailors who prepared new dress uniforms for them, complete with decorations and sewn-on rank insignia. Since Jerry Severson had served in an airborne unit in Vietnam, he wanted his dress-uniform trousers "tailored" in compliance with airborne tradition. When it wasn't, Severson was more than disappointed:

> I was Airborne and proud of it, and I was proud of my uniform, and I wanted my uniform tailored. I said, "I'll stay right here. You can feed me forever, but I'm not leaving till I get my uniform tailored."
>
> At that point I didn't care. I had come back to the States after all that and they wouldn't grant me a simple request. That's just exactly what I thought. I was ready to pay the gal to do it. She was up there sewing all the patches on. All she had to do was turn the pants inside out and run a seam down them inside and out.

It was to be the last battle Severson fought for the 173d Airborne Brigade, and he had every intention of winning it. He did. "I looked decent when I left the base," he said, flashing a smile.

The last step in the processing for soldiers being discharged was a visit to the paymaster. Most men received a substantial sum because many had opted to draw only a small portion of their salary each month during their year in Vietnam.

Once they were clothed, fed, paid, and given orders or discharge papers, they headed through the exits and off to the airport terminals for the last leg of the journey home. Although they did not anticipate victory parades or smiling glances, neither did they suspect that they would encounter hostility. Nevertheless, many men were faced with tangible proof that there were people in America who did not welcome Vietnam veterans.

The men were told to avoid confrontations with antiwar protesters. When Capt. Robert Steenlage arrived in California in December 1968, he was told not to wear a uniform off post. He also remembered being able to rent wigs to disguise soldiers' military haircuts. A midwesterner and a West Point graduate, Captain Steenlage simply couldn't believe that his own countrymen would treat soldiers in that fashion. He soon discovered how wrong he was:

> We went off base that evening and people were outside the gate and in the nearby community. They gave it to us hard. That was tough to take.
> "Why do you love war—why do you kill people?"
> "We hate you! Why don't you go back?"
> "What did you volunteer for?"
> No matter what you said to them, it was no use. I assumed there was no sense talking to them.
> "You deserved to die!"
> There were all kinds of swear words. They threw things—garbage. It was just a shock. It was really hard to believe. Coming home was worse than being there in many ways. It was horrible because coming from the Midwest and Iowa and being patriotic and believing in

all that. . . . This was the last straw. I just couldn't believe it. Once I got home I didn't get it too bad, but it is still hard to think about.

By 1968, many returning veterans were concealing their identity as soldiers, wearing uniforms only when necessary, in order to avoid sneers and callous remarks from onlookers. Michael Jackson, as was common among returnees in the later years of the war, went to the airport in civilian clothing. "You had to wear your uniform to get the military discount," he explained, "so, when you hit the airport, you went to the john and changed into uniform."

Dwight Reiland and his traveling companions made their way to Seattle-Tacoma International Airport without incident. In fact, discouraging words were the last thing on their minds at six in the morning. Reiland had a three-hour wait that began smoothly enough. But then he noticed that:

> A woman kept looking at us kind of funny and we were just puffed up and proud as peacocks; you know, the returning heroes. I misjudged her attention. I thought that she was thinking, These are just like my boys back home. Then she made a remark to one of the guys. I didn't know the guy she actually said it to; he was just right there by me. She said, "You guys coming home from Vietnam, are you?"
>
> Guy says, "Yeah." He was just tickled and everything.
>
> She says, "Well, you weren't in with any of those men that were killing those babies and children, were you?"
>
> Jeez! Everybody was shocked. Here we thought she thought we were probably pretty neat and instead she suspected that we were baby killers. . . .
>
> Everybody moved away from her. Nobody wanted that kind of a hassle. We were too happy at that point to let that bring us down. We were going home!

Ed Hoban didn't see any protesters, but he did suffer what he considered a great injustice in the airport lounge. "I wanted to get a drink," he stated with a trace of lingering bitterness, "and they turned me down because I was under age." He recalled thinking at the time, "Fight a damn war and they won't even let you drink when you get back." The sober expoint man caught his flight and headed home.

Whether they were headed for San Francisco or Shell Rock, Iowa, home itself lived up to every expectation. Steve Fredrick remembered that the Iowa cornfields never looked better. Layne Anderson hitchhiked the final leg of his trip to Blair, Wisconsin. His mother didn't know of his "seven-day drop" and was not expecting him. He walked through the door and into the living room, where she was reading the paper. Lacking better words for the occasion, he simply stated the obvious: "Hi, Mom, I'm home!"

Coming home was not merely a matter of walking through a doorway from one world into another. There were old habits, feelings, and reflexes to recondition. At the end of Dan Krehbiel's first day at home, he suddenly became very frightened that it might simply be a dream.

> I was really scared that I would wake up. I was sure I was dreaming. When people say that, usually they don't really mean it. I had never meant it before, but this was true. I was convinced that I would wake up. When I was in Vietnam I had two dreams at different times that were so real that I cried when I woke up. One of them was talking to my mother on the stairway in the house. Then I woke up and we were out on ambush. I was just heartbroken. The other one was with my brother at home again and I woke up from that and it felt just the same. So when I was home I remember riding around town in a civilian car and I suddenly started to cry and I said, "I'm going to wake up. I know it. I can't take this." I was really nuts for about two or three hours. Then my brother calmed me down. I hadn't been to sleep yet.

Tom Magedanz performed a ritual of sorts that helped to reassure him. "If you were smoking in Vietnam," he explained, "you just didn't light a cigaret at night because snipers could see you. So I went out at night on my folks' front lawn and lit my cigarette lighter and held it up above my head. I can do this now! I thought. I don't have to worry about anything. It was just a relief to . . . be able to not be afraid."

They had survived to face the rest of their lives, and many sensed that whatever else they came up against, it would likely seem pale in comparison to what they had so recently endured. Reflecting on his Vietnam experience, Dan Krehbiel was more than a little amazed that he had been able to endure it at all. The war has remained a source of strength throughout his life. Whenever things get difficult, he said, he reminds himself that, "This is nothing compared to Vietnam and what I was feeling then."

The experience reminded Krehbiel of an expression from his childhood: "Eating the toad!" It meant doing something that was really horrible. Vietnam, he decided, was like "eating the toad first thing in the morning; absolutely nothing could be worse than that the rest of the day. I ate the toad, and now I'm okay."

The life that the Vietnam veterans had spent in their years as combat soldiers was over. Leaving it behind and getting on with their lives would be next. Many tried not to look back. Charles Moskos discovered that soldiers who returned to the United States seldom wrote to those still in Vietnam, and those still in combat rarely corresponded with friends who had DEROS'd to The World. Friendships that had once been as cohesive as the red clay of the Central Highlands began to fade.[1] Dwight Reiland knew how it was, even though he never intended it to be that way:

> You had all these intentions. . . . God! You thought you would never, ever forget those guys. You were going to stay in touch. "We'll have to get back in touch at Christmas," and all that. You believed it at the time. You thought, Hey, I'm never going to forget this guy. And now I can't remember the names of some of the people. Once you got out of there, it didn't lessen those friendships you established, but that was a whole different world. That was there. Now you are home and things

are back to normal. Maybe you didn't intend it but that world just got farther and farther away.

But there were also, as Paul Meringolo discovered, "different things which kept the memory of Vietnam alive: different people, various events, circumstances. . . . I have always thought that if my best friend hadn't been killed, if he had lived, somehow I would have come to terms with Vietnam and assimilated my experiences into my life much more easily. But I'll never really know. . . ."

Leonard Dutcher arrived home from Vietnam on 13 June 1968. News of his impending arrival had preceded him:

133A CDT JUN 6 68 MA022 M
M TLA004 WUB021 CTA009 MM CT WA024 XV
GOVT PDB4
EXTRA
FAX WASHINGTON DC 4 1151P EDT

MR & MRS RICHARD M. DUTCHER DONT
DLVR BTWN 10PM & 6 AM DONT PHONE
   RT 2 MELROSE WIS THE SECRETARY OF THE
ARMY HAS ASKED ME TO EXPRESS HIS DEEP
REGRET THAT YOUR SON, SERGEANT
LEONARD E. DUTCHER, DIED IN VIETNAM ON
2 JUNE 1968 AS A RESULT OF WOUND
RECEIVED WHILE ENROUTE TO NIGHT
DEFENSIVE POSITION WHEN ENGAGED
HOSTILE FORCE IN FIREFIGHT. PLEASE
ACCEPT MY DEEPEST SYMPATHY. THIS
CONFIRMS PERSONAL NOTIFICATION MADE
BY A REPRESENTATIVE OF THE SECRETARY
OF THE ARMY
   KENNETH G WICKHAM MAJOR GENERAL
USA F63 THE ADJUTANT GENERAL (1246).[2]

APPENDIX

List of Interview Subjects

U.S. Army Infantry Veterans

Major Command/ Name	Combat Unit	RVN Tour Dates
1st Cavalry Division		
Barker, Gerry	B/1-8th Cav.	Sept. 65–Nov. 65
	C/2-8th Cav	Nov. 66–May 67
Musser, Terry	B/2-8th Cav	Sept. 65–April 66
*Emery, Robert	A/1-9th Cav	Dec. 65–April 66
Schultz, Tom	C/2-7th Cav.	Aug. 68–Aug. 69
Hoelzen, Randy	C/2-7th Cav	May 69–April 70
Gerrits, Paul	C/2-7th Cav.	Feb. 70–March 71
1st Infantry Division		
Johnson, Jerry	C/2-28th Inf.	Nov. 68–Nov. 69
I Field Force		
Roberts, Mike	B/1-50th Inf.	July 70–Sept. 71
4th Infantry Division		
Janick, Vernon	B/1-8th Inf.	Sept. 66–Aug. 68
Meil, Mike	B/1-10th Cav.	April 67–April 68
Merrell, John	B/1-14th Inf.	Nov. 68–Nov. 69
Keeling, Bob	A/2-8th Mech.	Nov. 69–Nov. 70
5th Infantry Division (Mechanized)		
Hill, Larry	HHC/1-77th Arm.	March 70–Jan. 71
5th Special Forces Group		
*Leanna, Ray		1961
		April 66–April 69
Barker, Gerry		1968–1970
9th Infantry Division		
*Tople, Terry	E/5-60th Mech.	Aug. 68–Feb. 69
Neely, Jon	C/2-47th Mech.	Nov. 68–Nov. 69

| Kurtz, Doug | 3d Bde. Airboat Plt./ 39th Cav. Plt. (ACV) | May 69–Sept. 70 |
| Putnam, Donald | A/2-47th Mech. | Oct. 69–Aug. 70 |

23d Infantry "Americal" Division

Meringolo, Paul	B/1-52d Inf.	Aug. 67–Aug. 68
Vetterkind, Jerry	C/1-52d Inf.	Oct. 67–Oct. 68
Anderson, Layne	D/5-46th Inf.	Aug. 68–Feb. 69
Boehm, Paul	D/5-46th Inf.	Aug. 68–March 69
*Whitebird, Francis	B&C/2-1st Inf.	March 69–Oct. 70
*Foell, Dennis	D/3-21st Inf.	March 69–April 70
Johnson, R. Bruce	C/4-3d Inf.	Jan. 70–Dec. 70
*Gates, Larry	C/5-46th Inf.	Oct. 70–April 71
Hoban, Ed	F/8th Cav.	March 71–Jan. 72

25th Infantry Division

Williams, Willie	A/2-27th Inf.	Jan. 66–Dec. 66
Olstad, Glen	B/4-23d Mech.	Feb. 68–Feb. 69
Harken, William	2-27th Inf.	Sept. 68–Jan. 69
Krehbiel, Dan	D/2-14th Inf.	June 69–June 70

101st Airborne Division (Airmobile)

*Roubideaux, Tom	C/2-502d Inf.	Aug. 65–June 66
*Raysor, James	E/1-327th Inf.	April 66–Aug. 67
Fredrick, Steve	B/3-187th Inf.	Sept. 68–May 69
Good, Bryan	D/1-327th Inf.	Dec. 69–Nov. 70
Jackson, Michael	D/2-327th Inf.	Dec. 69–Aug. 70
Reiland, Dwight	D/1-327th Inf.	March 71–Jan. 72

173d Airborne Brigade

| Severson, Jerry | E/1-17th Cav. | June 66–Aug. 67 |
| Musser, Terry | HHC/1-503d Inf. | April 67–Feb. 68 |

199th Light Infantry Brigade

| *Birhanzel, Thomas | 2-3d Inf | Nov. 69–Aug. 70 |

U.S. Marine Corps Infantry Veterans

Major Command/ Name	Combat Unit	RVN Tour Dates

1st Marine Division

Freitag, Jack	F/2/1st Marines	June 66–July 67
*Olson, Vince	1/1st Marines	June 67–Feb. 68
Stanton, James	HQ/1/1st Marines	Jan. 68–Aug. 70
*Moran, Robert Jr.	Recon/1/1st Marines	April 69–March 70

Yushta, Jeff	B/1/5th Marines	July 69–Aug. 70
*Magedanz, Thomas	E/2/7th Marines	July 69–July 70
Shepardson, Terry	M/3/5th Marines	Aug. 69–May 70

3d Marine Division

Yaeger, Phil	M/3/4th Marines	July 66–July 67
*Korkow, Kenneth	B/1/26th Marines	Jan. 68–March 68
Bonesteel, Robert	HQ/9th Marines	Oct. 67–Nov. 68

III Marine Amphibious Force

| Meyer, John | 1st CAP/2d CAG | April 70–Oct. 70 |
| *Trimble, Donald | 5th CAP/2d CAG | Jan. 71–May 71 |

Non-Infantry Combat Veterans

Major Command/ Name	Combat Unit	RVN Tour Dates
1st Logistical Command		
Carlisle, David	26th Gen. Spt. Grp.	April 68–June 69
4th Infantry Division		
Steenlage, Robert	124th Sig. Bn	Dec. 67–Dec. 68
16th Aviation Group		
*Gates, Larry		April 71–Oct. 71
17th Aviation Group		
*Johnson, Deane	61st Avn. Co. (AHC)	Sept. 68–Sept. 69
	238th Avn. Co. (AWC)	Sept. 69–Sept. 70
Miller, Glenn	57th Avn. Co. (AHC)	Jan. 72–Dec. 72
101st Airborne Division (Airmobile)		
*Hansen, David	101st Avn. Bn.	Feb. 69–Feb. 70

*Denotes interviews conducted by the South Dakota Vietnam Veterans Oral History Project. All other interviews were conducted by the author.

Glossary

AK-47: Lightweight Soviet- or Chinese-built 7.62mm assault rifle.

Arc light: Slang for a high-altitude B-52 heavy bombing mission.

Arty: Slang for artillery.

Blooper: Slang for the M79 grenade launcher.

Blues: Slang for an aerorifle platoon.

Boom-boom girl: Prostitute.

Boonies: The jungle, or simply the field.

Boot: A marine who has not yet completed basic training. In Vietnam the term was used as a synonym for newness.

Bouncing betty: Land mines that bounce into the air about chest high before exploding.

Bunkers: Protective shelters, usually below ground, reinforced with timber and steel and covered with sandbags or ammunition boxes filled with soil. Enemy bunkers were usually holes covered with heavy logs and packed with earth, serving the same purpose.

Bush: See boonies.

Bush hat: A broad-brimmed hat made of green cloth, often worn in the field in place of the much heavier and hotter steel helmet.

C-4: Plastic explosive used for a variety of tasks. Field soldiers often ignited small pieces to heat rations, a hazardous practice at best.

C-130: A high-wing, four-engine turboprop cargo plane able to operate from unimproved landing strips of medium length. Cargo is loaded through a large rear door that lowers as a ramp for access to the interior.

Camp Alpha: The processing center for soldiers arriving in Vietnam through the base at Long Binh. Home of the 90th Replacement Battalion.

Charlie: Slang for Viet Cong, derived from the phonetic alphabet designation for VC: "Victor Charlie."

Charm school: Slang for in-country training given to newly arrived soldiers.

Cherry: Slang for a newly arrived soldier.

Chieu-Hoi: Enemy soldier who turned himself in.

Chinook (CH-47): A large twin-rotor transport helicopter.

Claymore: An antipersonnel mine that fires hundreds of steel ball bearings when detonated by a trip wire or hand-held control.

Cobra (AH-1G): A sleek, fast attack helicopter armed with rockets, machine guns, and grenade launchers, used in ground support roles.

Combined Action Teams: Marine units that worked with South Vietnamese militia forces in the defense of villages and hamlets. Units lived and worked closely with the villagers they were sent to protect.

Company: A military unit ranging in size from 120 to 200 men, although often understrength in Vietnam by 25 percent or more. Usually commanded by a captain.

Concertina wire: Protective wire with sharpened steel barbs used to secure the perimeters of military installations and fortified positions. An apron or area of "tanglefoot" (crisscrossed barbed wire) was often laid between rolls of concertina wire.

Conscientious objector: A person opposed to serving in the military due to moral and/or ethical considerations.

Corpsman: Navy medical personnel, assigned to Marine Corps field units to administer emergency first-aid. Called "Doc." The senior naval hospital corpsman in a marine company was known as the "Senior Squid" and supervised the other corpsmen.

Crew chief: Man in charge of fueling and maintenance on a helicopter. On helicopters employing them he also served as a door gunner.

Daisy-chain: A series of booby traps linked together to detonate simultaneously.

Dap: A very complex and elaborate ritual handshake used by African-American soldiers.

Detonating cord (det cord): A flexible, braided cotton tube filled with explosive used to clear trees and other obstacles from landing zones.

Deuce-and-a-half: A standard 2 1/2-ton truck.

"Diddy bopping": Slang—a soldier who is not paying attention to what he is doing; laxness or carelessness.

Dink: An enemy soldier.

Dinky-dao (*dien cai dau*): Vietnamese for crazy.

Door gunners: The men who operate machine guns from helicopters, so named because their gun position is usually in the open doorway of the aircraft.

Drill instructor: Basic training sergeant.

Dustoff: A medevac helicopter. The name derived from the radio call sign of the first medical helicopter evacuation unit in Vietnam.

Elephant grass: Coarse tall grass with very sharp edges found in most open areas of Vietnam not under cultivation.

EM club: Enlisted men's club. A bar and recreation facility for soldiers under the rank of sergeant. NCOs and officers had their own clubs.

F-4 Phantom: Powerful jet fighter-bomber.

Fatigues: A soldier's work uniform.

Firebase: A temporary artillery installation set up to provide fire support for infantry operations in the area.

Flak jacket: An armored vest designed to prevent wounds from shell fragments.

Frag: A slang reference to murdering superior officers, NCOs, or fellow soldiers.

Freedom bird: The airplane on which a soldier flew home from Vietnam.

Forward observer: Directs artillery or air strikes by radio from the point of contact. Accompanies the infantry in the field.

Four-deuce: A 4.2-inch mortar.

Furlough: Leave.

GI bill: A term for the benefits, usually financial, awarded to those who have served in the armed forces. Most commonly such benefits are tied to education programs and home loans.

Green Beret: Nickname for U.S. Army's Special Forces soldiers, derived from their distinctive headgear. The men were specially trained in counterinsurgency operations, primarily working with indigenous people.

Greenie: Slang for a soldier new to Vietnam.

Grunt: Slang for an infantry soldier, either army or marine.

Gunship: Slang for an attack helicopter.

Helmet cover: A camouflage cloth cover for the helmet. It is reversible: a green side for jungles and a brown side for dry areas.

Huey (UH-1): Utility helicopter used primarily for troop transport and medical evacuation. The older C model was often used as a gunship.

Hump: A patrol or march out in the field.

Indirect fire: Fire not directly aimed at a target by line of sight.

Infusion: Transferring soldiers from one unit to another.

Jump wings: A badge given to soldiers who graduate from parachute school after completing airborne training.

Jungle boots: Combat boots with canvas uppers to allow better ventilation for wet feet. The lower parts were made of leather coated with a rubberized material that did not rot as quickly. A steel plate in the sole guarded against *punji* sticks. A soldier would wear out several pair during a typical tour.

Kit Carson Scout: A former VC or NVA soldier who voluntarily accompanied American units in the field acting as an advisor and interpreter.

Klick: One kilometer.

Land of the Big PX: America.

Landing zone: Where helicopters unload their cargo of men or materiel.

Leatherneck: A marine.

Loach: A light observation helicopter (LOH).

Log bird: A logistics (resupply) helicopter.

Lottery system: A revised method of conscription in which eligible males were selected on the basis of their date of birth from a random drawing.

M14: The 7.62mm rifle issued to GIs before the M16 was developed.

M16: Standard-issue, lightweight American assault rifle. Fires a 5.56mm bullet.

M60: A lightweight 7.62mm machine gun with ammunition that is linked together in a belt and fed into the weapon. The standard machine gun used by army and marine infantry units in Vietnam.

M79: A breech-loading, single-shot 40mm grenade launcher.

Main force: North Vietnamese Army units or Viet Cong units that were stronger and much better equipped for more conventional military action than their guerrilla counterparts.

Mamasan: Slang for any Vietnamese woman older than a child.

Mechanized unit: An infantry unit mounted on armored vehicles.

Medevac: Aerial medical evacuation of wounded from the field.

Napalm: A highly combustible, jellied petroleum substance dropped from the air in canisters (*na*phthenic acid and *palm*etate).

Newbie: A soldier or marine newly arrived in Vietnam.

Number 1: Slang for anything very, very good!

Number 10: Slang for anything very, very bad. When the state of Wisconsin dedicated a highway in honor of its Vietnam Veterans, it unwittingly chose Highway 10.

N'uoc mam: A repulsive-smelling Vietnamese condiment made by fermenting fish heads in water.

Oki: Marine slang for Okinawa.

Overrun: Overwhelming a defensive position.

Pacification: An allied program to secure the civilian population of South Vietnam from Viet Cong terror and increase the loyalty of peasants toward the government of Vietnam.

Parris Island: The Marine Corps training center on the East Coast. Marines sent to San Diego are usually referred to as "Hollywood" marines.

Platoon: Military unit consisting of from two to four squads and numbering approximately twenty-five to forty-five men. Usually commanded by a lieutenant.

Point man: The man in a maneuvering infantry unit who leads the way.

Poncho liner: Lightweight nylon quiltlike liner cut to fit inside a military poncho. Used mostly as bedding.

PRC-25: Portable backpack FM radio used in the field. Called the "Prick 25" by grunts.

Punji **pit:** A camouflaged pit containing sharpened bamboo spears. Most were small sticks intended to cause leg and foot wounds.

Recon by fire: To fire weapons into surrounding foliage to see if enemy soldiers are hiding there. To search out an enemy in likely locations with firepower.

Remington Raiders: Clerk-typists or soldiers in other safe rear-echelon occupations.

Repo-Depot: Slang for the replacement units where new troops are processed and assigned to duty with operational units.

Rock 'n roll: To fire a weapon on automatic.

Round: One bullet, shell, or shot of any kind.

Rucksack: A backpack. The standard through much of the war was the ALICE system, which consisted of a lightweight nylon pack fitted to an aluminum pack frame.

Sampan: A small wooden Vietnamese boat.

Sappers: VC or NVA who infiltrated firebases and base camps.

Satchel charge: An explosive charge carried by sappers in an attack on fixed installations.

Scuttlebutt: Rumors.

Search and destroy: Type of military operation designed to locate and destroy enemy military forces.

Selective Service: The U.S. government agency responsible for procuring manpower in time of war.

Sham: To avoid work or danger in the field or in the rear.

Short-timer: A soldier nearing the end of his tour in Vietnam.

Sit-rep: Short for situation report.

Skate: See sham.

Slick: Slang for a Huey helicopter used to carry troops.

Slope: Slang for an Asian.

Staging: Final processing and refresher training for marines preparing to depart for Vietnam.

Starlight Scope: A night-vision device that intensifies available light, allowing a soldier to see in the dark. Everything seen in the scope has a green tint.

Subic Bay: Large navy base located in the Philippines.

The World: Home.

Thump gun: Nickname for the M79 grenade launcher.

Toe-popper: A small booby trap usually consisting of a rifle or machine-gun bullet inside a tube in the ground pointing upward. The bullet fires when stepped on.

Tracers: Incendiary bullets that leave a bright trail that allows soldiers to "trace" the path of the round to its target. American tracers are red; Soviet-made tracers are green or white.

Vietnamization: America's policy under President Nixon to turn over the actual conduct of the war to South Vietnam's military and, through a series of graduated troop withdrawals, end American involvement.

Web gear: A suspender-like harness and belt to which an individual's personal equipment is attached. The straps distribute the weight of the load over a larger area, making it easier and less fatiguing to carry.

List of Abbreviations

AIT Advanced Individual Training
AO Area of Operation
APC armored personnel carrier
ARVN Army of the Republic of Vietnam
BITS Basic Infantry Training School
BX base exchange (navy and Marine Corps)
CAG Combined Action Group
CAP Combined Action Platoon
CO commanding officer
C's C rations

CS riot-control tear gas
CYA cover your ass
DEROS date eligible for return from overseas (army)
DMZ demilitarized zone (border between North and South Vietnam)
DOW died of wounds
FNG fucking new guy
FO forward observer
FSB fire support base
HE high explosive
HQ headquarters
ITR Infantry Training Regiment (USMC)
KCS Kit Carson Scout
KIA killed in action
LAW light antitank weapon
LP listening post
LRRP long-range reconnaissance patrol
LST Landing Ship, Tank
LZ landing zone
MACV Military Assistance Command Vietnam
MEDCAP Medical Civic Action Program
MIA missing in action
MOS Military Occupational Specialty
NCO noncommissioned officer
NDP night defensive position
NVA North Vietnamese Army
OJT on-the-job training
PAVN People's Army of Vietnam
POW prisoner of war
PX post exchange (army and air force)
R&R rest and recreation
RIF reconnaissance in force
ROKs Republic of Korea soldiers and marines
RPG rocket-propelled grenade
RTD rotation date (marines)
RTO radio/telephone operator
SOP standard operating procedure
TacAir tactical air support
TOC Tactical Operations Center
USARV U.S. Army Vietnam
VC Viet Cong
WIA wounded in action
XO executive officer

Notes

Chapter 1

1. Leonard Dutcher to his parents, 25 April 1966. Original copies of this and other Dutcher letters cited are in the possession of his sister, Mrs. Betty Ronke, Melrose, Wis.

2. Lawrence Baskir and William Strauss, *Chance and Circumstances: The Draft, the War, and the Vietnam Generation* (New York: Alfred A. Knopf, 1978), 60; Charles Moskos, *The American Enlisted Man: The Rank and File in Today's Military* (New York: Russell Sage Foundation, 1970), 136. Moskos cites American casualties while on patrol as 67 percent.

3. Moskos, *American Enlisted Man,* 147.

4. Ibid.

5. Ibid., 184.

6. S. L. A. Marshall as quoted by Lt. Col. John G. Fowler, Jr., "Combat Cohesion in Vietnam," *Military Review,* 59, no. 12 (December 1979); Neil Sheehan as quoted in *Time,* 30 May 1969, 27.

7. James A. Raysor, interview by Thomas C. Magedanz, Pierre, S.Dak., 15 December 1985, South Dakota Vietnam Veterans' Oral History Project, VNP-33, Vietnam Veterans Association Inc. and The Robinson Museum, Pierre (hereafter cited as S.Dak. Project). Subsequent quotes by Raysor are from this interview unless otherwise cited.

8. Donald Putnam, interview by author, Green Bay, Wis., 9 December 1989. James Ebert Vietnam Veterans' Oral History Collection, EVP-30, Special Collections, McIntyre Library, University of Wisconsin-Eau Claire (hereafter cited as Ebert Collection). Subsequent quotes by Putnam are from this interview unless otherwise cited.

9. Dan W. Krehbiel, interview by author, Melrose, Wis., 6 April

1984. Ebert Collection, EVP-3. Subsequent quotes by Krehbiel are from this interview unless otherwise cited.

10. Edmund M. Hoban, interview by author, Melrose, Wis., 21 June 1990. Ebert Collection, EVP-38. Subsequent quotes by Hoban are from this interview unless otherwise cited.

11. Paul Boehm, interview by author, Green Bay, Wis., 9 December 1989. Ebert Collection, EVP-31. Subsequent quotes by Boehm are from this interview unless otherwise cited.

12. Phillip E. Yaeger, interview by author, La Crosse, Wis., 25 July 1989. Ebert Collection, EVP-15. Subsequent quotes by Yaeger are from this interview unless otherwise cited.

13. Michael R. Jackson, interview by author, Madison, Wis., 12 October 1989. Ebert Collection, EVP-25. Subsequent quotes by Jackson are from this interview unless otherwise cited.

14. *Life,* December 1966, 43.

15. Gerry H. Barker, interview by author, Melrose, Wis., 6 December 1989. Ebert Collection, EVP-28. Subsequent quotes by Barker are from this interview unless otherwise cited.

16. Moskos, *American Enlisted Man,* 116–17.

17. Willie Williams, interview by author, Madison, Wis., 12 October 1989. Ebert Collection, EVP-26. Subsequent quotes by Williams are from this interview unless otherwise cited.

18. Robert L. Emery, interview by Thomas C. Magedanz, Mission, S.Dak., 18 August 1985. S.Dak. Project, VNP-28. Subsequent quotes by Emery are from this interview unless otherwise cited.

19. Robert H. Moran, Jr., interview by Thomas C. Magedanz, Pierre, S.Dak., 7 August 1985. S.Dak. Project, VNP-26. Subsequent quotes by Moran are from this interview unless otherwise cited.

20. Loren Baritz, *Backfire* (New York: Random House, 1985; Ballantine Books, 1985), 278. See also the Notre Dame survey from Baskir and Strauss, 9.

21. "Social Incidence of Vietnam Casualties," *Armed Forces and Society,* 2 (May 1976). Reprinted in Baskir and Strauss, *Chance and Circumstance,* 9–10.

22. William C. Westmoreland, *A Soldier Reports* (New York: Doubleday, 1976; Dell, 1981), 391–92.

23. Robert Bruce Johnson, interview by author, La Crosse, Wis., 14 June 1990. Ebert Collection, EVP-37. Subsequent quotes by R. Bruce Johnson are from this interview unless otherwise cited.

24. Terry M. Musser, interviews by author, Melrose, Wis., 15 March 1984 and 12 June 1989. Ebert Collection, EVP-11. Subse-

quent quotes by Musser are from these interviews unless otherwise cited.

25. Vernon Janick, interview by author, Coon Valley, Wis., 17 July 1989. Ebert Collection, EVP-13. Subsequent quotes by Janick are from this interview unless otherwise cited.

26. James L. Stanton, Jr., interview by author, Melrose, Wis., 10 January 1990. Ebert Collection, EVP-32. Subsequent quotes by Stanton are from this interview unless otherwise cited.

27. Gerald L. Severson, interviews by author, Melrose, Wis., 2 April 1984 and 21 February 1989. Ebert Collection, EVP-4. Subsequent quotes by Severson are from these interviews unless otherwise cited.

28. Kenneth A. Korkow, interview by Thomas C. Magedanz, Pierre, S.Dak., 7 May 1985. S.Dak. Project, VNP-15. Subsequent quotes by Korkow are from this interview unless otherwise cited.

29. Moskos, *American Enlisted Man,* 161.

30. Michael K. Meil, interview by author, Melrose, Wis., 6 September 1989, Ebert Collection, EVP-21. Subsequent quotes by Meil are from this interview unless otherwise cited.

31. David C. Carlisle, interview by Thomas C. Magedanz and author, Pierre, S.Dak., 22 April 1990. Ebert Collection, EVP-36 and S.Dak. Project, VNP-35. Subsequent quotes by Carlisle are from this interview unless otherwise cited.

32. Thomas Magedanz to author, 29 August 1990.

33. Randall W. Hoelzen, interview by author, La Crosse, Wis., 12 March 1991. Ebert Collection, EVP-41. Subsequent quotes by Hoelzen are from this interview unless otherwise cited.

34. Terry L. Shepardson, interview by author, Melrose, Wis., 26 February 1989. Ebert Collection, EVP-8. Subsequent quotes by Shepardson are from this interview unless otherwise cited.

35. John M. Merrell, interview by author, Melrose, Wis., 1 May 1989. Ebert Collection, EVP-10. Subsequent quotes by Merrell are from this interview unless otherwise cited.

36. Thomas C. Magedanz, interview by Robert M. Hinckey, Pierre, S.Dak., 5 May 1985. S.Dak. Project, VNP-14. Subsequent quotes by Magedanz are from this interview unless otherwise cited.

37. Larry J. Hill, interview by author, Blair, Wis., 14 November 1989. Ebert Collection, EVP-34. Subsequent quotes by Hill are from this interview unless otherwise cited.

38. Moskos, *American Enlisted Man,* 23. As the war progressed, the mood of young adults and the marketing strategy of toy companies seems to have changed. The epitome of this was probably the

sale of a "Beat the Draft" board game released in 1970. The idea behind the game, according to *Games* magazine, was to "move around a Day-Glo board picking up potential deferments, attempting to avoid Sgt. Jones at the Army's Induction Center. Reach the age of 26 and you're home free!" "Call our Bluff," *Games,* August, 1991, 48.

39. Paul T. Meringolo, interview by author, Worcester, Mass., 24 August 1989. Ebert Collection, EVP-20. Subsequent quotes by Meringolo are from this interview unless otherwise cited.

40. Vincent R. Olson, interview by Thomas C. Magedanz, Hyde County, S.Dak., 16 September 1985. S.Dak. Project, VNP-29. Subsequent quotes by Olson are from this interview unless otherwise cited.

41. Richard Ogden, *Green Knight, Red Mourning* (New York: Zebra Books, 1985), 17.

42. Jeffrey Yushta, interview by author, La Crosse, Wis., 2 August 1989. Ebert Collection, EVP-17. Subsequent quotes by Yushta are from this interview unless otherwise cited.

43. Deane L. Johnson, interview by Thomas C. Magedanz, Pierre, S.Dak., 14 May 1985. S.Dak. Project, VNP-16. Subsequent quotes by Johnson are from this interview unless otherwise cited.

44. Baskir and Strauss, *Chance and Circumstance,* 52, 54.

45. Donald D. Trimble, interview by Thomas C. Magedanz, Pierre, S.Dak., 2 October 1985. S.Dak. Project, VNP-30. Subsequent quotes by Trimble are from this interview unless otherwise cited.

46. Glenn R. Miller, interview by Thomas C. Magedanz and author, Pierre, S.Dak., 20 April 1990. Ebert Collection, EVP-35 and S.Dak. Project, VNP-34. Subsequent quotes by Miller are from this interview unless otherwise cited.

47. Gloria Emerson, *Winners and Losers* (New York: Random House, 1972), 51, 59.

48. Baskir and Strauss, *Chance and Circumstance,* 51; see also Thomas C. Thayer, *War Without Fronts: The American Experience in Vietnam* (Boulder, Colo.: Westview Press, 1985), 114. Thayer shows that Marine Corps reservists made up about 6 percent of all marines killed in action (KIA) in Vietnam (816 out of 12,936). Army reservists totaled 2,695 soldiers killed (9 percent of the total of 30,595 servicemen who died in Vietnam due to hostile causes). The National Guard lost 72 KIAs, with the Kentucky National Guard and the town of Bardstown being hit particularly hard. Battery C, 2d Howitzer Battalion, 138th Field Artillery, was called to active duty on 13 May 1968 and sent to Vietnam. Five men from the battery

were killed in an attack launched on Fire Support Base Tomahawk near Phu Bai on 19 June 1969. See Gloria Emerson, *Winners and Losers,* 139–40.

49. John E. Meyer, interview by author, Melrose, Wis., 25 February 1989. Ebert Collection, EVP-9. Subsequent quotes by Meyer are from this interview unless otherwise cited.

50. Baskir and Strauss confirm Meyer's suspicions in *Chance and Circumstance,* 53.

51. Willard Waller, *The Veteran Comes Back* (New York: Dryden Press, 1944), 93–110, 180–82. Reprinted in Charles R. Figley and Seymour Leventman, ed., *Strangers at Home: Vietnam Veterans Since the War* (New York: Praeger, 1980), 45.

52. Dwight N. Reiland, interview by author, Clarion, Iowa, 9 September 1989. Ebert Collection, EVP-22. Subsequent quotes by Reiland are from this interview unless otherwise cited.

53. Baskir and Strauss, *Chance and Circumstance,* 5. During 1965, approximately one-third of the men in the army's twenty-five infantry battalions were draftees. The Marine Corps' fourteen infantry battalions were filled predominantly with volunteers. Statistics on draftee casualties are from Emerson and are reprinted in *Winners and Losers,* 254. The statistics originated with *The Discarded Army: Veterans After Vietnam,* by Paul Starr with James Henry and Raymond Bonner (New York: Charterhouse Books, 1973).

54. Starr, *The Discarded Army,* 8–9. The 70 percent draftee statistic for a 1970 rifle company is in Emerson, *Winners and Losers,* 254–55. Loren Baritz cites a figure of 88 percent for infantry riflemen in *Backfire,* 278.

55. Moskos, *The American Enlisted Man,* 52.

56. *In Pursuit of Equity: Who Serves When Not All Serve?* Report of the National Advisory Commission on Selective Service (February 1967), 17, and Table 5.2, 133.

57. U.S. Department of Defense, Selective Service, "You and the Draft" (Washington: Government Printing Office, 29 March 1967), 5.

58. Baskir and Strauss, *Chance and Circumstance,* 9.

59. *In Pursuit of Equity,* 19.

60. Douglas A. Kurtz, interview by author, Melrose, Wis., 27 September 1989. Ebert Collection, EVP-24. Subsequent quotes by Kurtz are from this interview unless otherwise cited.

61. *In Pursuit of Equity,* 9. The reversal of the draft sequence was announced in *Time,* 10 March 1967.

62. Ibid., 26.

63. Baritz, *Backfire,* 278.

64. Baskir and Strauss, *Chance and Circumstance,* 22.

65. William Harken, interview by author, Waverly, Iowa, 15 August 1989. Ebert Collection, EVP-19. Subsequent quotes by Harken are from this interview unless otherwise cited.

66. Thomas Schultz, interview by author, Sumner, Iowa, 2 March 1984. Ebert Collection, EVP-2. Subsequent quotes by Schultz are from this interview unless otherwise cited.

67. Stephen E. Fredrick, interview by author, Melrose, Wis., 29 February 1984. Ebert Collection, EVP-1. Subsequent quotes by Fredrick are from this interview unless otherwise cited.

68. Baskir and Strauss based their statistics on a comparison of nationwide college enrollment trends between 1965 and 1972. Data for their study came from the *Statistical Abstract of the US, 1973,* Table 203, 130. *Chance and Circumstance,* 29, 32. The New York examples are from *In Pursuit of Equity,* 27, 98.

69. Thomas C. Birhanzel, interview by Deane Johnson, Pierre, S.Dak., 27 April 1985. S.Dak. Project, VNP-12. Subsequent quotes by Birhanzel are from this interview unless otherwise cited.

70. Unpublished manuscript of personal Vietnam reflections and experiences. Original in the private collection of Thomas Schultz, Sumner, Iowa, 3.

71. Jon A. Neely, interview by author, Rochester, Pa., 12 January 1990. Ebert Collection, EVP-33. Subsequent quotes by Neely are from this interview unless otherwise cited.

72. Waller, *The Veteran,* reprinted in Figley and Leventman, *Strangers at Home,* 43.

Chapter 2

1. Leonard Dutcher to his parents, 7 October 1966.

2. "You'll Need to Know This if You're in Vietnam," *Newsweek,* 11 April 1966, 33.

3. Gwynne Dyer, *War* (New York: Crown, 1985), 109–10.

4. Thomas Magedanz to his parents, 16 February 1969, private collection of Thomas Magedanz, Pierre, S.Dak.

5. First Lieutenant Dennis R. Owczarski to Walter Fredrick, Jr., 23 September 1967, private collection of Stephen Fredrick, Melrose, Wis.

6. Jeffrey Beatty to his mother, 20 December 1965, private collection of Mrs. Corrine Hovre-Hill, Blair, Wis.

7. Peter Barnes, *Pawns: The Plight of the Citizen Soldier* (New York: Knopf, 1972), 86.

8. Stephen Fredrick to his parents, 2 October 1967.

9. Thomas Magedanz to his parents, 28 February 1969.

10. Stephen Fredrick to his parents, 2 October 1967.

11. Dyer, *War,* 112.

12. Larry Iwasko to his mother, 21 September 1967, private collection of Mrs. Dorothy Iwasko, Elmhurst, Ill.

13. Thomas Magedanz, unpublished reflections on Vietnam, June 1983. Hereafter referred to as Magedanz Reflections.

14. Ibid.

15. After World War II, sociologist Eli Ginzburg did a study on the correlation of socioeconomic and educational backgrounds and its relation to combat performance. His study showed that soldiers with some college education were five times more likely to perform well in combat than high school dropouts, and men who finished high school were three times more likely to perform better than those without a high school education. Based on his study the military instituted a series of aptitude tests and rated applicants' scores in one of five categories. The lowest of the AFQT categories is Category V, which automatically disqualifies the person from military service. Categories I, II, and III were clearly acceptable. The question came with Category IV.

During the Vietnam War, Defense Secretary Robert S. McNamara instituted Project 100,000, which sought to use the military as a mechanism for social engineering and the rehabilitation of the undereducated and disadvantaged. Under this program, men in Category IV who had previously been classified as substandard (the tenth to thirteenth percentile) were accepted for military training. Between 1966 and 1968 this translated into 240,000 substandard recruits, 41 percent of whom were black and half of whom had IQs below 85. Not only did the program not remediate its members, but during the Vietnam era men with the poorest educational background had the highest likelihood of serving in combat. Baskir and Strauss rightly point out that these men indirectly kept the better-educated and privileged draft-age males safe and gave President Johnson more draftable people without the undesirable alternative of mobilizing reserves or conscripting deferred persons. Baskir and Strauss, *Chance and Circumstance,* 122–26.

16. Michael Roberts, interview by author, 27 September 1989,

Webster City, Iowa. Ebert Collection, EVP-27. Subsequent quotes by Roberts are from this interview unless otherwise cited.

17. Terry Tople, interview by Thomas C. Magedanz, Fort Pierre, S.Dak., 28 March 1985. S.Dak. Project, VNP-8. Subsequent quotes by Tople are from this interview unless otherwise cited.

18. Stephen Fredrick to his parents, 9 October 1967.

19. Ibid., 30 October 1967.

20. Ibid., 6 November 1967.

21. Eddie P. Austin, personal diary, 29 August 1966 and 6 November 1966. Photocopy of the original in author's personal collection.

22. Thomas Magedanz wrote at the end of his training, "Well, only 1½ weeks left here. We are supposed to graduate April 17 if everything goes right. That day I'm going to buy two or three boxes of candy and eat it all." Thomas Magedanz to his parents, 6 April 1969.

23. Maj. Gen. John E. Kelly, commander, 2d Armored Division, Fort Hood, Tex., to Mrs. Corrine Hovre, 23 December 1965, private collection of Mrs. Corrine Hovre-Hill, Blair, Wis.

24. Paul Gerrits, interview by author, Green Bay, Wis., 10 December 1989. Ebert Collection, EVP-29. All subsequent quotes by Gerrits are from this interview unless otherwise cited.

Chapter 3

1. Leonard Dutcher to his parents, 17 January 1967.

2. Moskos, *American Enlisted Man,* 56–57.

3. Thomas Magedanz to George "Doc" Connor, 17 May 1969. Original in private collection of Tom Magedanz, Pierre, S.Dak., 1.

4. Tim O'Brien, *If I Die in a Combat Zone* (New York: Bantam Doubleday Dell, 1969; Laurel Edition, 1987), 58.

5. Dyer, *War,* 103.

6. Thomas Magedanz, notes from conversations with author, 22 April 1990, Pierre, S.Dak.

7. Stephen Fredrick to his parents, 22 January 1968. Originals of each style mentioned are in private collection of Stephen Fredrick, Melrose, Wis.

8. Thomas Magedanz, caption to photograph in personal scrapbook, October 1970.

9. Stephen Fredrick to his parents, 25 November 1967.

10. Richard Holmes, *Acts of War: The Behavior of Men in Battle* (New York: Macmillian Inc., 1986; Free Press, 1989), 42.

11. Bryan Good, interview by author, Elroy, Wis., 5 March 1991. Ebert Collection, EVP-40. Subsequent quotes by Good are from this interview unless otherwise cited.

12. Norman Cousins as quoted in an essay by Jack Freitag titled "Lessons of 'Nam," printed in the La Crosse *Tribune* (date unknown). Copy in private papers of Jack Freitag, La Crosse, Wis.

13. Jack Freitag, interview by author, La Crosse, Wis., 24 July 1989. Ebert Collection, EVP-14. Subsequent quotes by Freitag are from this interview unless otherwise cited.

14. Wayne R. Eisenhart, "You Can't Hack It Little Girl: A Discussion of the Covert Psychological Agenda of Modern Combat Training," *Journal of Social Issues,* 31, no. 4 (Fall 1975): 18.

15. *Your Tour in Vietnam,* AFIF 181, 16mm (Department of Defense, Armed Forces Information Service, 1970). Also, *Know Your Enemy: Viet Cong,* AFIF 172, 16mm (Department of Defense, Armed Forces Information Service, 1970).

16. Rick Atkinson, *The Long Gray Line: The American Journey of West Point's Class of 1966* (Boston: Houghton Mifflin, 1989), 135.

17. Jeffrey L. Beatty to his mother, 8 April 1966.

18. "Armed Forces Quick Kill," *Time,* 14 July 1967, 16.

19. Stephen Fredrick to his parents, 8 January 1968.

20. Leonard Dutcher to his parents, 1 August 1967.

21. Ibid., 4 June 1966.

22. Thomas C. Magedanz to his parents, 7 June 1969.

23. Layne Anderson, interview by author, Blair, Wis., 26 June 1989. Ebert Collection, EVP-12. All subsequent quotes by Anderson are from this interview unless otherwise cited.

24. Andrew F. Krepinevich, Jr., *The Army and Vietnam* (Baltimore: Johns Hopkins University Press, 1986), 5.

25. Atkinson, *Long Gray Line,* 129.

26. Thomas Magedanz to his parents, 3 May 1969.

27. Stephen Fredrick to his parents, 2 May 1968.

28. Ibid., 22 January 1968. Paul Striepe died 3 January 1968.

29. Mark Lane, *Conversations With Americans* (New York: Simon and Schuster, 1970).

30. Moskos, *American Enlisted Man,* 75.

31. Eugene B. Sledge, *With the Old Breed at Peleliu and Okinawa* (Novato, Calif.: Presidio Press, 1981), 41.

Chapter 4

1. Leonard Dutcher to his parents, 3 October 1967.

2. Thomas L. Roubideaux, interview by Thomas C. Magedanz, Pierre, S.Dak., 20 June 1985. S.Dak. Project, VNP-19. Subsequent quotes by Roubideaux are from this interview unless otherwise cited.

3. Several popular antiwar posters of the day used this theme.

4. Stephen T. Banko III, "The Search for the Living Stream: Vietnam Veterans as Casualties of Peace," a speech delivered at the Nicholas School, Buffalo, N.Y., 12 November 1984, *Vital Speeches of the Day* (1 January 1985), 167.

5. Lieutenant Colonel Kenneth R. Pierce, "The Battle of the Ia Drang Valley," *Military Review,* 69, no. 1 (January 1989): 89–90.

6. Atkinson, *Long Gray Line,* 202–203. Also, Shelby L. Stanton, *The Rise and Fall of an American Army* (Novato, Calif.: Presidio Press, 1985; New York: Dell 1986), 74–75. Additional information on the training and mobilization of the 9th Infantry Division comes from a manuscript study prepared by the Center of Military History, Washington, D.C., entitled *Army Systems of Basic Training, 1919–1974,* 22–24.

7. Stanton, *Rise and Fall,* 186.

8. Shelby L. Stanton, *Vietnam Order of Battle* (New York: Galahad Books, 1986), 333.

9. Ibid., 260–61.

10. Thomas C. Magedanz to his parents, 20 July 1969.

11. Stanton, *Rise and Fall,* 65.

12. Jeffrey L. Beatty to his mother, 6 March 1966.

13. For a more detailed account of the voyage of the 1st Brigade, 1st Cavalry Division, to Vietnam in 1965 on the USNS *Geiger,* see Col. Kenneth D. Mertel, *Year of the Horse—Vietnam* (New York: Exposition Press, 1968; Bantam Doubleday, 1990), 28–41.

14. Jerry Vetterkind, interview by author, Strum, Wis. VHS videocassette recording of slides with narrative by the subject, 17 April 1991, private collection of author.

15. Mertel, *Year of the Horse,* 31.

16. Jeffrey L. Beatty to his mother, 8 August 1966.

17. Leonard Dutcher to his parents, 24 October 1967.

18. Stephen Fredrick to his parents, 19 August 1968.

19. Holmes, *Acts of War,* 86.

20. Guenter Lewy, *America in Vietnam* (New York: Oxford Univ. Press, 1978), 156, 158.

21. Baskir and Strauss, *Chance and Circumstance,* 13, 113–14.

22. Larry Gates, interview by Thomas C. Magedanz, Pierre, S.Dak., 2 March 1985. S.Dak. Project, VNP-1. All subsequent quotes by Gates are from this interview unless otherwise cited.

23. O'Brien, *If I Die,* 73.

24. Jeffrey L. Beatty to his mother, 6 and 27 March 1966.

25. Stephen Fredrick to his parents, 19 August 1968.

26. Thomas Schultz, unpublished manuscript, 1.

27. Keith Walker, *A Piece of My Heart* (Novato, Calif.: Presidio Press, 1985; New York: Ballantine Books, 1987), 299.

28. Charles R. Anderson, *The Grunts* (Novato, Calif.: Presidio Press, 1976; New York: Berkley Books, 1976), 15.

Chapter 5

1. Leonard Dutcher to his parents, 26 October 1967.

2. Ibid.

3. Charles Gadd, *Line Doggie* (Novato, Calif.: Presidio Press, 1987; New York: Pocket Books, 1989), 19.

4. Gary McKay, *In Good Company: One Australian's War in Vietnam* (Sydney, Aus.: Allen and Unwin, 1987), 102.

5. Ibid., 72.

6. Stuart A. Herrington, *Silence Was a Weapon: The Vietnam War in the Villages* (Novato, Calif.: Presidio Press, 1982; New York: Ivy Books, 1987), 254.

7. Josh Cruze, as quoted in Kim Willenson, *The Bad War* (New York: New American Library, 1987), 6.

8. Moskos, *American Enlisted Man,* 98.

9. *Your Tour in Vietnam,* 16mm motion picture. The conditions of poverty encountered in Vietnam were consistent with those found in most of the Third World and resulted only in part from the war itself. Most men tried to maintain good relations with the civilians they encountered, even if it was only joking around with the little children or the soda girls. When Tom Magedanz served with the Peace Corps in the Philippines, he encountered similar squalor and noted that a few Peace Corps volunteers actually became abusive and had to be sent home. (Tom Magedanz to the author, 19 July 1990.)

10. Stanton, *Vietnam Order of Battle,* 197. One additional sub-depot of the 90th Replacement Battalion, called Camp Alpha, was located at Saigon's Ton Son Nhut Airport.

11. Atkinson, *Long Gray Line,* 291.

12. Carl D. Rogers, tape-recorded message, 12 March 1966. Reprinted in *Vietnam Voices,* John Clark Pratt, ed. (New York: Viking Penguin Books, 1984), 221–22.

13. Moskos, *American Enlisted Man,* 147.

14. Roger Kaplan, "Army Unit Cohesion in Vietnam: A Bum Rap," *Parameters,* 17, no. 3 (September 1987): 60.

15. The average four-day wait for processing is a rough estimate based on interviews conducted by the author.

16. Robert Keeling, interview by author, Clarion, Iowa, 9 September 1989. Ebert Collection, EVP-23. All subsequent quotes by Keeling are from this interview unless otherwise cited.

17. James McDonough, *Platoon Leader* (Novato, Calif.: Presidio Press, 1985; New York: Bantam Books, 1985), 15.

18. Thomas Magedanz to author, 29 August 1990.

19. Lewy, *America in Vietnam,* 147–48. However, Thayer in *War Without Fronts,* 115–16, indicates that the total number of American deaths in Quang Tri Province was slightly higher than those for Quang Nam Province, but his chart excludes the year 1965, which saw numerous operations in the Da Nang area.

20. Thayer, *War Without Fronts,* 115–16; see also Table 11.10.

21. In 1969, Tay Ninh Province, on the Cambodian border north and west of Saigon, represented the locale with the highest American death toll. Operating in Tay Ninh Province was as dangerous overall as serving in most areas of Military Region 1, and was statistically more dangerous than serving in the Central Highlands of Military Region 2. Thayer, *War Without Fronts,* 115, and Lewy, *America in Vietnam,* 147.

22. Thayer, *War Without Fronts,* 13.

23. Ibid., 13, 19.

24. Francis Whitebird, interview by Thomas C. Magedanz, Pierre, S.Dak, 31 January and 18 March 1985. S.Dak. Project, VNP-4. All subsequent quotes by Whitebird are from this interview unless otherwise cited.

25. Thomas Magedanz to his parents, 1 August 1969.

26. The 9th Infantry Division's base camp was built on a platform of 17 million yards of dredged material 2.8 meters above the Kinh Xang Canal just west of My Tho. It included a 54-acre basin for LSTs, a 1,500-foot airstrip, 21,000 square yards of maintenance apron with 174 helicopter revetments, and 5 large hangars. There was also a 351,000-gallon fuel storage area with 24 refueling points. Some 12,500 men could be housed in the base area. The base camp was self-contained, with a 6,000-kilowatt hardened power plant,

27,000-gallon per hour water purification plant, a protected Medical Unit Self-Contained Transportable (MUST), and 13.5 miles of cement-stabilized roadways. Officially completed 15 June 1969 at a cost of $8 million, the base was named Dong Tam, meaning "Friendship." Lieutenant General Julian J. Ewell and Maj. Gen. Ira A. Hunt, *Sharpening the Combat Edge: The Use of Analysis to Reinforce Military Judgment,* Vietnam Studies (Washington, D.C.: Government Printing Office, 1974), 72, 74.

27. Gary Thorson to Prof. Edward Peterson, Wisconsin State University River Falls, January 1969, 1.

28. Glen Olstad, interview by author, La Crosse, Wis., 8 August 1989. Ebert Collection, EVP-18. All subsequent quotes by Olstad are from this interview unless otherwise cited.

29. Thomas Schultz, unpublished manuscript, 4.

30. Thomas Magedanz to his parents, 1 August 1969.

Chapter 6

1. Leonard Dutcher to his parents, 30 October 1967.

2. Gadd, *Line Doggie,* 16. Boot and newbie were terms commonly applied to Marine Corps replacements. Greenie, cherry, FNG, turtle, and other names were indiscriminantly used by all services.

3. Johnnie Clark, *Guns Up!* (New York: Ballantine Books, 1984), 9.

4. Dennis G. Foell, interview by Thomas C. Magedanz, Pierre, S.Dak., 28 February 1985. S.Dak. Project, VNP-6. Subsequent quotes by Foell are from this interview unless otherwise cited.

5. Thomas Schultz, unpublished manuscript of first days in Vietnam. Original in writer's possession.

6. O'Brien, *If I Die,* 84.

7. Roger Hoffman, "Nicknames," *New York Times Magazine* (12 May 1985): 58.

8. Magedanz Reflections, June 1983.

9. The M60's 7.62mm ammunition weighed more per round than the M16's 5.56mm ammunition. Tim O'Brien, "The Things They Carried," *Esquire* (August 1968): 78.

10. John D. Bergen, *Military Communications: A Test for Technology,* The U.S. Army in Vietnam (Washington, D.C.: Center of Military History, 1986), 253–54.

11. Ibid.

12. Robert Bonesteel, interview by author, Eau Claire, Wis., 16 June 1992. Ebert Collection, EVP-42. Subsequent quotes by Bonesteel are from this interview unless otherwise cited.

13. Holmes, *Acts of War,* 26.

14. Clark, *Guns Up!,* 49.

15. Statement made by Maj. Gen. Edwin B. Wheeler, chief of staff for Headquarters, Marine Corps, as quoted in Graham A. Cosmas and Lt. Col. Terrence P. Murray, *U.S. Marines in Vietnam: Vietnamization and Redeployment 1970–1971* (Washington D.C.: U.S. Marine Corps History and Museums Division, 1986), 352. Fifty to 60 percent of all marines had a two-year enlistment; thus they were trained, served in Vietnam, and were discharged very rapidly. Ibid.

16. Moskos, *American Enlisted Man,* 154.

17. Leonard Dutcher to his parents, 16 February 1968.

18. Ibid., 17 and 19 February 1968.

19. Ibid., 29 March 1968.

20. Thayer, *War Without Fronts,* Table 11.6, 113.

21. Ibid., 114, 118–19. Part of the increased odds afforded by survival were, as Thayer points out, the result of a learning curve that each new arrival had to repeat. But the practice of removing old-timers from the field, combined with the six-month tour in the field for most junior officers, also had an impact.

22. Statistics are from "Department of Defense Casualty Figures for South East Asia," November 1986, 10. See also, Lt. Col. Charles R. Shrader, *Amicicide: The Problem of Friendly Fire in Modern War* (Fort Leavenworth, Kans.: U.S. Army Command and General Staff College, December 1982), xi–xii.

23. Data on the Korean War comes from Frank A. Reister, *Effects of Type of Operation and Tactical Action on Major Unit Casualty and Morbidity Experience—Korean War* (Washington, D.C., May 1969), tables 18 and 19. Work cited in Shrader, *Amicicide,* xi and 111–12.

24. Jeffrey Beatty to his mother, 11 August 1966.

Chapter 7

1. Leonard Dutcher to his parents, 7 November 1967.

2. John Dollard, *Fear in Battle* (Washington, D.C.: Infantry Journal, 1944), as quoted in Holmes, *Acts of War,* 141.

3. Sledge, *With the Old Breed,* 19.

4. Magedanz Reflections, 2 June 1983, 18.

5. Holmes, *Acts of War,* 140.

6. Austin diary, 1 February 1967. Photocopy in private collection of Jack Freitag.

7. John Sack, *"M"* (New York: Esquire, 1966; Avon, 1985), 156.

8. Dollard, as quoted in Holmes, *Acts of War,* 205, 207.

9. Thayer, *War Without Fronts,* 45; see also Table 5.1, 49.

10. CIA notes from National Security Study Memorandum 1, "The Situation in Vietnam—CIA Studies for a National Security Study Memorandum," noted that of the almost two million allied small-unit operations conducted in Vietnam during the years 1967 and 1968, less than 2 percent resulted in contact with the enemy. Lewy, *America in Vietnam,* 83.

11. Thomas Schultz, unpublished memoir, 4.

12. Magedanz Reflections, 1972, 7.

13. Robert Steenlage, interview by author, Galesville, Wis., 15 August 1990. Ebert Collection, EVP-39. Subsequent quotes by Steenlage are from this interview unless otherwise cited.

Chapter 8

1. Leonard Dutcher to his parents, 5 December 1967.

2. Ambrose Bierce, "Horseman in the Sky," reprinted in *Ambrose Bierce's Civil War* (Washington, D.C.: Gateway Regnery, 1986), 78.

3. The column by Ernie Pyle in *Stars and Stripes* was read aloud during Larry Gates's interview with Thomas Magedanz. The original source of the passage is unknown.

4. A study of American soldiers in Italy in 1944 established that 31 percent averaged less than four hours of sleep a night and another 56 percent averaged less than six hours. Lieutenant Colonel H. L. Thompson as quoted in Holmes, *Acts of War,* 124.

5. Ron Flesch, *Redwood Delta* (New York: Berkley Books, 1988), 135.

6. Tom Magedanz recalled the following C-ration meals as being standard fare during his tour in 1969–70: turkey loaf, boned turkey, chicken and noodles, spaghetti with ground meat, beans and meatballs, beef slices with potatoes and gravy, beef with spiced sauce, chopped ham and eggs, ham and lima beans, pork slices with juices, canned beefsteak, sliced ham, and beans and franks. It seemed to Magedanz that there were usually a dozen varieties of meals and that occasionally new offerings would appear. Veterans serving early in the war could recall only about six different meals.

7. The creation of the mad minute was attributed to Lt. Col. Hal Moore, commander of the 1st Battalion, 7th Cavalry, at LZ X-Ray during the Ia Drang Valley campaign in the fall of 1965. See Lt. Gen. Harold G. Moore and Joseph L. Galloway, *We Were Soldiers Once and Young* (New York: Random House, 1992), 191.

8. Advertisement in *Time,* June 1967.

9. Soldiers in the 1st Cavalry Division who dyed their fatigues with the unit patches and insignia still attached found them to come out looking black green. According to J. D. Coleman, this gave division headquarters the idea for "subdued" patches and insignia that would be more difficult to see in the jungle. According to Coleman, the 1st Cavalry had subdued patches manufactured in Japan, and its soldiers were the first to wear them in Vietnam. The idea was adopted by other units and eventually came into practice armywide during the Vietnam War. J. D. Coleman, *Pleiku: The Dawn of Helicopter Warfare in Vietnam* (New York: St. Martin's Press, 1988), 42.

Some units did not surrender their traditional colored insignia until late in the war. Sergeant Steve Fredrick, for example, was adamant that the unit he served with, the 3d Battalion, 187th Infantry Regiment of the 101st Airborne, was still wearing the colored "Screaming Eagle" insignia in 1969 when he rotated homed.

10. Clark, *Guns Up!,* 57.

11. Magedanz Reflections, 1971, 1.

12. David Hansen, interview by Thomas C. Magedanz, Pierre, S.Dak., 11 April 1985. S.Dak. Project,VNP-10. Subsequent quotes by Hansen are from this interview unless otherwise cited.

13. Leonard Dutcher to his parents, 21 November 1967.

14. Atkinson, *Long Gray Line,* 263.

15. O'Brien, "Things They Carried," *Esquire,* 81.

16. Stephen Fredrick to his parents, 15 September 1968.

17. Stanley Goff and Robert Sanders with Clark Smith, *Brothers: Black Soldiers in the Nam* (Novato, Calif: Presidio Press, 1982; New York: Berkley Books, 1985), 145.

18. Gadd, *Line Doggie,* 91. Bernard Fall, *Last Reflections on a War* (New York: Doubleday, 1967), 245. The marine officer confided to Fall, "Most of us are wearing prophylactics on patrol to prevent that because it is painful as hell." Stories of the notorious "tree leech" were in many cases most likely false, a way in which old-timers entertained themselves at the expense of new replacements. Convincing a cherry to wear a rubber into the bush on his first operation was considered quite a coup. However, Bernard Fall was not a newcomer to Vietnam, and Richard MacLeod was sharing his

story with Matthew Brennan, who had served in the same unit as MacLeod. See Matthew Brennan, ed., *Headhunters: Stories from the 1st Squadron, 9th Cavalry in Vietnam, 1965–1971* (Novato, Calif.: Presidio Press, 1987), 230–31. S. L. A. Marshall recounted a similar incident in *Ambush* (Nashville: Battery Press, 1983; New York: Jove, 1988), 214. Whether any or all of the "leech entrenching" stories are true is left to the reader to decide.

19. Magedanz Reflections, 1974, 10.

20. Anderson, *The Grunts*, 78–79, and Jack Estes, *A Field of Innocence* (New York: Warner Books, 1987), 56.

21. Dr. Joseph Sperrazza (known as the father of penetrating wound analysis) maintained in 1980 that casualties could be reduced about 20 percent by wearing flak jackets. He cited a study done during the Vietnam War in which army experts using wound analysis data from 1967–69 found that among eight thousand battle casualties, about 80 percent of American deaths resulted from wounds to the head, neck, and chest. *Chicago Tribune* Sunday Edition, Section 5 (6 November 1988): 15.

Use of flak jackets among army units was optional because of studies such as those done by generals Ira A. Hunt and Julian J. Ewell, which determined that: "Some people derived considerable psychological assurance from them . . ." However, "wound data and 'flak jacket saves' " demonstrated that the 9th Infantry Division was not "saving many casualties with their use. Thus the 9th Division made their use optional."

Some experts felt that the better mobility gained by not wearing the jackets resulted in fewer casualties, but this was never established. The common practice was to give jackets to the point man and others up front and rotate those positions—or pass the jackets—to hold down fatigue. Ewell and Hunt, *Sharpening the Combat Edge*, 90–91.

22. Anderson, *The Grunts*, 54.

23. Magedanz Reflections, 1972, 2.

24. Thomas Magedanz to his parents, 8 August 1969. See also Magedanz Reflections, 1974, 11.

25. Clark, *Guns Up!*, 146.

26. Goff, Sanders, and Smith, *Brothers*, 159.

27. Magedanz Reflections, 1972, 2.

28. Anderson, *The Grunts*, 40.

Chapter 9

1. Leonard Dutcher to his parents, 9 January 1968. Dutcher's best friend was killed by an antipersonnel mine encountered while moving up a ridgeline. The platoon's new lieutenant ignored Sergeant Dutcher's desire to stand off from the hill until morning. The men moved as carefully as possible, but they were tired and vigilance dropped off. Dutcher's friend the machine gunner sat down on a "bouncing betty," which killed him. The platoon RTO, Paul Meringolo, recalled how the men, and particularly Sergeant Dutcher, were not angered at the Viet Cong, however, so much as they were "enraged at the platoon leader for being so irresponsible having the platoon come up and secure the area as opposed to waiting as he had hoped we would. Dutcher was yelling at the platoon leader in various terms and he had to be actually restrained by the other guys from really assaulting the platoon leader."

2. Between 1965 and the end of 1968, only three hundred out of more than eight thousand enemy attacks were at or above the battalion level. Later in the war, large-scale enemy assaults became even less common. From 1969 until 1972, the number of enemy battalion-sized attacks dropped to only forty-nine and did not increase again until the Communist Easter Offensive of 1972—after most American ground forces had been withdrawn. See Thayer, *War Without Fronts*, 44.

3. In a survey of 2,845 legionnaires who served in Southeast Asia compiled for *American Legion Magazine* (December 1988), 19 percent responded that they had experienced high levels of combat, 38 percent rated their combat experience as moderate, and 43 percent rated their experience as low.

A senate committee found—using techniques developed by the Center for Research Policy—that of 1,176 Vietnam veterans surveyed, 30 percent reported heavy exposure to combat, 38 percent rated their exposure as moderate, and 31 percent felt that their exposure was light. Senate Committee on Veterans Affairs, "Myths and Realities: A study of attitudes toward Vietnam Era Veterans," Compiled by the Veterans Administration (Washington, D.C.: July 1980).

4. Marshall, *Ambush,* 136.

5. Raphael G. "Ray" Leanna, interview by Thomas C. Magedanz, Hughes County, S.Dak., 27 June 1985, S.Dak. Project, VNP-20. All subsequent quotes by Leanna are from this interview unless otherwise cited.

6. Lewy, *America in Vietnam,* 83.

7. Thayer, *War Without Fronts,* 91.

8. As quoted, ibid.

9. Dale Bertsch, interview by Thomas C. Magedanz, Pierre, S.Dak., 11 June 1985. S.Dak. Project, VNP-18. Subsequent quotes by Bertsch are from this interview unless otherwise cited.

10. Magedanz Reflections, 1 June 1983, 15.

11. Austin diary, 9 November 1966.

12. Lewy, *America in Vietnam,* 309.

13. Krepinevich, *Army and Vietnam,* 201.

14. Capt. Francis J. West, Jr., *Small Unit Actions in Vietnam: Summer 1966* (Washington, D.C.: Marine Corps History and Museums Division, 1967), 3, 7.

15. Magedanz Reflections, 23 May 1983, 16.

16. Combined Intelligence Center, Vietnam, *What a Platoon Leader Should Know about the Enemy's Jungle Tactics* (U S. Military Assistance Command, Vietnam, 1967), 45.

17. West, *Small Unit Actions,* 6.

18. *What a Platoon Leader Should Know,* 23, 25.

19. Department of the Navy, USMC, *Professional Knowledge Gained From Operational Experience in Vietnam. Special Issue: Mines and Boobytraps,* 1969-393-899/S 7102 (Washington, D.C.: Government Printing Office, May-June 1969), 45.

20. Ibid., 3.

21. Donn A. Starry, *Mounted Combat in Vietnam,* Vietnam Studies (Washington, D.C.: Department of the Army, 1978), 79.

22. Starry, *Mounted Combat,* 79.

23. Lewy, *America in Vietnam,* 101.

24. Cosmas and Murray, *Vietnamization and Redeployment,* 257–58.

25. Department of the Army, *Boobytraps,* FM 5-31 (Washington, D.C.: Government Printing Office, 14 September 1965).

26. Flesch, *Redwood Delta,* 81.

27. O'Brien, *If I Die,* 126.

28. Ibid., 125.

29. Anderson, *The Grunts,* 162.

30. O'Brien, *If I Die,* 122.

31. Austin diary, 10 November 1966.

32. Magedanz interview and Reflections, 17 August 1983, 26.

33. Holmes, *Acts of War,* 210.

34. *What a Platoon Leader Should Know,* 5.

35. Ibid., 15. See also Lt. Col. Albert Garland, ed., *Infantry in*

Vietnam: Small Unit Actions in the Early Days: 1965–66 (Nashville: Battery Press, 1982; New York: Jove, 1985), 71.

36. Ibid., 7, 15.

37. Marshall, *Ambush,* 138, 148–49.

38. Charles R. Smith, *U.S. Marines in Vietnam: High Mobility and Stand-down 1969* (Washington, D.C.: Marine Corps History and Museums Division, 1988), 195.

39. Holmes, *Acts of War,* 210.

40. Thayer, *War Without Fronts,* 47. (Statistic is based on 15,000 incidents per year, 40 per day.)

41. Ibid.

42. The 1st Platoon took the bulk of the initial assault wave and was forced from its defensive position on the company's perimeter. When the lieutenant in command of the platoon fell back, only five members of the platoon could initially be found. Eventually others turned up, but Sergeant Williams estimated that about one-third of the company was killed or wounded, and many of those casualties were concentrated in the portion of his platoon that remained within the perimeter that evening. See Garland, *Infantry in Vietnam,* 156.

Chapter 10

1. Leonard Dutcher to his parents, 12 December 1967.

2. Stephen Fredrick to his parents, 23 September 1968.

3. Ward Just, *To What End: Report From Vietnam* (Boston: Houghton Mifflin, 1968), 71.

4. Richard Sexton, reprinted in *Vietnam Voices,* 212.

5. Anderson, *The Grunts,* 158.

6. Flesch, *Redwood Delta,* 15.

7. McDonough, *Platoon Leader,* 15.

8. Stephen Fredrick, "Patrol," *The Castle* (Waverly, Iowa: Wartburg College, Autumn 1969), 14.

9. Stephen Fredrick to his parents, September 1968.

10. Holmes, *Acts of War,* 218.

11. Paul Fussell, *Wartime: Understanding and Behavior in the Second World War* (New York: Oxford Univ. Press, 1989), 282.

12. Stephen Fredrick to his father, 26 December 1968.

13. David Sartori to Prof. Edward M. Peterson, 23 January 1969. Original in the Special Collections, McIntyre Library, University of Wisconsin-Eau Claire.

14. Pfc. Dan Evans, "A Grunt—Waits, Watches and Sometimes Dies," *Pacific Stars and Stripes*, 25 February 1971, 2.

15. David Sartori to Prof. Edward M. Peterson, 23 January 1969, 4.

16. U.S. Department of Defense, *U.S. Casualties in Southeast Asia: Statistics as of November 11, 1986* (Washington, D.C.: Government Printing Office, 1986), 10.

17. Dollard, *Fear in Battle,* 12, 18.

18. Jeffrey Beatty to his mother, 17 November 1966; see also U.S. Army Record of Personal Effects for Jeffrey Beatty, RA 17 738 701, 30 March 1967, 1.

19. Moskos, *American Enlisted Man,* 142–43; see also Charles Moskos, "The Combat Soldier in Vietnam," *Journal of Social Issues,* 31, no. 4 (Fall 1975): 32.

20. Dr. Martin Luther King as quoted in Marvin E. Gettleman, Jane Franklin, Marilyn Young, and H. Bruce Franklin, *Vietnam and America: A Documented History* (New York: Grove Press, 1985), 311.

21. Fussell, *Wartime,* 141.

22. Michael Lanning, *Vietnam, 1969–1970: A Company Commander's Journal* (New York: Ivy Books, 1988), 30.

23. Ibid.

24. Fussell, *Wartime,* 140.

25. Just, *To What End,* 26–27.

26. Ibid., 29.

27. Baritz, *Backfire,* 171.

28. Austin diary, 12 December 1966.

29. Ogden, *Green Knight, Red Mourning,* 275.

Chapter 11

1. Leonard Dutcher to his parents, 29 March 1968.

2. Paul Meringolo to Mrs. Betty Ronke, 18 October 1988.

3. Anderson, *The Grunts,* 38.

4. Matthew Brennan, *Brennan's War: Vietnam 1965–1969* (Novato, Calif.: Presidio Press, 1985; New York: Pocket Books, 1985), 32.

5. The 5,260 is derived from data in tables 11.12 and 11.11, in Thayer, *War Without Fronts,* 117–18. The other figures are from pages 115 and 119.

6. A more detailed account of this incident is found in Brennan, *Headhunters,* 25–28.

7. As contacts dropped in 1968, the 9th Division's field commanders felt that the preparation of each LZ alerted the enemy and gave him time to evade. The division abandoned preparatory fires and found that the tactic worked successfully. Gunships instead were moved outside LZs to engage escaping enemy soldiers. See Ewell and Hunt, *Sharpening the Combat Edge,* 92–93.

8. Leonard Dutcher to his parents, 10 November 1967.

9. Magedanz Reflections, 1972, 2.

10. Stanton, *Order of Battle,* 8.

11. Ibid., 9, 14.

12. The enemy had agents and informants who worked themselves into positions of power in the South Vietnamese government and military. According to military analyst Guenter Lewy, "The work of these agents was simplified by the extreme carelessness which for a long time characterized the planning and preparation of large American operations." Lewy, *America in Vietnam,* 61, 64.

13. John D. Bergen, *Military Communications: A Test for Technology,* U.S. Army in Vietnam (Washington, D.C.: Center of Military History, 1986), 403.

14. Krepinevich, *Army and Vietnam,* 201; Lewy, *America in Vietnam,* 99.

15. Lewy, *America in Vietnam,* 100.

16. Thayer, *War Without Fronts,* 79.

17. Marvin E. Gettleman, Jane Franklin, Marylin Young, and Bruce Franklin, ed., *Vietnam and America: A Documented History* (New York: Grove Press, Inc., 1985), 461.

18. Thayer, *War Without Fronts,* 83–84.

19. CS gas derived its name from the initials of its inventors: B. B. Corson and R. W. Stoughton. By 1969, 13.7 million pounds of CS gas had been used in Vietnam. The United States had a stronger gas called DM that was removed from use in Vietnam because it caused some fatalities. See Lewy, *America in Vietnam,* 248–49, 252.

20. Magedanz Reflections, 1972, 6.

21. Lewy, *America in Vietnam,* 77.

22. MACV Directive 381–21, 26 December 1967, Tab B to Appendix 1, Annex A, as quoted ibid., 78.

23. Ibid., 79.

24. Ibid., 75, 78.

25. Stanton, *Rise and Fall,* 259.

26. Gadd, *Line Doggie,* 220.

27. Just, *To What End,* 72.

28. Lewy, *America in Vietnam,* 81.

29. Thayer, *War Without Fronts,* 102.

30. Lewy, *America in Vietnam,* 84.

31. Thayer, *War Without Fronts,* 104, 107. The largest concentration of enemy KIAs, 35 percent, was in I Corps (Military Region 1). Regions 3 and 4 accounted for another 20 percent each.

32. Lewy, *America in Vietnam,* 68.

Chapter 12

1. Leonard Dutcher to his parents, 3 April 1968.

2. John W. Dower, *War Without Mercy: Race and Power in the Pacific War* (New York: Pantheon Books, 1986), 12.

3. Stephen T. Banko, III, "Search for the Living Stream," *Vital Speeches of the Day,* 1 January 1985, 167.

4. Philip Caputo, *A Rumor of War* (New York: Holt, Rinehart and Winston, 1977; Ballantine Books, 1978), xviii.

5. John Ellis as quoted in Fussell, *Wartime,* 281.

6. What was obvious to the men in Vietnam was later supported by a poll of Vietnam veterans after the war; the heavier the combat a solder experienced, the more likely he was to become thrilled by the fighting. The proportion of Vietnam veterans saying they liked the thrill of being in a war rose from 9 percent among those seeing light action to 21 percent of those who saw heavy combat. Veteran's Administration, *Myths and Realities: A Study of Attitudes Toward Vietnam Era Veterans.* Submitted to the Committee on Veterans Affairs, U.S. Senate. (Washington, D.C.: Government Printing Office, July 1980), 15, 21.

7. Caputo, *Rumor of War,* xviii.

8. Lanning, *Company Commander's Journal,* 36. The "kill or be killed" aspects of World War II in the Pacific are probably best understood in the context of John Dower's *War Without Mercy,* especially pages 10–13.

9. Eric Sevareid is mentioned in Lewy, *America in Vietnam,* 308. The quote from correspondent Edgar L. Jones appeared in an article titled "One War is Enough," *Atlantic Monthly,* February 1946, 48–53. Other examples appear in Dower, *War Without Mercy,* 61–70.

10. As quoted in Fussell, *Wartime,* 117.

11. As quoted in Harry G. Summers, Jr., "The Battle of the Ia

Drang Valley," *American Heritage* (February-March 1984): 57. Such acts as those Jack Smith described were common in other actions as well. The corpses of seventy-eight Americans killed in action near Dak To in 1967 bore evidence that the NVA had gouged out eyes and severed ring fingers. One survivor managed to feign death even as his finger was removed. Other American dead were found with bullet holes in their foreheads—marks of execution. Atkinson, *Long Gray Line,* 235, 249.

12. Austin diary, 20 January 1967.

13. Stephen Fredrick to the author, 13 August 1991.

14. Gadd, *Line Doggie,* 235.

15. Rudyard Kipling as quoted in Peter Vansittart, *Voices from the Great War* (New York: Avon Books, 1985), 15.

16. Magedanz Reflections, 1971, 7. Magedanz noted in later correspondence that this event occurred several months after the marine base at LZ Ross had been hit by sappers. The platoon, in his opinion, was angered with this particular brand of elite hard-core NVA, and the men's actions resulted from those emotions getting out of hand. Thomas Magedanz to author, 11 October 1991.

17. Lanning, *Company Commander's Journal,* 106. Michael Jackson and Stephen Fredrick of the 101st Airborne Division both recalled ace of spades calling cards and both specified Bicycle brand. Paul Gerrits frequently saw 1st Cavalry Division patches deposited on enemy KIAs. The practice also was mentioned frequently throughout Matthew Brennan's memoirs. The practice was undoubtedly taken to its most barbaric extremes by the man in Richard Ford III's LRRP unit who, along with removing gold teeth, left wallet-sized photos of himself on the dead. See Wallace Terry, *Bloods: An Oral History of the Vietnam War by Black Veterans* (New York: Ballantine Books, 1984), 44.

18. Clark, *Guns Up!* 63.

19. The concept of counting coup has been misused in this context. Among the native American tribes, the act did not require killing nor even injuring an enemy—but simply facing him at close range in order to establish one's bravery.

20. S. L. A. Marshall, *Pacific Stars and Stripes,* 25 February 1971, 11.

21. Magedanz Reflections, June 1983, 19.

22. Col. Sharon I. Richie, "Combat Nurses: You Won't Be Alone," *Military Review,* 69, no. 1 (January 1989): 68.

23. John Ellis, *Cassino: Hollow Victory* (New York: McGraw-Hill, 1984), 29.

Chapter 13

1. Leonard Dutcher to his parents, 9 April 1967.

2. Larry Iwasko to his mother, 3 September 1968. Original in the private collection of Mrs. Dorothy Iwasko.

3. West, *Small Unit Actions*, 37.

4. Magedanz Reflections, 1971, 9.

5. The margin of error may be as high as 25 percent. See Lewy, *America in Vietnam*, 272–73.

6. Ogden, *Green Knight, Red Mourning*, 96. Paul Meringolo said that he happened upon the human remains of similar "executions," noting: "We were later to find out that when the North Vietnamese would come into a village, they would quite often decapitate or use various other methods of killing some of the villagers to put the fear of God into them for cooperating with the Americans rather than helping the VC."

7. Ibid., 98.

8. *Time* (15 December 1967): 32–34.

9. As quoted in Lewy, *America in Vietnam*, 276.

10. Magedanz Reflections, 1971, 8.

11. James A. Amodt to Dr. George Garlid and Dr. C. C. Smith, 1 September 1968. Special Collections, McIntyre Library, University of Wisconsin-Eau Claire.

12. Austin diary, 29 September 1966.

13. Ibid., 20 March 1967.

14. Anderson, *The Grunts*, 203.

15. As quoted in Willenson, *The Bad War*, 63.

16. The lieutenant referred to was Charles J. Gains. A mustang is an officer who was an enlisted man before being commissioned.

17. O'Brien, *If I Die*, 21.

18. Just, *To What End*, 150–51, 153.

19. Cosmas and Murray, *Vietnamization and Redeployment*, 348.

20. When Sergeant Williams returned home from his first tour of duty during Christmas 1966, he and his wife saw Sergeant Wolmack's release from captivity on television.

21. David Kohler and James Wensyel, "Our First Southeast Asian War," *American History Illustrated*, 24, no. 7 (January-February 1990): 28.

22. As quoted in Bill McCloud, "What Should We Tell Our Children About Vietnam?" *American Heritage*, 39, no. 4 (May-June 1988): 58.

23. Lanning, *Company Commander's Journal*, 214.

24. Anderson, *The Grunts,* 203

25. James Martin Davis, "Vietnam: What It Was Really Like," *Military Review*, 69, no. 1 (January 1989): 36.

26. Lewy, *America in Vietnam,* 325.

27. Lewy estimates that about 250,000 South Vietnamese civilians were killed during allied operations during the course of the war. An additional 39,000 were killed by Communist forces. This amounts to roughly 20 percent of the deaths in Southeast Asia on all sides, by both combatants and noncombatants, based on a total of 1.3 million dead. See ibid., 451.

Thomas Thayer's calculations are quite complicated but approximate Lewy's. Thayer estimates that some 195,000 civilians were killed between 1965 and 1972. He cites the estimate of the U.S. Senate Subcommittee to Investigate Problems Connected with Refugees and Escapees, which placed the number of civilian war deaths at 415,000 killed and an additional 935,000 wounded. Using either estimate, Thayer notes, civilian casualties were approximately one-half of 1 percent or less of the population for any given year, and although he emphasizes the tragic nature of such losses, he believes that perspective is important. See Thayer, *War Without Fronts,* 125–29.

28. Stanton, *Rise and Fall,* 179.

29. Eddie P. Austin to his parents, 17 April 1967. Photocopy in author's collection.

30. Austin diary, 9 April 1967.

31. Austin diary, 19 April 1967.

Chapter 14

1. Leonard Dutcher to his parents, 1 June 1968.

2. Fussell, *Wartime,* 282; Charles Moskos, "The Combat Soldier in Vietnam," *Journal of Social Issues,* 31, no. 4 (Fall 1975): 32. A soldier's preoccupation with his time remaining in country was often evident in his letters. Marine Larry Iwasko, for example, included in roughly half of his letters the exact number of days he had remaining to serve beginning with 373 days and ending with 10. Leonard Dutcher also made frequent reference to his days remaining, beginning at 300.

3. Max Hastings, *The Korean War* (New York: Simon and Schuster, 1987), 284.

4. Ibid., 284.

5. Ibid., 277.

6. Sledge, *With the Old Breed,* 295.

7. Moskos, "Combat Soldier in Vietnam," 32.

8. James Goodwin, Psy. Ph.D., reprinted in Tom Williams, Psy. Ph.D., *Post Traumatic Stress Disorders of the Vietnam Veteran: Observations and Recommendations for the Psychological Treatment of the Veteran and His Family* (Cincinnati: Disabled American Veterans, 1980), 11.

9. Leonard Dutcher to his parents, 13 April 1968.

10. Gadd, *Line Doggie,* 238.

11. Steve Fredrick to his parents, mid-February 1969.

12. Ibid., late February 1969.

13. O'Brien, *If I Die,* 171. Layne Anderson served in a sister company during the same time period but saw things differently. Perhaps his observations were less sympathetic, or, after twenty years, less accurate, but in Anderson's memory, "They were giving the rear jobs to the blacks. If they didn't, there would be charges of prejudice." Tom Birhanzel, who served in a different brigade in the 23d (Americal) Division, agreed with Anderson's observations. "When we went to the rear [Chu Lai], there was a lot of talk about how many blacks were serving out in the field, and the whites were getting all the good jobs, but in my area I found that to be exactly the opposite," he explained.

14. Comdr. George L. Jackson, "Constraints of the Negro Civil Rights Movement on American Military Effectiveness," *Naval War College Review* (January 1970): 100–107. Reprinted in Gettleman, et al., *Vietnam and America,* 317–22.

15. Baskir and Strauss, *Chance and Circumstance,* 8; Thayer, *War Without Fronts,* 114.

16. Steve Fredrick to his parents, late February 1969.

17. Gadd, *Line Doggie,* 223.

18. Steve Fredrick to his parents, 4 May 1969.

19. Ibid., May 1969.

20. Ibid., May 1969.

21. Larry Iwasko to his mother, 26 June 1968.

22. Ibid., 3 September 1968.

23. Magedanz Reflections, 1971, 5.

24. Steve Fredrick to his parents, 8 May 1969.

25. Gadd, *Line Doggie,* 249.

Epilogue

1. Moskos, "Combat Soldier in Vietnam," 29.
2. Telegram, The Adjutant General to Mr. and Mrs. Richard Dutcher, Melrose, Wis., 6 June 1968. Original in the private collection of Mrs. Betty Ronke, Melrose, Wis.

Selected Bibliography

Interviews

James Ebert Vietnam Veterans' Oral History Collection. Special Collections, McIntyre Library, University of Wisconsin-Eau Claire. Transcripts and tapes of the following interviews conducted by the author are on file:

Anderson, Layne D. EVP-12. 26 June 1989. Blair, Wis.
Barker, Gerry H. EVP-28. 6 December 1989. Melrose, Wis.
Boehm, Paul. EVP-31. 9 December 1989. Green Bay, Wis.
Bonesteel, Robert, EVP-42. 16 June 1992. Eau Claire, Wis.
Carlisle, David C. EVP-36. 22 April 1990. Pierre, S.Dak.
Fredrick, Stephen E. EVP-1. 29 February 1984. Melrose, Wis.
Freitag, Jack. EVP-14. 24 July 1989. La Crosse, Wis.
Gerrits, Paul E. EVP-29. 10 December 1989. Green Bay, Wis.
Good, Bryan L. EVP-40. 5 March 1991. Elroy, Wis.
Harken, William. EVP-19. 15 August 1989. Waverly, Iowa.
Hill, Larry J. EVP-34. 14 November 1989. Blair, Wis.
Hoban, Edmund M. EVP-38. 21 June 1990. Melrose, Wis.
Hoelzen, Randall W. EVP-41. 12 March 1991. La Crosse, Wis.
Jackson, Michael R. EVP-25. 12 October 1989. Madison, Wis.
Janick, Vernon. EVP-13. 17 July 1989. Coon Valley, Wis.
Johnson, Jerome R. EVP-16. 28 July 1989. Clarion, Iowa.
Johnson, Robert Bruce. EVP-37. 14 June 1990. La Crosse, Wis.
Keeling, Robert L. EVP-23. 9 September 1989. Clarion, Iowa.
Krehbiel, Dan W. EVP-3. 6 April 1984. Melrose, Wis.
Kurtz, Douglas A. EVP-24. 27 September 1989. Melrose, Wis.
Meil, Michael K. EVP-21. 6 September 1989. Melrose, Wis.
Meringolo, Paul T. EVP-20. 24 August 1989. Worcester, Mass.
Merrell, John M. EVP-10. 1 May 1989. Melrose, Wis.
Meyer, John E. EVP-9. 25 February 1989. Melrose, Wis.

Miller, Glenn R. EVP-35. 20 April 1990. Pierre, S.Dak.
Musser, Terry M. EVP-11. 15 March 1984 and 12 June 1989. Melrose, Wis.
Neely, Jon A. EVP-33. 12 January 1990. Rochester, Pa.
Olstad, Glen M. EVP-18. 8 August 1989. La Crosse, Wis.
Putnam, Donald. EVP-30. 9 December 1989. Green Bay, Wis.
Reiland, Dwight N. EVP-22. 9 September 1989. Clarion, Iowa.
Roberts, Michael L. EVP-27. 27 September 1989. Webster City, Iowa.
Schultz, Thomas. EVP-2. 2 March 1984. Sumner, Iowa.
Severson, Gerald L. EVP-4. 2 April 1984 and 21 February 1989. Melrose, Wis.
Shepardson, Terry L. EVP-8. 26 February 1989. Melrose, Wis.
Stanton, James L. Jr., EVP-32. 10 January 1990. Melrose, Wis.
Steenlage, Robert. EVP-39. 15 August 1990. Galesville, Wis.
Williams, Willie. EVP-26. 12 October 1989. Madison, Wis.
Yaeger, Phillip E. EVP-15. 25 July 1989. La Crosse, Wis.
Yushta, Jeffrey. EVP-17. 2 August 1989. La Crosse, Wis.

South Dakota Vietnam Veterans' Oral History Project. Vietnam Era Veterans Association, Inc., and the Robinson Museum, Pierre, S.Dak. Transcripts and tapes of the following interviews are on file:

Birhanzel, Thomas C. VNP-12. 27 April 1985. Pierre, S.Dak.
Carlisle, David C. VNP-35. 22 April 1990. Pierre, S.Dak.
Emery, Robert L. VNP-28. 18 August 1985. Mission, S.Dak.
Foell, Dennis G. VNP-6. 28 February 1985. Pierre, S.Dak.
Gates, Larry F. VNP-1. 4 September 1984 and 2 March 1985. Pierre, S.Dak.
Hansen, David H. VNP-10. 11 April 1985. Pierre, S.Dak.
Johnson, Deane L. VNP-16. 14 May 1985. Pierre S.Dak.
Korkow, Kenneth A. VNP-15. 7 May 1985. Pierre, S.Dak.
Magedanz, Thomas C. VNP-14. 5 May 1985. Pierre, S.Dak.
Miller, Glenn R. VNP-34. 20 April 1990. Pierre, S.Dak.
Moran, Robert H. Jr., VNP-26. 7 August 1985. Pierre, S.Dak.
Olson, Vincent R. VNP-29. 16 September 1985. Hyde County, S.Dak.
Raysor, James A. VNP-33. 15 December 1985. Pierre, S.Dak.
Roubideaux, Thomas L. VNP-19. 20 June 1985. Pierre, S.Dak.
Tople, Terry A. VNP-8. 28 March 1985. Fort Pierre, S.Dak.
Trimble, Donald D. VNP-30. 2 October 1985. Pierre, S.Dak.

Whitebird, Francis G. VNP-4. 31 January 1985 and 18 March 1985. Pierre, S.Dak.

Correspondence

Amodt, James A. Letter to Dr. George Garlid and Dr. C. C. Smith. Special Collections, McIntyre Library, University of Wisconsin-Eau Claire.

Austin, Eddie P. Letter to his parents and diary kept in training and Vietnam. Photocopies in private collection of the author.

Beatty, Jeffrey L. Letters to his mother. Also condolence letters from the military and correspondence pertaining to personal disposition of personal effects, burial, and escort of body. Private collection of Mrs. Corrine Hovre-Hill, Blair, Wis.

Cook, Leonard. Letters to Mr. and Mrs. Richard Dutcher. Private collection of Mrs. Betty Ronke, Melrose, Wis.

Dutcher, Leonard. Letters to his parents and sister. Private collection of Mrs. Betty Ronke, Melrose, Wis.

Fredrick, Stephen. Letters to his parents. Private collection of Stephen Fredrick, Melrose, Wis.

Iwasko, Larry. Letters to his mother. Private collection of Mrs. Dorothy Iwasko, Elmhurst, Ill.

Magedanz, Thomas. Letters to his parents. Private collection of Thomas Magedanz, Pierre, S.Dak.

Meringolo, Paul. Letters to Mrs. Betty Ronke. Private collection of Mrs. Betty Ronke, Melrose, Wis.

Pellegriti, Joseph. Letters to Mr. and Mrs. Richard Dutcher and Mrs. Betty Ronke. Private collection of Mrs. Betty Ronke, Melrose, Wis.

Sartori, David. Letters to Dr. E. M. Peterson. Special Collections, McIntyre Library, University of Wisconsin-Eau Claire.

Thorson, Gary E. Letter to Dr. E. M. Peterson. Special Collections, McIntyre Library, University of Wisconsin-Eau Claire.

Vidalez, Tony. Letters to Mr. and Mrs. Richard Dutcher. Private collection of Mrs. Betty Ronke, Melrose, Wis.

Government Publications and Films

Bergen, John D. *Military Communications: A Test for Technology.* The U.S. Army in Vietnam. Washington, D.C.: Center of Military History, 1986.

Cosmas, Graham A., and Lt. Col. Terrence P. Murray. *U.S. Marines in Vietnam: Vietnamization and Redeployment 1970–1971*. Washington, D.C.: U.S. Marine Corps History and Museums Division, 1986.

Ewell, Lt. Gen. Julian J., and Maj. Gen. Ira A. Hunt. *Sharpening the Combat Edge: The Use of Analysis to Reinforce Military Judgment*. Vietnam Studies. Washington, D.C.: Government Printing Office, 1974.

Flemming, Keith V., Jr., Lt. Col. Lane Rogers, and Maj. Gary L. Telfer. *U.S. Marines in Vietnam: Fighting the North Vietnamese, 1967*. Washington D.C.: U.S. Marine Corps History and Museums Division, 1984.

Hoang, Ngoc Lung. *Intelligence*. Indochina Monographs. Washington, D.C.: Center of Military History, 1982.

Ott, Maj. Gen. David E. *Field Artillery, 1954–1973*. Vietnam Studies. Washington, D.C.: Department of the Army, 1975.

Shrader, Lt. Col. Charles R. *Amicicide: The Problem of Friendly Fire in Modern War*. Fort Leavenworth, Kans.: U.S. Army Command and General Staff College, December 1982.

Shulimson, Jack. *U.S. Marines in Vietnam: An Expanding War, 1966*. Washington, D.C.: U.S. Marine Corps History and Museums Division, 1982.

Smith, Charles R. *U.S. Marines in Vietnam: High Mobility and Standdown 1969*. Washington, D.C.: U.S. Marine Corps History and Museums Division, 1988.

Starry, Gen. Donn A. *Mounted Combat in Vietnam*. Vietnam Studies. Washington, D.C.: Department of the Army, 1978.

West, Capt. Francis J., Jr. *Small Unit Action in Vietnam: Summer 1966*. Washington, D.C.: U.S. Marine Corps History and Museums Division, 1967.

Department of the Army. *Army Systems of Basic Training, 1919–1974*. Manuscript. Washington, D.C.: Center of Military History, 1974.

———. *Boobytraps*. FM 5-31. Washington, D.C.: Government Printing Office, 14 September 1965.

———. *Helpful Hints For Personnel Ordered to Vietnam*. DA Pam 608-16. Washington, D.C.: Government Printing Office, March, 1968.

———. *Rifle, M16A1, Part I: Care, Cleaning, and Lubrication*. Training Film no. TF 21-3907. Washington, D.C.: Army Training Command. 16mm motion picture.

———. *Rifle, M16A1, Part II: Field Expedients*. Training Film no.

TF 21-3908. Washington, D.C.: Army Training Command. 16mm motion picture.

———. *Training of Combat Replacements, 1940–1968.* Unpublished report. Fort Knox, Ky.: Special Planning Group, Headquarters, U.S. Army Training Center, Armor, 1968.

Department of Defense. *Know Your Enemy: The Viet Cong.* AFIF 172. Washington, D.C.: Armed Forces Information Service. 16mm motion picture.

———. *The Unique War.* AFIF 153. Washington, D.C.: Armed Forces Information Service. 16mm motion picture.

———. *Your Tour in Vietnam.* AFIF 181. Washington, D.C.: Armed Forces Information Service. 16mm motion picture.

———. *Black Americans in Defense of Our Nation.* Washington, D.C.: Government Printing Office, January 1985.

———. *A Pocket Guide to Vietnam.* DOD PG-21B. Washington, D.C.: Government Printing Office, November 1970.

———. *U.S. Casualties in Southeast Asia: Statistics as of November 11, 1986.* Washington, D.C.: Government Printing Office, 1986.

U.S. Military Assistance Command Vietnam, Combined Intelligence Center. *What a Platoon Leader Should Know about the Enemy's Jungle Tactics.* Japan: PPC, 1967.

Department of the Navy, USMC. *Professional Knowledge Gained From Operational Experience in Vietnam, Special Issue: Mines and Booby Traps.* 1969-393-899/S 7102. Washington, D.C.: Government Printing Office, May/June 1969.

U.S. Senate, Special Subcommittee on Alcohol and Narcotics. *Drug and Alcohol Abuse in the Military.* Washington, D.C.: Government Printing Office, 1970.

Veterans Administration. *Data on Vietnam Era Veterans.* Washington, D.C.: Office of Information Management and Statistics. April 1985.

———. *Myths and Realities: A Study of Attitudes Toward Vietnam Era Veterans.* Washington, D.C.: Government Printing Office, July 1980.

Books

Anderson, Charles R. *The Grunts.* Novato, Calif.: Presidio Press, 1976; New York: Berkley Books, 1976.

Atkinson, Rick. *The Long Gray Line: The American Journey of West Point's Class of 1966.* Boston: Houghton Mifflin, 1989.

Bain, David Haward. *Sitting in Darkness: Americans in the Philippines*. Boston: Houghton Mifflin, 1984.

Baritz, Loren. *Backfire*. New York: Random House, 1985; Ballantine Books, 1985.

Barnes, Peter. *Pawns: The Plight of the Citizen Soldier*. New York: Knopf, 1972.

Baskir, Lawrence M., and William A. Strauss. *Chance and Circumstance: The Draft, the War, and the Vietnam Generation*. New York: Knopf, 1978.

Brende, Joel O., and Erwin R. Parson. *Vietnam Veterans: The Road to Recovery*. New York: Plenum Press, 1985.

Brennan, Matthew. *Brennan's War: Vietnam 1965–1969*. Novato, Calif.: Presidio Press, 1985; New York: Pocket Books, 1985.

————, ed. *Headhunters: Stories from the 1st Squadron, 9th Cavalry in Vietnam 1965–1971*. Novato, Calif.: Presidio Press, 1987.

Caputo, Philip. *A Rumor of War*. New York: Holt, Rinehart and Winston, 1977, Ballantine Books, 1978.

Cash, John A., John Albright, and Allan W. Sandstrum. *Seven Firefights in Vietnam*. Washington, D.C.: Office of the Chief of Military History, 1970; New York: Bantam Books, 1985.

Clark, Johnnie M. *Guns Up!* New York: Ballantine Books, 1984.

Coleman, J. D. *Pleiku: The Dawn of Helicopter Warfare in Vietnam*. New York: St. Martin's Press, 1988.

————, ed. *The First Air Cavalry Division: August 1965 to December 1969*. Phouc Vinh: 1st Air Cavalry Division, 1970.

Cook, John L. *Dust Off*. New York: Bantam Books, 1988.

Currey, Cecil B. *Self-Destruction: The Disintegration and Decay of the U.S. Army During the Vietnam Era*. New York: Norton, 1981.

Dollard, John. *Fear in Battle*. 1st rev. ed. Washington, D.C.: Infantry Journal, June 1944.

Donovan, David. *Once a Warrior King: Memories of an Officer in Vietnam*. New York: Ballantine Books, 1985.

Dower, John W. *War Without Mercy: Race and Power in the Pacific War*. New York: Pantheon Books, 1986.

Downs, Frederick. *The Killing Zone*. New York: Norton, 1978.

Dyer, Gwynne. *War*. New York: Crown, 1985.

Edelman, Bernard, ed. *Dear America: Letters Home From Vietnam*. New York: The New York Vietnam Veteran's Memorial Commission and W. W. Norton, 1985; New York: Pocket Books, 1986.

Egendorf, Arthur. *Healing From the War: Trauma and Transformation After Vietnam*. Boston: Shambhala Publications, 1986.

Ellis, John. *Eye-Deep in Hell: Trench Warfare in World War I*. Baltimore: The Johns Hopkins Univ. Press, 1989.

Emerson, Gloria. *Winners and Losers: Battles, Retreats, Gains, Losses, and Ruins from a Long War*. New York: Random House, 1972.

Estes, Jack. *A Field Of Innocence*. New York: Warner Books, 1987.

Fall, Bernard B. *Last Reflections on a War*. New York: Doubleday, 1967.

———. *Street Without Joy*. Harrisburg, Pa.: Stackpole, 1967.

———. *The Two Vietnams: A Political and Military Analysis*. New York: Praeger, 1964.

Fallows, James. *National Defense*. New York: Random House, 1981.

Figley, Charles R., and Seymour Leventman. *Strangers at Home: Vietnam Veterans Since the War*. New York: Praeger, 1980.

Flesch, Ron. *Redwood Delta*. New York: Berkley Books, 1988.

Fuller, Tony and Peter Goldman. *Charlie Company: What Vietnam Did to Us*. New York: Newsweek, 1983.

Fussell, Paul. *Wartime: Understanding and Behavior in the Second World War*. New York: Oxford Univ. Press, 1989.

———, ed. *The Norton Book of Modern War*. New York: Norton, 1991.

Gabriel, Richard A., and Paul L. Savage. *Crisis in Command: Mismanagement in the Army*. New York: Hill and Wang, 1978.

Gadd, Charles. *Line Doggie: Foot Soldier in Vietnam*. Novato Calif.: Presidio Press, 1987; New York: Pocket Books, 1989.

Garland, Lt. Col. Albert N. (Ret.), ed. *Infantry in Vietnam: Small Unit Actions in the Early Days: 1965–1966*. Nashville, Tenn.: Battery Press, 1982; New York: Jove, 1985.

Gettleman, Marvin E., et al. *Vietnam and America: A Documented History*. New York: Grove Press, 1985.

Giblett, Noel, ed. *Homecomings: Stories from Australian Vietnam Veterans and Their Wives*. Perth, Aus.: Vietnam Veterans Counseling Service, 1987.

Goff, Stanley, Robert Sanders, and Clark Smith. *Brothers: Black Soldiers in the Nam*. Novato, Calif.: Presidio Press, 1982; New York: Berkley Books, 1985.

Greenberg, Martin H. and Augustus Richard Norton. *Touring Nam: The Vietnam War Reader*. New York: Bantam Books, 1989.

Hastings, Max. *The Korean War*. New York: Simon and Schuster, 1987.

Herrington, Stuart. *Silence Was a Weapon: The Vietnam War in the*

Villages. Novato, Calif.: Presidio Press, 1982; New York: Ivy Books, 1987.

Holmes, Richard. *Acts of War: The Behavior of Men in Battle*. New York: Macmillian, 1986; Free Press, 1989.

Hughes, Larry. *You Can See a Lot Standing Under a Flare in the Republic of Vietnam*. New York: Morrow, 1969.

Johnson, Bruce R. *Under the Southern Cross: A Feeling of War*. La-Farge, Wis.: Epitaph-News, 1989.

Just, Ward S. *Military Men*, New York: Knopf, 1970.

———. *To What End: Report from Vietnam*. Boston: Houghton Mifflin, 1968.

Kovic, Ron. *Born on the Fourth of July*. New York: Pocket Books, 1977.

Krepinevich, Andrew F., Jr. *The Army and Vietnam*. Baltimore: Johns Hopkins Univ. Press, 1986.

Lane, Mark. *Conversations with Americans*. New York: Simon and Schuster, 1970.

Lanning, Michael Lee. *Vietnam, 1969–1970: A Company Commander's Journal*. New York: Ivy Books, 1988.

Lewy, Guenter. *America in Vietnam*. New York: Oxford Univ. Press, 1978.

Ly Qui Chung, ed. *Between Two Fires: The Unheard Voices of Vietnam*. New York: Praeger, 1970.

McAulay, Lex. *The Battle of Long Tan*. Melbourne, Aus.: Century Hutchinson, 1976.

Magedanz, Thomas C., ed. *South Dakotans in Vietnam: Excerpts from the South Dakota Vietnam Veterans Oral History Project*. Pierre, S.Dak.: Vietnam Era Veterans Association and Robinson Museum, 1986.

Marshall, S. L. A. *Ambush: The Battle of Dau Tieng*. Nashville: Battery Press, 1983; New York: Jove, 1988.

Mason, Robert. *Chickenhawk*. New York: Viking, 1983.

McCann, William, ed. *Ambrose Bierce's Civil War*. Washington, D.C.: Regnery Gateway, 1986.

McDonough, James R. *Platoon Leader*. Novato, Calif.: Presidio Press, 1985; New York: Bantam Books, 1985.

McKay, Gary. *In Good Company: One Australian's War in Vietnam*. Sydney, Aus.: Allen and Unwin, 1987.

Mertel, Col. Kenneth D. *Year of the Horse—Vietnam: First Air Cavalry in the Highlands*. New York: Exposition Press, 1968; Bantam Books, 1990.

Moore, Lt. Gen. Harold G., and Joseph L. Galloway. *We Were Soldiers Once And Young.* New York: Random House, 1992.

Moskos, Charles C. *The American Enlisted Man: The Rank and File in Today's Military.* New York: Russell Sage Foundation, 1970.

O'Brien, Tim. *If I Die in a Combat Zone: Box Me Up and Ship Me Home.* New York: Dell, 1987.

Ogden, Richard E. *Green Knight, Red Mourning.* New York: Zebra Books, 1985.

Palmer, David Richard. *Summons of the Trumpet.* Novato, Calif.: Presidio Press, 1978; New York: Ballantine Books, 1978.

Parks, David. *G.I. Diary.* New York: Harper and Row, 1968.

Parrish, John A. *12, 20 & 5: A Doctor's Year in Vietnam.* New York: Dutton, 1972.

Perret, Geoffrey. *A Country Made by War.* New York: Random House, 1989.

Pisor, Robert. *The End of the Line: The Siege of Khe Sanh.* New York: Ballantine Books, 1982.

Pratt, John Clark. *Vietnam Voices: Perspectives on the War Years, 1941–1982.* New York: Penguin Books, 1984.

Pyle, Ernie. *Brave Men.* New York: Holt, 1944.

Sack, John. *"M."* New York: Esquire, 1966; Avon, 1985.

Santoli, Al. *Everything We Had.* New York: Random House, 1981; Ballantine Books, 1990.

Sheehan, Neil. *A Bright and Shining Lie: John Paul Vann and America in Vietnam.* New York: Random House, 1988.

Spector, Ronald H. *Eagle Against the Sun: The American War with Japan.* New York: Free Press, 1985.

Stanton, Shelby L. *Vietnam Order of Battle.* New York: Galahad Books, 1986.

———. *The Rise and Fall of an American Army: U.S. Ground Forces in Vietnam, 1965–1973.* Novato, Calif.: Presidio Press, 1985; New York: Dell, 1986.

Terry, Wallace. *Bloods: An Oral History of the Vietnam War by Black Veterans.* New York: Ballantine Books, 1984.

Thayer, Thomas C. *War Without Fronts: The American Experience in Vietnam.* Boulder, Colo.: Westview Press, 1985.

Vietnam Veterans Memorial Fund, Inc. *Vietnam Veterans Memorial Directory of Names.* Washington, D.C.: Vietnam Veteran Fund, August, 1985.

Walker, Keith. *A Piece of My Heart.* Novato, Calif.: Presidio Press, 1985; New York: Ballantine Books, 1987.

Ward, Joseph T. *Dear Mom: A Sniper's Vietnam*. New York: Ballantine Books, 1991.

Waterhouse, Larry G., and Mariann G. Wizard. *Turning the Guns Around: Notes on the G.I. Movement*. New York: Dell, 1971.

Westmoreland, William C. *A Soldier Reports*. New York: Doubleday, 1976; Dell, 1981.

Willenson, Kim. *The Bad War: An Oral History of the Vietnam War*. New York: New American Library, 1987.

Williams, Tom, Psy.D. *Post-Traumatic Stress Disorders of the Vietnam Veteran: Observations and Recommendations for the Psychological Treatment of the Veteran and His Family*. Cincinnati: Disabled American Veterans, 1980.

Periodicals

"A New High." *Grunt Free Press*. July 1971, 14.

Banko, Stephen T. III. "The Search for the Living Stream: Vietnam Veterans as Casualties of Peace." *Vital Speeches of the Day* 51, no. 6 (1 January 1985): 166–68.

Belenky, Lt. Col. Gregory Lucas, et al. "Battle Stress: The Israeli Experience." *Military Review* 65, no. 7 (July 1985): 28–37.

Broyles, William, Jr. "The Road to Hill 10." *Atlantic Monthly*. April 1985, 90–96.

"Call Our Bluff." *Games*. August 1991, 48.

Chilcoat, George W. "The Images of Vietnam: A Popular Music Approach." *Social Education* 49, no. 6 (October 1985): 601–603.

Davis, James Martin. "Vietnam: What It Was Really Like." *Military Review* 69, no. 1 (January 1989): 34–44.

Eisenhart, Wayne R. "You Can't Hack It Little Girl: A Discussion of the Covert Psychological Agenda of Modern Combat Training." *Journal of Social Issues* 31, no. 4 (Fall 1975): 13–23.

Evans, Pfc. Dan. "A Grunt—Waits, Watches and Sometimes Dies." *Pacific Stars and Stripes*. 25 February 1971, 2–3.

Evans, David. "Defense Department Experts Aiming to Decrease Battlefield Casualty Rates." *Chicago Tribune*. 6 November 1988, Section 5, 15.

Fowler, Lt. Col. John G., Jr. "Combat Cohesion in Vietnam." *Military Review* 59, no. 12 (December 1979): 22–31.

Frazier, Ian. "The War as We Knew It." *Atlantic Monthly*. May 1986, 40–41.

Fredrick, Steve. "Ambush." *The Wartburg College Castle* 22 (Autumn 1969): 14–16.

Harris, Robert F. "There is a Santa Claus!" *Leatherneck*. December 1988, 51.

Hersh, Seymour M. "The Decline and Near Fall of the U.S. Army." *National Review*. December 1972, 58–65.

Hoffman, Roger. "Nicknames." *New York Times Magazine*. 12 May 1985, 58.

Jordan, Bob. "Sapper Attack!: The Battle for Cam Le Bridge." *Leatherneck*. September 1988, 23.

Kaplan, Roger. "Army Unit Cohesion in Vietnam: A Bum Rap." *Parameters* 17, no. 3 (September 1987): 58–67.

Knowlton, Maj. William A., Jr. "Cohesion and the Vietnam Experience." *Military Review* 66, no. 5 (May 1986): 56–64.

Kohler, David R. and James W. Wensyel. "Our First Southeast Asian War." *American History Illustrated* 24, no. 7 (January-February 1990): 18–30.

Lane, William K., Jr. "Vietnam Vets Without Hollywood, Without Tears." *The Wall Street Journal*. 26 July 1988, 20.

Lifton, Robert Jay. "The Gook Syndrome and Numbered Warfare." *Saturday Review*. December 1972, 66–72.

Linden, Eugene. "Fragging and Other Withdrawal Symptoms: The Demoralization of an Army." *Saturday Review*. 8 January 1972, 12–17.

McArthur, George. "The Alienated GI: Cause of Anguish for the Army." *Pacific Stars and Stripes*. Date unknown, 1971, 12.

McCloud, Bill. "What Should We Tell Our Children About Vietnam?" *American Heritage* 39, no. 4 (May-June 1988): 55–77.

Mannion, Dennis M. "Christmas at Khe Sanh." *Leatherneck*. December 1988, 44–45.

Marshall, S. L. A. "The Case Against Blanket War Crimes Charges." *Pacific Stars and Stripes*. 25 February 1971, 11.

Martin, Thad. "The Black Vietnam Vet: Still Looking for Respect." *Ebony*. April 1986, 123–24.

Moskos, Charles C., Jr. "The Combat Soldier in Vietnam." *Journal of Social Issues* 31, no. 4 (1975): 25–37.

Norman, Michael. "Rites of Passage." *New York Times Magazine*. 23 October 1983, 78.

O'Brien, Tim. "The Things They Carried." *Esquire*. August 1986, 76–81.

Pierce, Lt. Col. Kenneth R. "The Battle of the Ia Drang Valley." *Military Review* 69, no. 1 (January 1989): 87–97.

Pilisk, Marc. "The Legacy of Vietnam." *Journal of Social Issues* 31, no. 4 (1975): 3–12.

"The Human Cost of Vietnam," *American Legion*. December 1988, 38–42.

Richie, Col. Sharon I. "Combat Nurses: You Won't Be Alone." *Military Review* 69, no. 1 (January 1989): 65–73.

Sack, John. "The Education of a Young Lieutenant." *Esquire*. June 1983, 260–62.

Spiller, Roger J. "Isen's Run: Human Dimensions of Warfare in the 20th Century." *Military Review* 68, no. 5 (May 1988): 30–32.

Stanton, Shelby. "Lessons Learned or Lost: Air Cavalry and Airmobility." *Military Review* 69, no. 1 (January 1989): 74–86.

Summers, Harry G., Jr. "The Battle of the Ia Drang Valley." *American Heritage* 35, no. 1 (February-March 1984): 51–58.

"The Real War? An Interview with Paul Fussell." *American Heritage* 40, no. 7 (November 1989): 126–38.

Wilson, William. "I had Prayed to God that This Thing Was Fiction." *American Heritage* 41, no. 1 (February 1990): 44–53.

"You'll Need to Know This if You're in Vietnam." *Newsweek*. 11 April 1966, 33.

Index

483

ground, 235, 320; types of
described, 318
Operations: Cedar Falls, 319; Crazy
Horse, 318, 321; Double Eagle,
319; Eagle Claw, 318; Hastings,
136, 318; Hickory, 363;
Jefferson-Glenn, 318; Junction
City, 273–74, 385; Masher-White
Wing, 250, 318; Prairie and
Prairie II, 318; Starlight, 318
Oskings, Keith, 402
out-processing, 405–21

Parris Island, 44
patriotism, 14, 62, 113–14
Patterson, Cpl. Bill, 395
Peleliu, 74
Phantoms. *See* F-4 Phantom jets
Philippines Insurrection, 386
Phouc Thanh, 107
Phouc Vinh, 243
Phu Bai, 11, 20–31, 116, 120, 127,
336, 403
Phuthan massacre, 372
Pinkville, 319, 380
Plain of Reeds, 210, 306–7, 388
Pleiku, 91, 127, 158–59, 181, 412,
416
pointman, 147–48
PRC-25 radio, 144, 201–2
prisoners of war, 349–57, 384–85;
ARVN, 247–48; shooting of
wounded, 350–51; torture of,
142, 357–58, 363
psychological breakdown, 281
psychological preparation in field,
206
Pueblo incident, 19
Pulaski, Robert, 336–37
Puller, Chesty, 65
punji stakes, 177, 236–37, 241,
279, 377, 389; jungle boot
resistance to, 196, 327; locations
of, 237–38
Purple Heart (decoration), 33, 41,
400

Putnam, Donald, 3, 33–34, 58, 80,
142–43, 173, 193, 219–20, 223,
253, 284, 300, 311, 314–15, 357,
358, 361, 382, 385, 423
Pyle, Ernie, 189

Quan Loi, 117
Quang Nam Province, 118
Quang Ngai Province, 118, 372
Quang Tin Province, 118
Quang Tri, 116, 120
Quang Tri Province, 118
Que Son Valley, 251, 348, 357,
391–92
Qui Nhon, 377
quick-kill shooting technique,
66–67

Ranger School, 63
Raysor, James A., 3, 8, 36, 353–54,
388–89
reaction to combat, 274–75
rear jobs, 398–405
reconnaissance units, 230, 388–89
recruiters, 17
reenlisting, 402–15, 424
Reiland, Dwight N., 21, 26, 28, 42,
47, 74, 81, 93, 104, 114, 116,
120, 130–31, 133–34, 149, 154,
167–68, 201, 207–8, 211–12,
229, 237, 248, 286, 296, 328,
336–37, 401–2, 417, 424, 426,
428–29
relocation operations, 389; effect
on GIs, 389–90
REMFs, 225
replacement depot, 106, 110,
114–15, 117, 138
replacements, 131, 142, 151, 156;
mistakes by, 154–55, 157–58;
self-consciousness of, 134
reserves (all branches), 19; Marine
Reserves as percent of KIA,
446n
resupply, 198, 207
revenge, 353, 362, 391

On the front lines with the
bravest men in the bloodiest
year of the war

WARRIORS

An Infantryman's Memoir of Vietnam

by Robert Tonsetic

It was the tumultuous year 1968, and Robert Tonsetic was Rifle Company commander of the 4th Battalion, 12th Infantry in Vietnam. He took over a group of grunts demoralized by defeat but determined to get even. Through the legendary Tet and May Offensives, he led, trained, and risked his life with these brave men, and this is the thrilling, brutal, and honest story of his tour of duty. Tonsetic tells of leading a seriously undermanned ready-reaction force into a fierce, three-day battle with a ruthless enemy battalion; conducting surreal night airmobile assaults and treks through fetid, pitch-black jungles; and relieving combat stress by fishing with hand grenades and joyriding in Hueys.

Published by Presidio Press
Available wherever books are sold

Seventy-seven deadly days
in combat

WEST DICKENS AVENUE

A Marine at Khe Sanh

by John Corbett

In January 1968, John Corbett and his fellow leathernecks of the 26th Marine Regiment fortified a remote outpost at a place in South Vietnam called Khe Sanh. Within days of their arrival, twenty thousand North Vietnamese soldiers surrounded the base. What followed over the next seventy-seven days became one of the deadliest fights of the Vietnam War—and one of the greatest battles in military history.

"In this short, readable account, Corbett describes his days at Khe Sanh in almost dispassionate prose and in great detail. . . . effectively convey[ing] the siege from a Marine grunt's point of view."
—*Publishers Weekly*

Published by Presidio Press
Available wherever books are sold